CHASING AFTER Aoi Koshiba

4

Created by
Hazuki Takeoka

Manga by
Fly

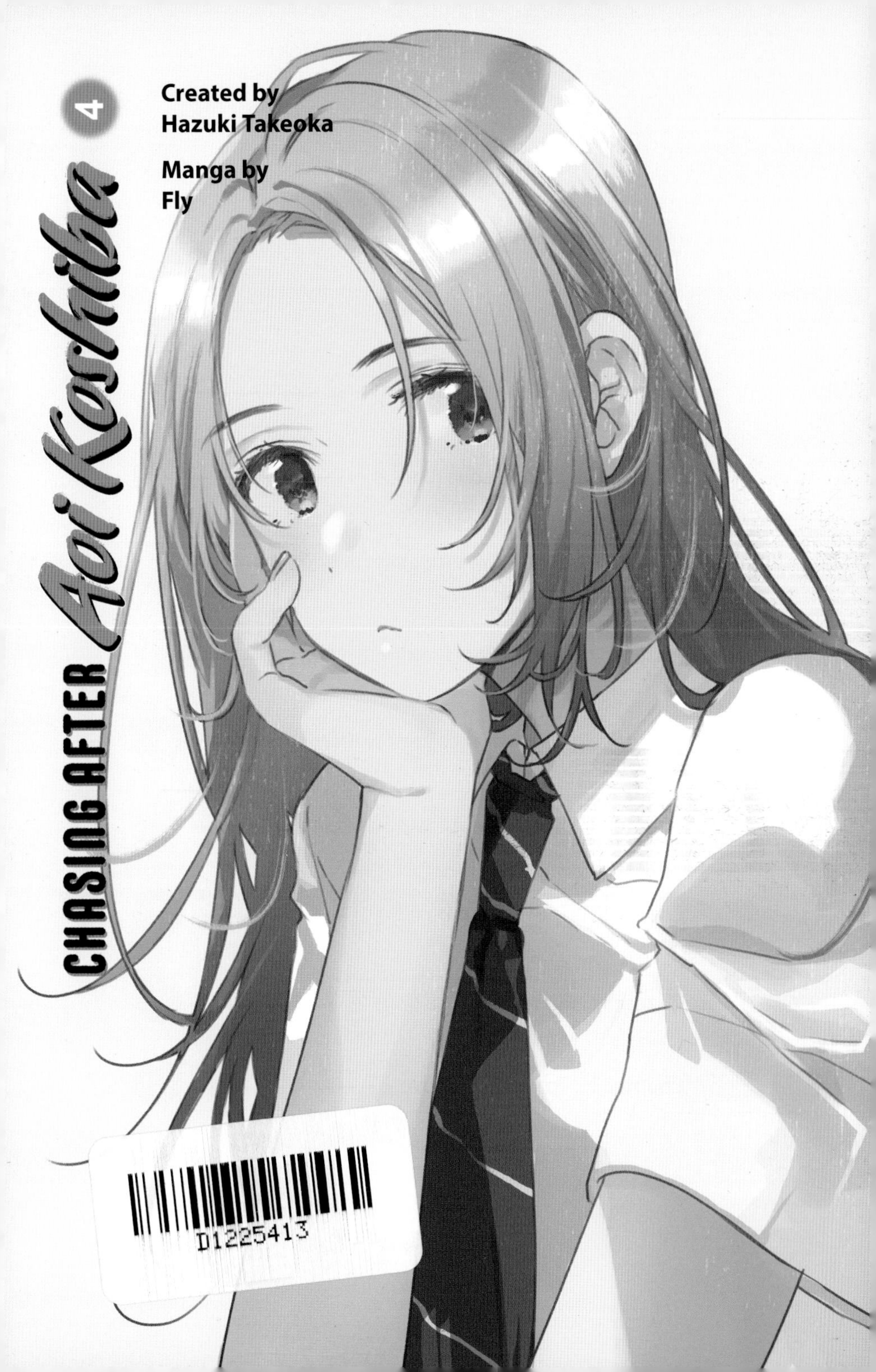

c o n t e n t s

Chapter 25:
Mutual Love (Part 1)

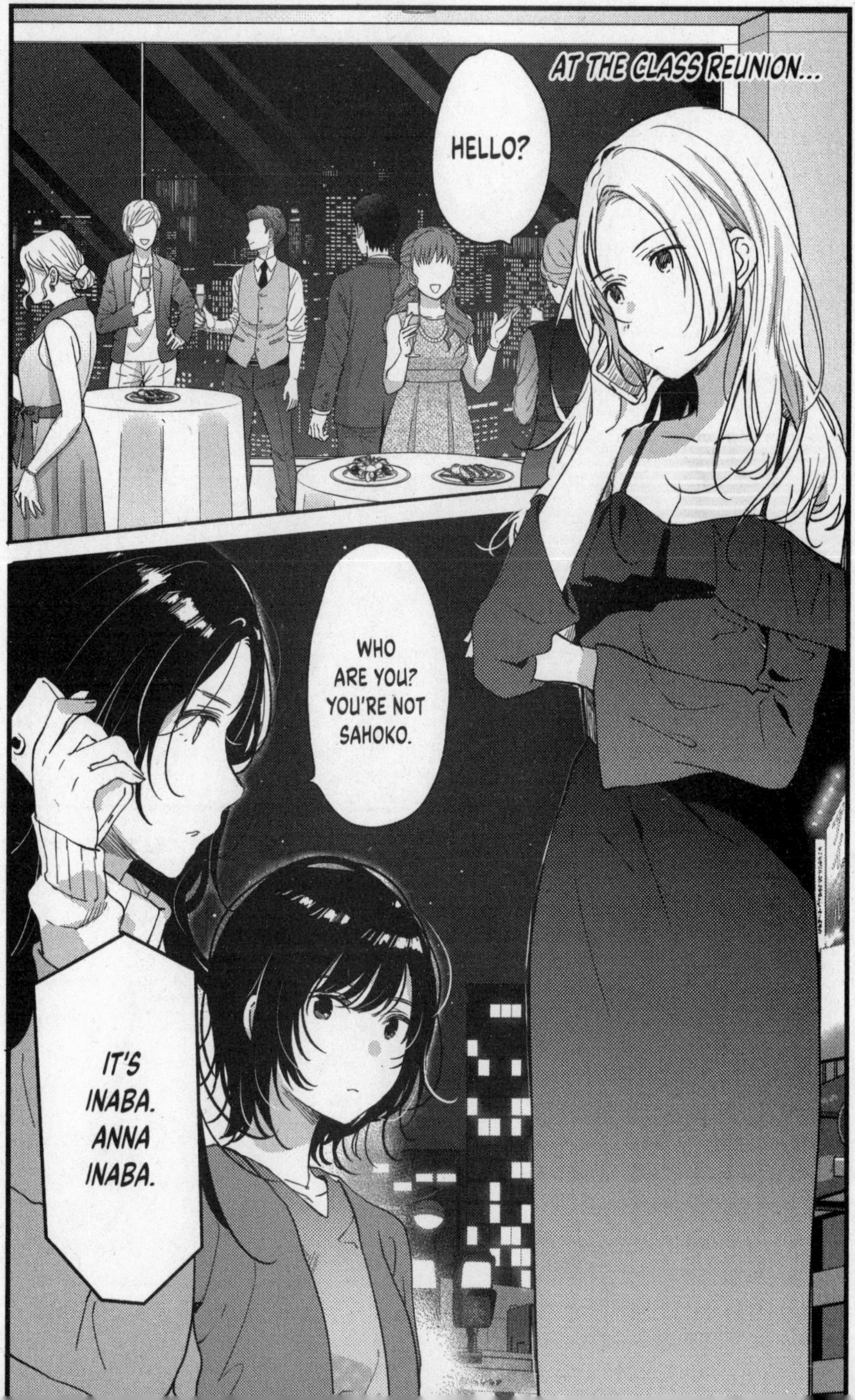
AT THE CLASS REUNION...
HELLO?
WHO ARE YOU? YOU'RE NOT SAHOKO.
IT'S INABA. ANNA INABA.

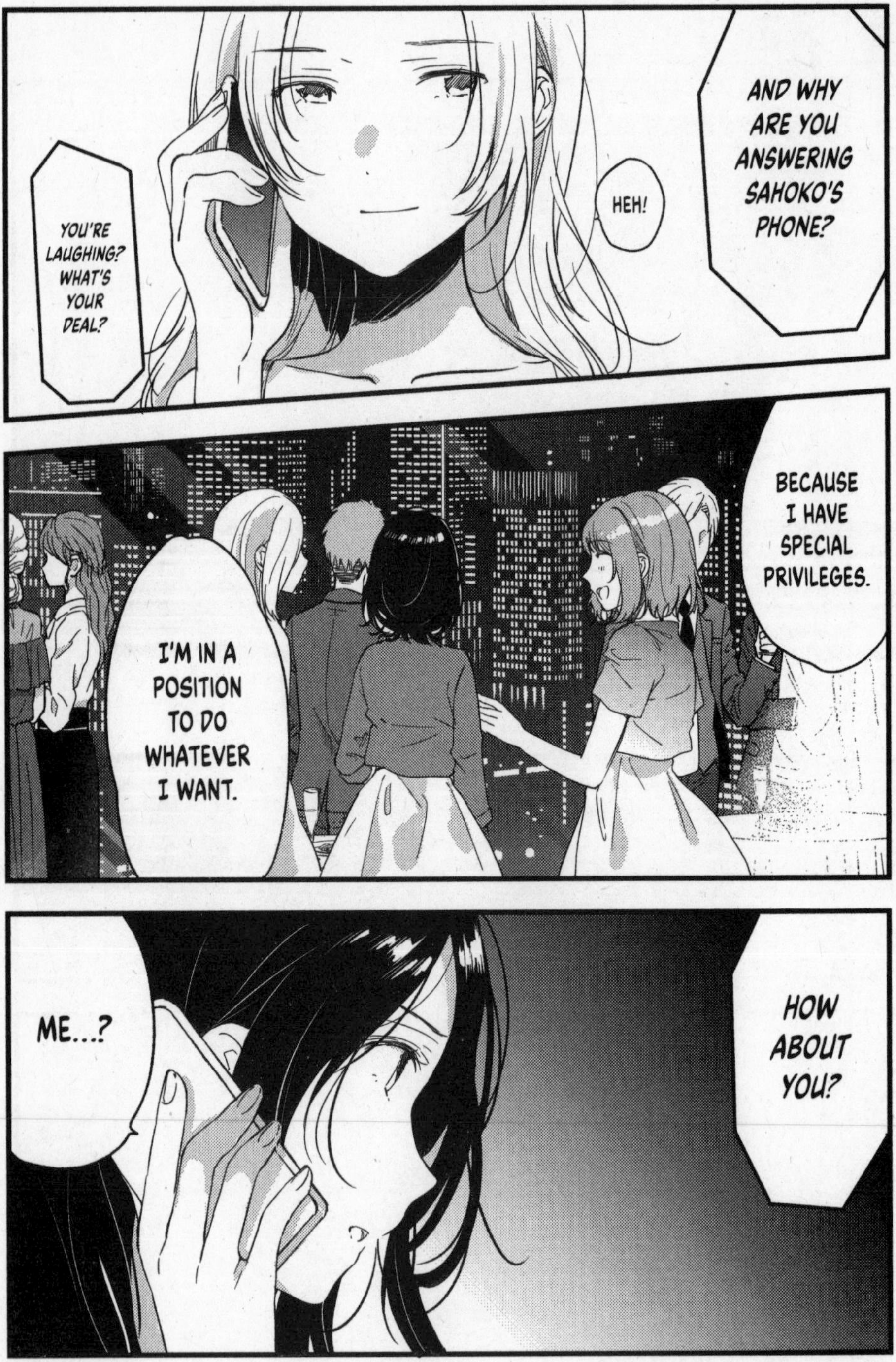
AND WHY ARE YOU ANSWERING SAHOKO'S PHONE?
HEH!
YOU'RE LAUGHING? WHAT'S YOUR DEAL?
BECAUSE I HAVE SPECIAL PRIVILEGES.
I'M IN A POSITION TO DO WHATEVER I WANT.
HOW ABOUT YOU?
ME...?

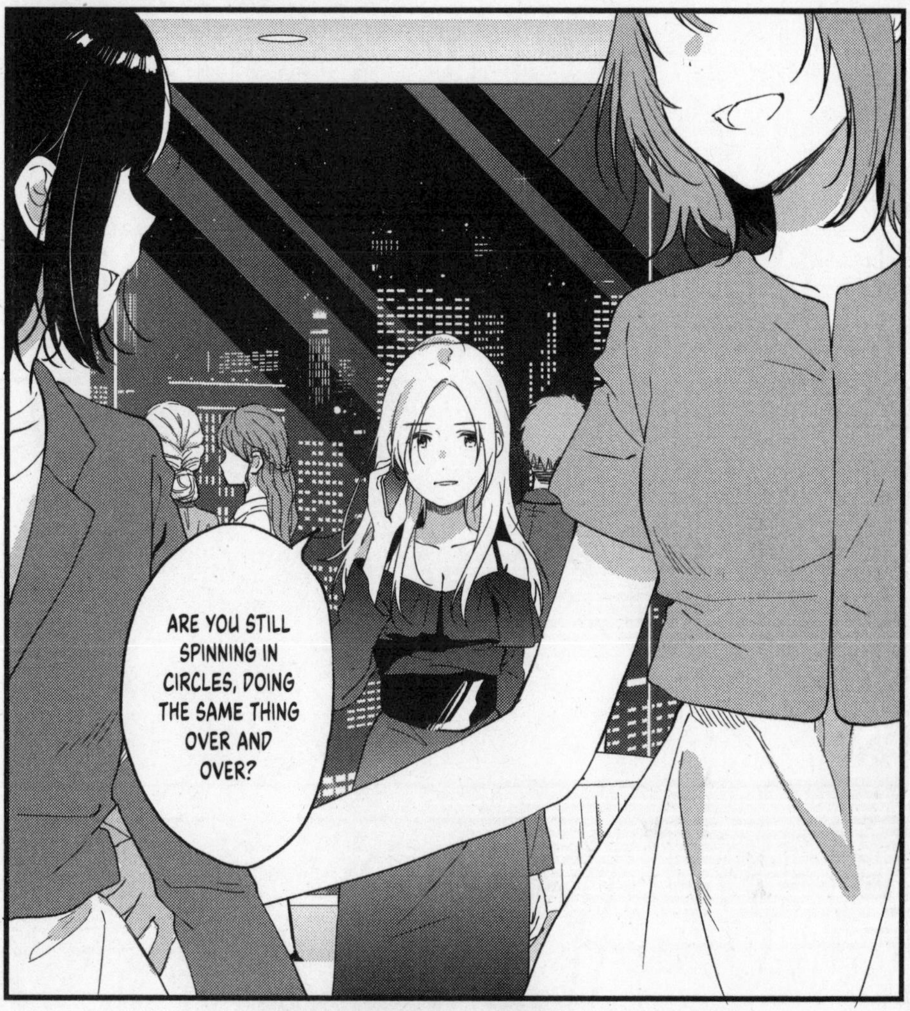
ARE YOU STILL SPINNING IN CIRCLES, DOING THE SAME THING OVER AND OVER?

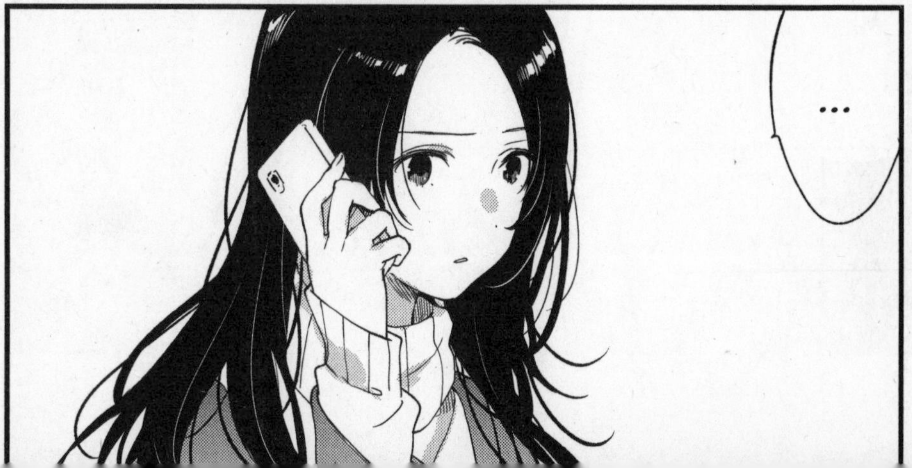
...

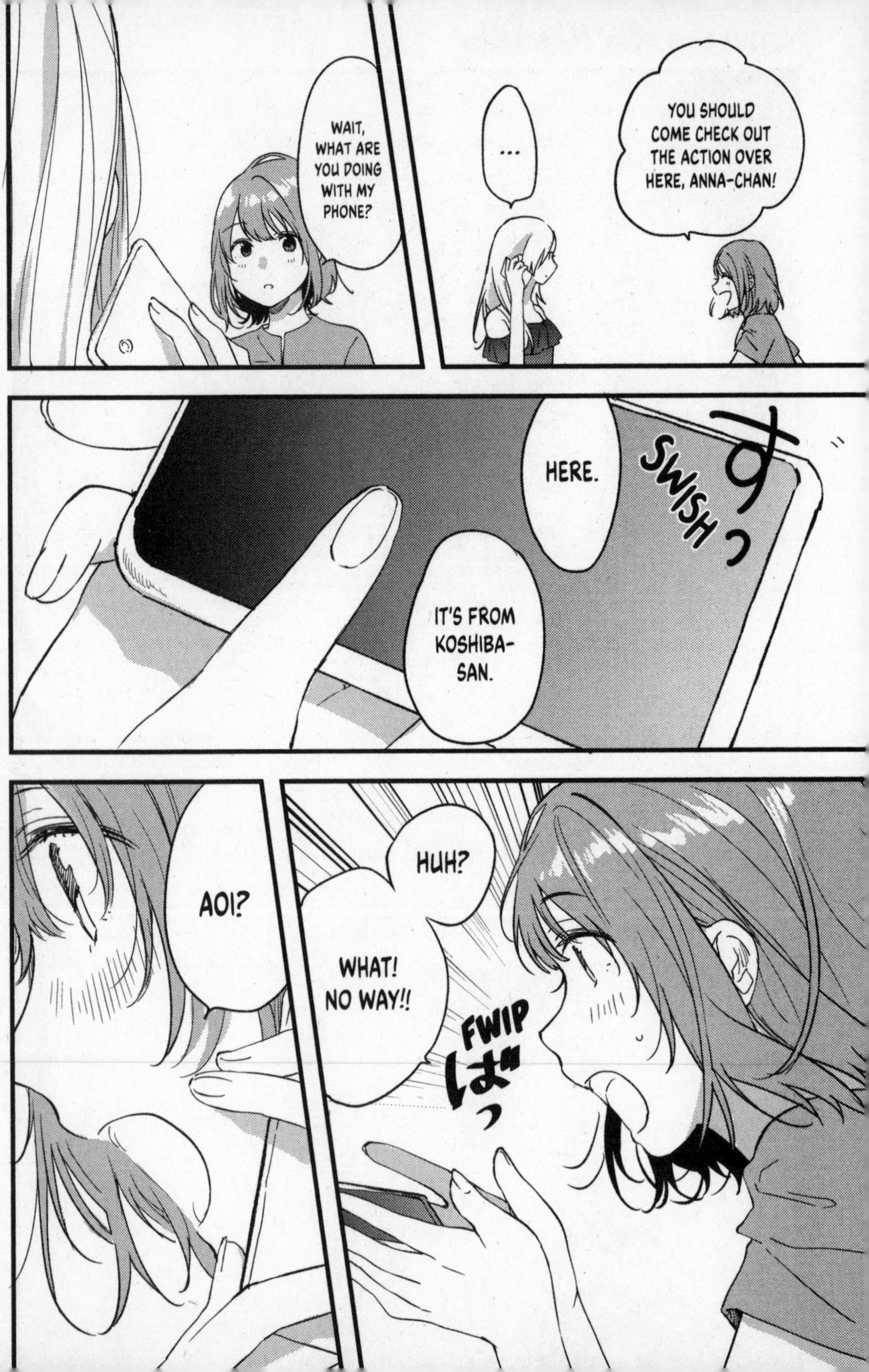
YOU SHOULD COME CHECK OUT THE ACTION OVER HERE, ANNA-CHAN!
...
WAIT, WHAT ARE YOU DOING WITH MY PHONE?
SWISH
すっ
HERE.
IT'S FROM KOSHIBA-SAN.
HUH?
WHAT! NO WAY!!
FWIP
ばっ
AOI?

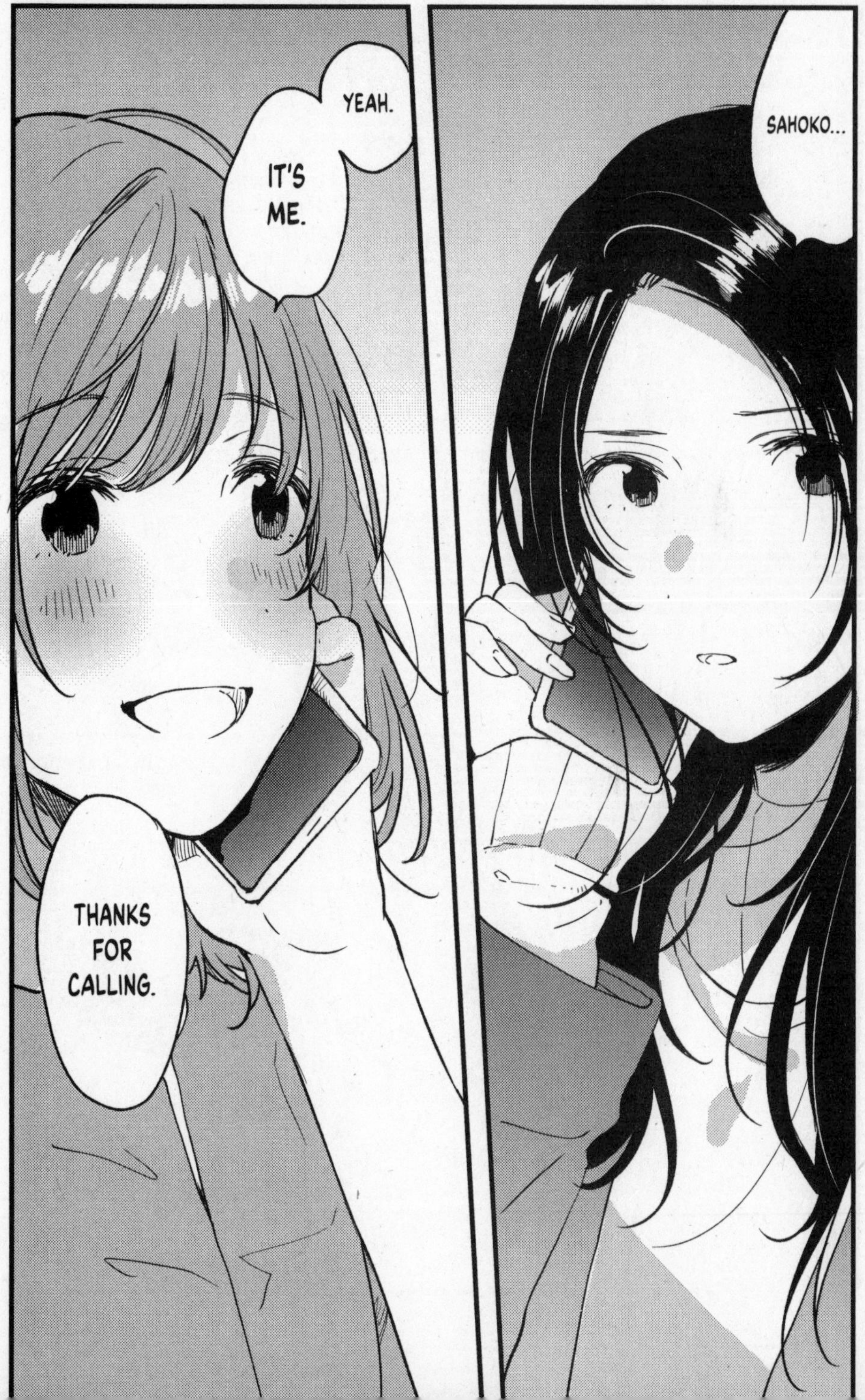
SAHOKO...
YEAH.
IT'S ME.
THANKS FOR CALLING.

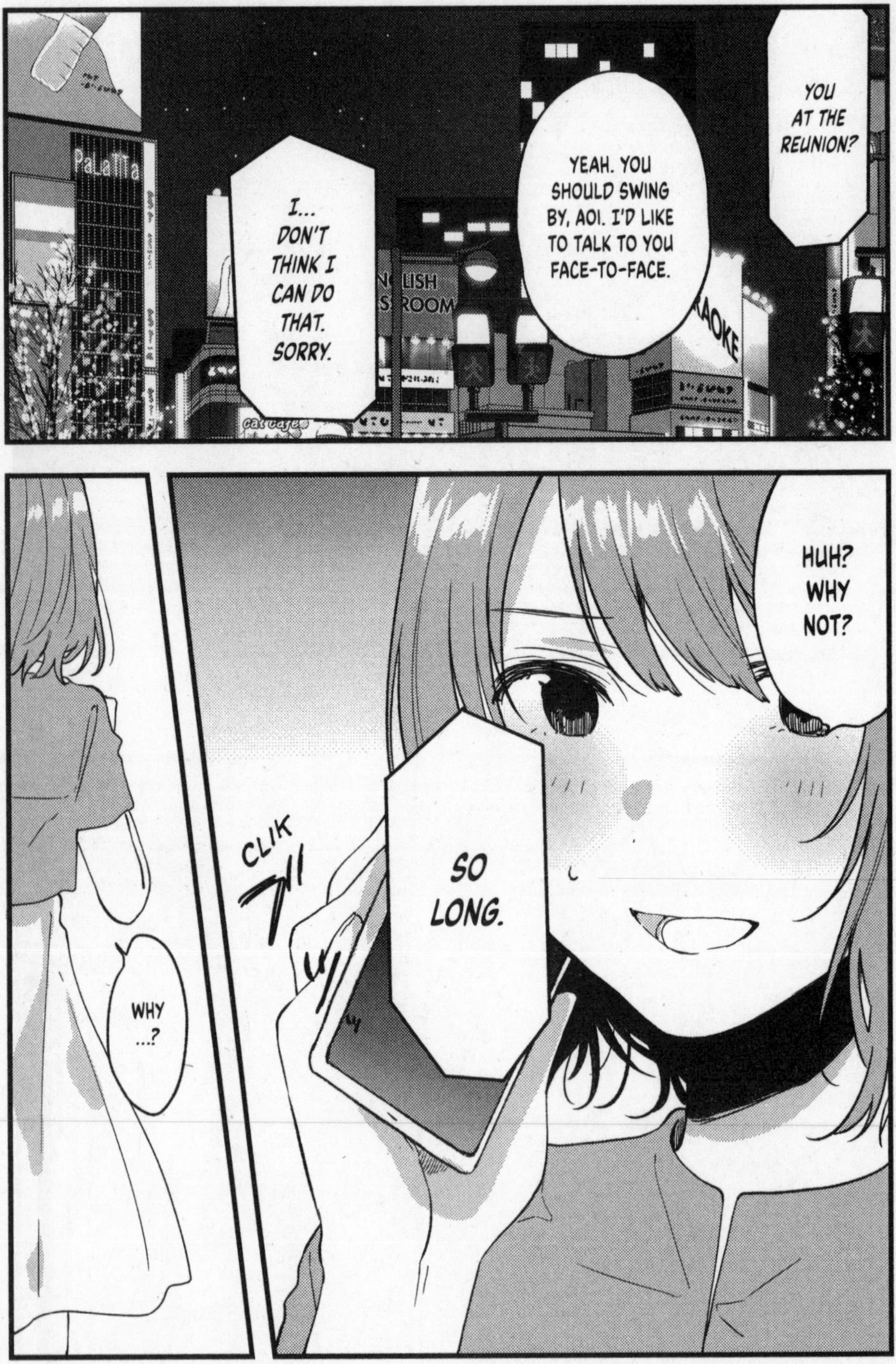
YOU AT THE REUNION?
YEAH. YOU SHOULD SWING BY, AOI. I'D LIKE TO TALK TO YOU FACE-TO-FACE.
I... DON'T THINK I CAN DO THAT. SORRY.
HUH? WHY NOT?
SO LONG.
CLIK
WHY ...?

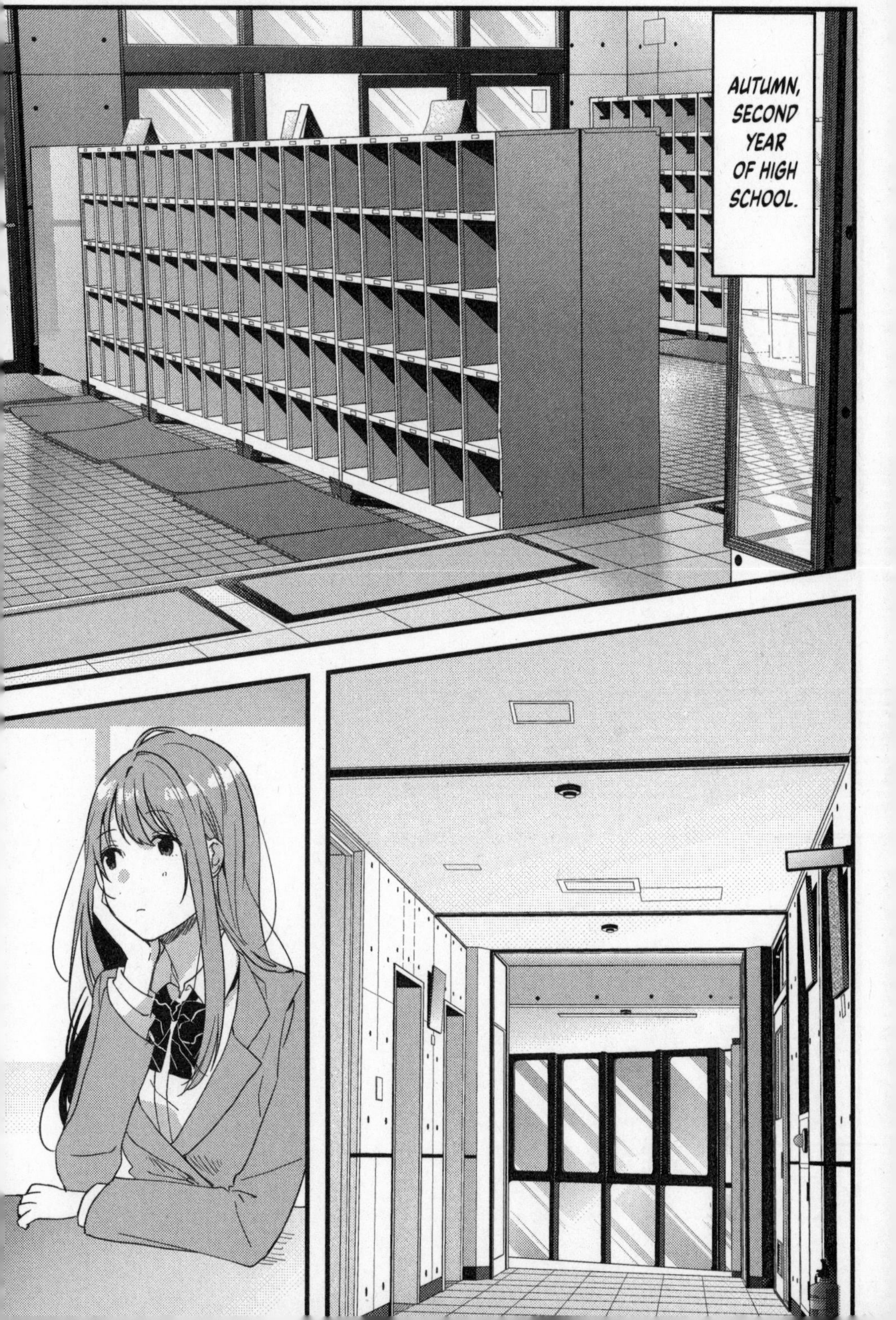
AUTUMN, SECOND YEAR OF HIGH SCHOOL.

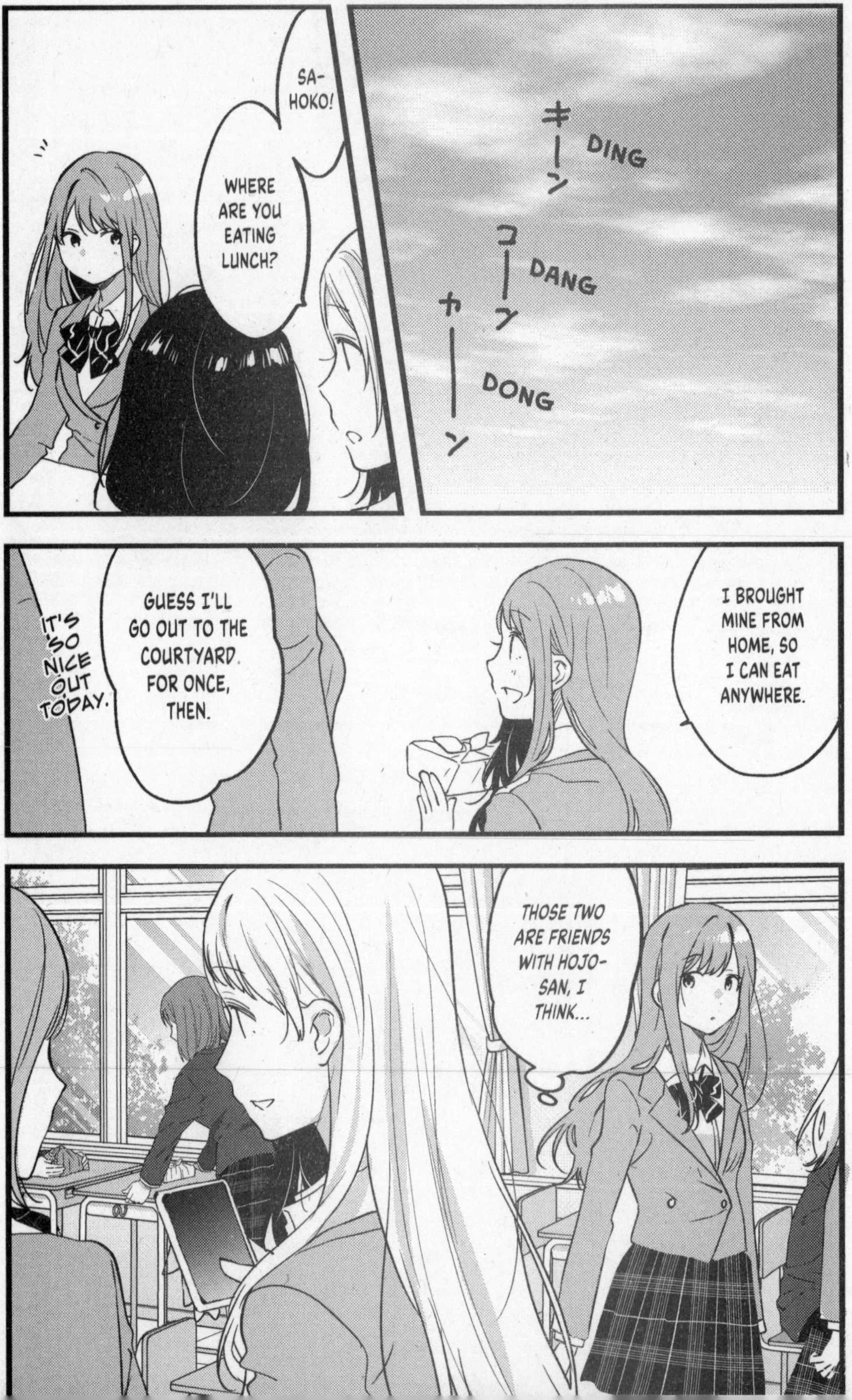
キーン
DING
コーン
DANG
カーン
DONG
SA-HOKO!
WHERE ARE YOU EATING LUNCH?
I BROUGHT MINE FROM HOME, SO I CAN EAT ANYWHERE.
GUESS I'LL GO OUT TO THE COURTYARD FOR ONCE, THEN.
IT'S SO NICE OUT TODAY.
THOSE TWO ARE FRIENDS WITH HOJO-SAN, I THINK...

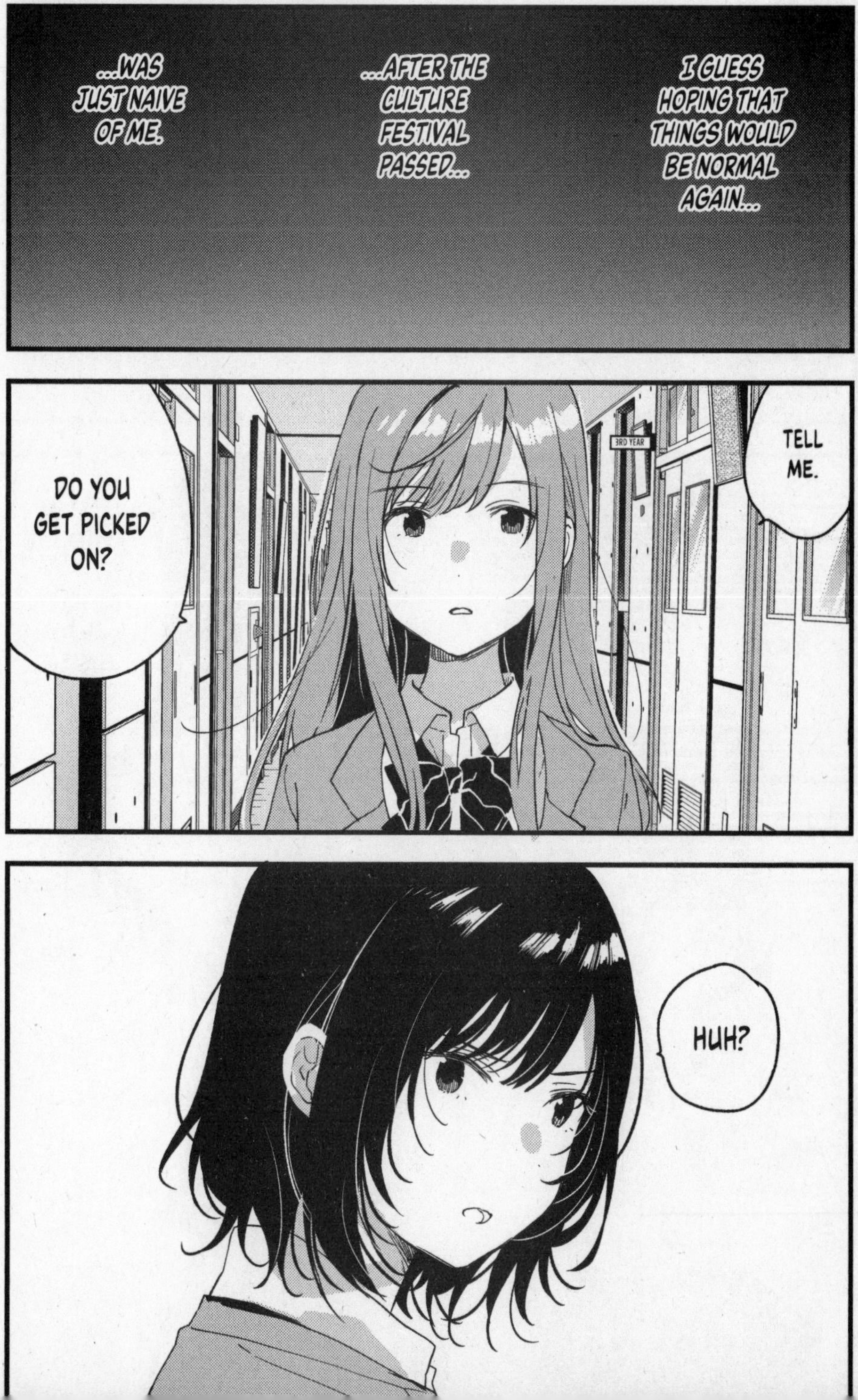
I GUESS HOPING THAT THINGS WOULD BE NORMAL AGAIN...
...AFTER THE CULTURE FESTIVAL PASSED...
...WAS JUST NAIVE OF ME.
3RD YEAR
TELL ME.
DO YOU GET PICKED ON?
HUH?

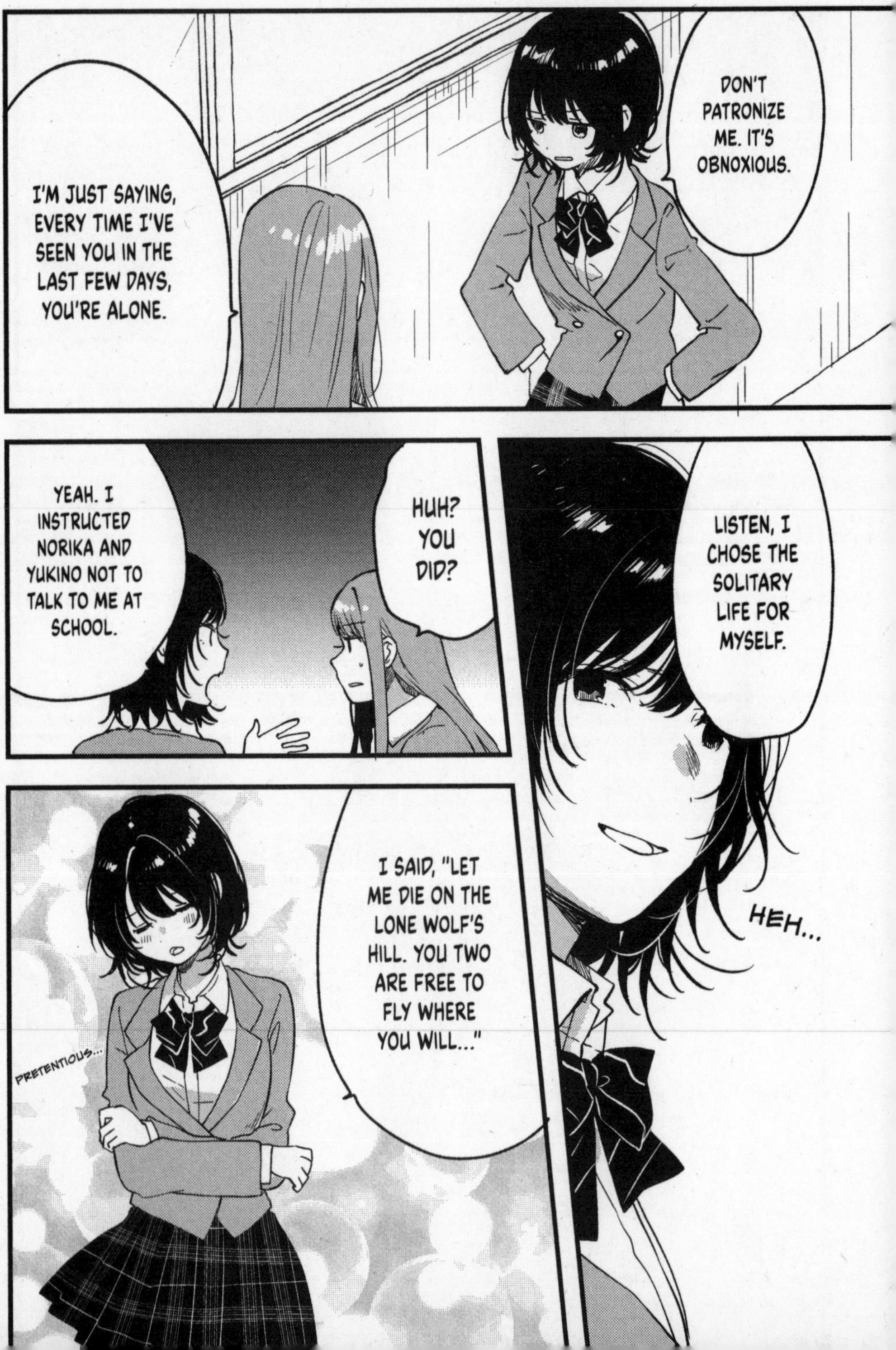
DON'T PATRONIZE ME. IT'S OBNOXIOUS.
I'M JUST SAYING, EVERY TIME I'VE SEEN YOU IN THE LAST FEW DAYS, YOU'RE ALONE.
LISTEN, I CHOSE THE SOLITARY LIFE FOR MYSELF.
HEH...
HUH? YOU DID?
YEAH. I INSTRUCTED NORIKA AND YUKINO NOT TO TALK TO ME AT SCHOOL.
I SAID, "LET ME DIE ON THE LONE WOLF'S HILL. YOU TWO ARE FREE TO FLY WHERE YOU WILL..."
PRETENTIOUS...

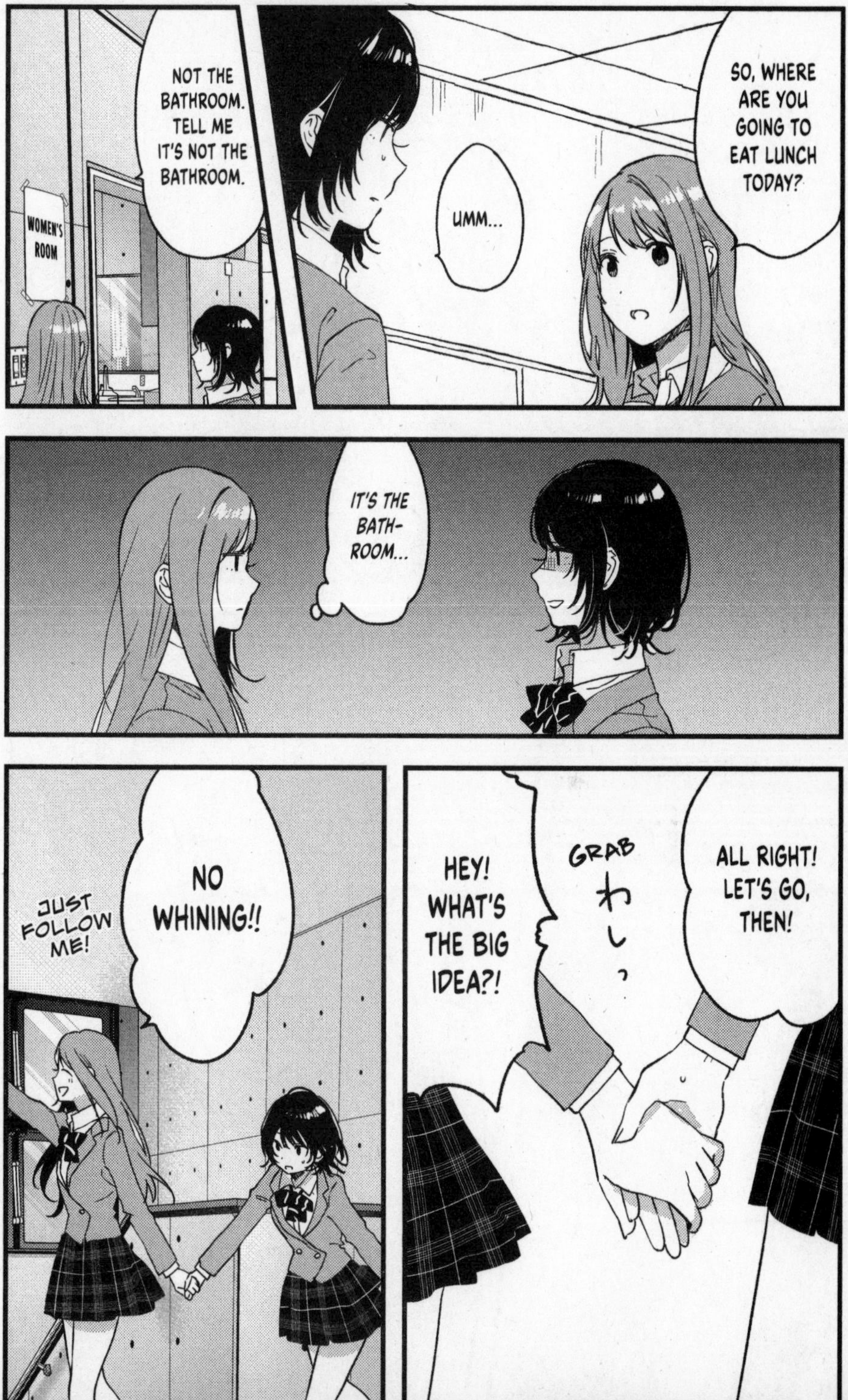
SO, WHERE ARE YOU GOING TO EAT LUNCH TODAY?
UMM...
NOT THE BATHROOM. TELL ME IT'S NOT THE BATHROOM.
WOMEN'S ROOM
IT'S THE BATH-ROOM...
ALL RIGHT! LET'S GO, THEN!
GRAB
わしっ
HEY! WHAT'S THE BIG IDEA?!
NO WHINING!!
JUST FOLLOW ME!

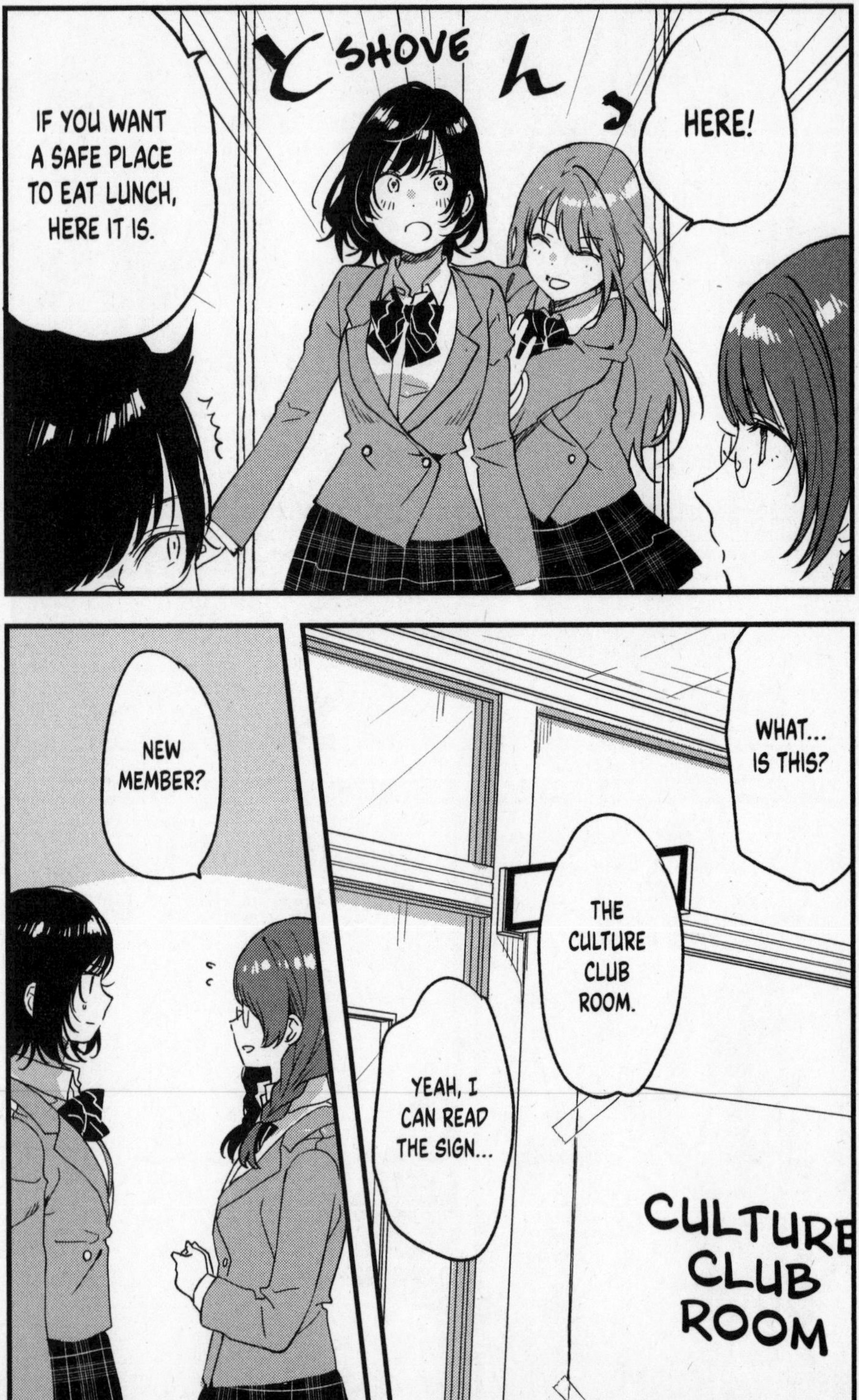
HERE!
SHOVE
IF YOU WANT A SAFE PLACE TO EAT LUNCH, HERE IT IS.
WHAT... IS THIS?
THE CULTURE CLUB ROOM.
YEAH, I CAN READ THE SIGN...
CULTURE CLUB ROOM
NEW MEMBER?

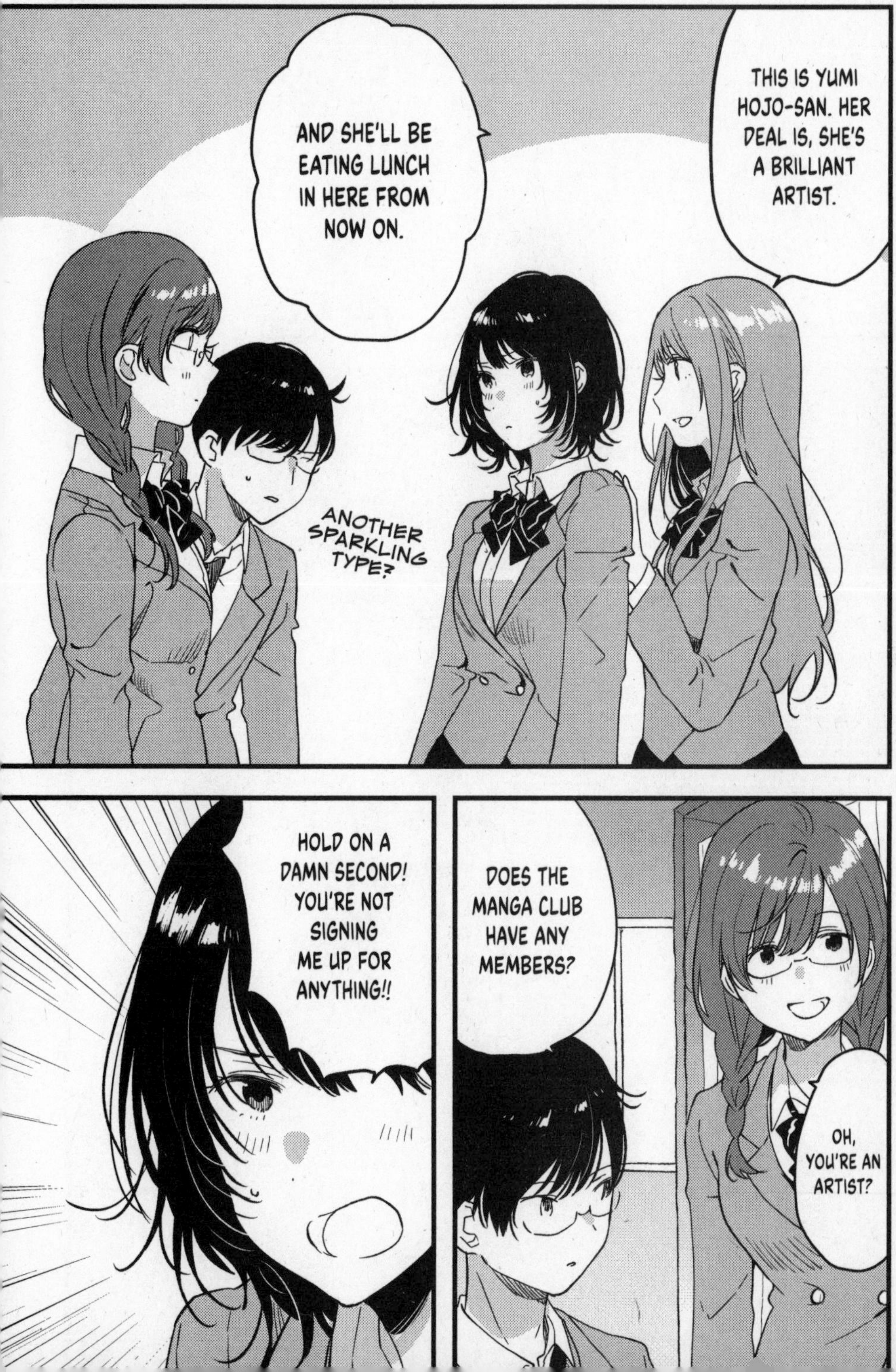
THIS IS YUMI HOJO-SAN. HER DEAL IS, SHE'S A BRILLIANT ARTIST.
AND SHE'LL BE EATING LUNCH IN HERE FROM NOW ON.
ANOTHER SPARKLING TYPE?
DOES THE MANGA CLUB HAVE ANY MEMBERS?
OH, YOU'RE AN ARTIST?
HOLD ON A DAMN SECOND! YOU'RE NOT SIGNING ME UP FOR ANYTHING!!

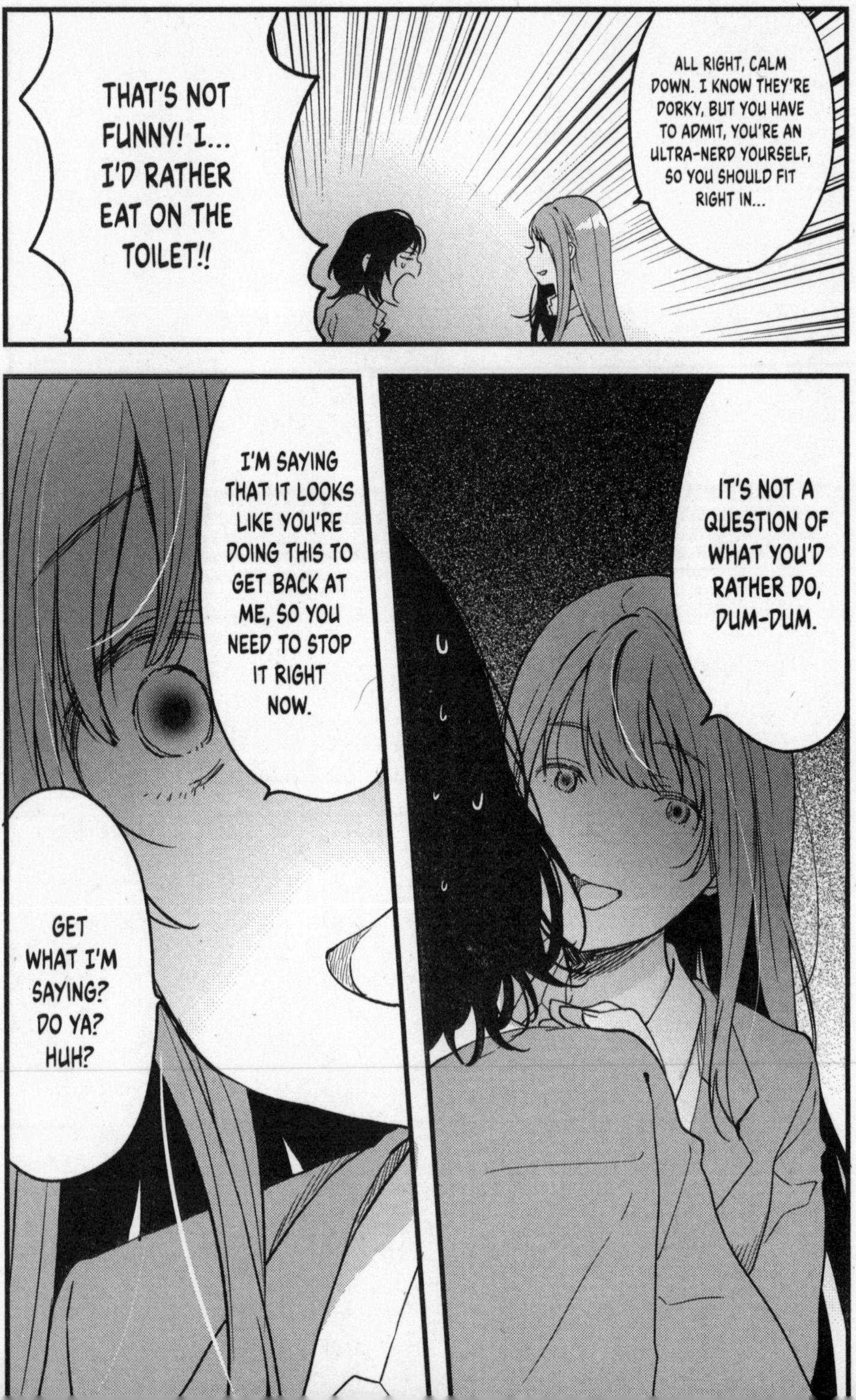
ALL RIGHT, CALM DOWN. I KNOW THEY'RE DORKY, BUT YOU HAVE TO ADMIT, YOU'RE AN ULTRA-NERD YOURSELF, SO YOU SHOULD FIT RIGHT IN...
THAT'S NOT FUNNY! I... I'D RATHER EAT ON THE TOILET!!
IT'S NOT A QUESTION OF WHAT YOU'D RATHER DO, DUM-DUM.
I'M SAYING THAT IT LOOKS LIKE YOU'RE DOING THIS TO GET BACK AT ME, SO YOU NEED TO STOP IT RIGHT NOW.
GET WHAT I'M SAYING? DO YA? HUH?

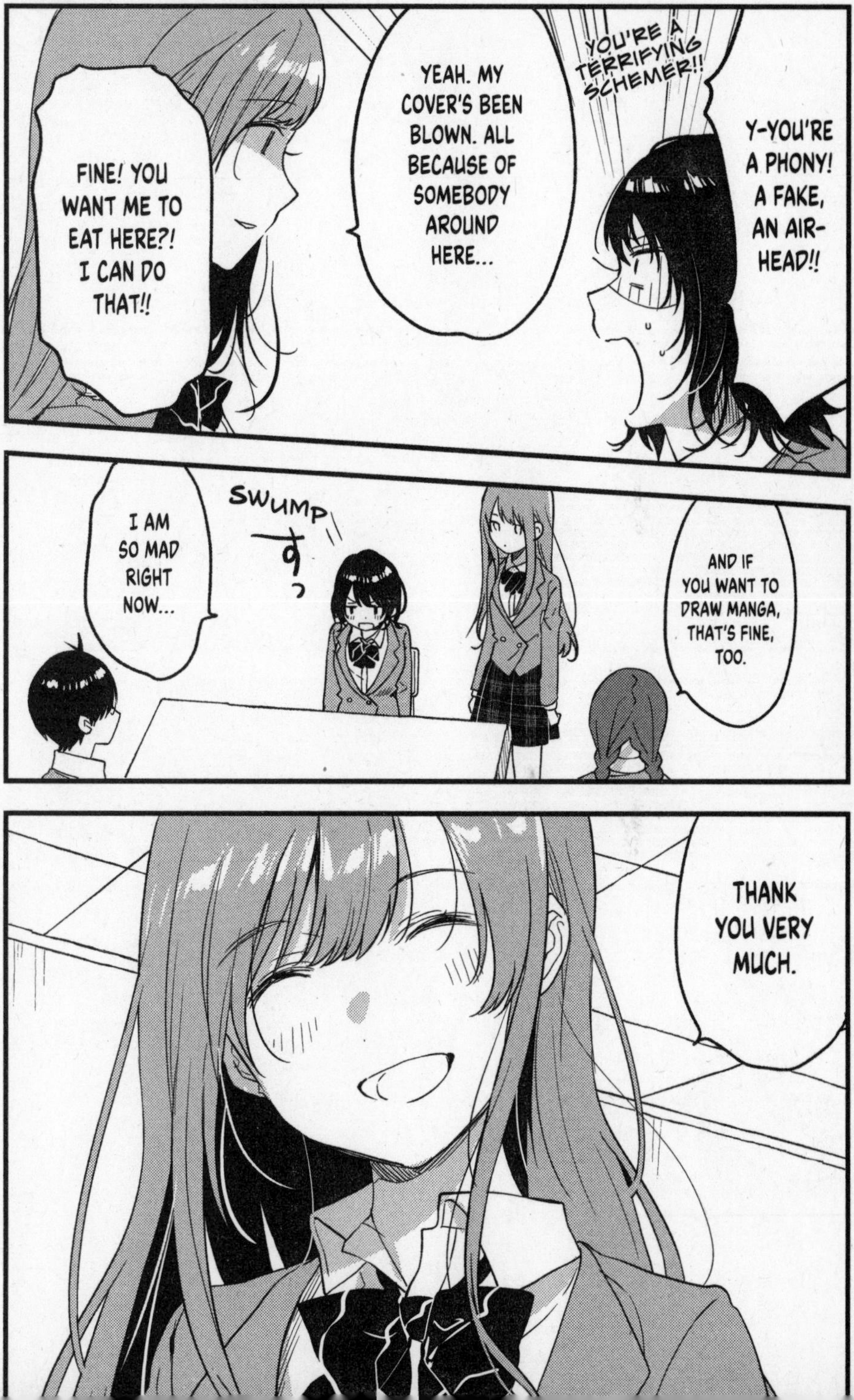
YOU'RE A TERRIFYING SCHEMER!!
Y-YOU'RE A PHONY! A FAKE, AN AIR-HEAD!!
YEAH. MY COVER'S BEEN BLOWN. ALL BECAUSE OF SOMEBODY AROUND HERE...
FINE! YOU WANT ME TO EAT HERE?! I CAN DO THAT!!
AND IF YOU WANT TO DRAW MANGA, THAT'S FINE, TOO.
SWUMP
すっ
I AM SO MAD RIGHT NOW...
THANK YOU VERY MUCH.

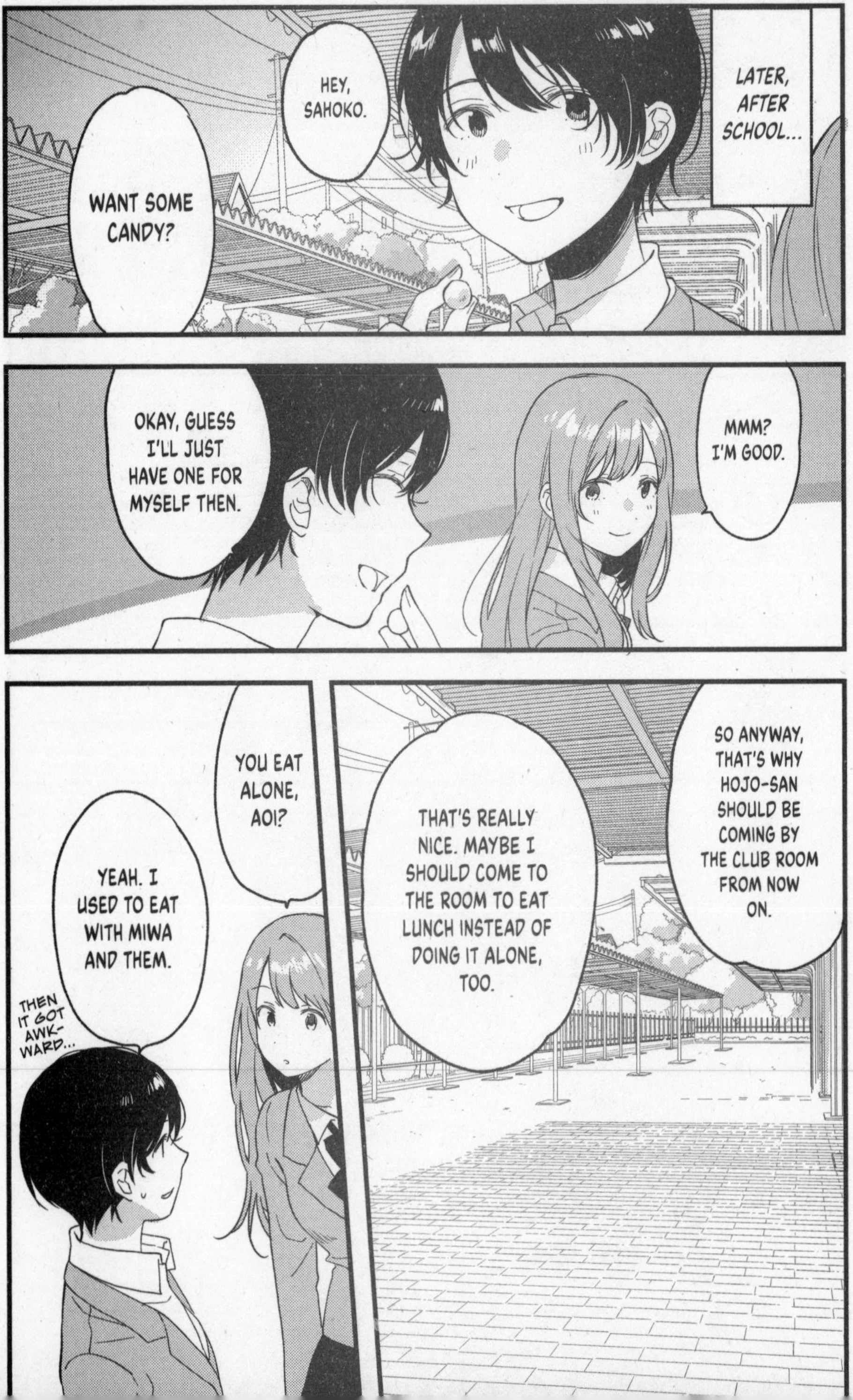
LATER, AFTER SCHOOL...
HEY, SAHOKO.
WANT SOME CANDY?
MMM? I'M GOOD.
OKAY, GUESS I'LL JUST HAVE ONE FOR MYSELF THEN.
SO ANYWAY, THAT'S WHY HOJO-SAN SHOULD BE COMING BY THE CLUB ROOM FROM NOW ON.
THAT'S REALLY NICE. MAYBE I SHOULD COME TO THE ROOM TO EAT LUNCH INSTEAD OF DOING IT ALONE, TOO.
YOU EAT ALONE, AOI?
YEAH. I USED TO EAT WITH MIWA AND THEM.
THEN IT GOT AWKWARD...

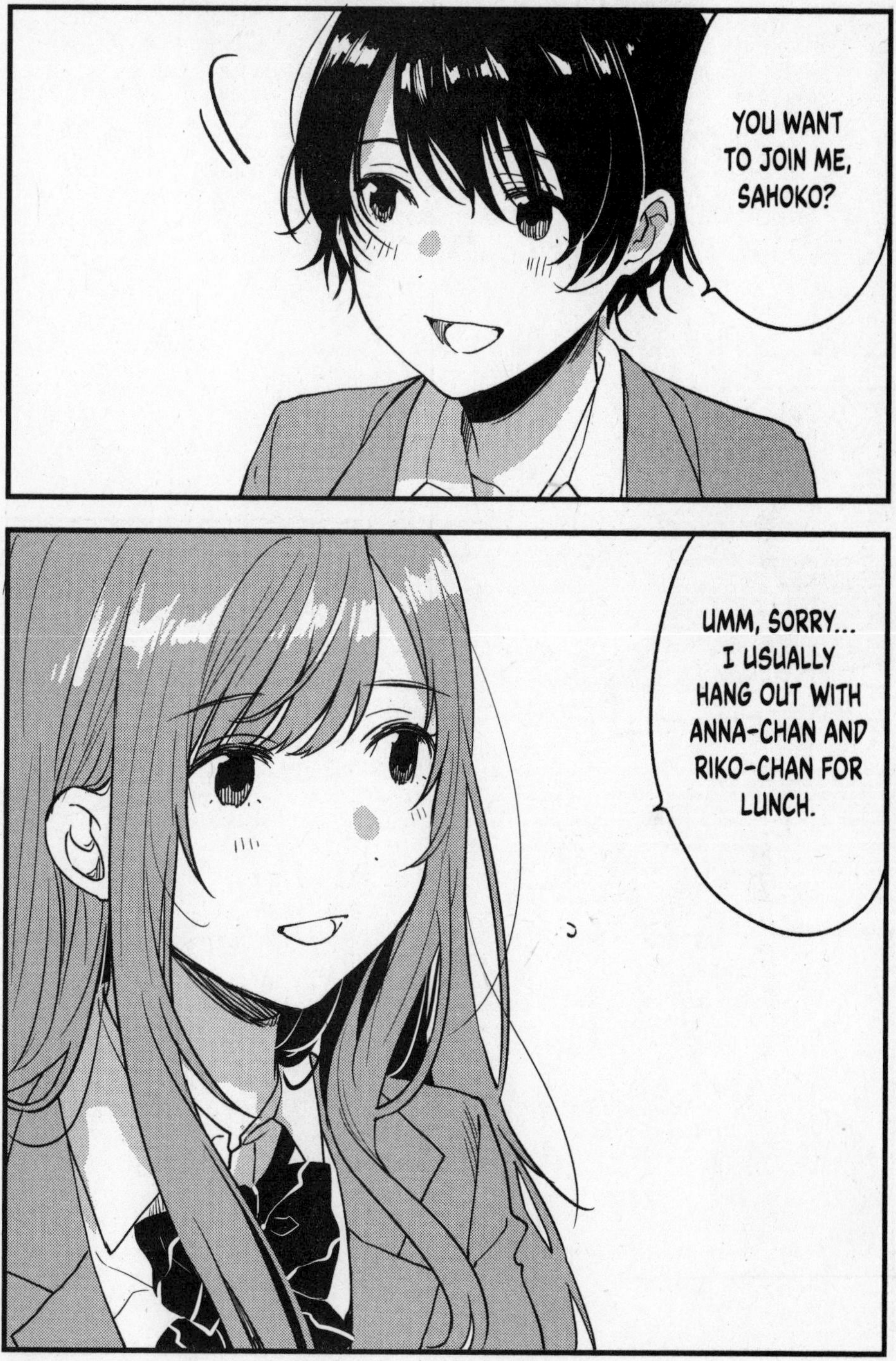
YOU WANT TO JOIN ME, SAHOKO?
UMM, SORRY... I USUALLY HANG OUT WITH ANNA-CHAN AND RIKO-CHAN FOR LUNCH.

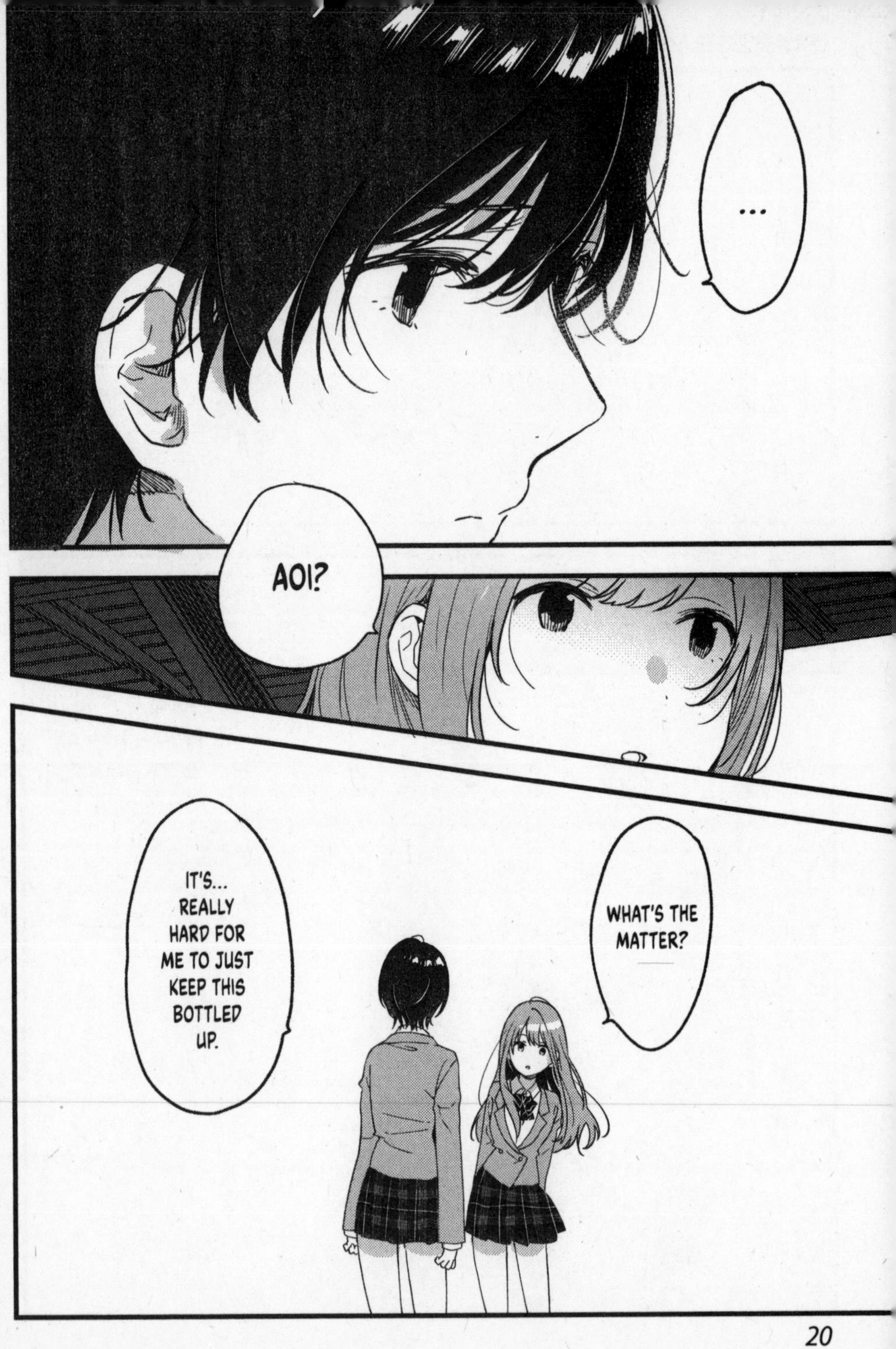
...
AOI?
WHAT'S THE MATTER?
IT'S... REALLY HARD FOR ME TO JUST KEEP THIS BOTTLED UP.

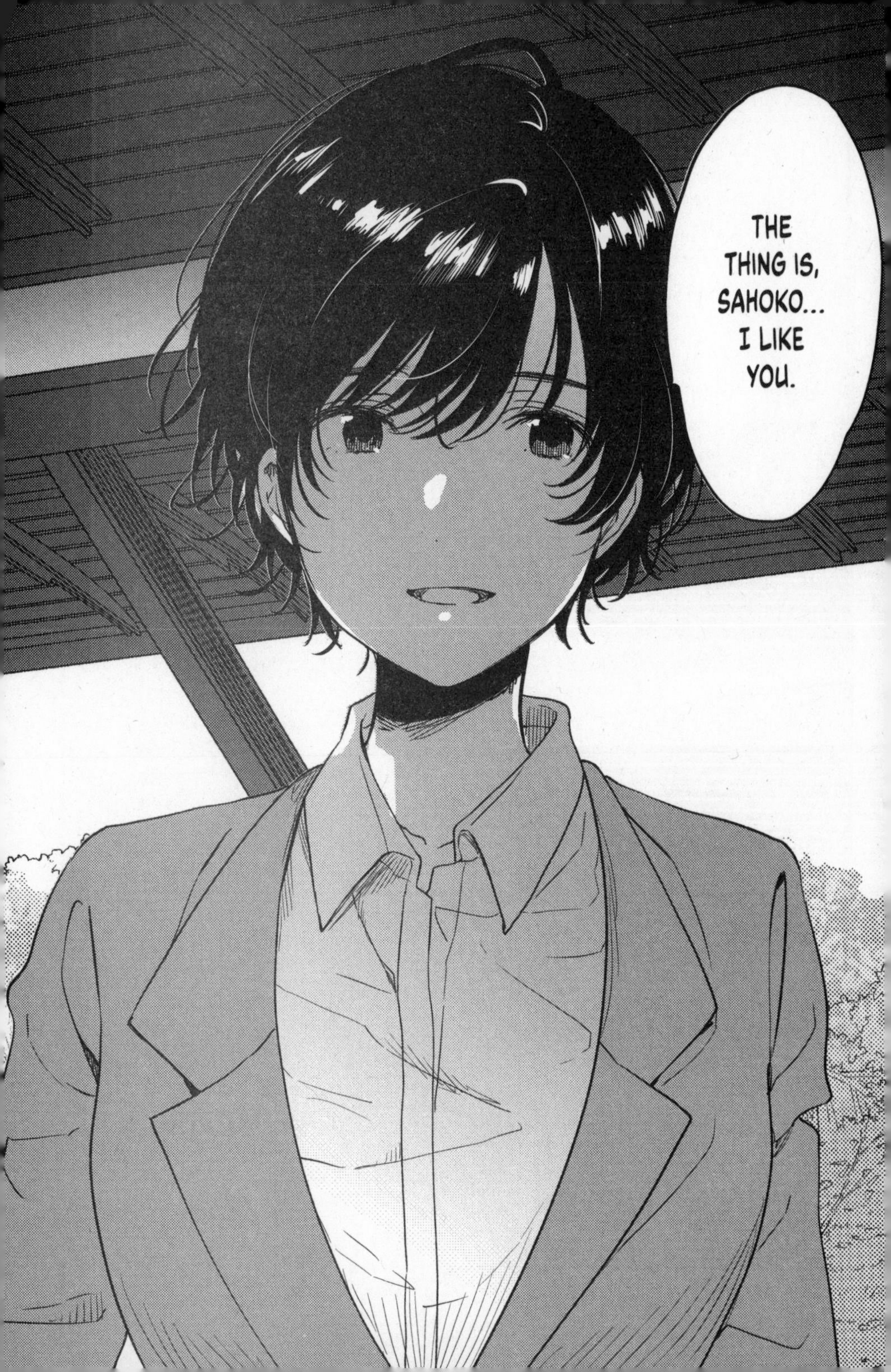
THE THING IS, SAHOKO... I LIKE YOU.

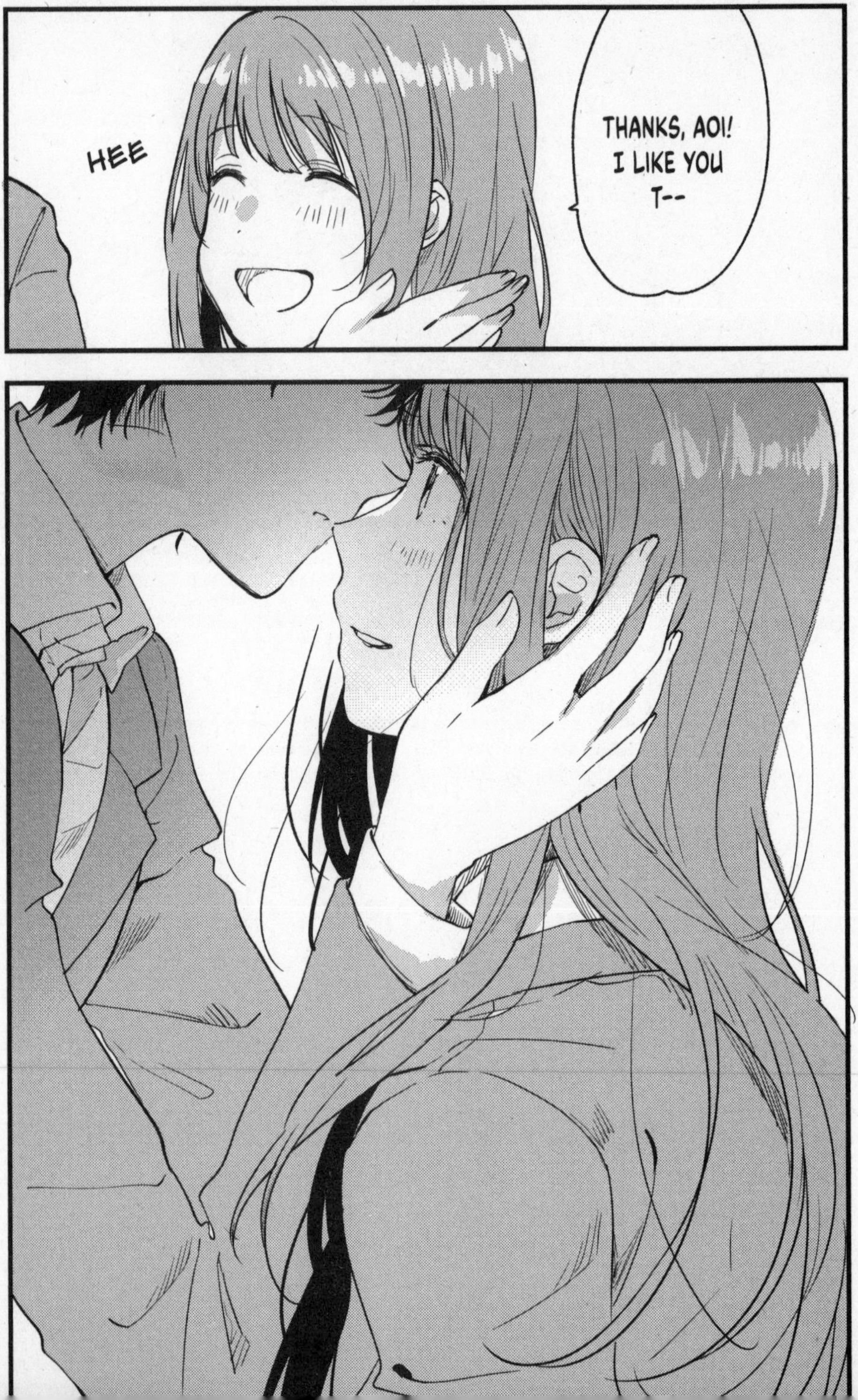
THANKS, AOI! I LIKE YOU T--
HEE

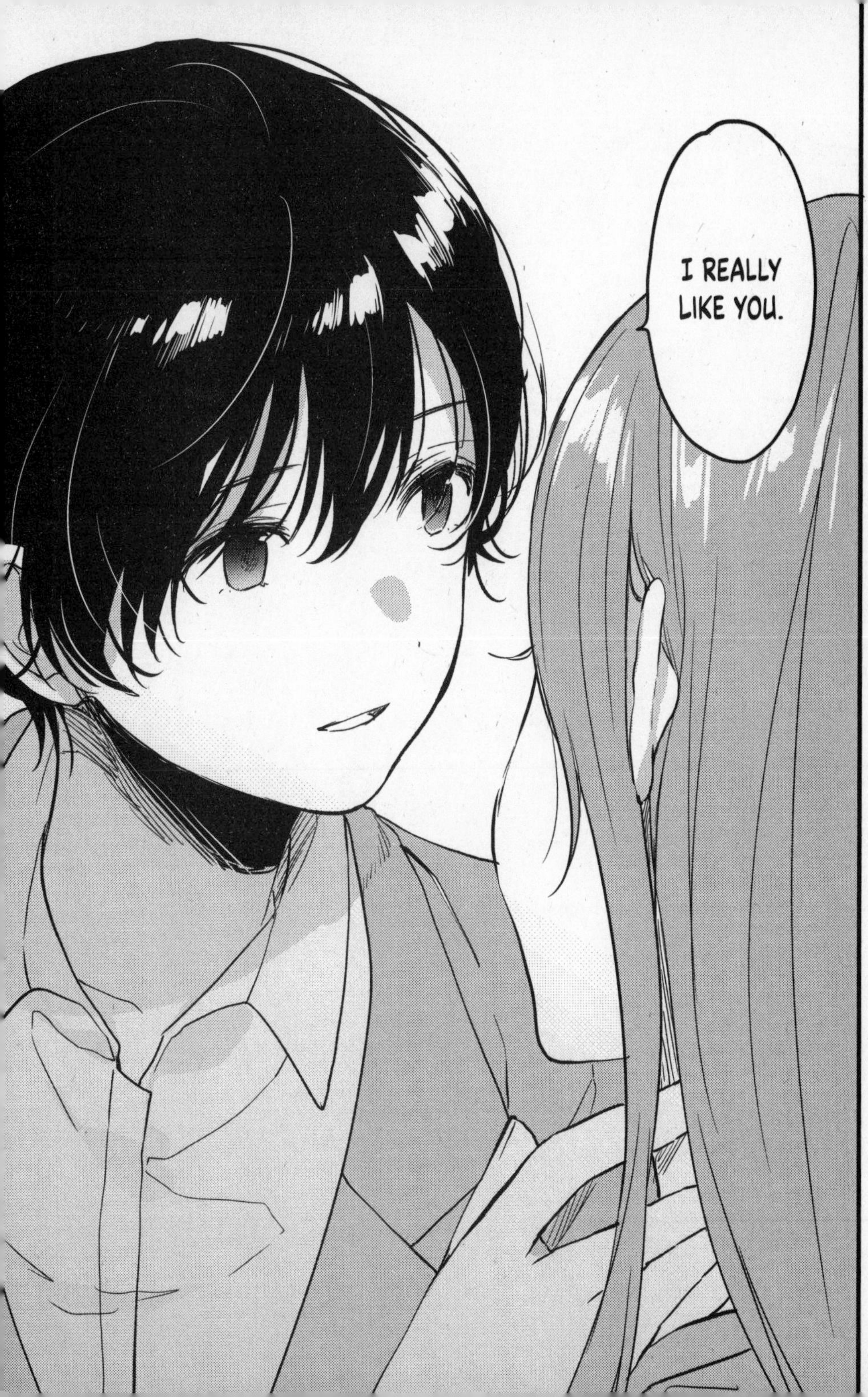
I REALLY LIKE YOU.

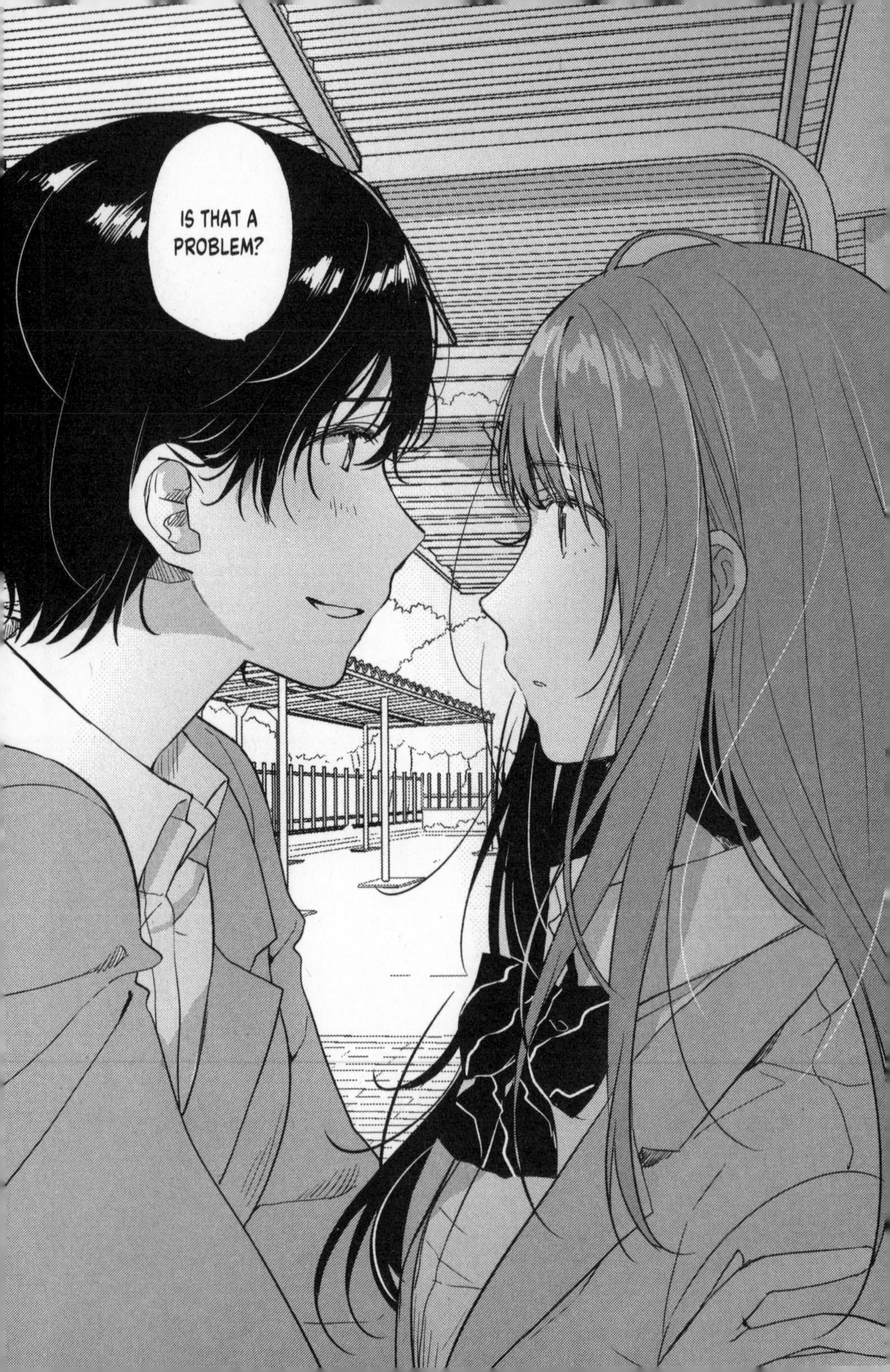
IS THAT A PROBLEM?

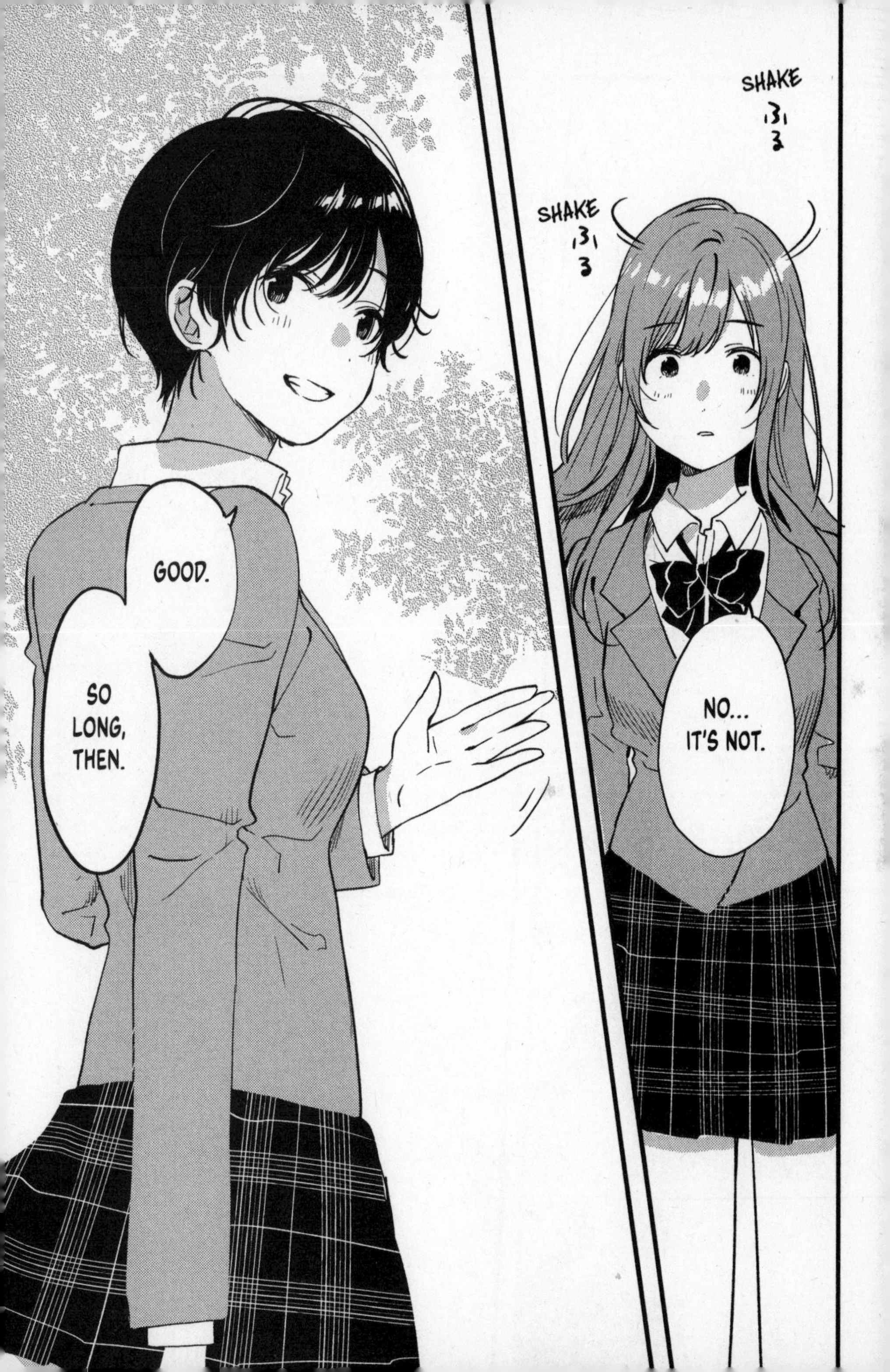
SHAKE
SHAKE
NO... IT'S NOT.
GOOD.
SO LONG, THEN.

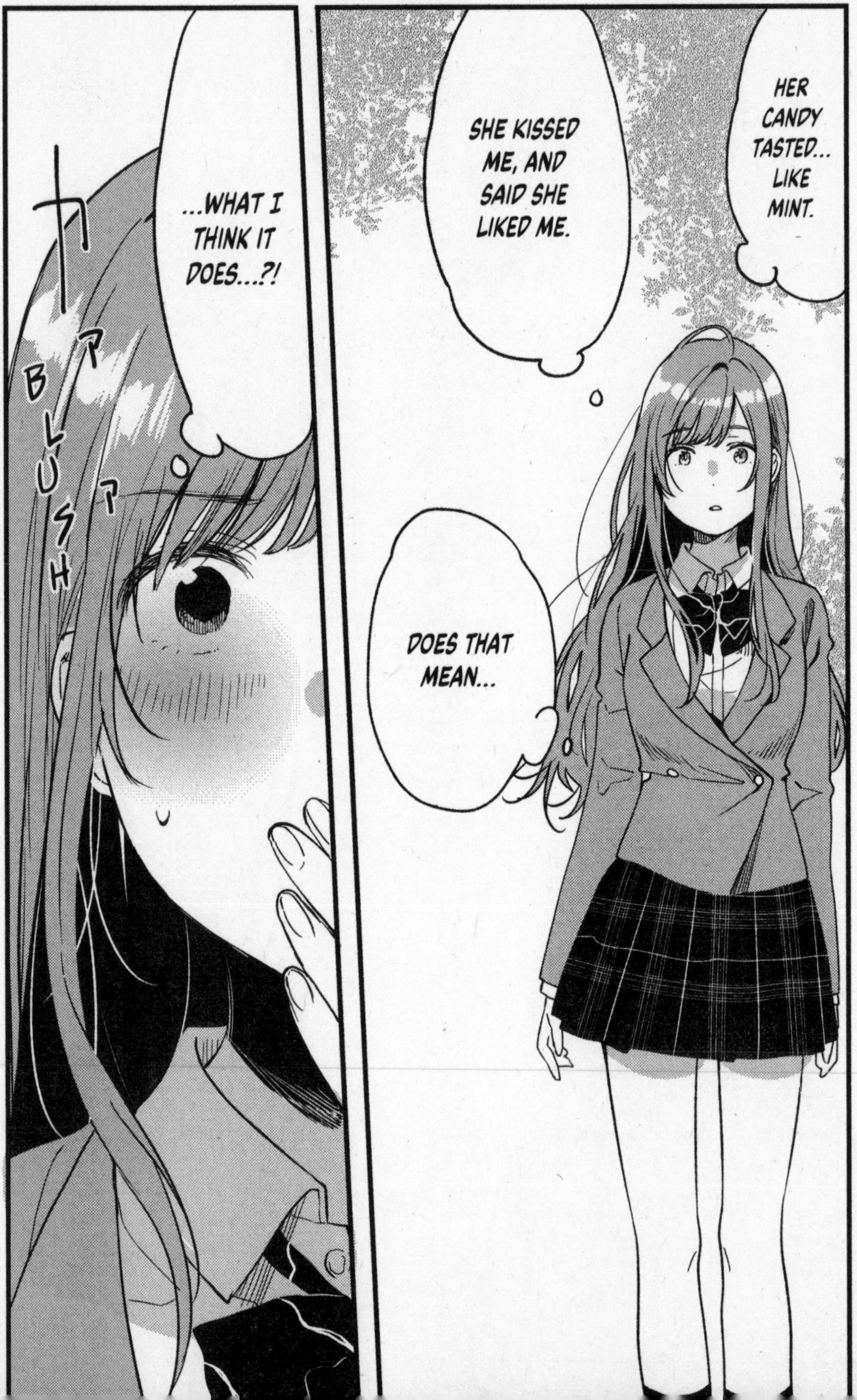
HER CANDY TASTED... LIKE MINT.
SHE KISSED ME, AND SAID SHE LIKED ME.
DOES THAT MEAN...
...WHAT I THINK IT DOES...?!
BLUSH

CHASING AFTER *Aoi Koshiba*

Autumn, Second Year of High School

CHASING AFTER *Aoi Koshiba*

Autumn, Second Year of High School

Chapter 26:
Mutual Love (Part 2)

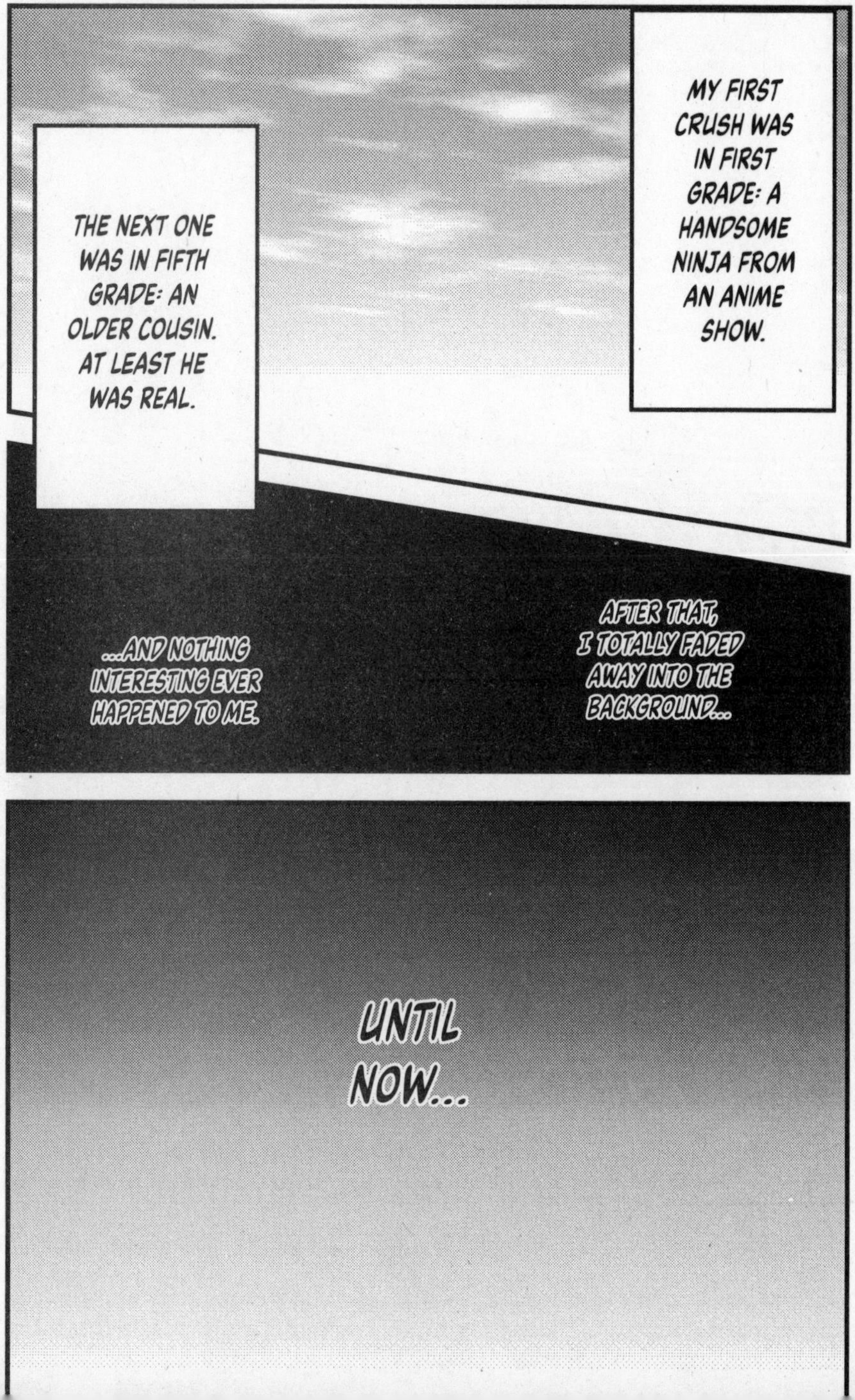
MY FIRST CRUSH WAS IN FIRST GRADE: A HANDSOME NINJA FROM AN ANIME SHOW.
THE NEXT ONE WAS IN FIFTH GRADE: AN OLDER COUSIN. AT LEAST HE WAS REAL.
AFTER THAT, I TOTALLY FADED AWAY INTO THE BACKGROUND...
...AND NOTHING INTERESTING EVER HAPPENED TO ME.
UNTIL NOW...

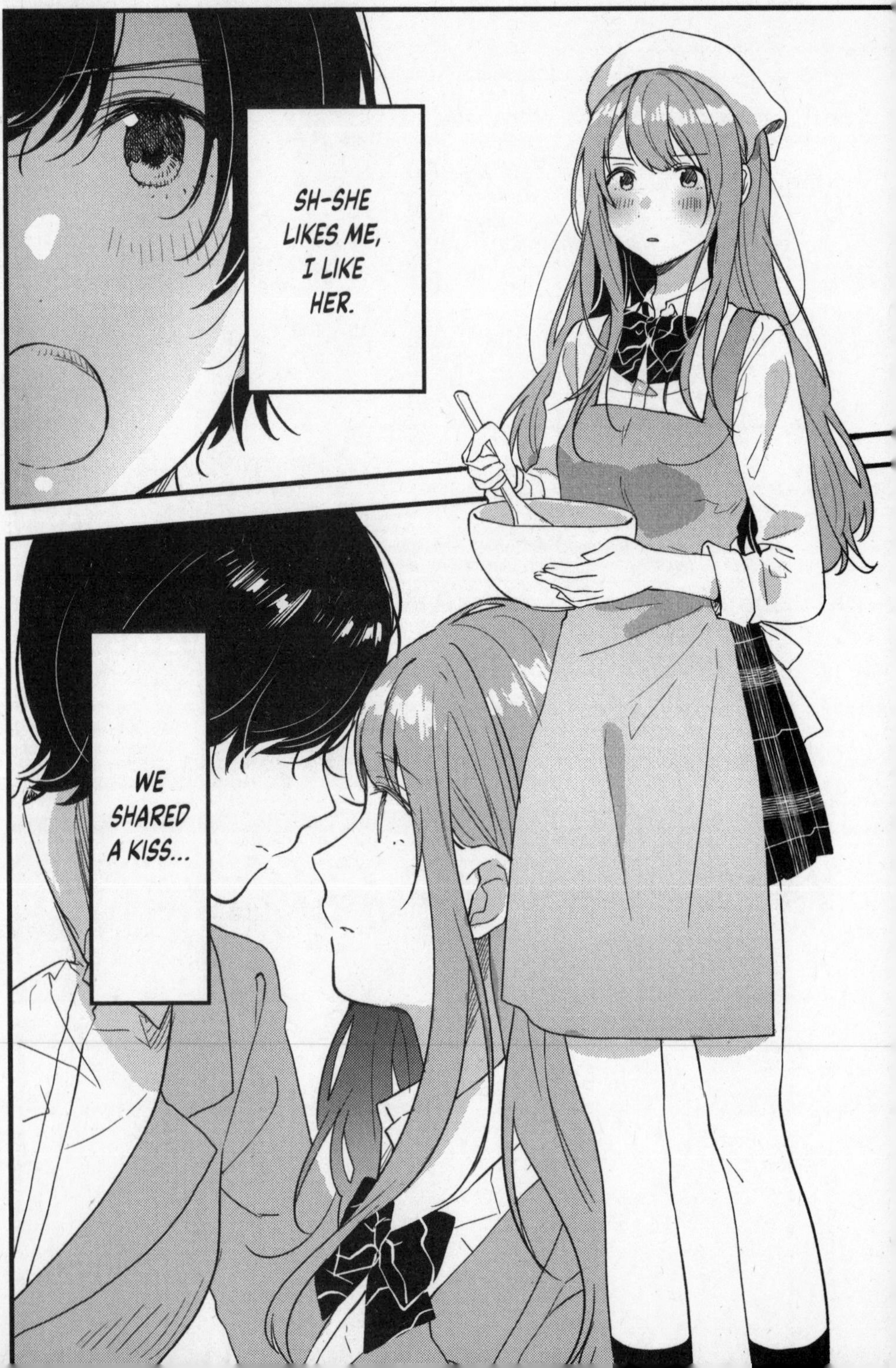
SH-SHE LIKES ME, I LIKE HER.
WE SHARED A KISS...

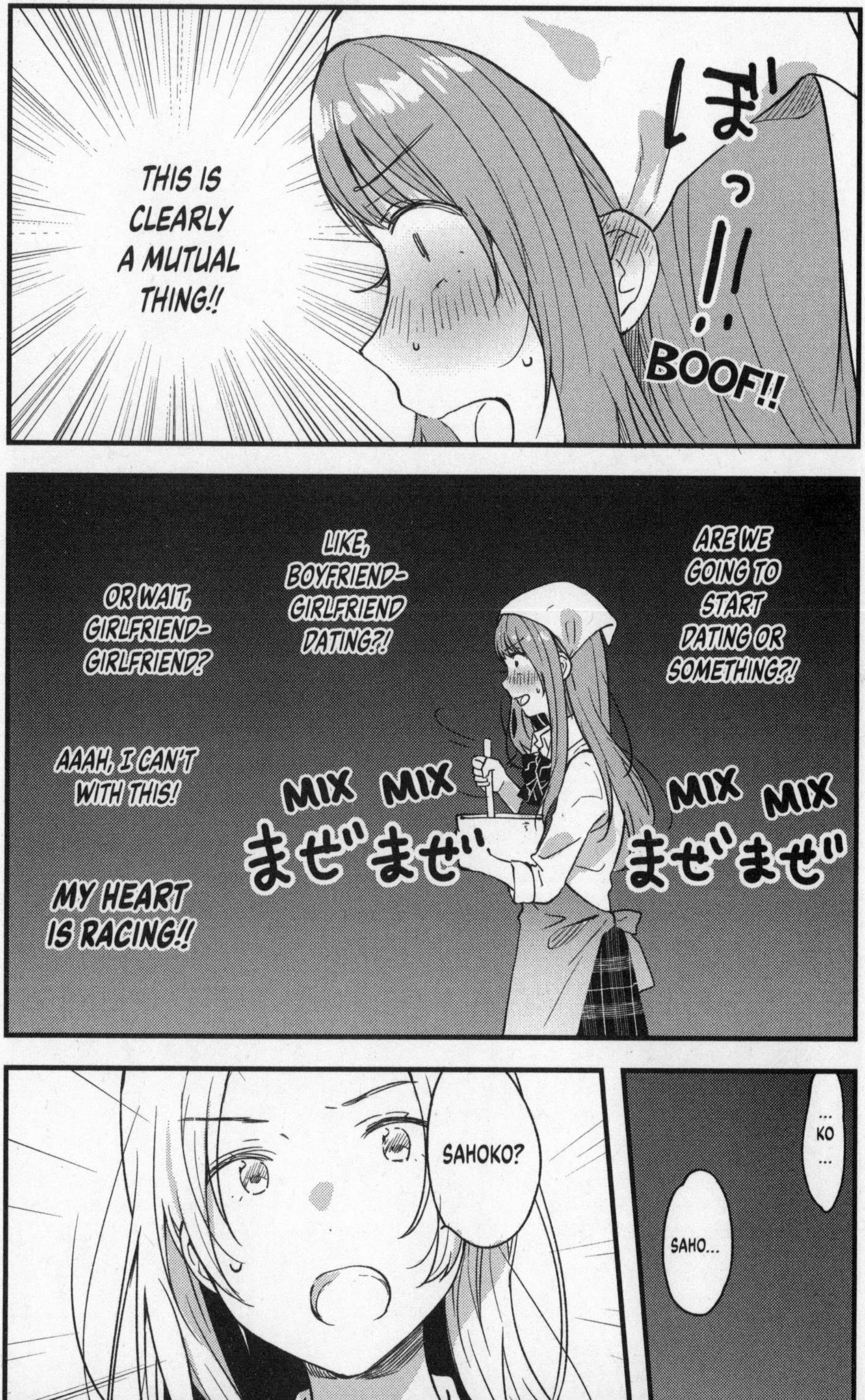
ぼっ!!
BOOF!!
THIS IS CLEARLY A MUTUAL THING!!
ARE WE GOING TO START DATING OR SOMETHING?!
LIKE, BOYFRIEND-GIRLFRIEND DATING?!
OR WAIT, GIRLFRIEND-GIRLFRIEND?
MIX MIX
まぜまぜ
MIX MIX
まぜまぜ
AAAH, I CAN'T WITH THIS!
MY HEART IS RACING!!
...KO...
SAHO...
SAHOKO?

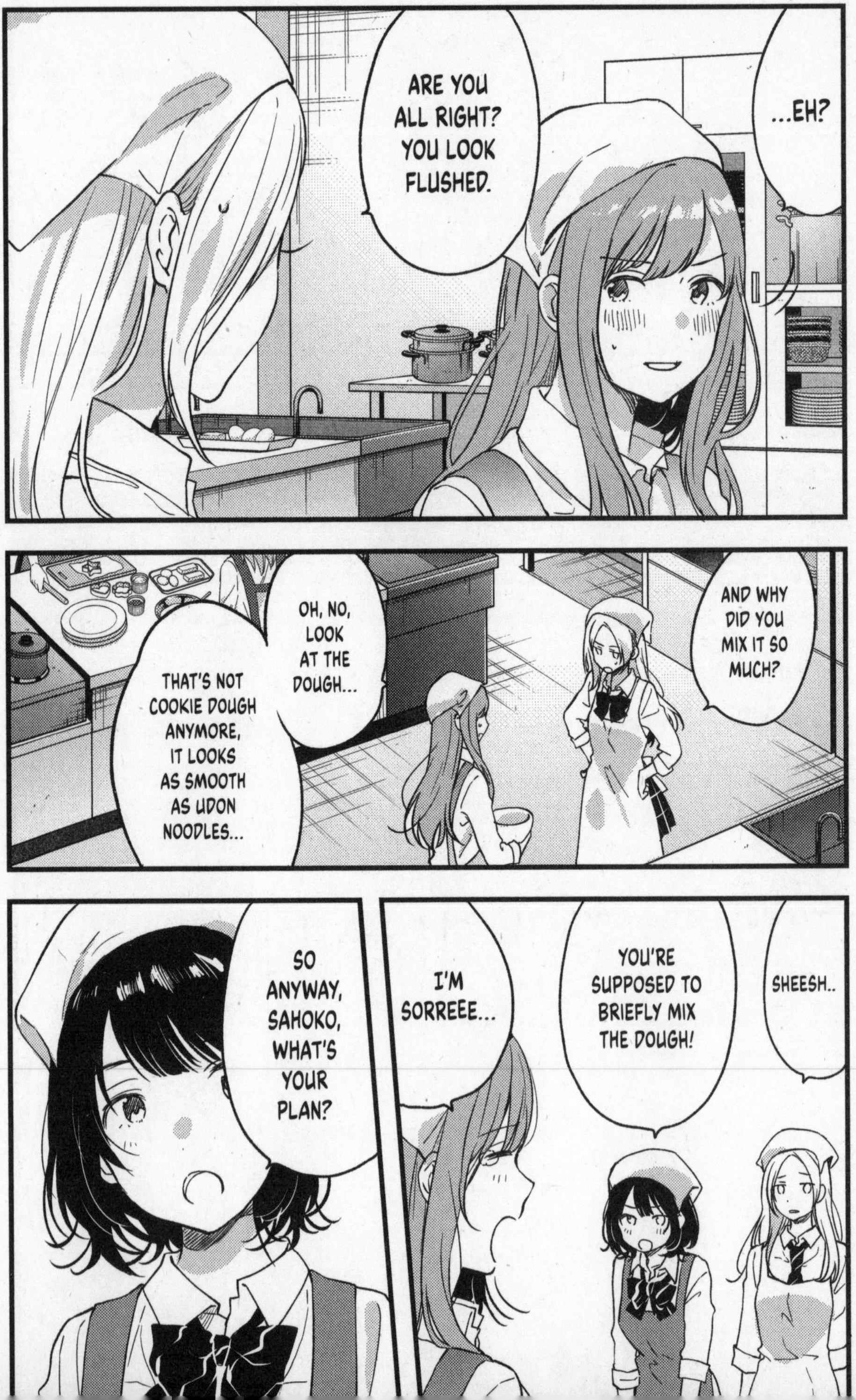
...EH?
ARE YOU ALL RIGHT? YOU LOOK FLUSHED.
AND WHY DID YOU MIX IT SO MUCH?
OH, NO, LOOK AT THE DOUGH...
THAT'S NOT COOKIE DOUGH ANYMORE, IT LOOKS AS SMOOTH AS UDON NOODLES...
SHEESH..
YOU'RE SUPPOSED TO BRIEFLY MIX THE DOUGH!
I'M SORREEE...
SO ANYWAY, SAHOKO, WHAT'S YOUR PLAN?

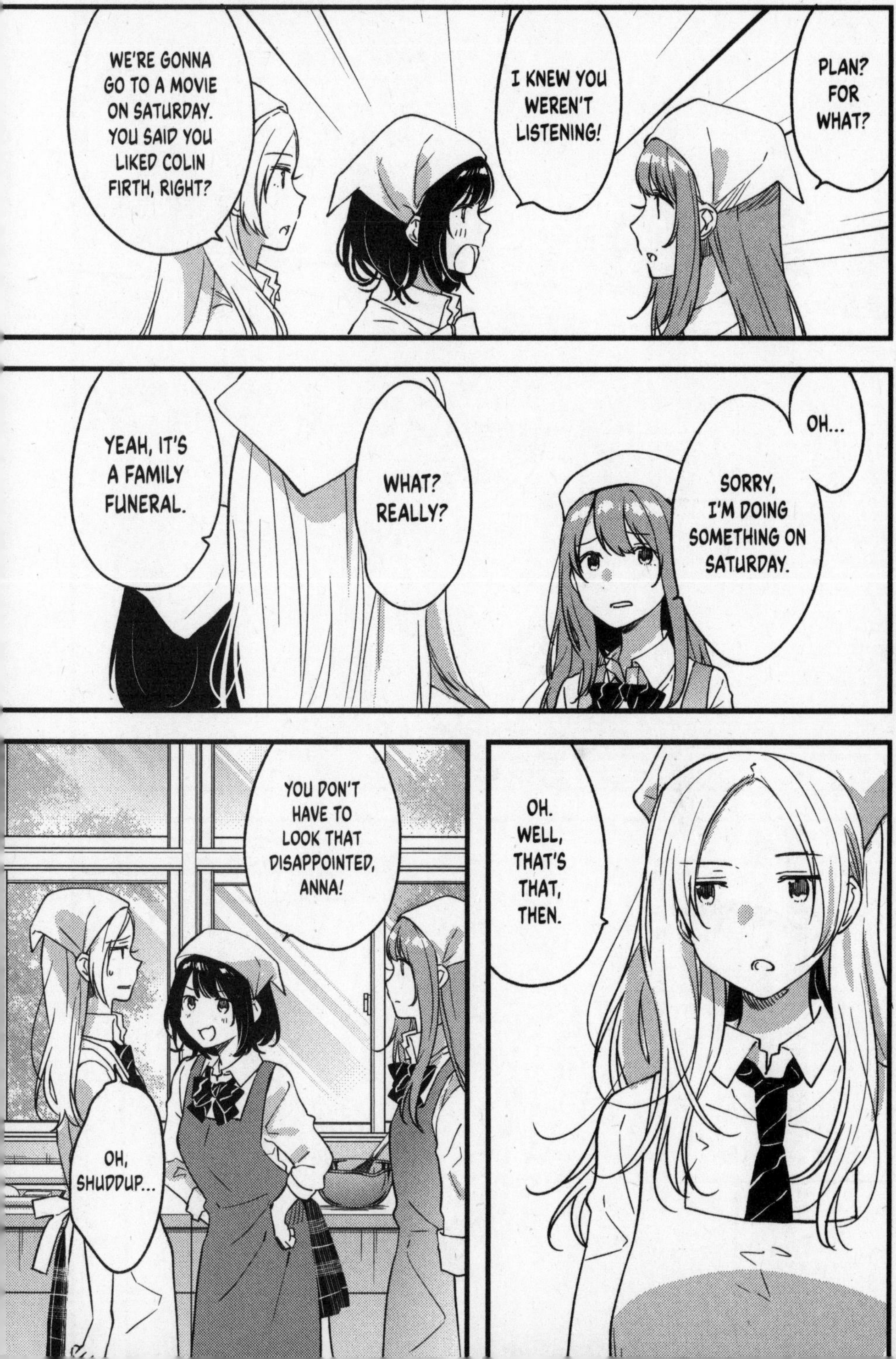
PLAN? FOR WHAT?
I KNEW YOU WEREN'T LISTENING!
WE'RE GONNA GO TO A MOVIE ON SATURDAY. YOU SAID YOU LIKED COLIN FIRTH, RIGHT?
OH...
SORRY, I'M DOING SOMETHING ON SATURDAY.
WHAT? REALLY?
YEAH, IT'S A FAMILY FUNERAL.
OH. WELL, THAT'S THAT, THEN.
YOU DON'T HAVE TO LOOK THAT DISAPPOINTED, ANNA!
OH, SHUDDUP...

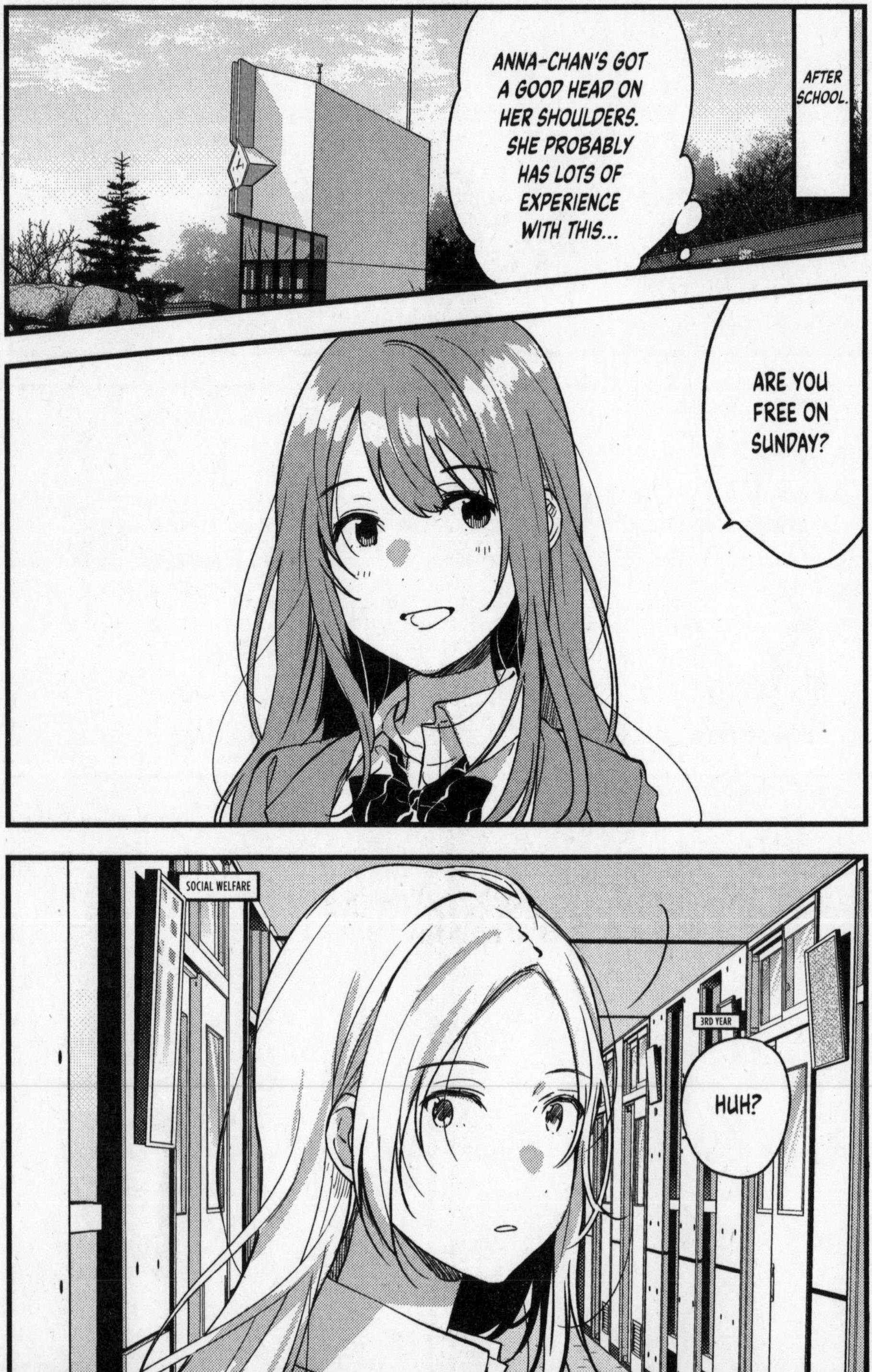
AFTER SCHOOL.
ANNA-CHAN'S GOT A GOOD HEAD ON HER SHOULDERS. SHE PROBABLY HAS LOTS OF EXPERIENCE WITH THIS...
ARE YOU FREE ON SUNDAY?
SOCIAL WELFARE
3RD YEAR
HUH?

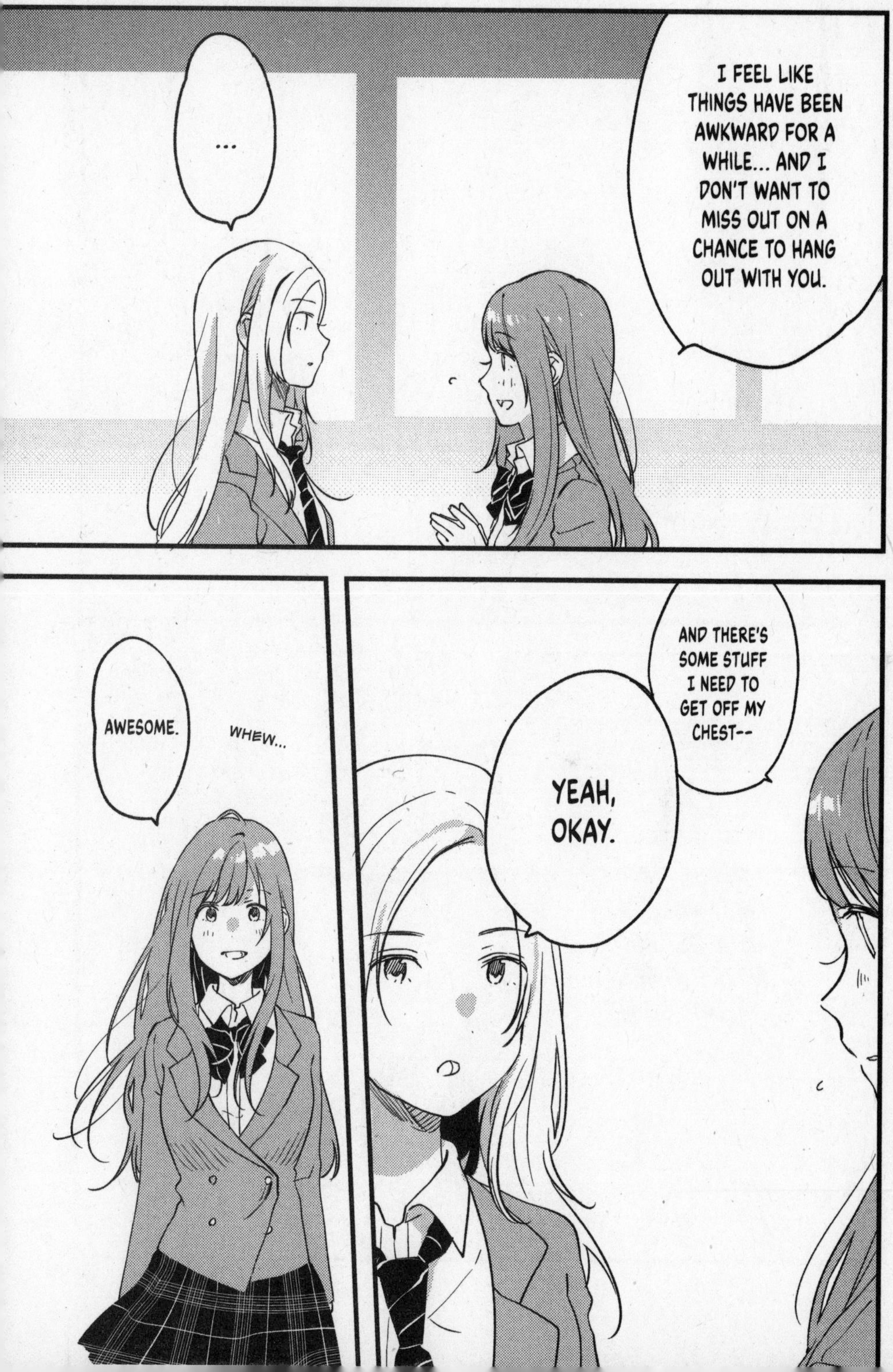
I FEEL LIKE THINGS HAVE BEEN AWKWARD FOR A WHILE... AND I DON'T WANT TO MISS OUT ON A CHANCE TO HANG OUT WITH YOU.
...
AND THERE'S SOME STUFF I NEED TO GET OFF MY CHEST--
YEAH, OKAY.
AWESOME.
WHEW...

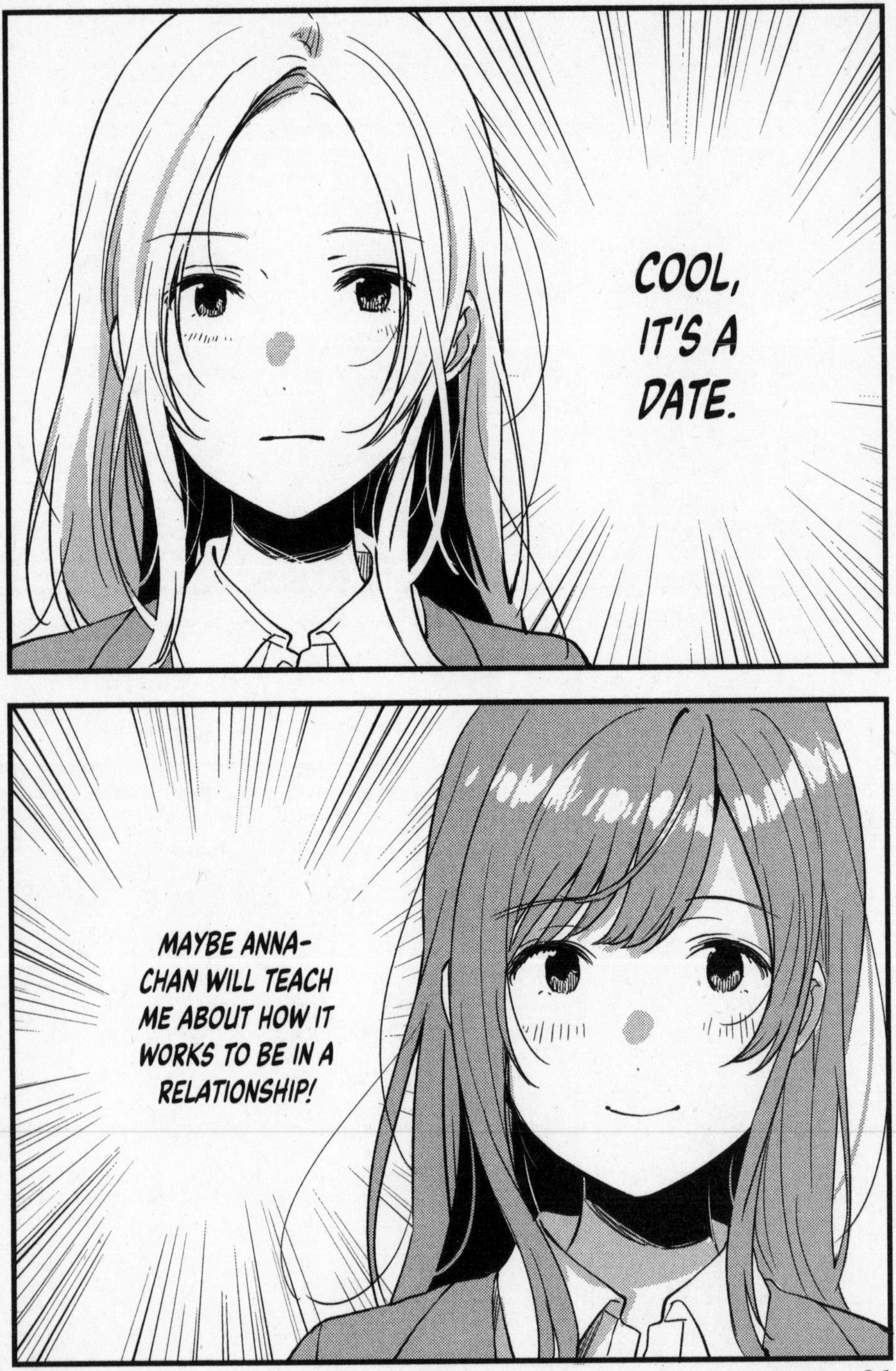
COOL, IT'S A DATE.
MAYBE ANNA-CHAN WILL TEACH ME ABOUT HOW IT WORKS TO BE IN A RELATIONSHIP!

CHASING AFTER *Aoi Koshiba*

Autumn, Second Year of High School

CHASING AFTER *Aoi Koshiba*

Autumn, Second Year of High School

Chapter 27:
Even After Opening Up (Part 1)

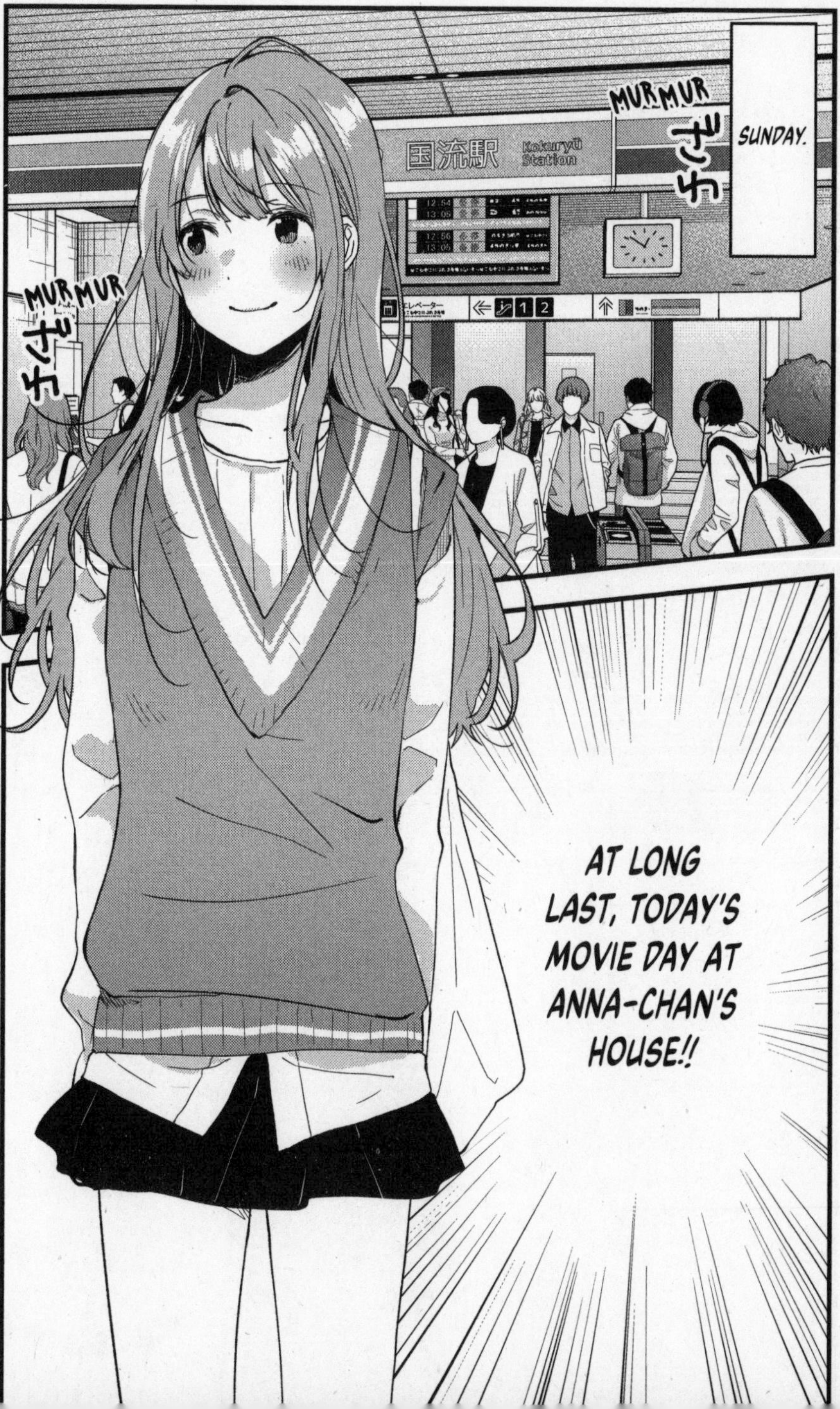
SUNDAY.
MURMUR
国流駅 Kokuryū Station
MURMUR
AT LONG LAST, TODAY'S MOVIE DAY AT ANNA-CHAN'S HOUSE!!

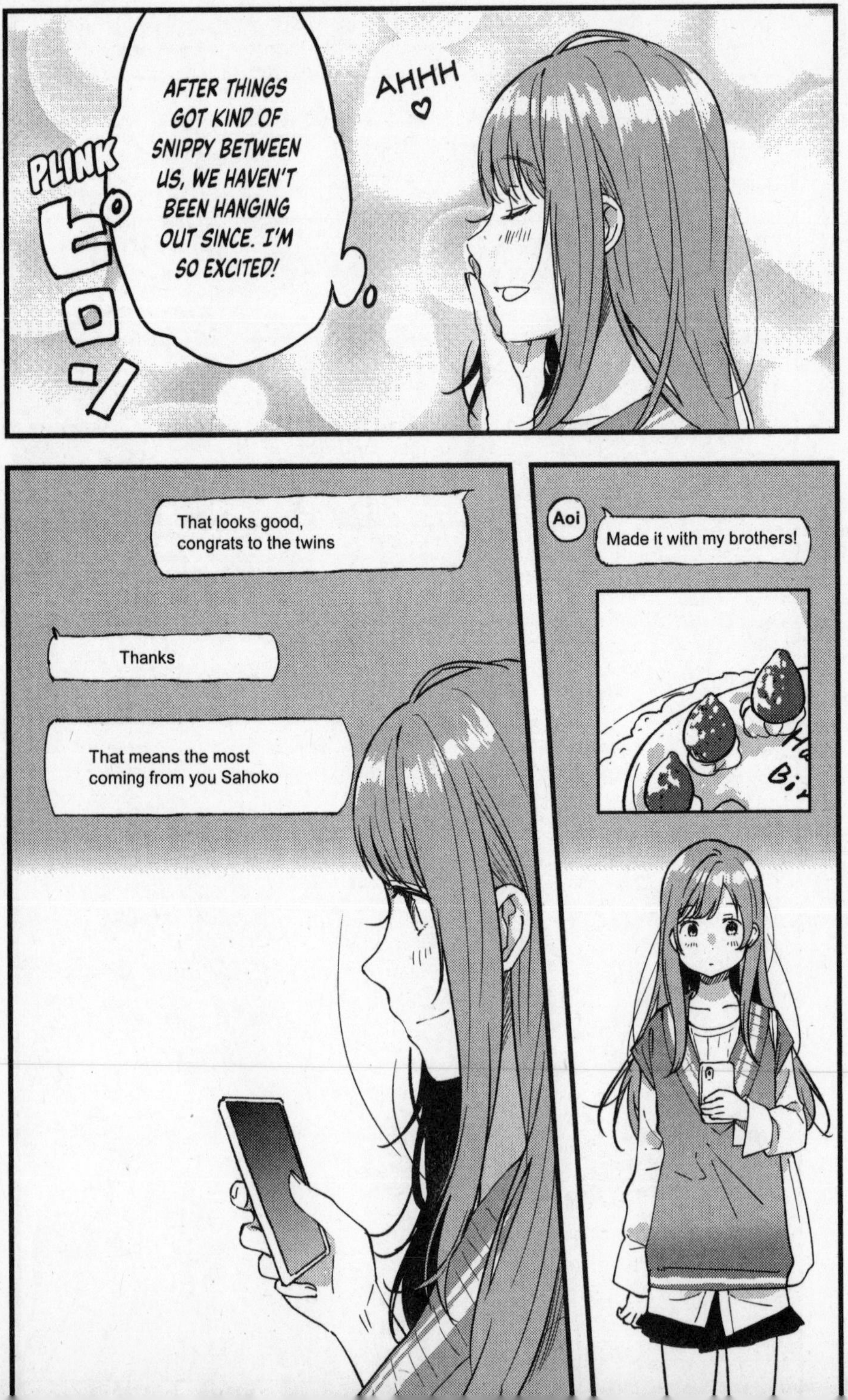
AHHH ♡
AFTER THINGS GOT KIND OF SNIPPY BETWEEN US, WE HAVEN'T BEEN HANGING OUT SINCE. I'M SO EXCITED!
PLINK
ピロン
Aoi
Made it with my brothers!
That looks good, congrats to the twins
Thanks
That means the most coming from you Sahoko

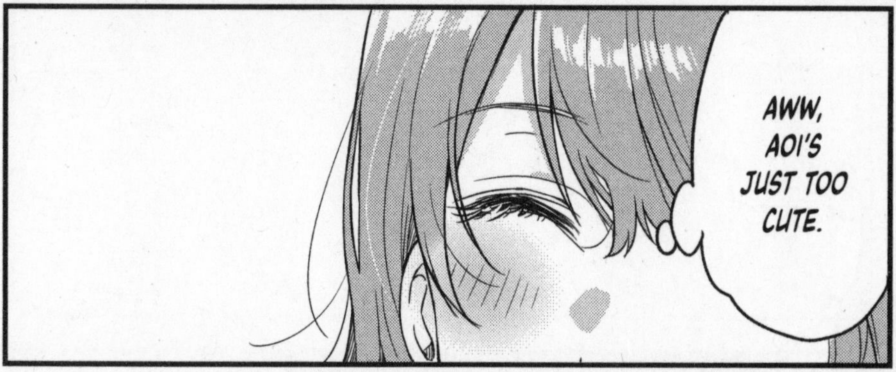
AWW, AOI'S JUST TOO CUTE.

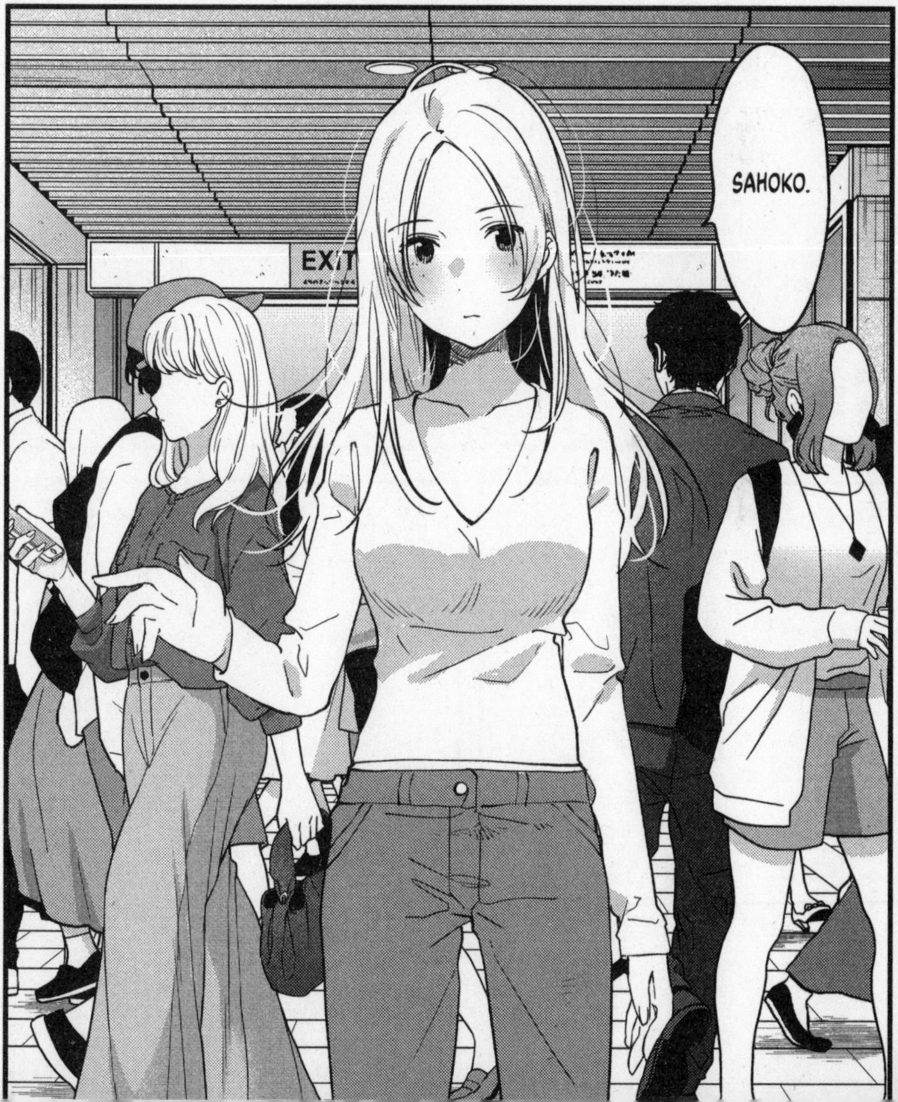
SAHOKO.
EXIT

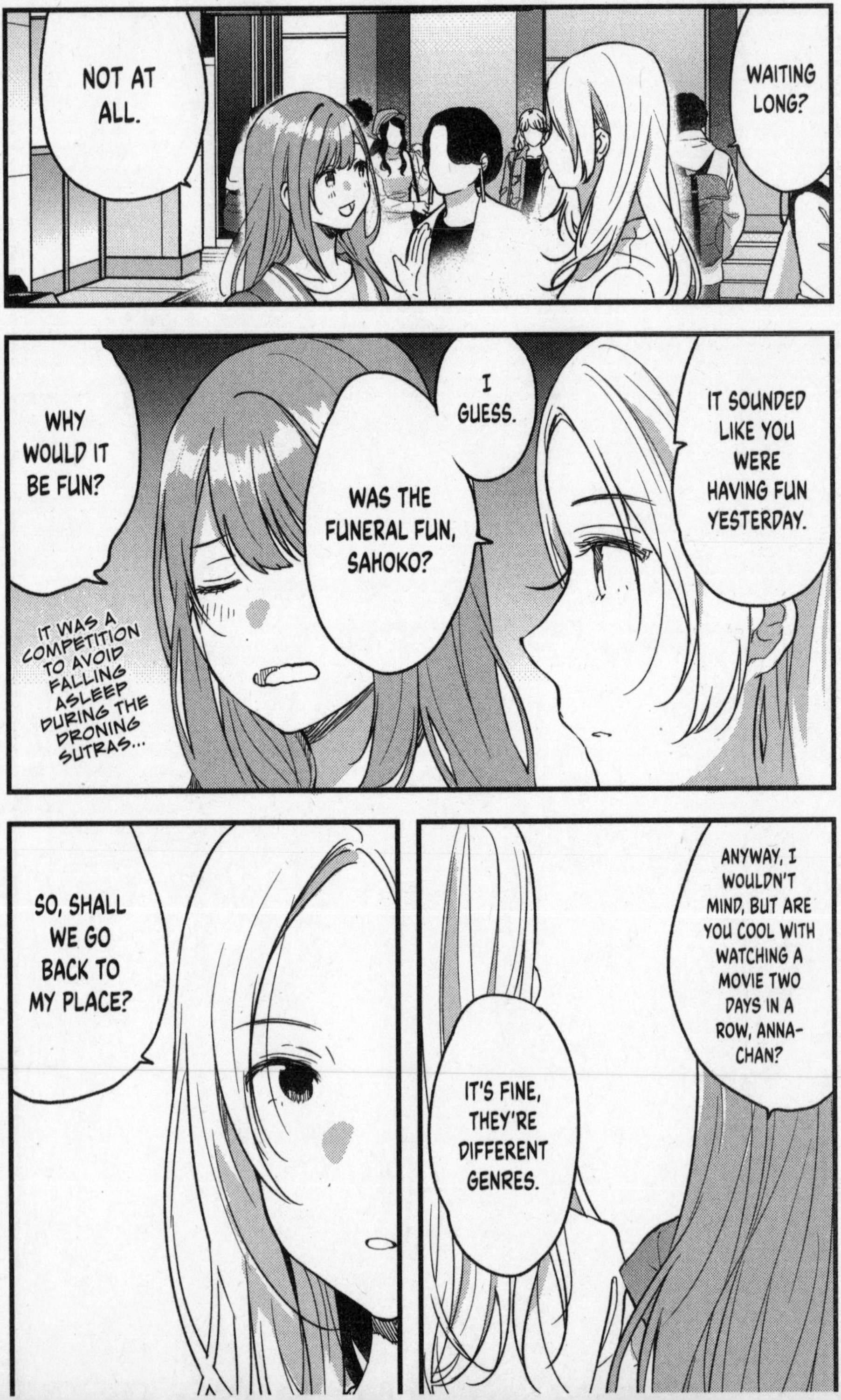
WAITING LONG?
NOT AT ALL.
IT SOUNDED LIKE YOU WERE HAVING FUN YESTERDAY.
I GUESS.
WAS THE FUNERAL FUN, SAHOKO?
WHY WOULD IT BE FUN?
IT WAS A COMPETITION TO AVOID FALLING ASLEEP DURING THE DRONING SUTRAS...
ANYWAY, I WOULDN'T MIND, BUT ARE YOU COOL WITH WATCHING A MOVIE TWO DAYS IN A ROW, ANNA-CHAN?
IT'S FINE, THEY'RE DIFFERENT GENRES.
SO, SHALL WE GO BACK TO MY PLACE?

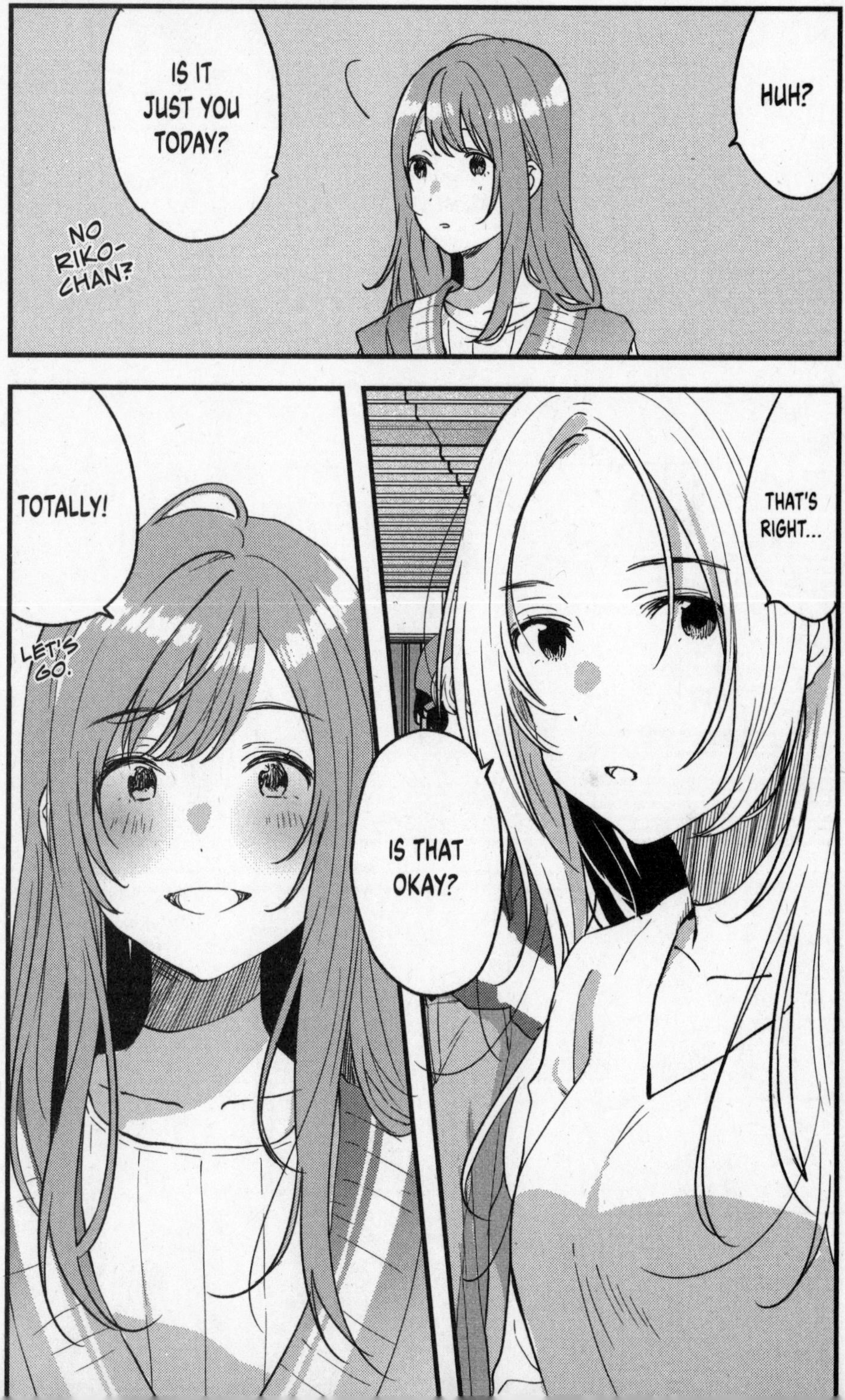
HUH?
IS IT JUST YOU TODAY?
NO RIKO-CHAN?
THAT'S RIGHT...
IS THAT OKAY?
TOTALLY!
LET'S GO.

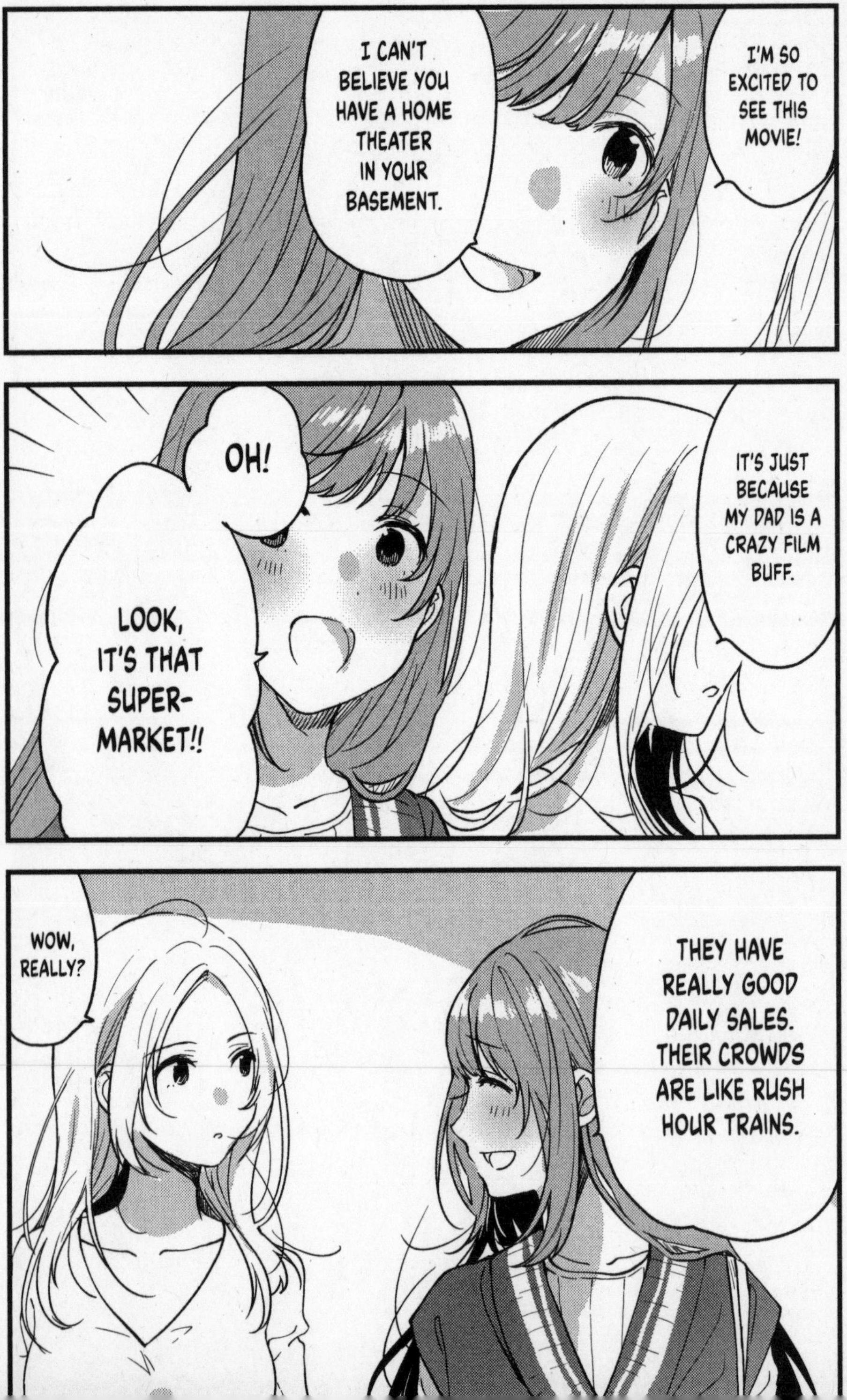
I'M SO EXCITED TO SEE THIS MOVIE!
I CAN'T BELIEVE YOU HAVE A HOME THEATER IN YOUR BASEMENT.
IT'S JUST BECAUSE MY DAD IS A CRAZY FILM BUFF.
OH!
LOOK, IT'S THAT SUPER-MARKET!!
THEY HAVE REALLY GOOD DAILY SALES. THEIR CROWDS ARE LIKE RUSH HOUR TRAINS.
WOW, REALLY?

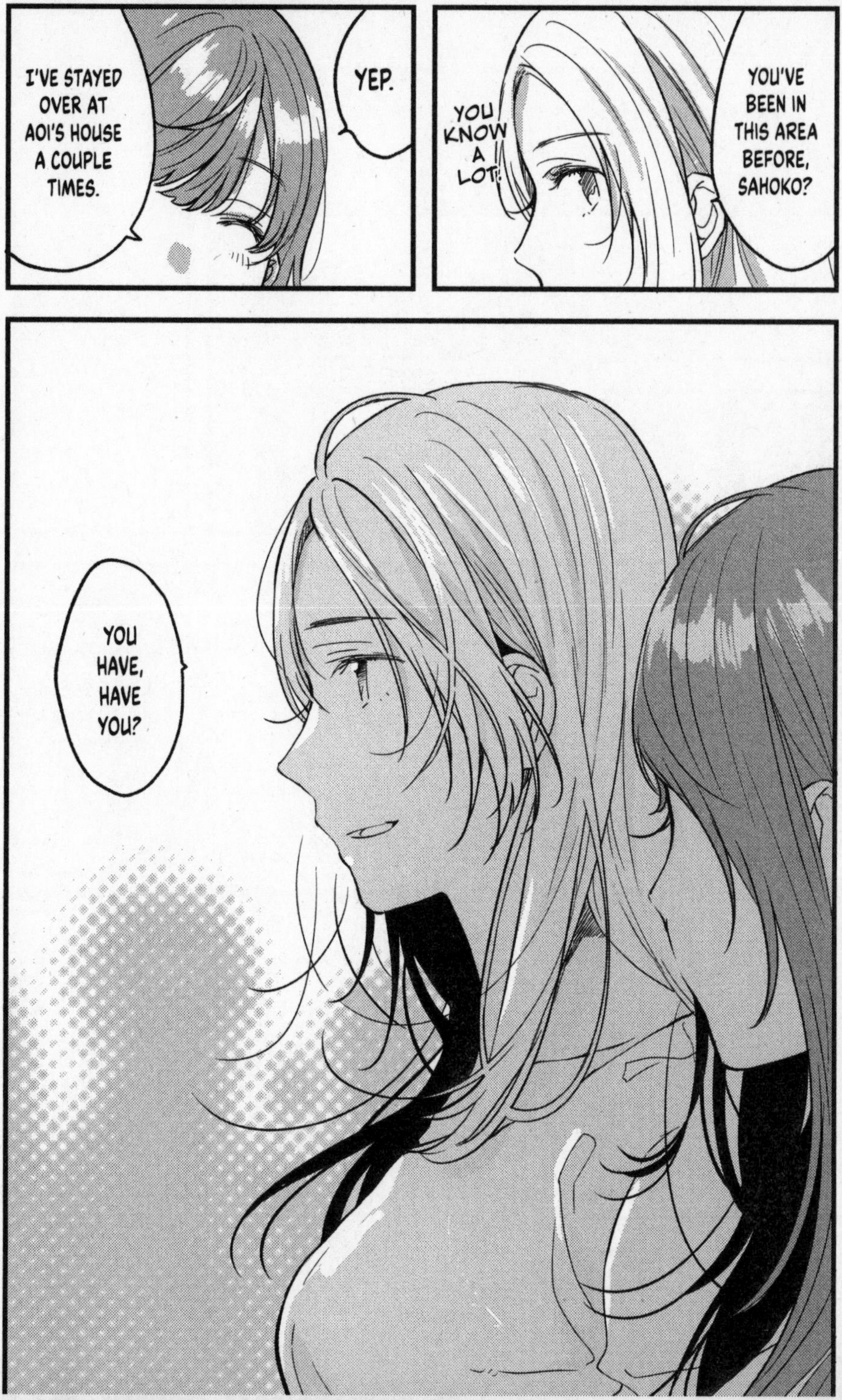
YOU'VE BEEN IN THIS AREA BEFORE, SAHOKO?
YOU KNOW A LOT!
YEP.
I'VE STAYED OVER AT AOI'S HOUSE A COUPLE TIMES.
YOU HAVE, HAVE YOU?

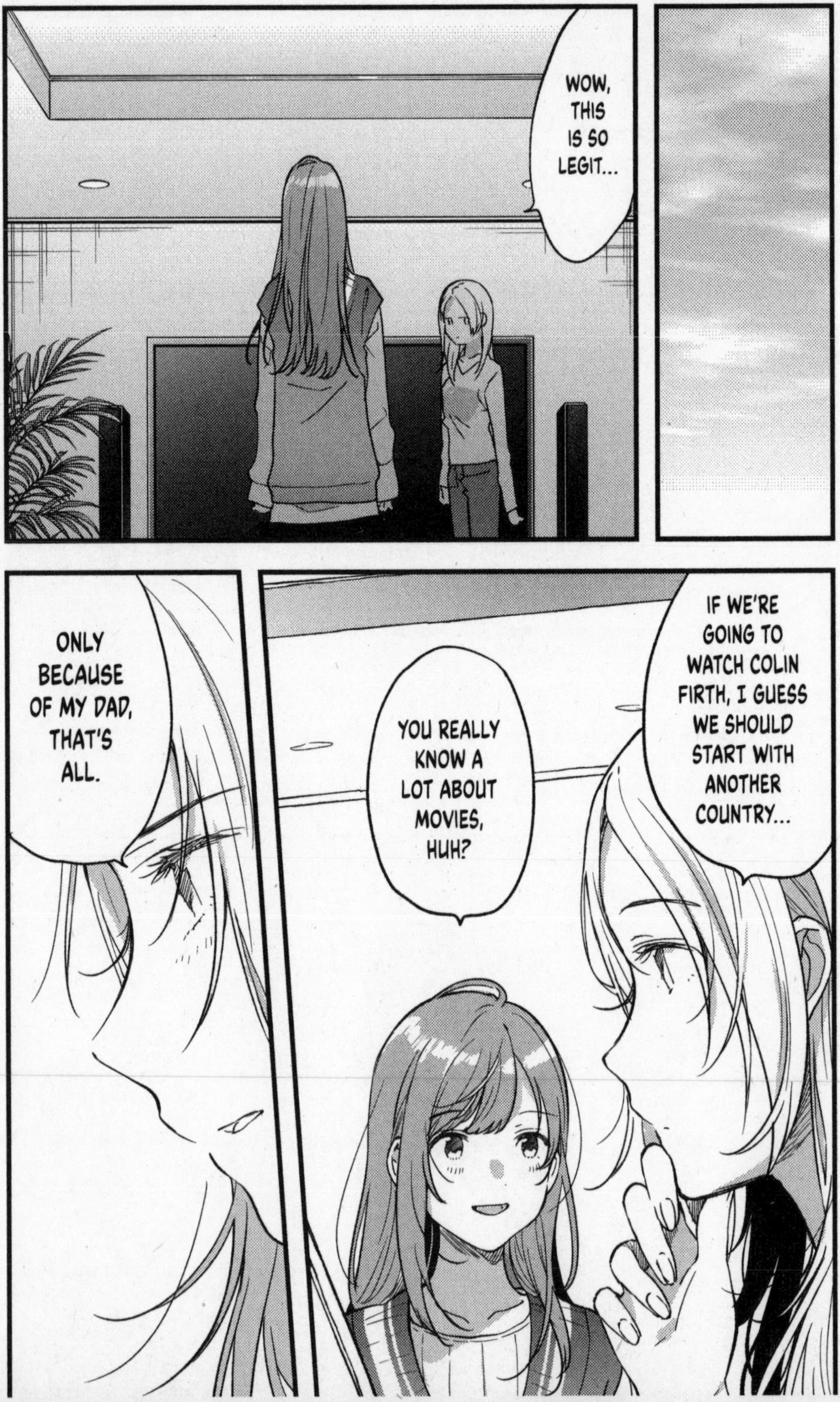
WOW, THIS IS SO LEGIT...
IF WE'RE GOING TO WATCH COLIN FIRTH, I GUESS WE SHOULD START WITH ANOTHER COUNTRY...
YOU REALLY KNOW A LOT ABOUT MOVIES, HUH?
ONLY BECAUSE OF MY DAD, THAT'S ALL.

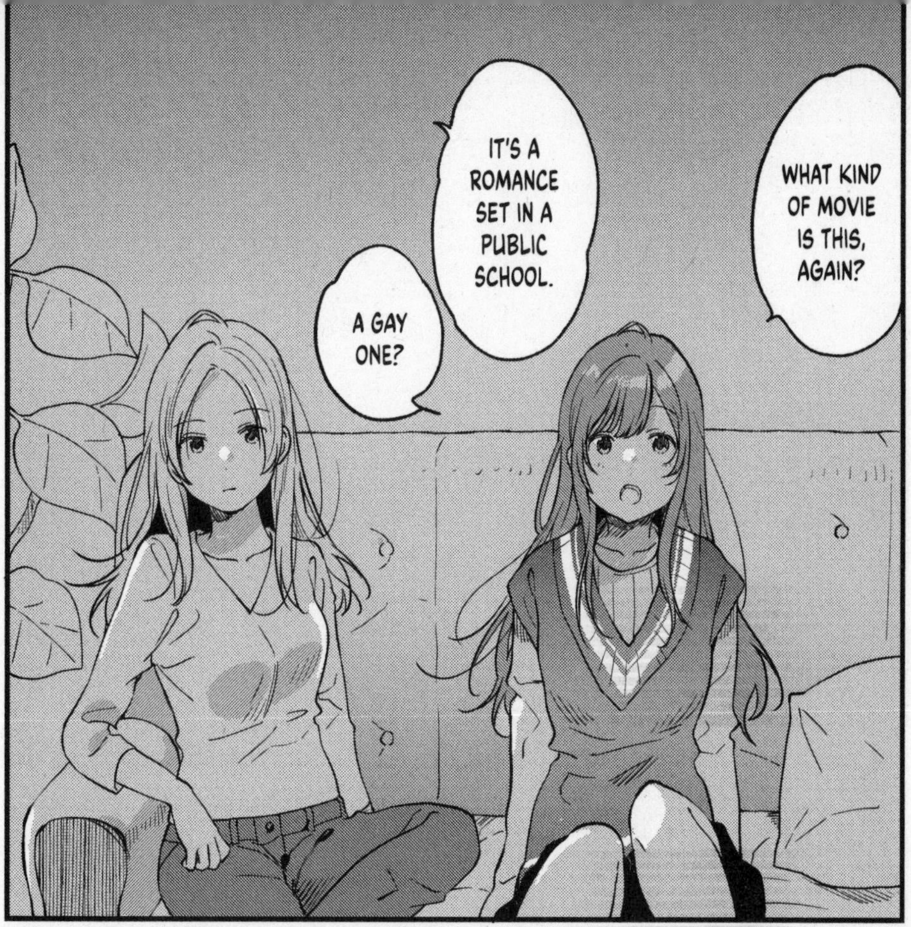
WHAT KIND OF MOVIE IS THIS, AGAIN?
IT'S A ROMANCE SET IN A PUBLIC SCHOOL.
A GAY ONE?

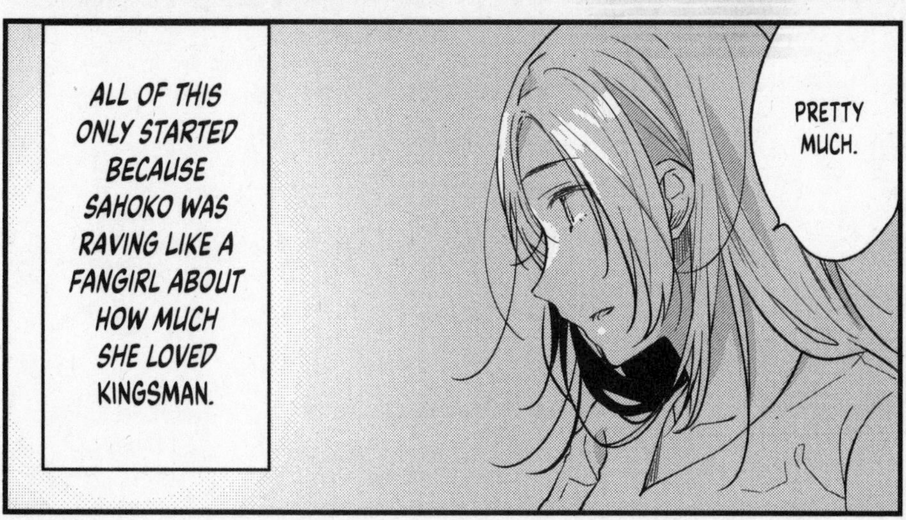
PRETTY MUCH.
ALL OF THIS ONLY STARTED BECAUSE SAHOKO WAS RAVING LIKE A FANGIRL ABOUT HOW MUCH SHE LOVED KINGSMAN.

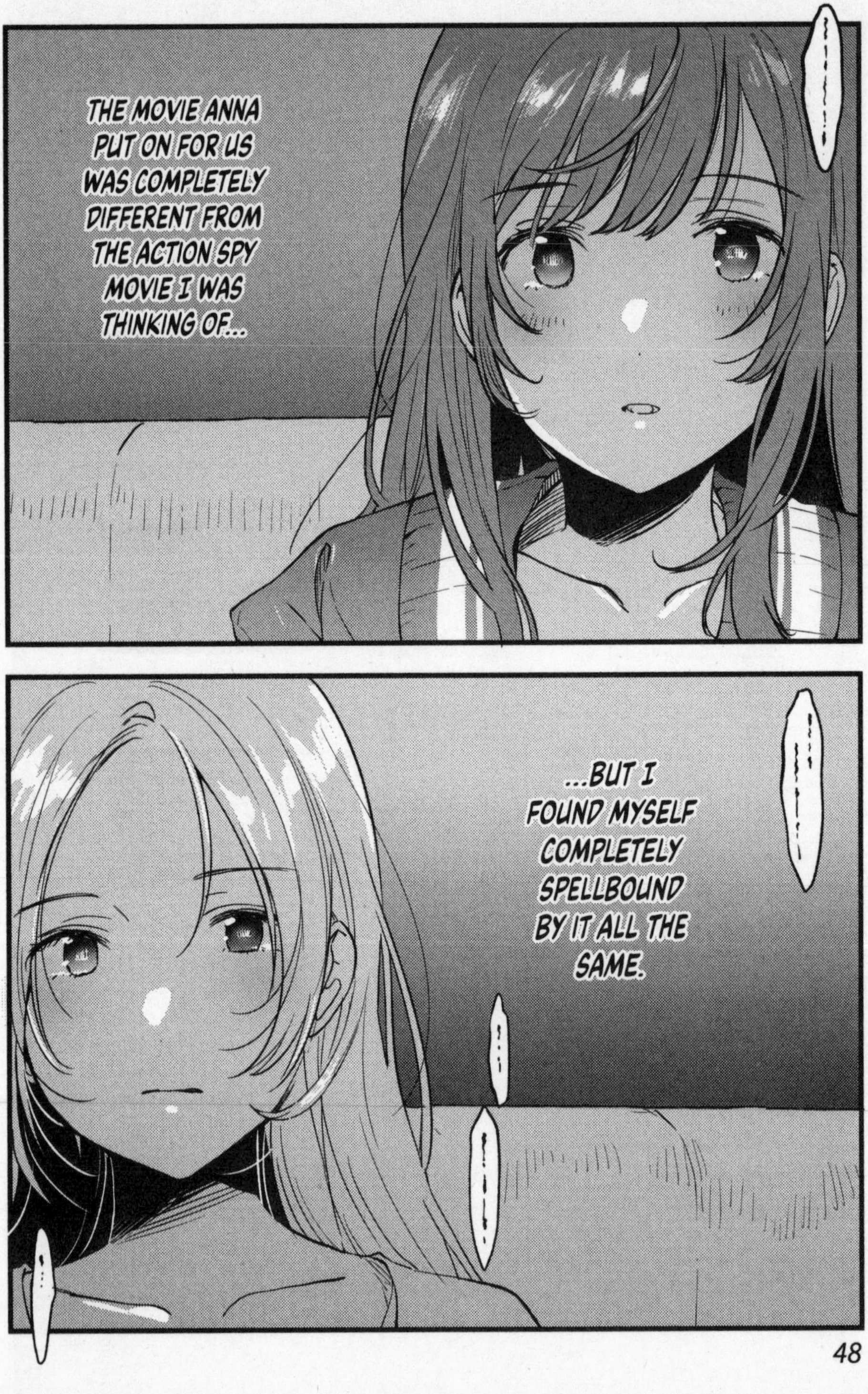
THE MOVIE ANNA PUT ON FOR US WAS COMPLETELY DIFFERENT FROM THE ACTION SPY MOVIE I WAS THINKING OF...
...BUT I FOUND MYSELF COMPLETELY SPELLBOUND BY IT ALL THE SAME.

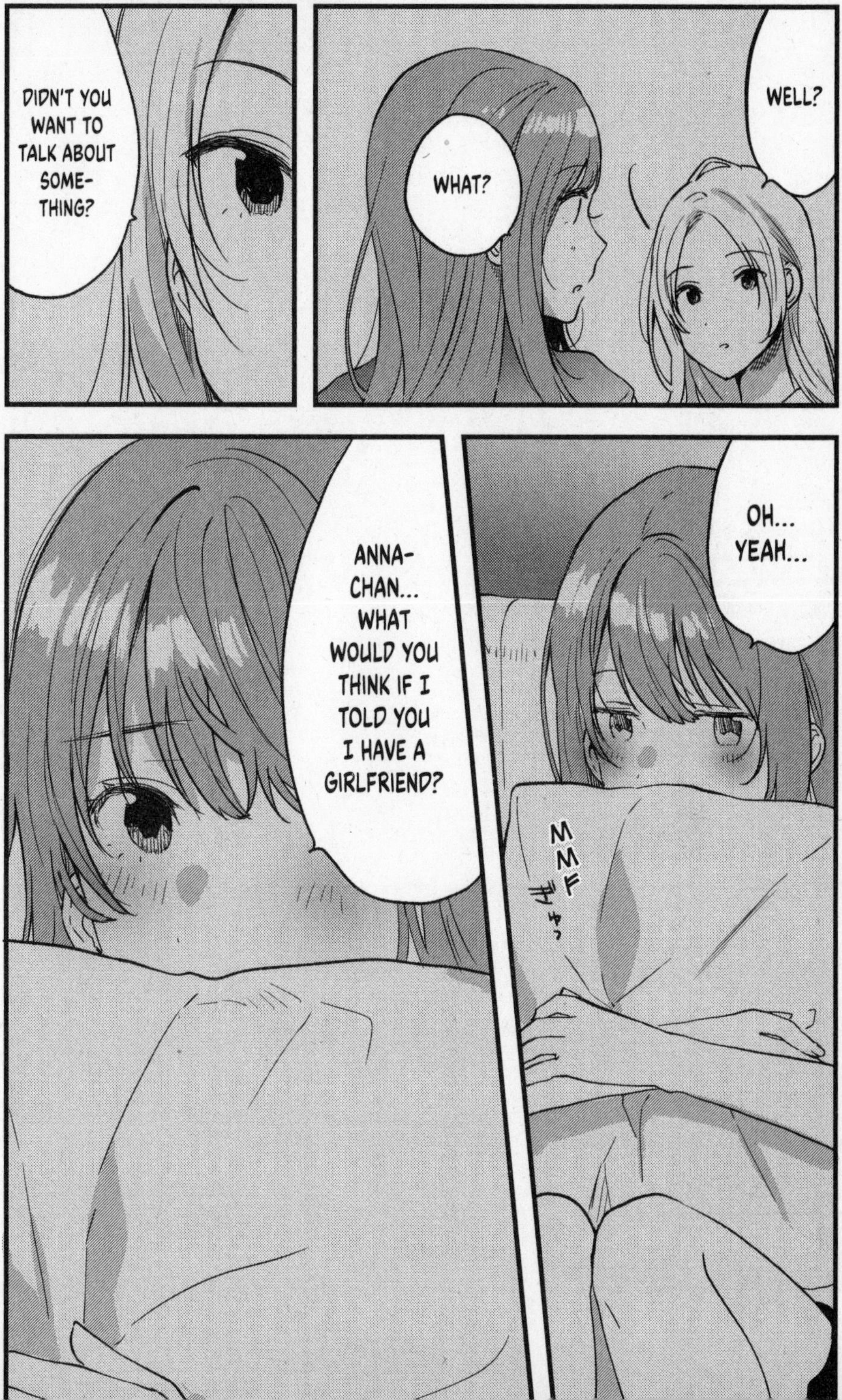
WELL?
WHAT?
DIDN'T YOU WANT TO TALK ABOUT SOME-THING?
OH... YEAH...
MMF
ANNA-CHAN... WHAT WOULD YOU THINK IF I TOLD YOU I HAVE A GIRLFRIEND?

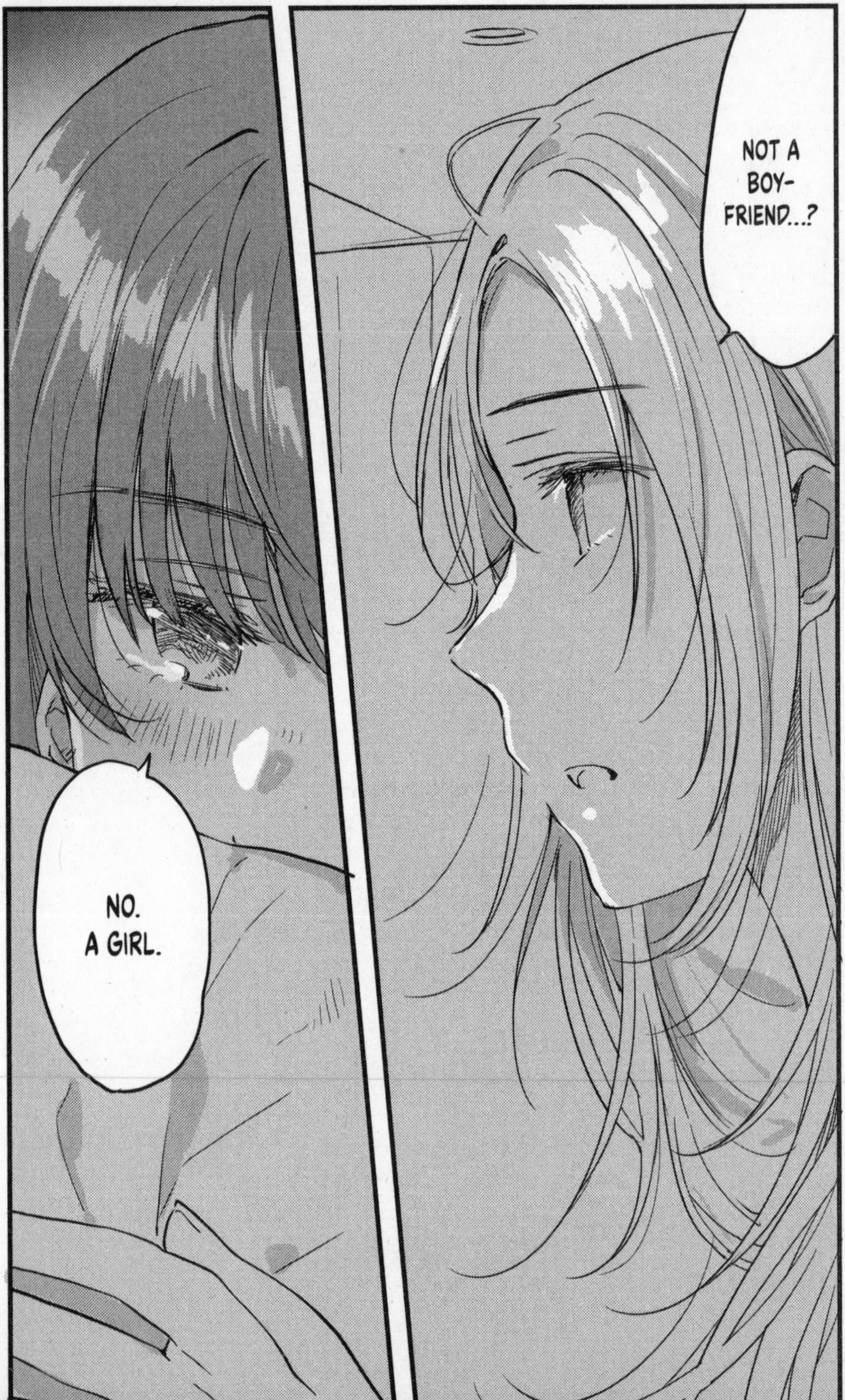
NOT A BOY-FRIEND...?
NO. A GIRL.

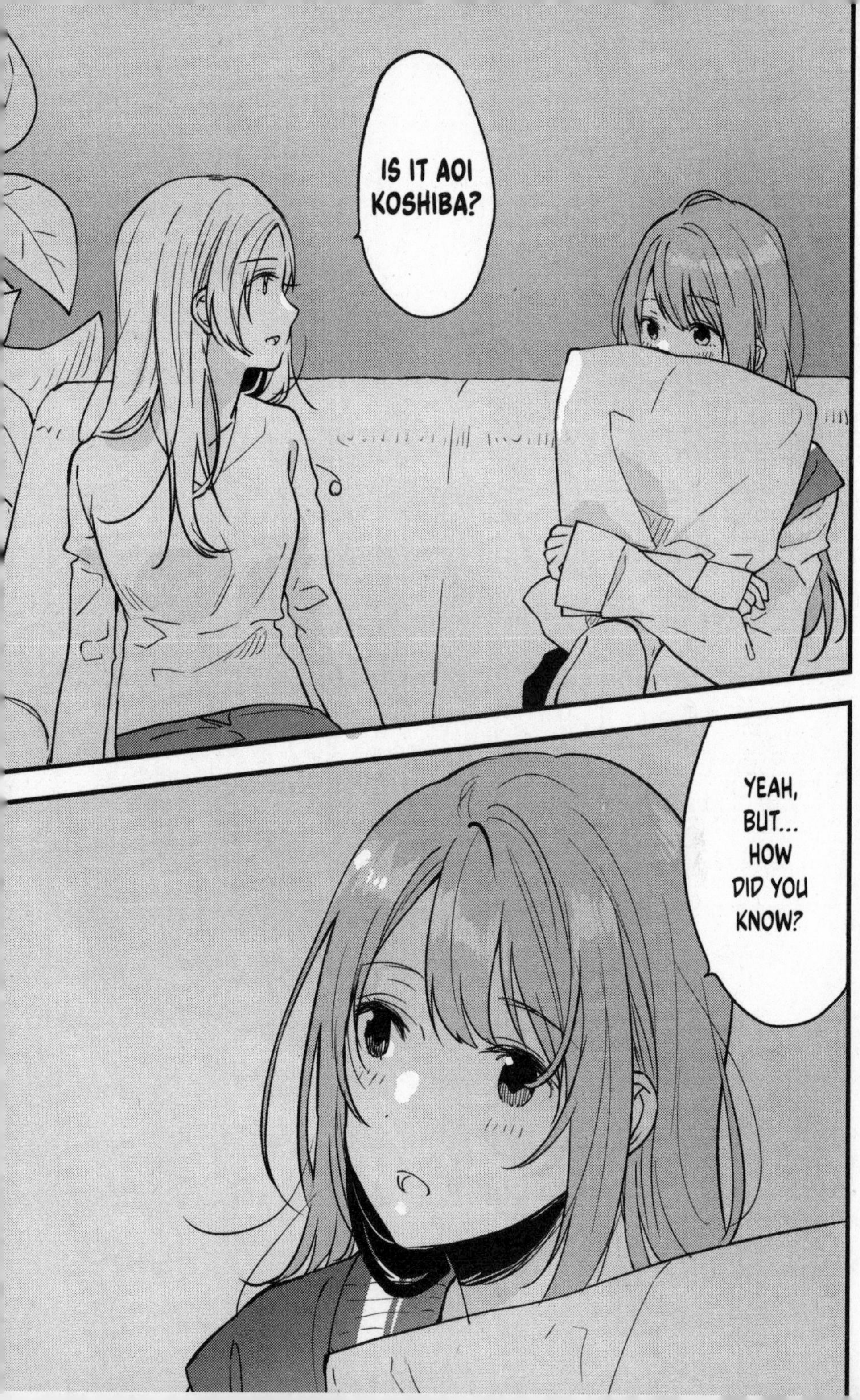
IS IT AOI KOSHIBA?
YEAH, BUT... HOW DID YOU KNOW?

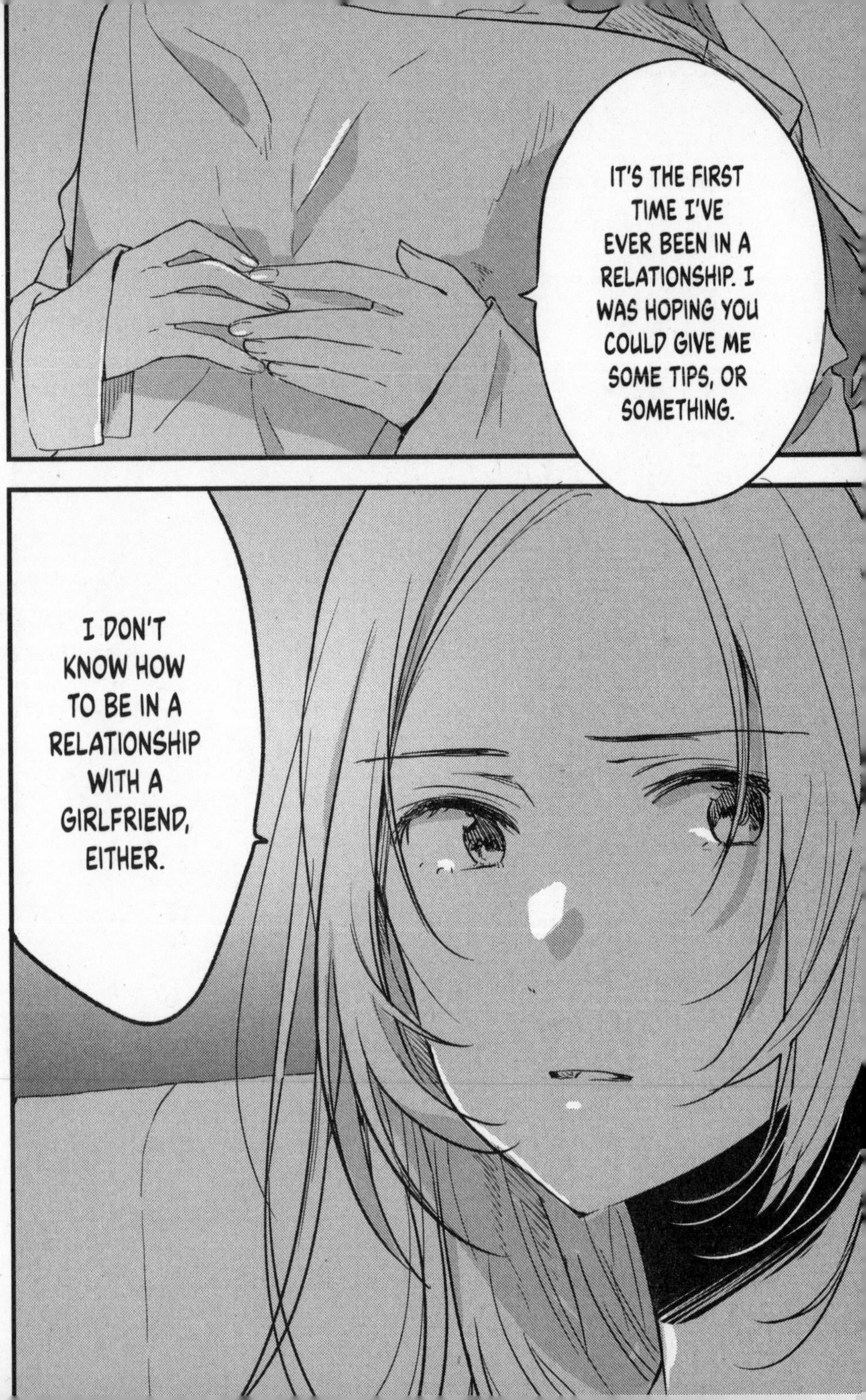
IT'S THE FIRST TIME I'VE EVER BEEN IN A RELATIONSHIP. I WAS HOPING YOU COULD GIVE ME SOME TIPS, OR SOMETHING.
I DON'T KNOW HOW TO BE IN A RELATIONSHIP WITH A GIRLFRIEND, EITHER.

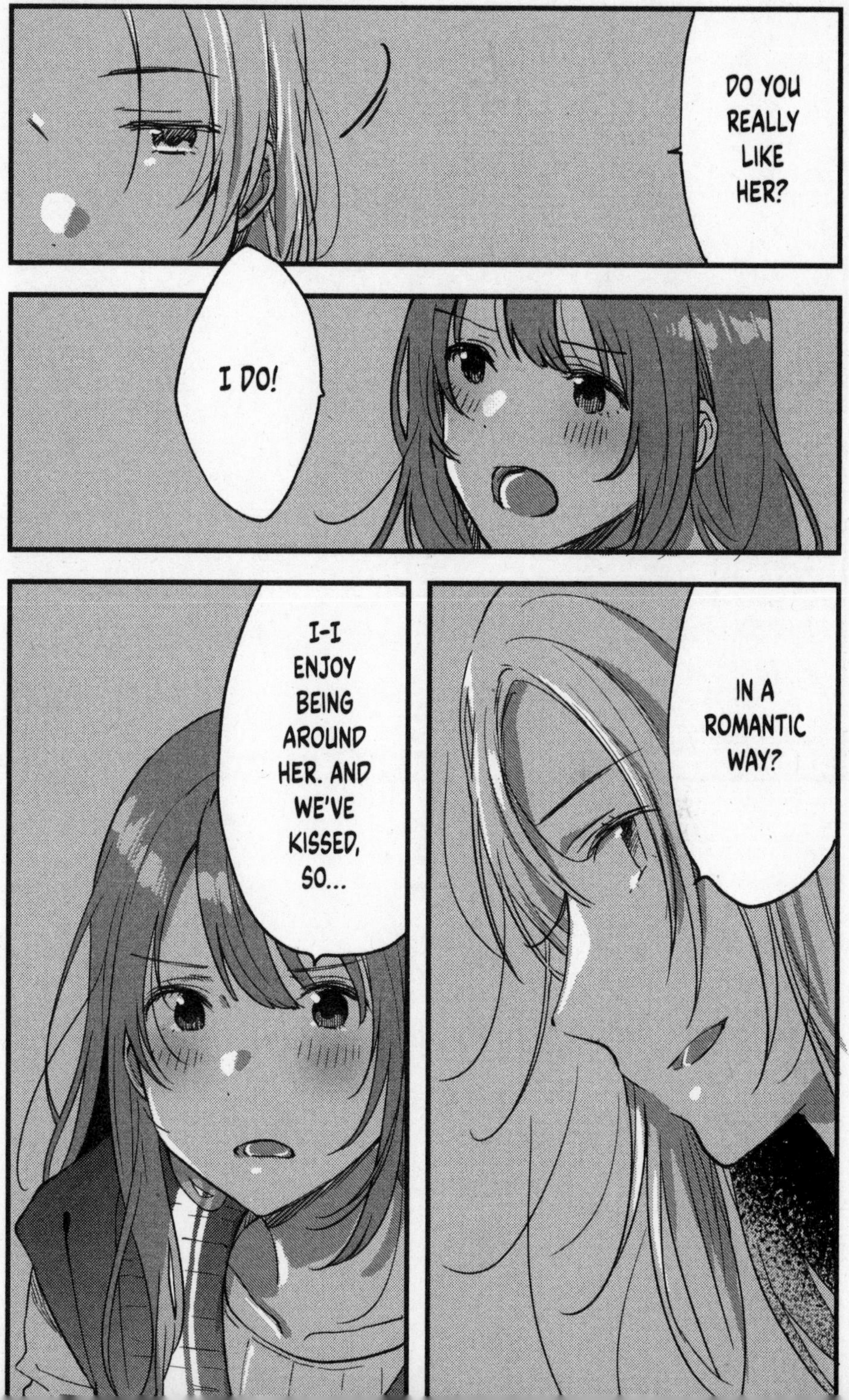
DO YOU REALLY LIKE HER?
I DO!
IN A ROMANTIC WAY?
I-I ENJOY BEING AROUND HER. AND WE'VE KISSED, SO...

YOU DON'T
KNOW A THING.

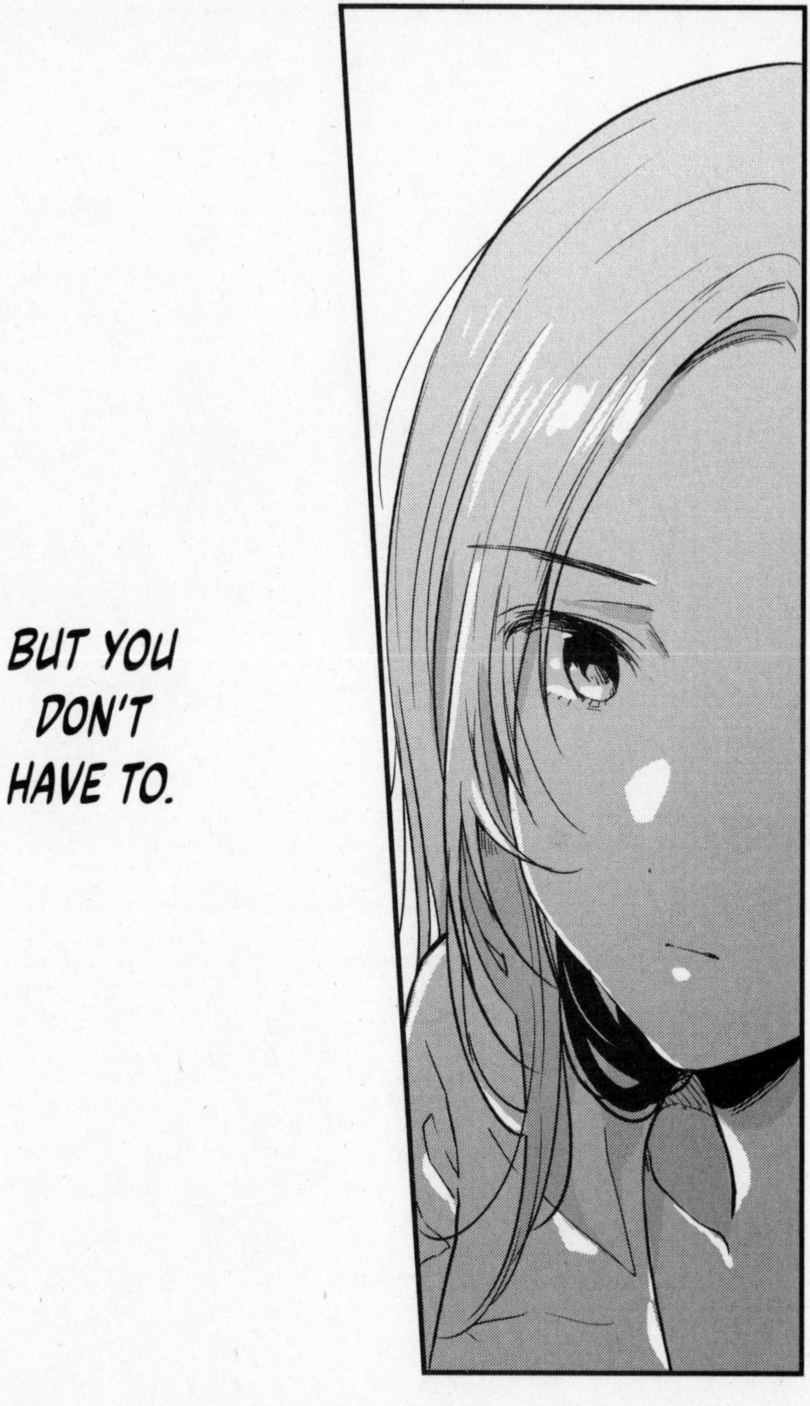
BUT YOU DON'T HAVE TO.

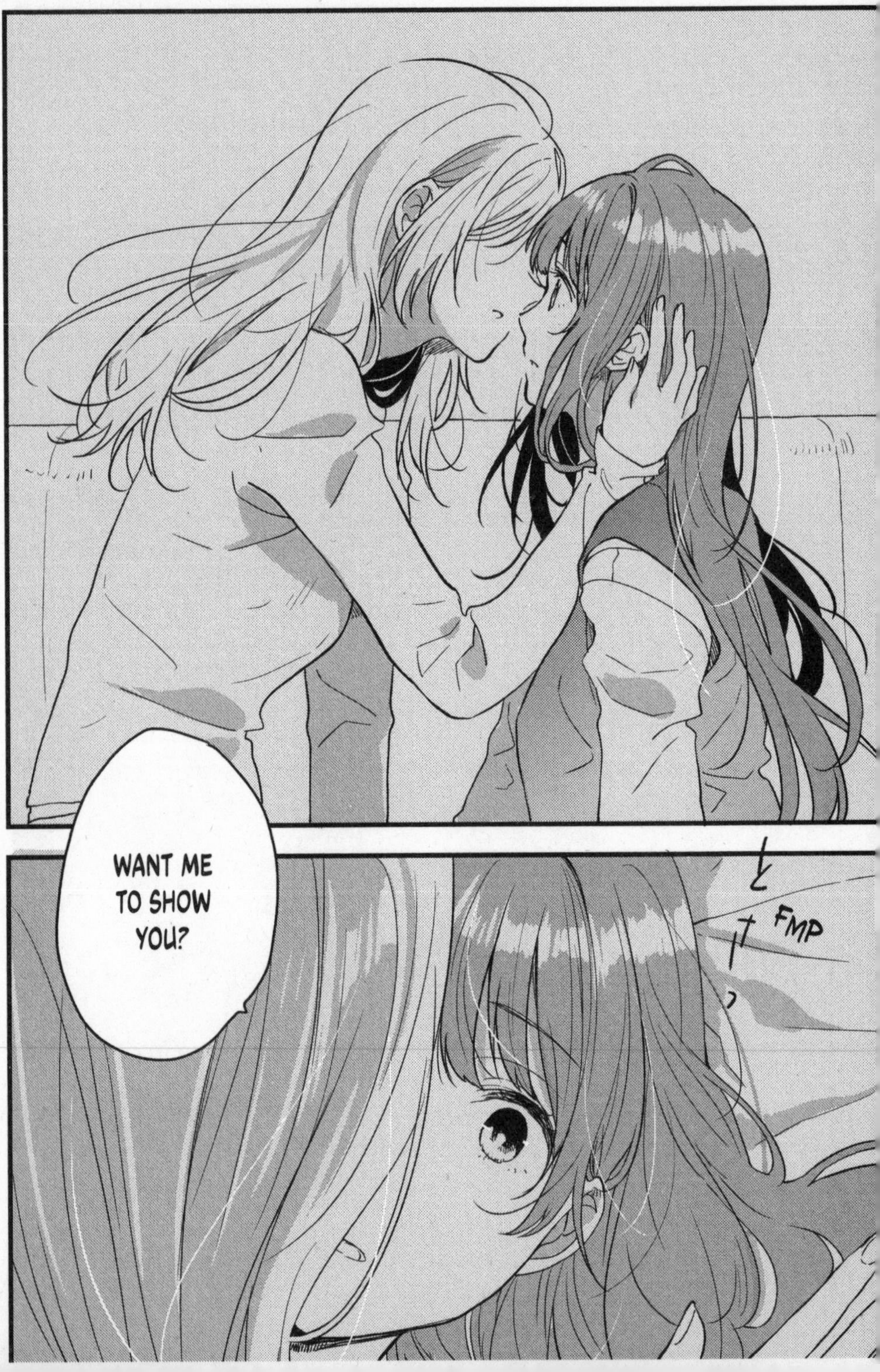
FMP
WANT ME TO SHOW YOU?

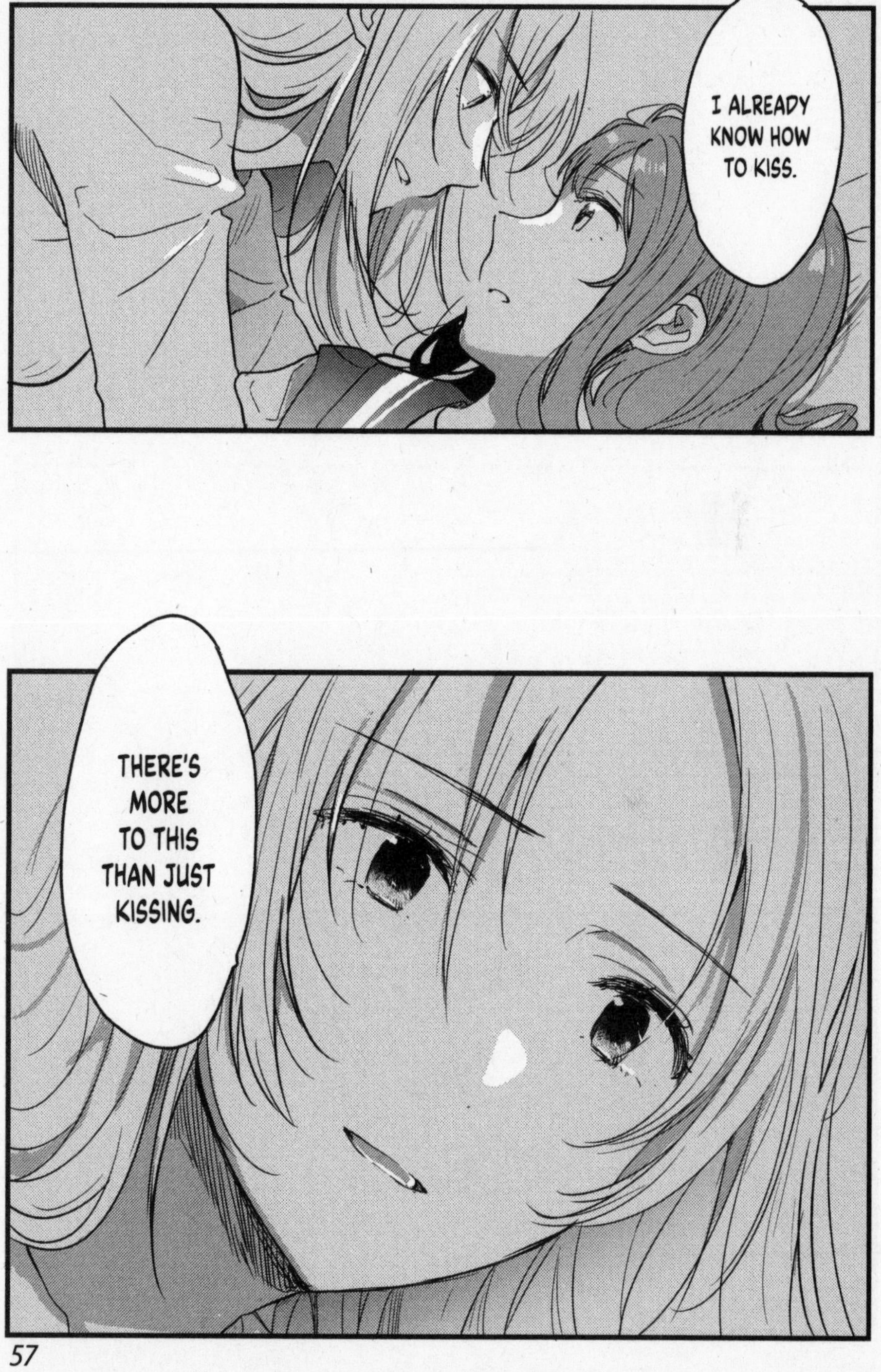
I ALREADY KNOW HOW TO KISS.
THERE'S MORE TO THIS THAN JUST KISSING.

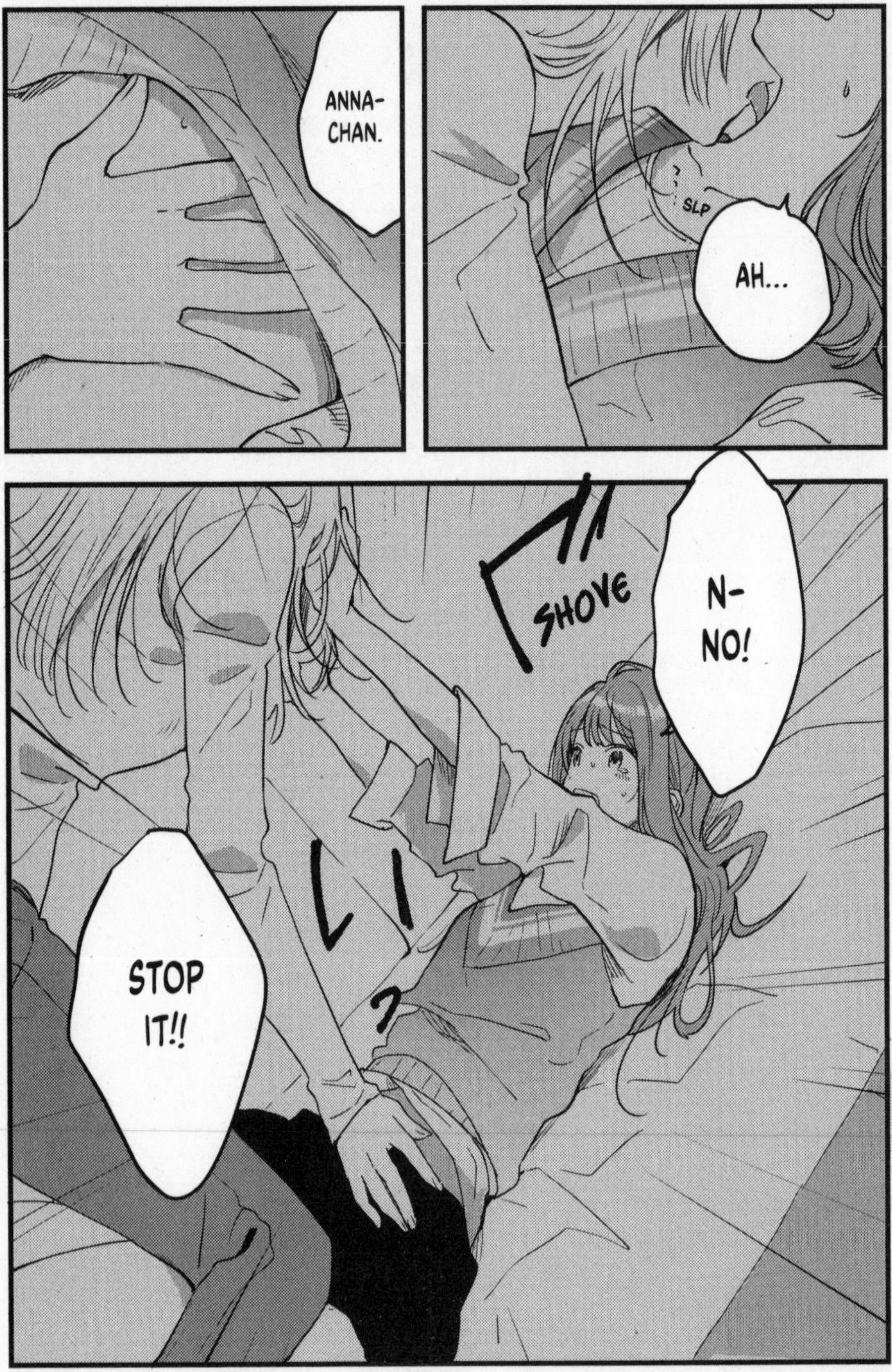
SLP
AH...
ANNA-CHAN.
N-NO!
SHOVE
STOP IT!!

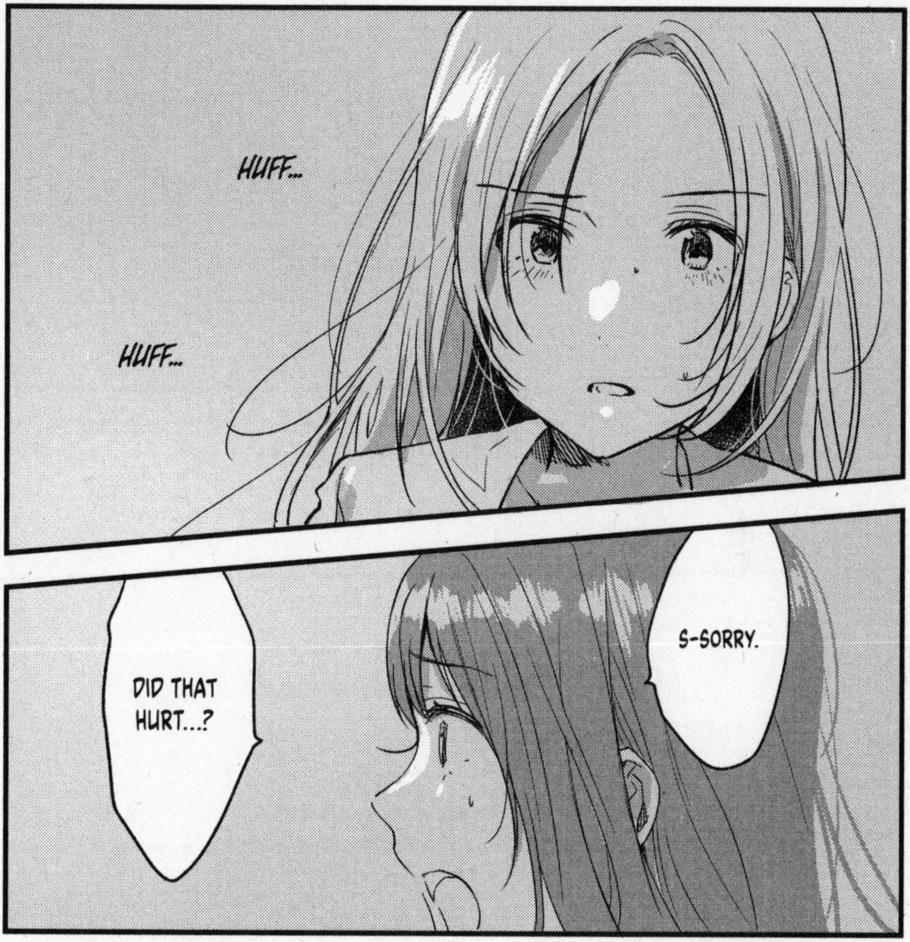
HUFF...
HUFF...
S-SORRY.
DID THAT HURT...?

IT DIDN'T WORK.

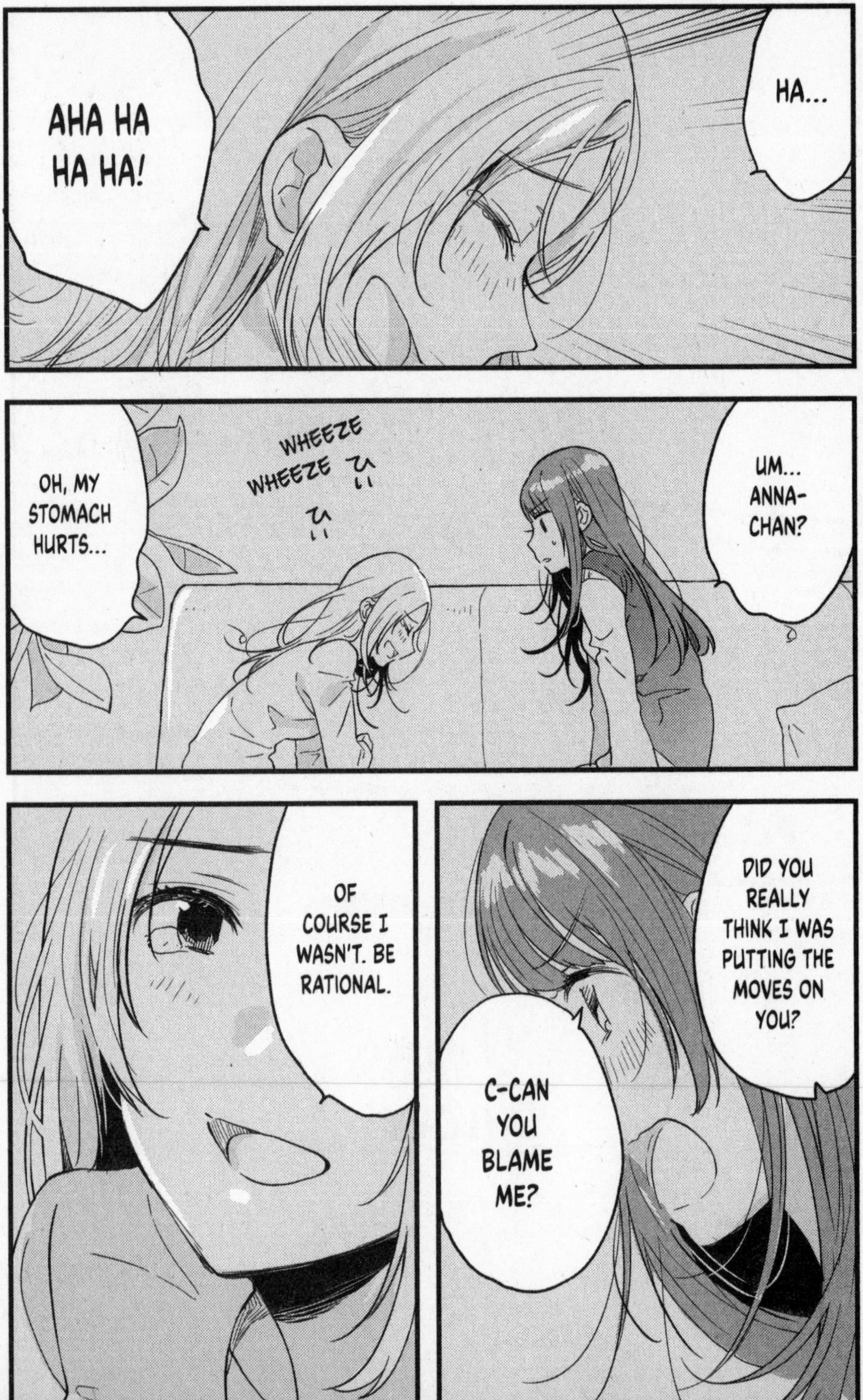
HA...
AHA HA HA HA!
UM... ANNA-CHAN?
WHEEZE WHEEZE
ひい ひい
OH, MY STOMACH HURTS...
DID YOU REALLY THINK I WAS PUTTING THE MOVES ON YOU?
C-CAN YOU BLAME ME?
OF COURSE I WASN'T. BE RATIONAL.

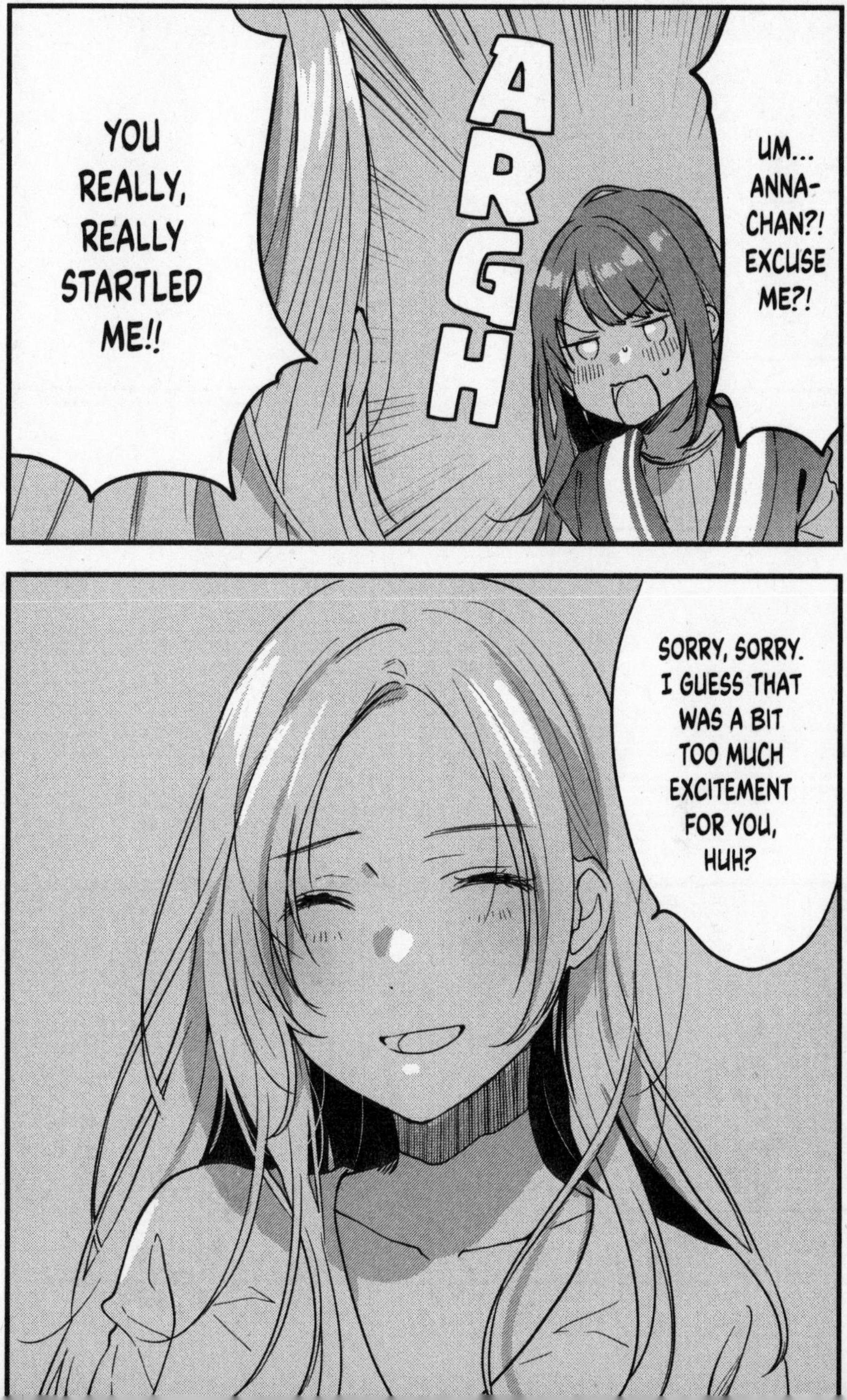
UM... ANNA-CHAN?! EXCUSE ME?!
ARGH
YOU REALLY, REALLY STARTLED ME!!
SORRY, SORRY. I GUESS THAT WAS A BIT TOO MUCH EXCITEMENT FOR YOU, HUH?

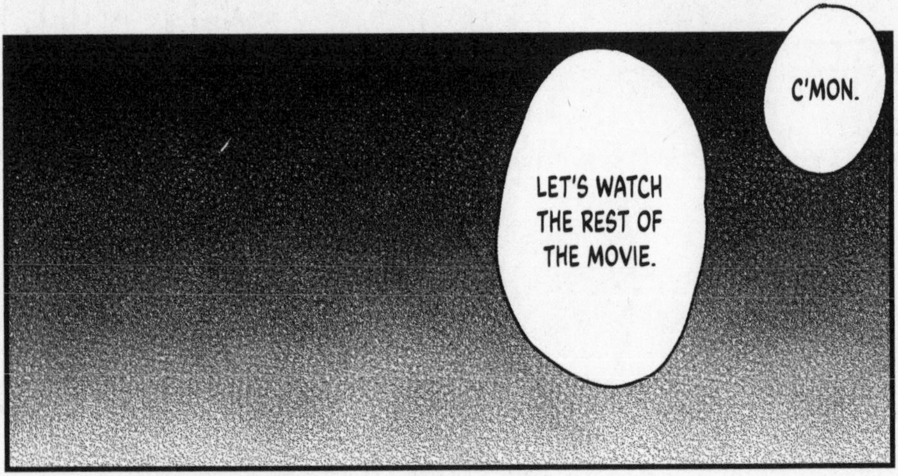
C'MON.
LET'S WATCH THE REST OF THE MOVIE.

I CAN'T BE AOI KOSHIBA.

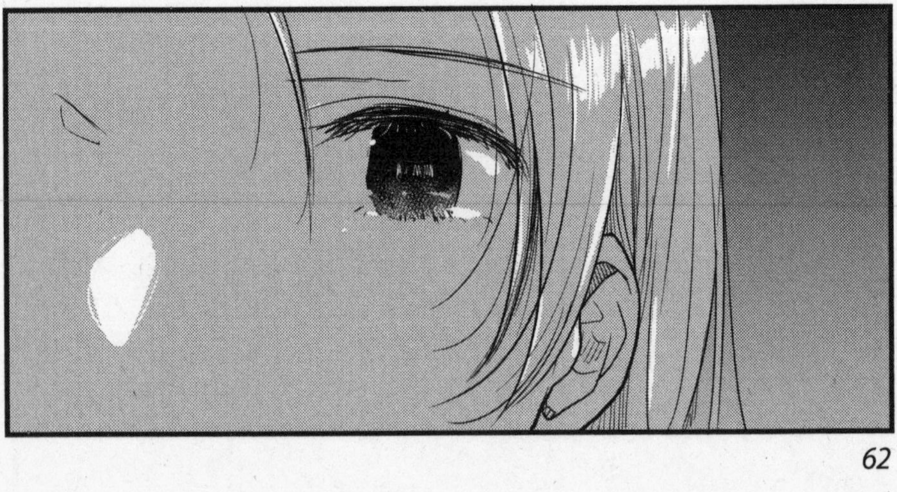

Chapter 28:
Even After Opening Up (Part 2)

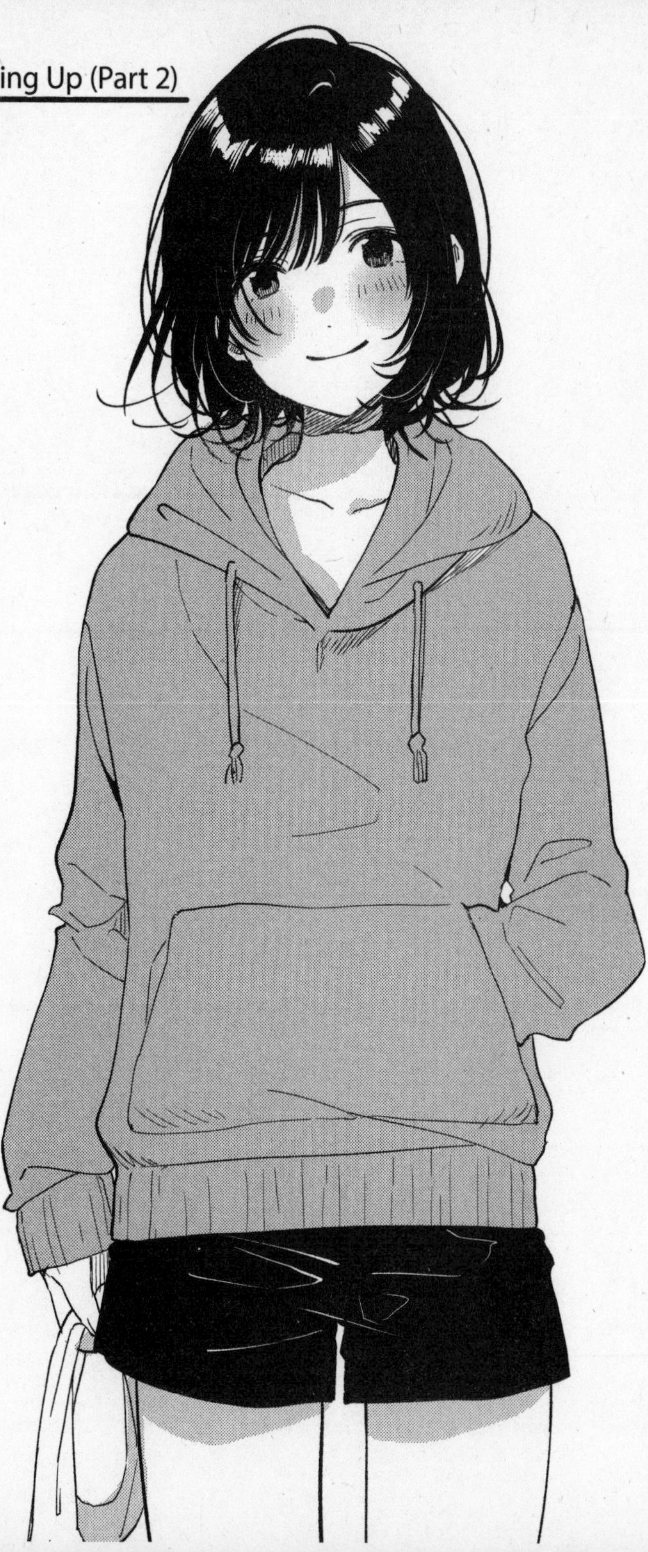

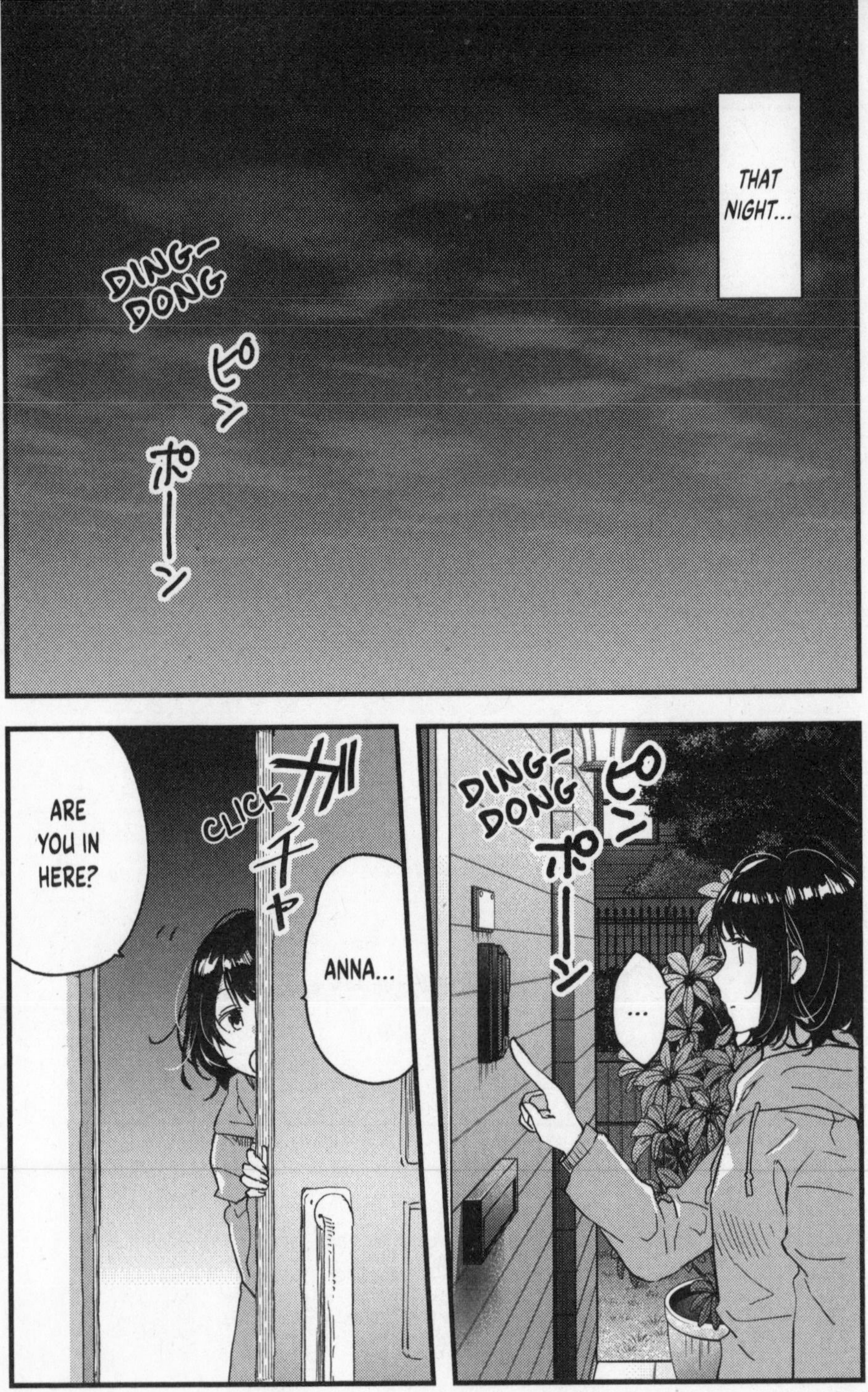
THAT NIGHT...
DING-DONG
ピンポーン
DING-DONG
ピンポーン
...
ガチャ
CLICK
ANNA...
ARE YOU IN HERE?

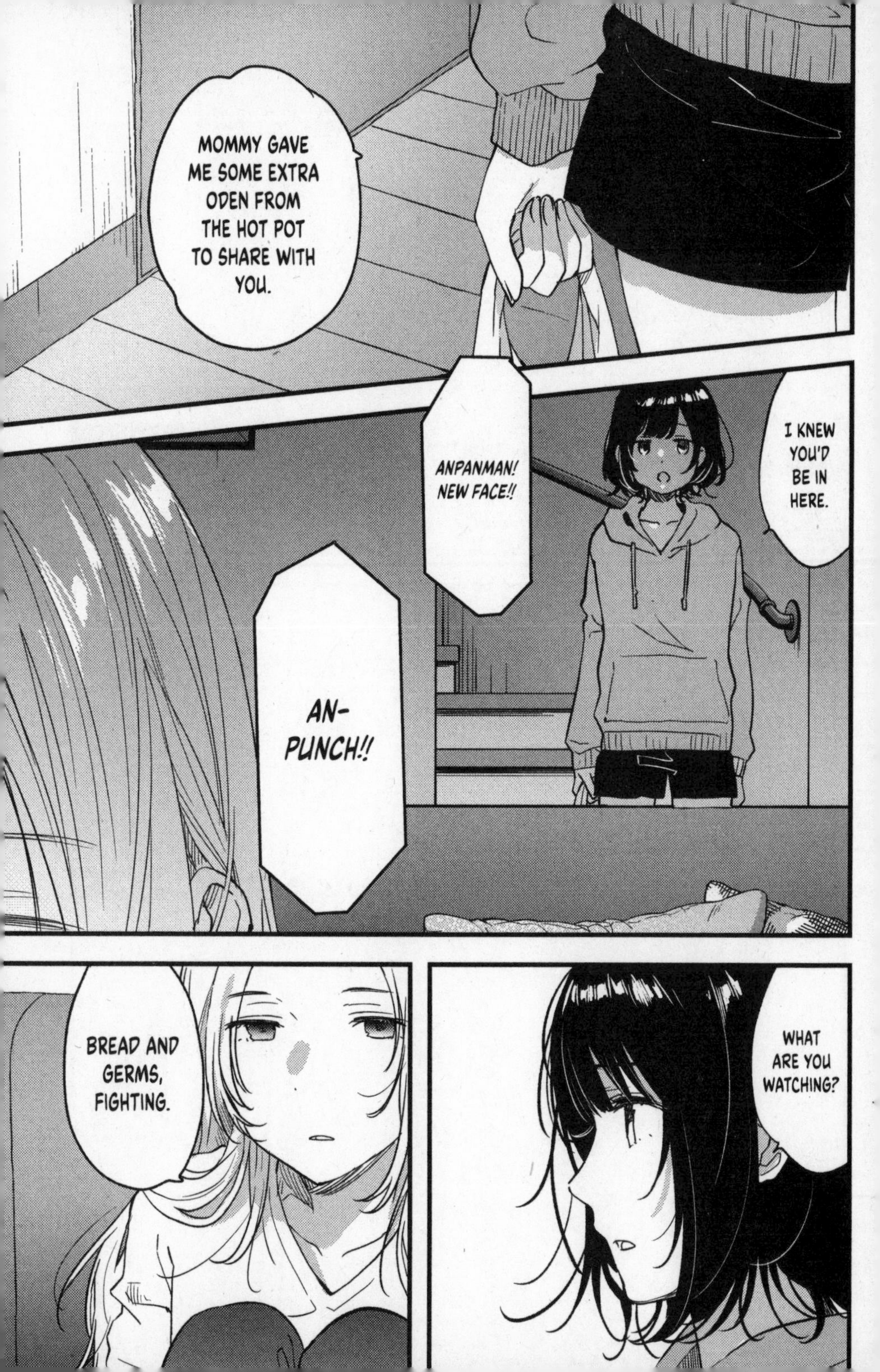
MOMMY GAVE ME SOME EXTRA ODEN FROM THE HOT POT TO SHARE WITH YOU.
I KNEW YOU'D BE IN HERE.
ANPANMAN! NEW FACE!!
AN-PUNCH!!
WHAT ARE YOU WATCHING?
BREAD AND GERMS, FIGHTING.

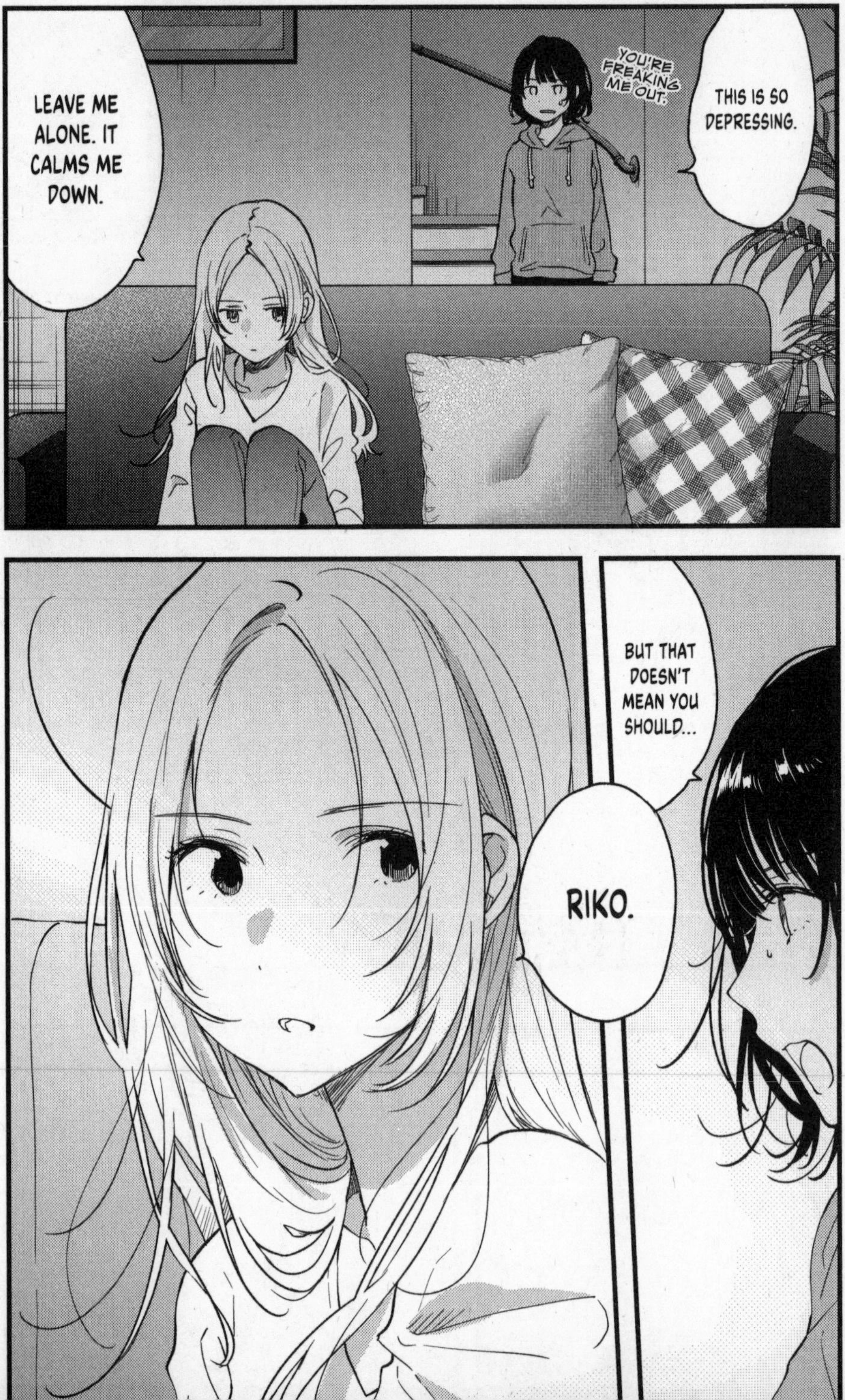
THIS IS SO DEPRESSING.
YOU'RE FREAKING ME OUT.
LEAVE ME ALONE. IT CALMS ME DOWN.
BUT THAT DOESN'T MEAN YOU SHOULD...
RIKO.

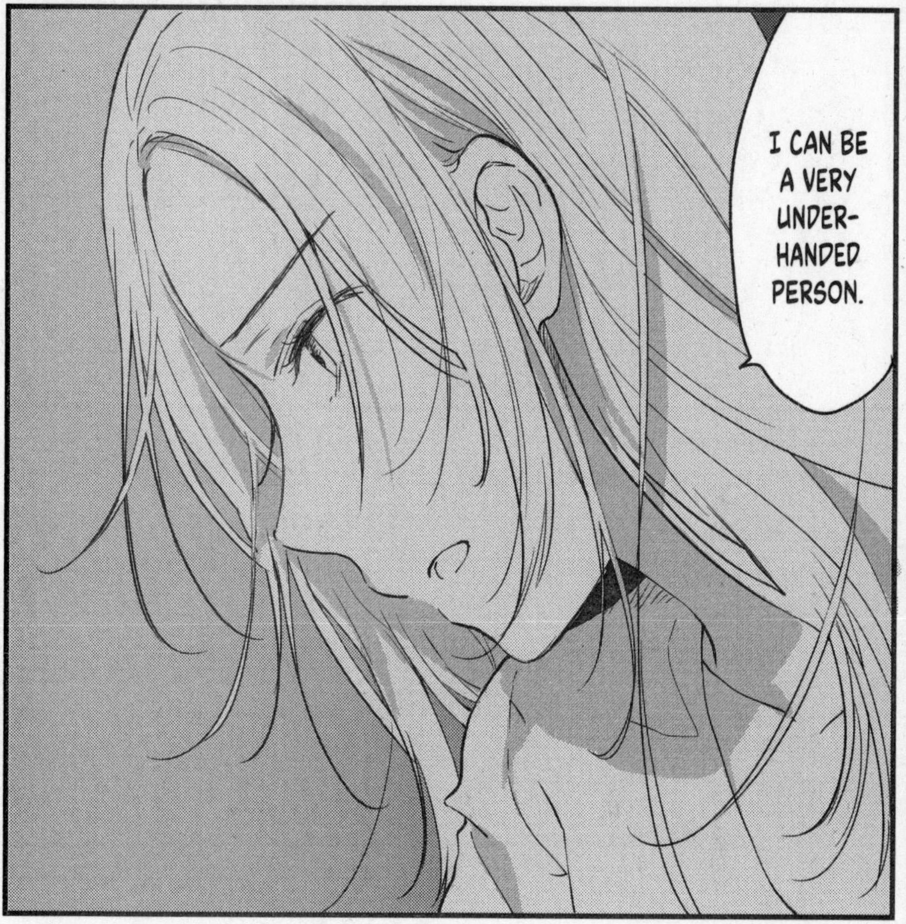
I CAN BE A VERY UNDER-HANDED PERSON.

I CHOOSE THE CHEAP AND DIRTY OPTION: BEING HER FRIEND.

BECAUSE THEN I CAN BE THERE FOREVER.

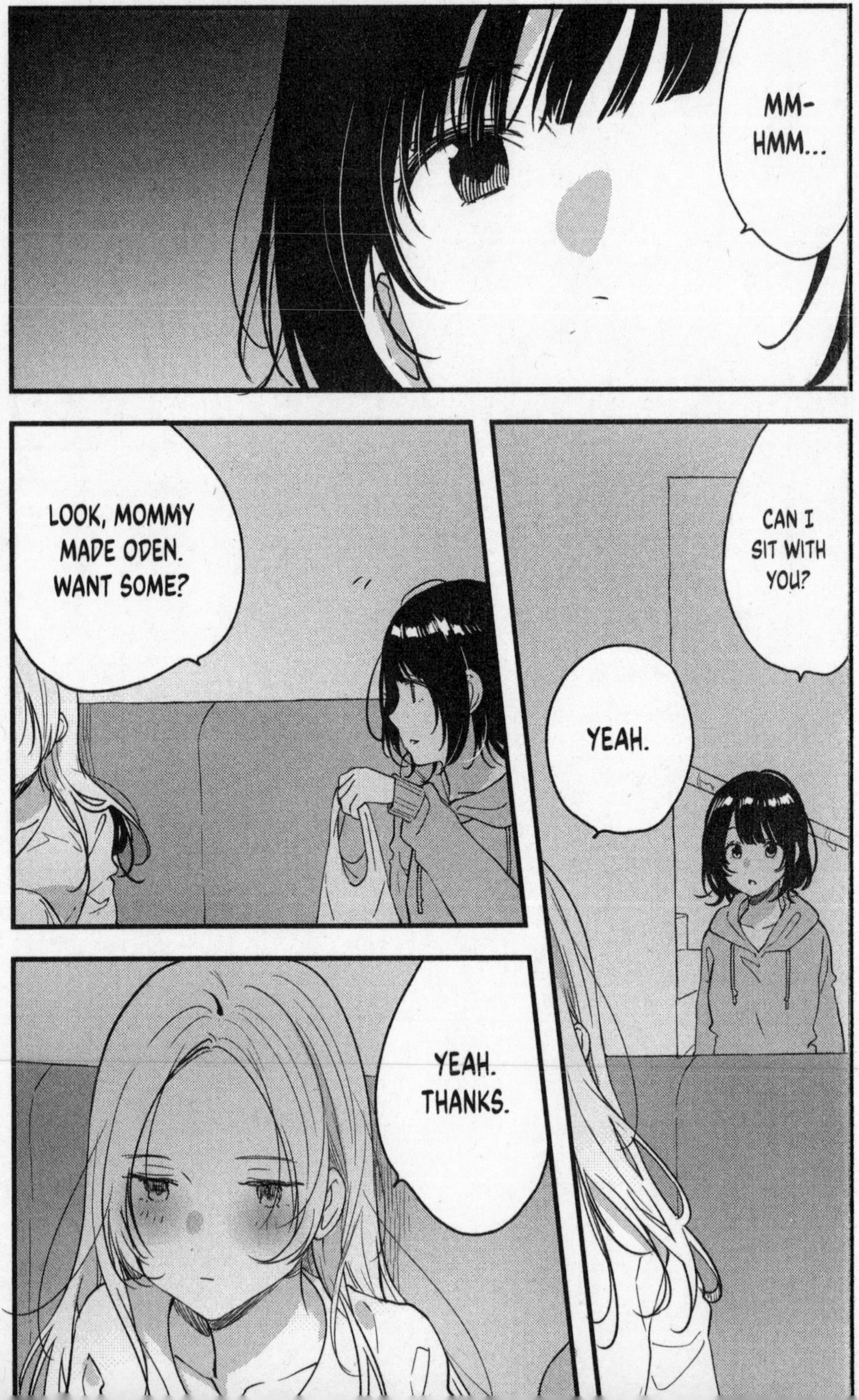
MM-HMM...
CAN I SIT WITH YOU?
YEAH.
LOOK, MOMMY MADE ODEN. WANT SOME?
YEAH. THANKS.

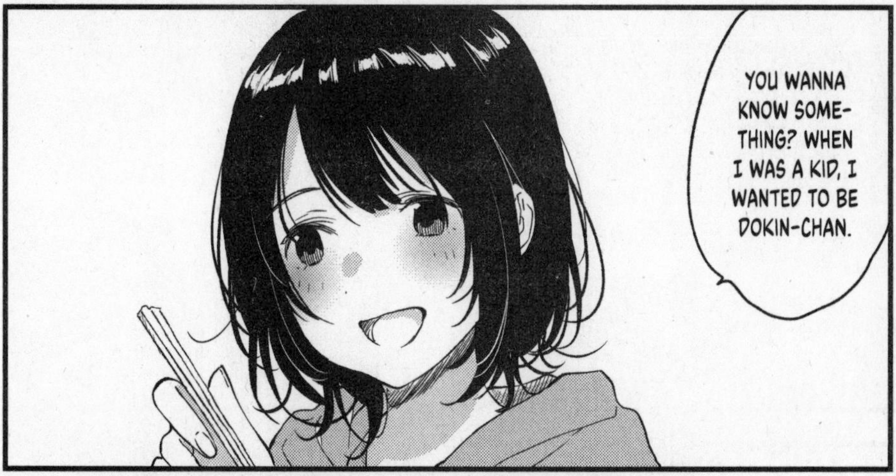
YOU WANNA KNOW SOME-THING? WHEN I WAS A KID, I WANTED TO BE DOKIN-CHAN.

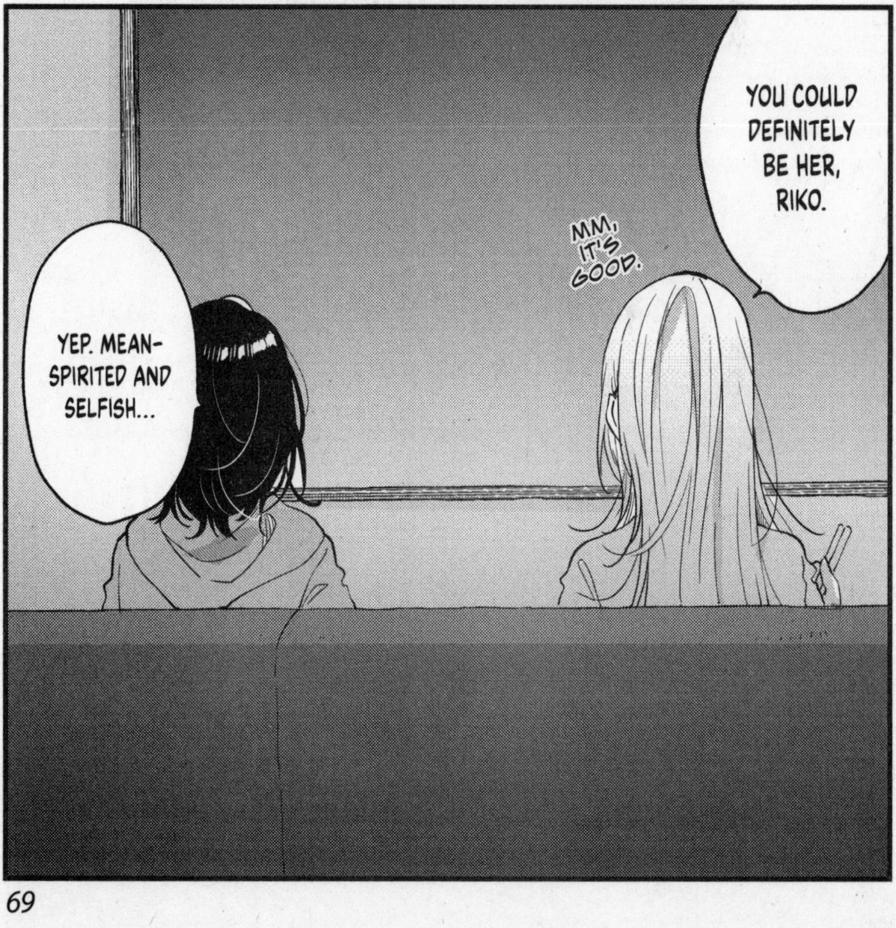
YOU COULD DEFINITELY BE HER, RIKO.
MM, IT'S GOOD.
YEP. MEAN-SPIRITED AND SELFISH...

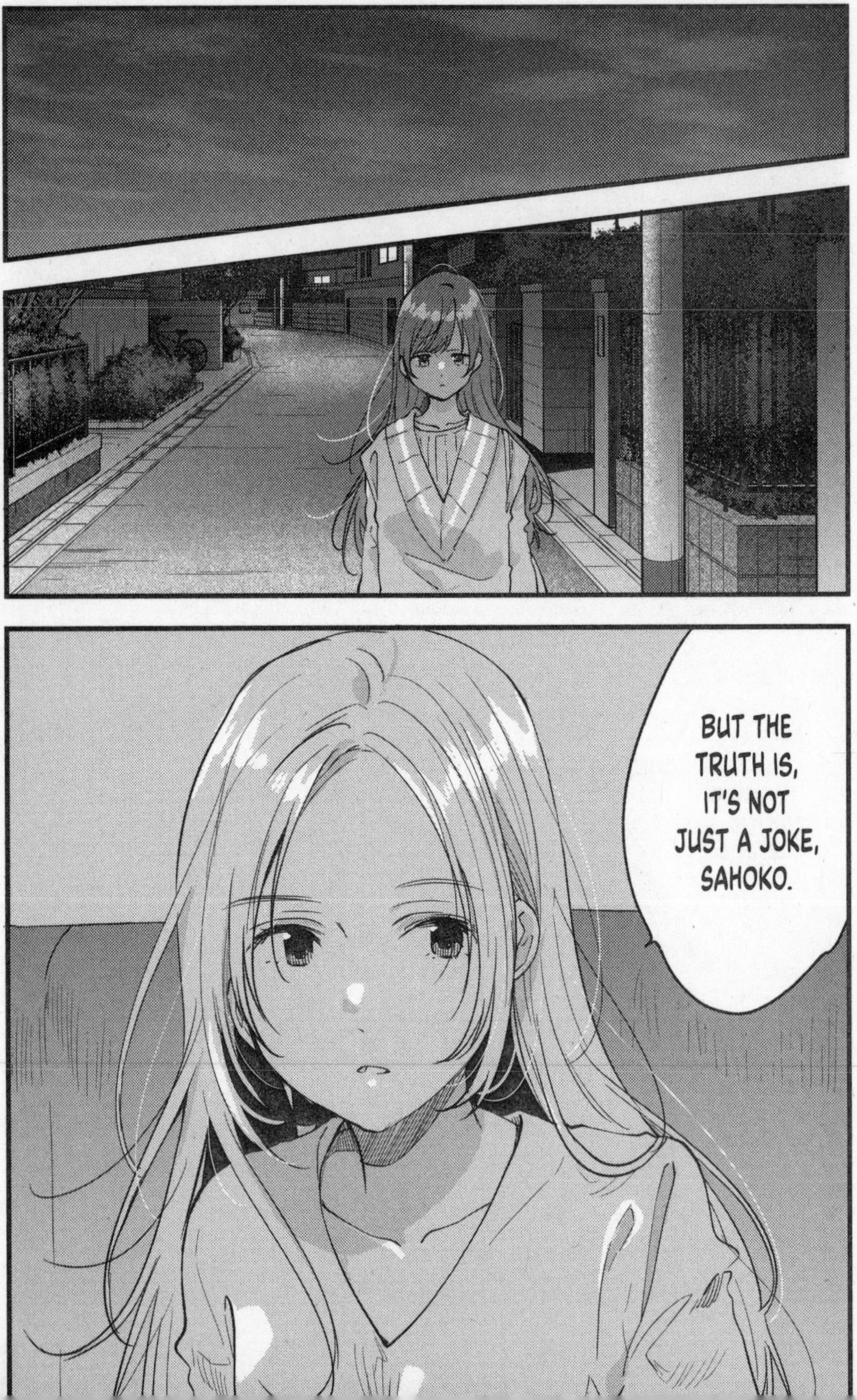
BUT THE TRUTH IS, IT'S NOT JUST A JOKE, SAHOKO.

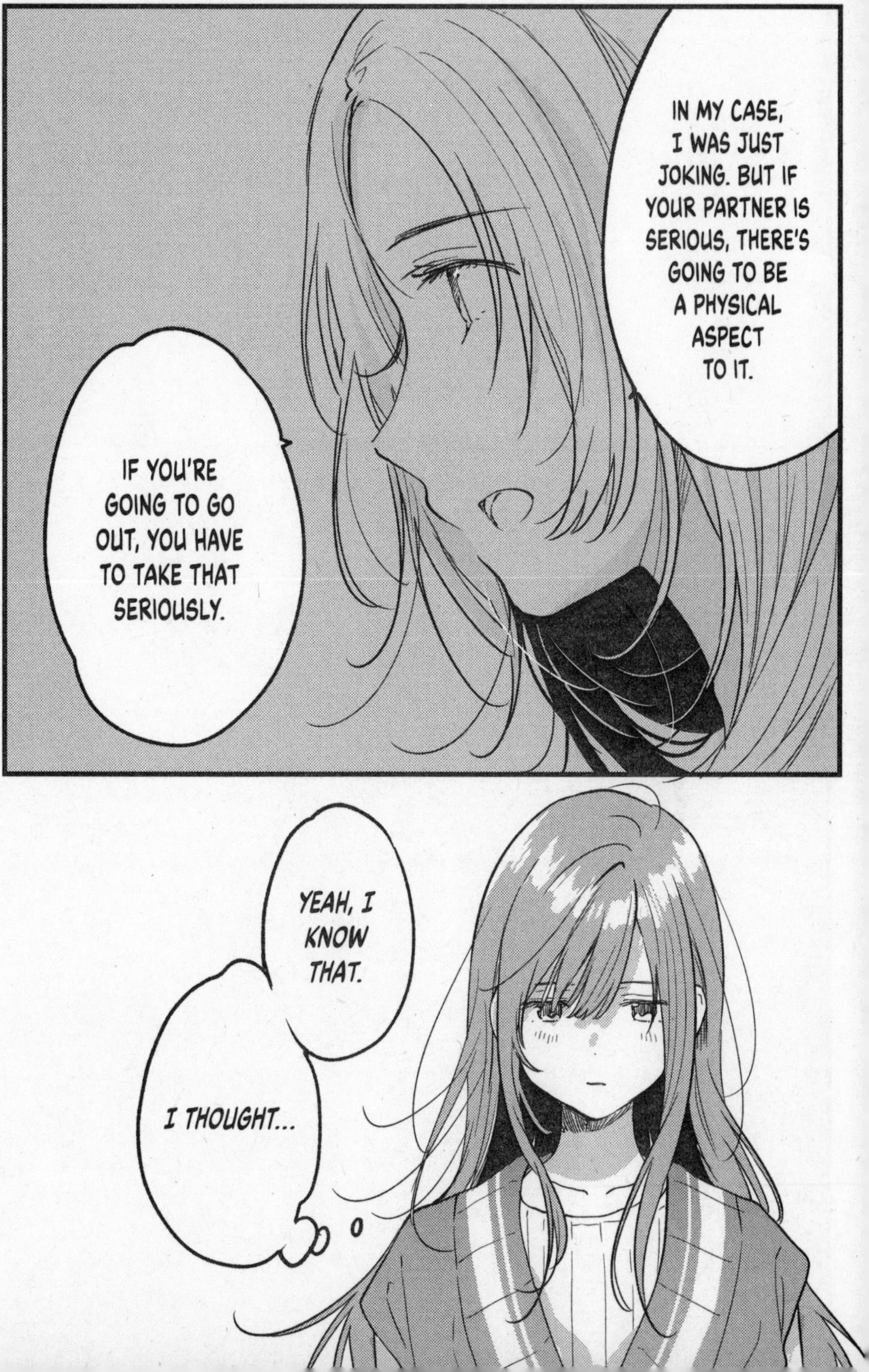
IN MY CASE, I WAS JUST JOKING. BUT IF YOUR PARTNER IS SERIOUS, THERE'S GOING TO BE A PHYSICAL ASPECT TO IT.
IF YOU'RE GOING TO GO OUT, YOU HAVE TO TAKE THAT SERIOUSLY.
YEAH, I KNOW THAT.
I THOUGHT...

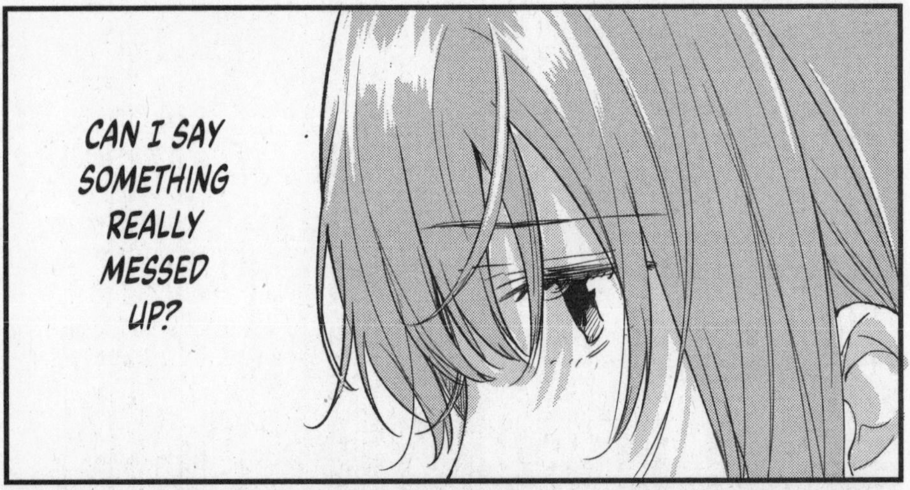
CAN I SAY SOMETHING REALLY MESSED UP?

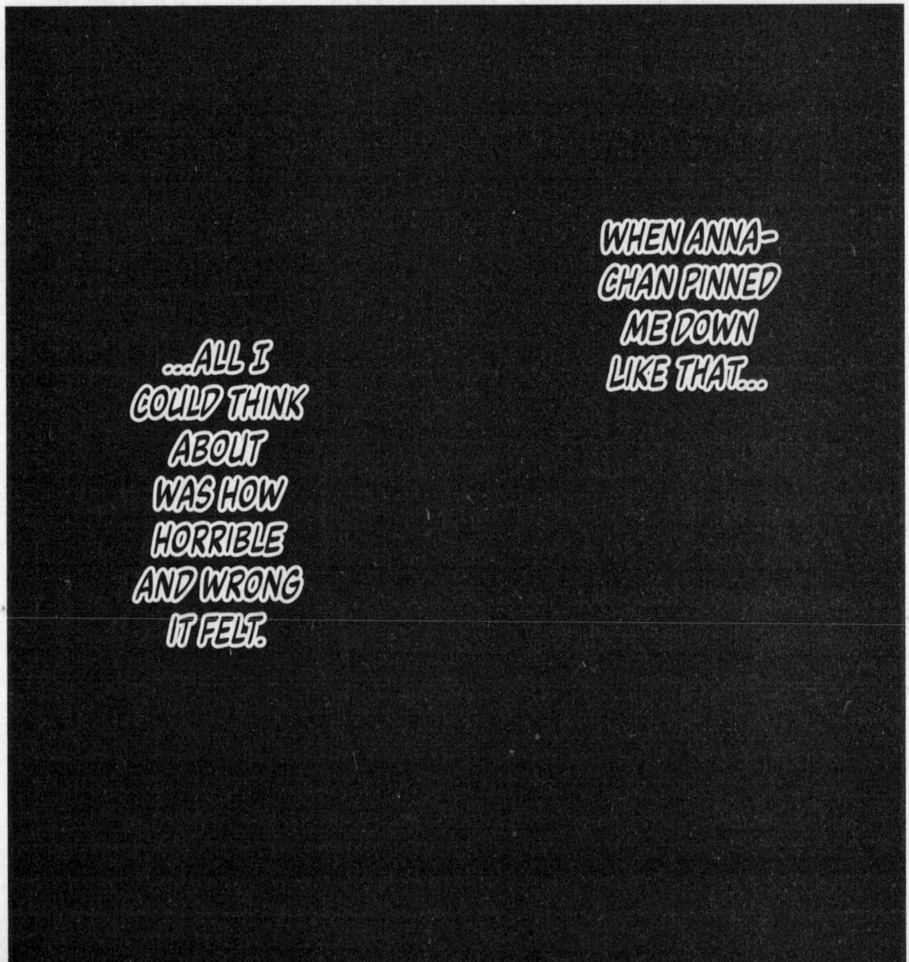
WHEN ANNA-CHAN PINNED ME DOWN LIKE THAT...
...ALL I COULD THINK ABOUT WAS HOW HORRIBLE AND WRONG IT FELT.

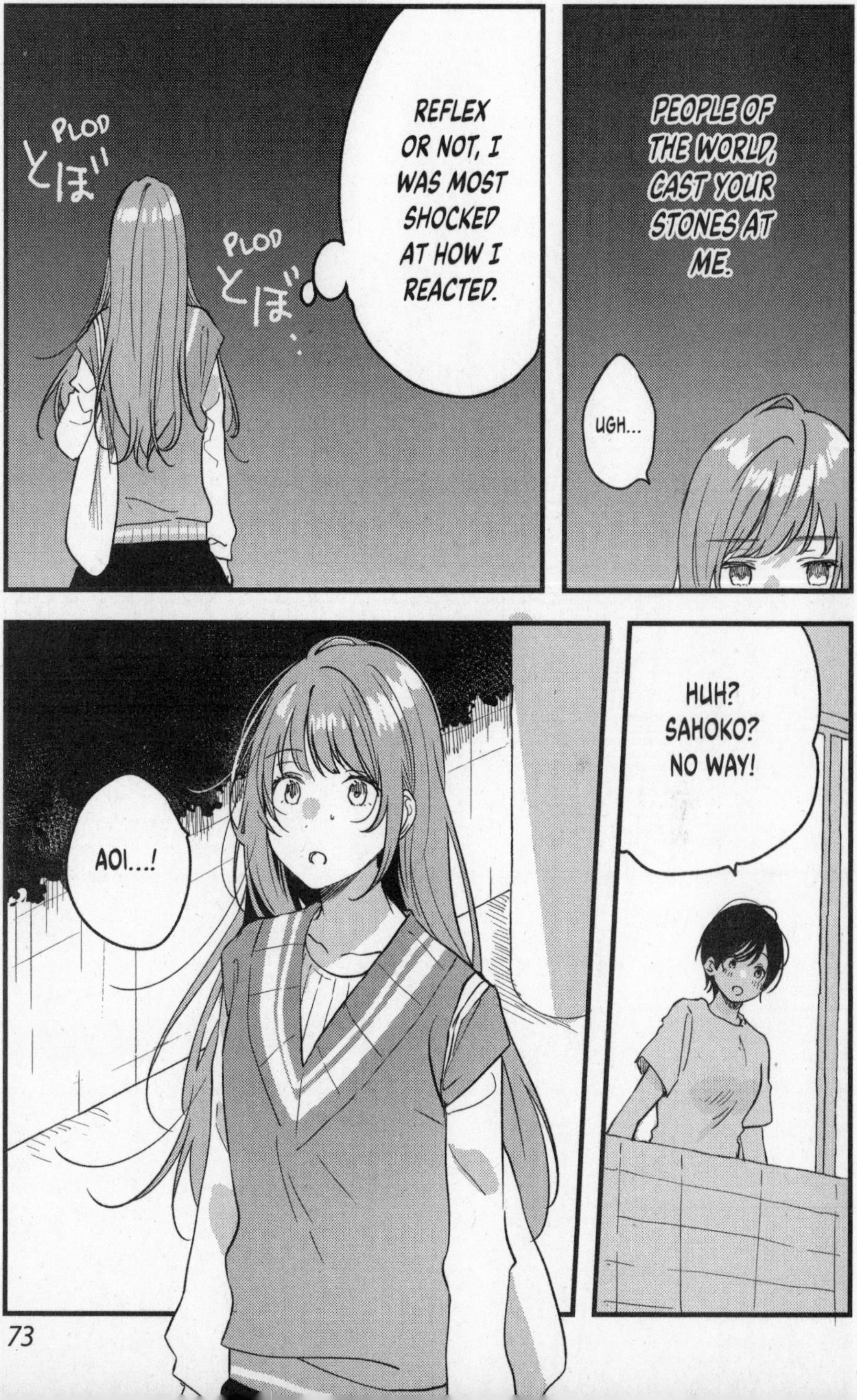
PEOPLE OF THE WORLD, CAST YOUR STONES AT ME.
UGH...
REFLEX OR NOT, I WAS MOST SHOCKED AT HOW I REACTED.
PLOD
とぼ
PLOD
とぼ
HUH? SAHOKO? NO WAY!
AOI...!

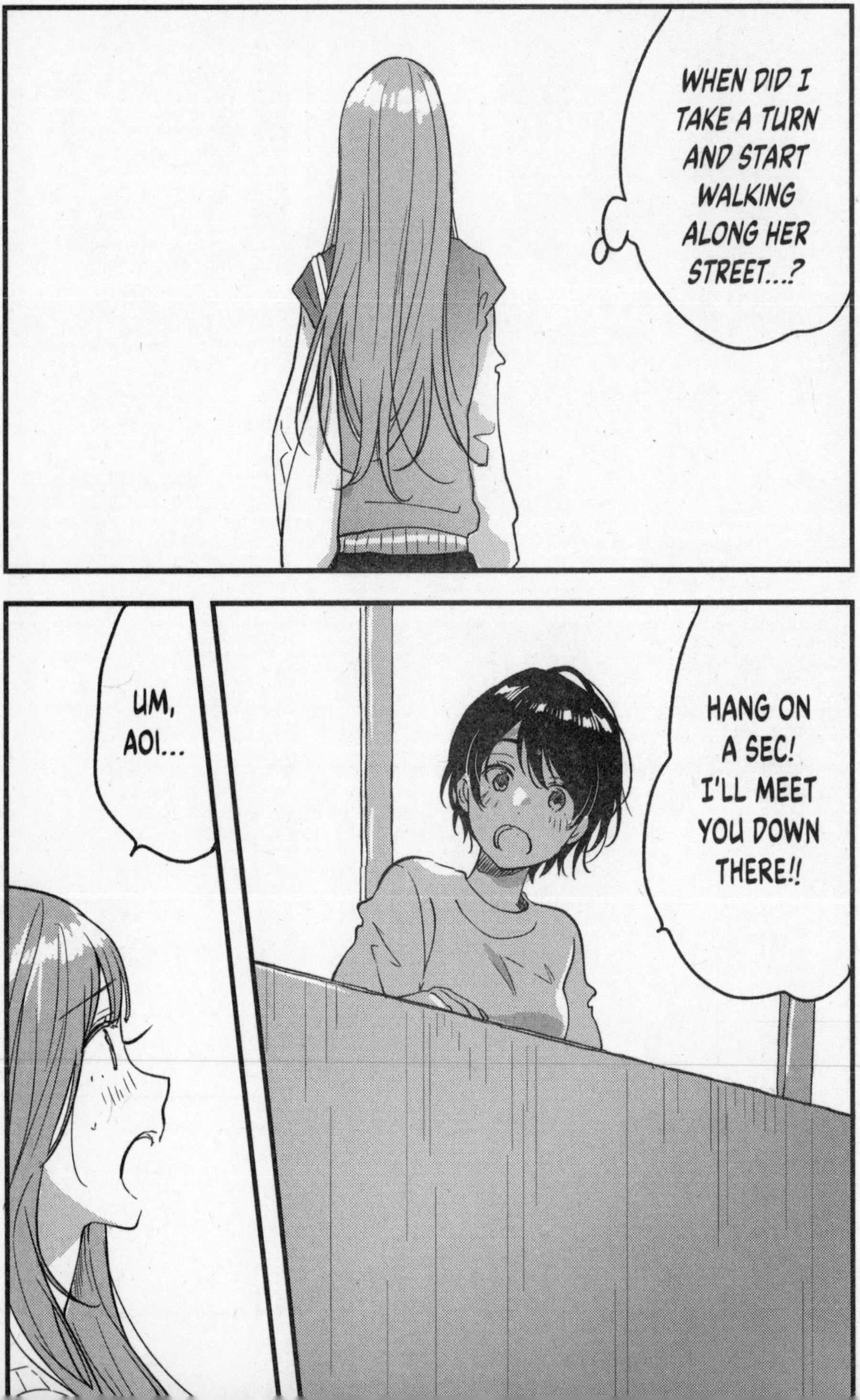
WHEN DID I TAKE A TURN AND START WALKING ALONG HER STREET...?
HANG ON A SEC! I'LL MEET YOU DOWN THERE!!
UM, AOI...

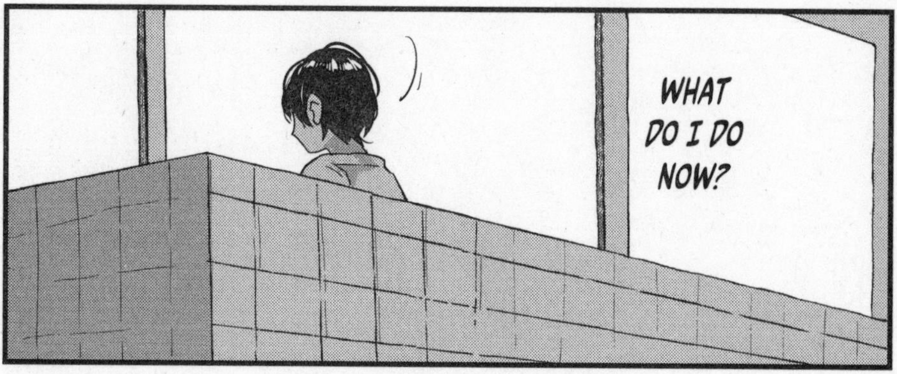
WHAT DO I DO NOW?

IT'S AOI, RADIANT AS EVER, AND ME, AT MY WORST SELF-LOATHING.

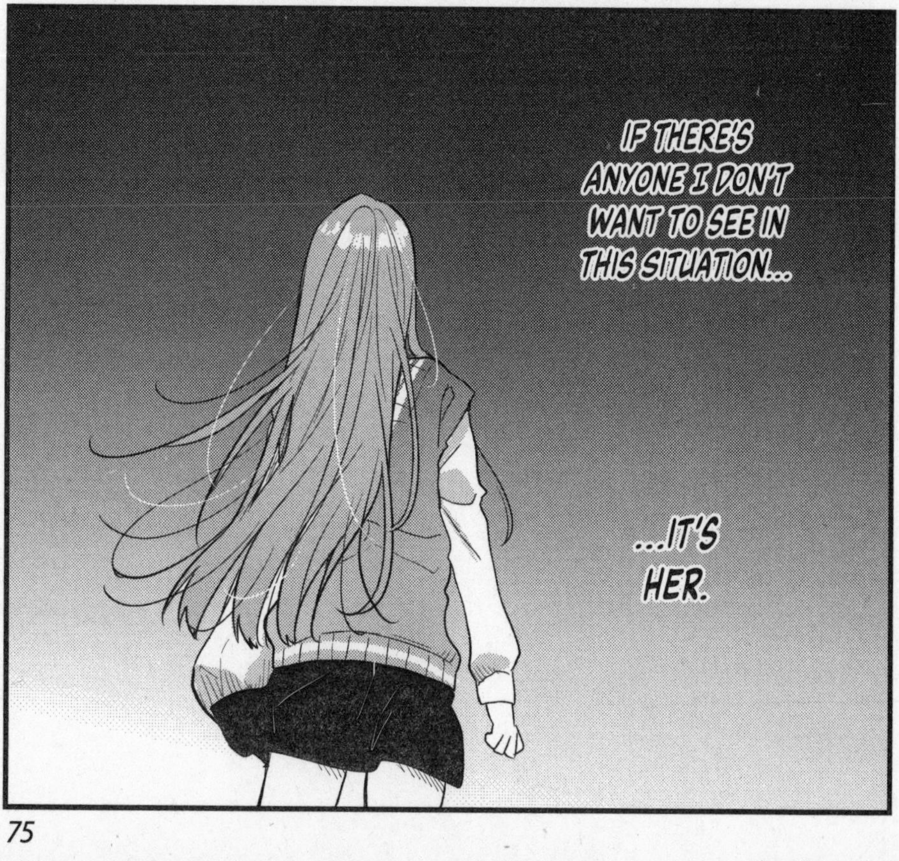
IF THERE'S ANYONE I DON'T WANT TO SEE IN THIS SITUATION...
...IT'S HER.

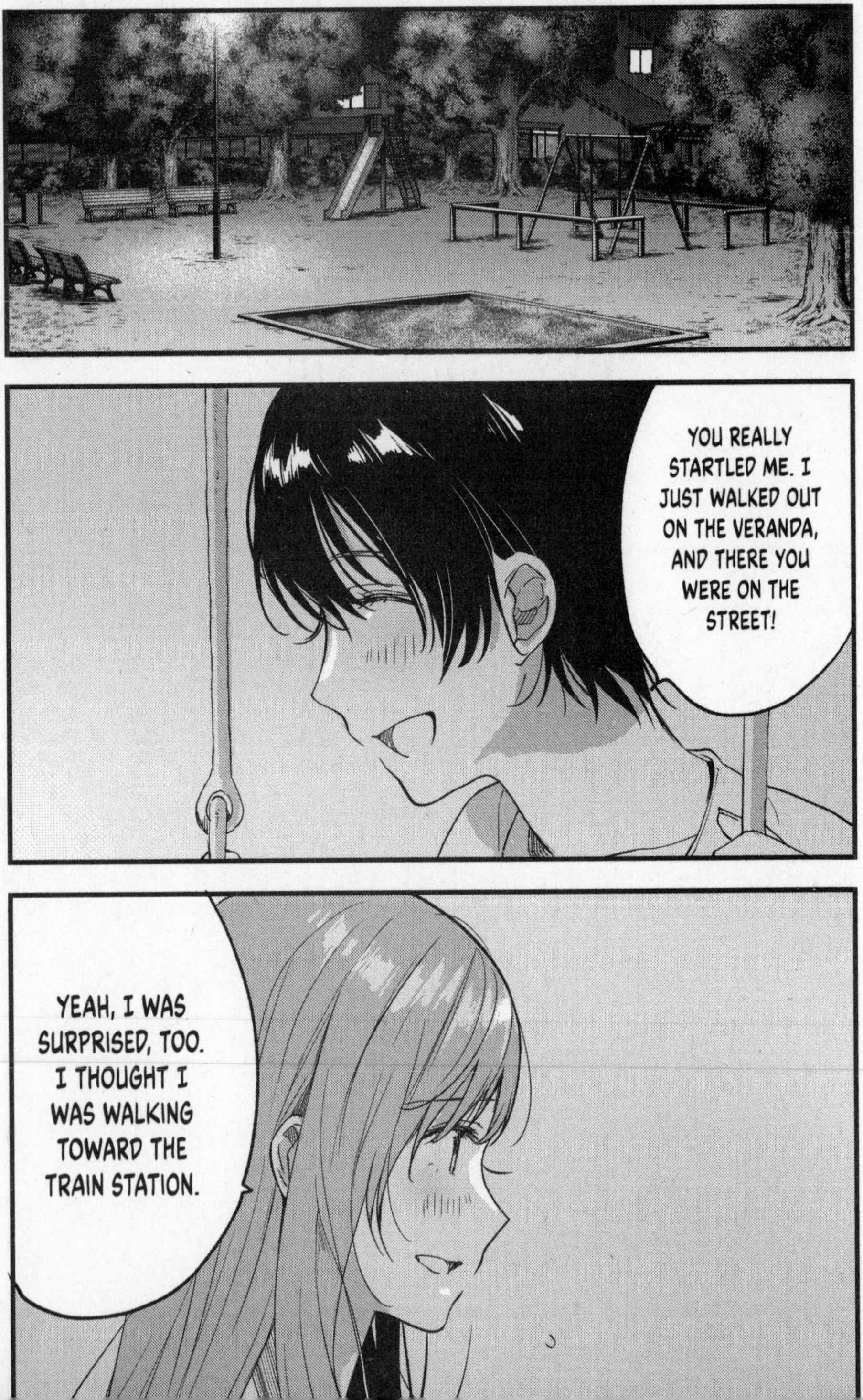
YOU REALLY STARTLED ME. I JUST WALKED OUT ON THE VERANDA, AND THERE YOU WERE ON THE STREET!
YEAH, I WAS SURPRISED, TOO. I THOUGHT I WAS WALKING TOWARD THE TRAIN STATION.

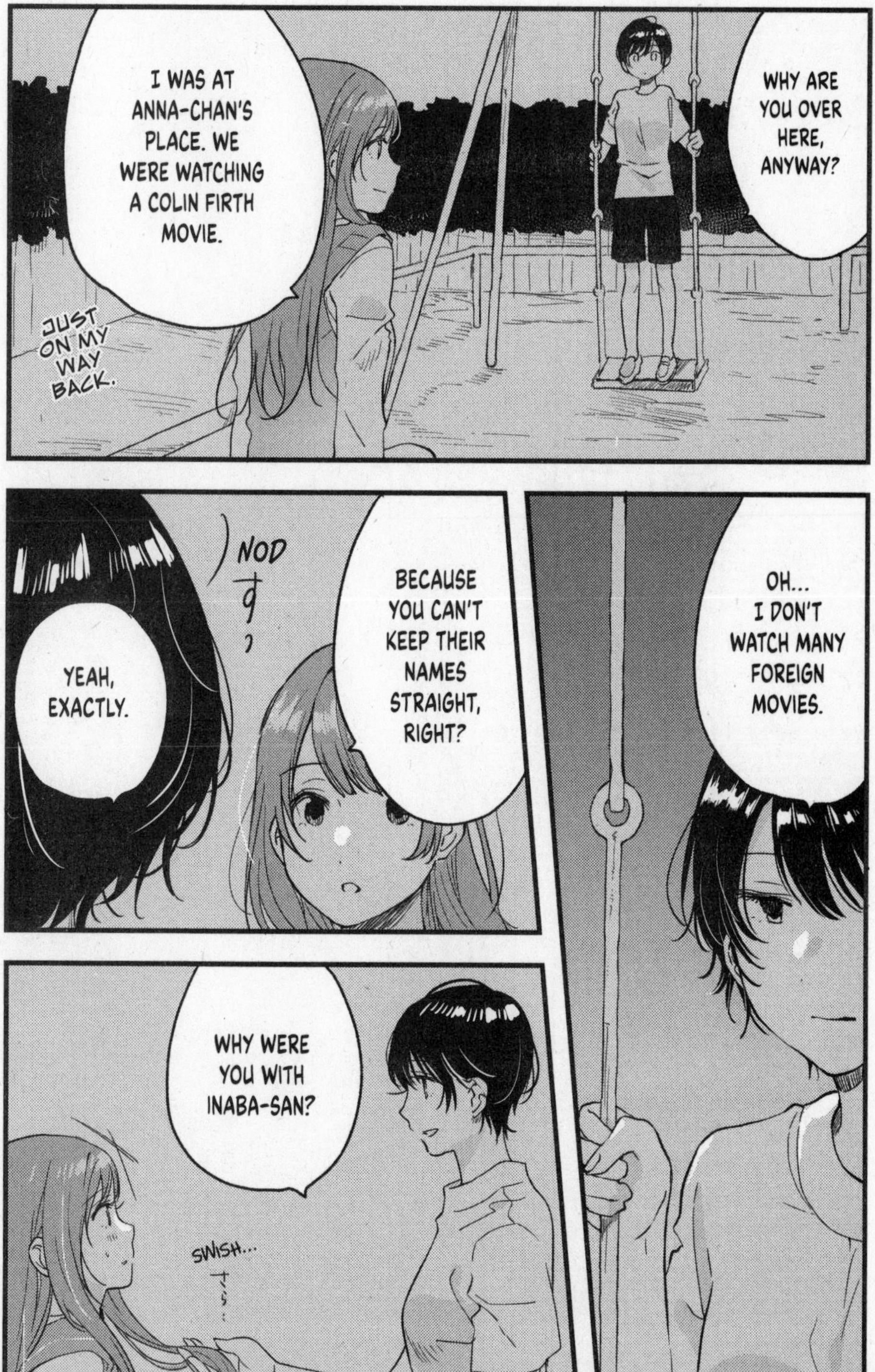
WHY ARE YOU OVER HERE, ANYWAY?
I WAS AT ANNA-CHAN'S PLACE. WE WERE WATCHING A COLIN FIRTH MOVIE.
JUST ON MY WAY BACK.
OH... I DON'T WATCH MANY FOREIGN MOVIES.
BECAUSE YOU CAN'T KEEP THEIR NAMES STRAIGHT, RIGHT?
NOD
YEAH, EXACTLY.
WHY WERE YOU WITH INABA-SAN?
SWISH...

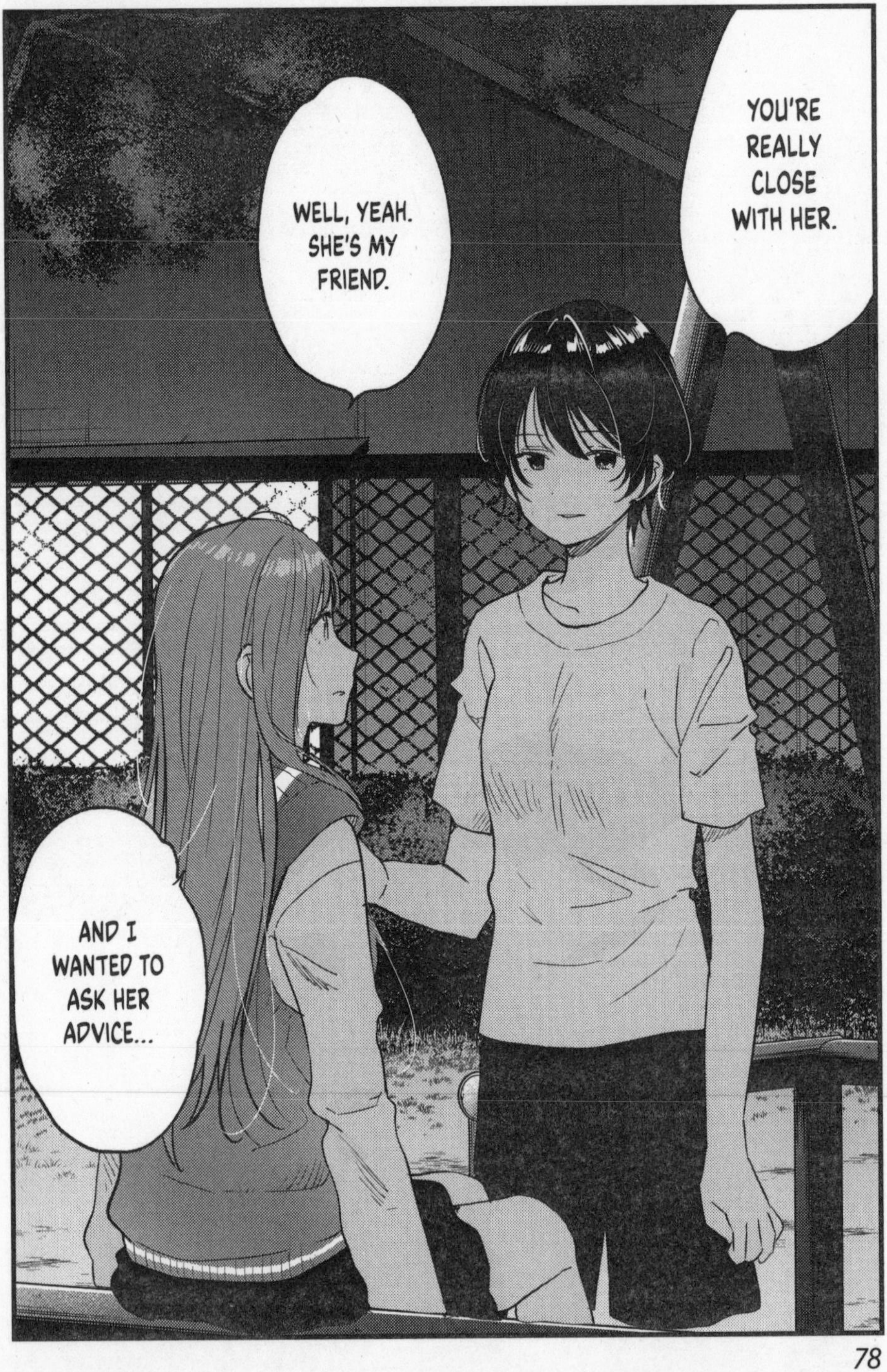
YOU'RE REALLY CLOSE WITH HER.
WELL, YEAH. SHE'S MY FRIEND.
AND I WANTED TO ASK HER ADVICE...

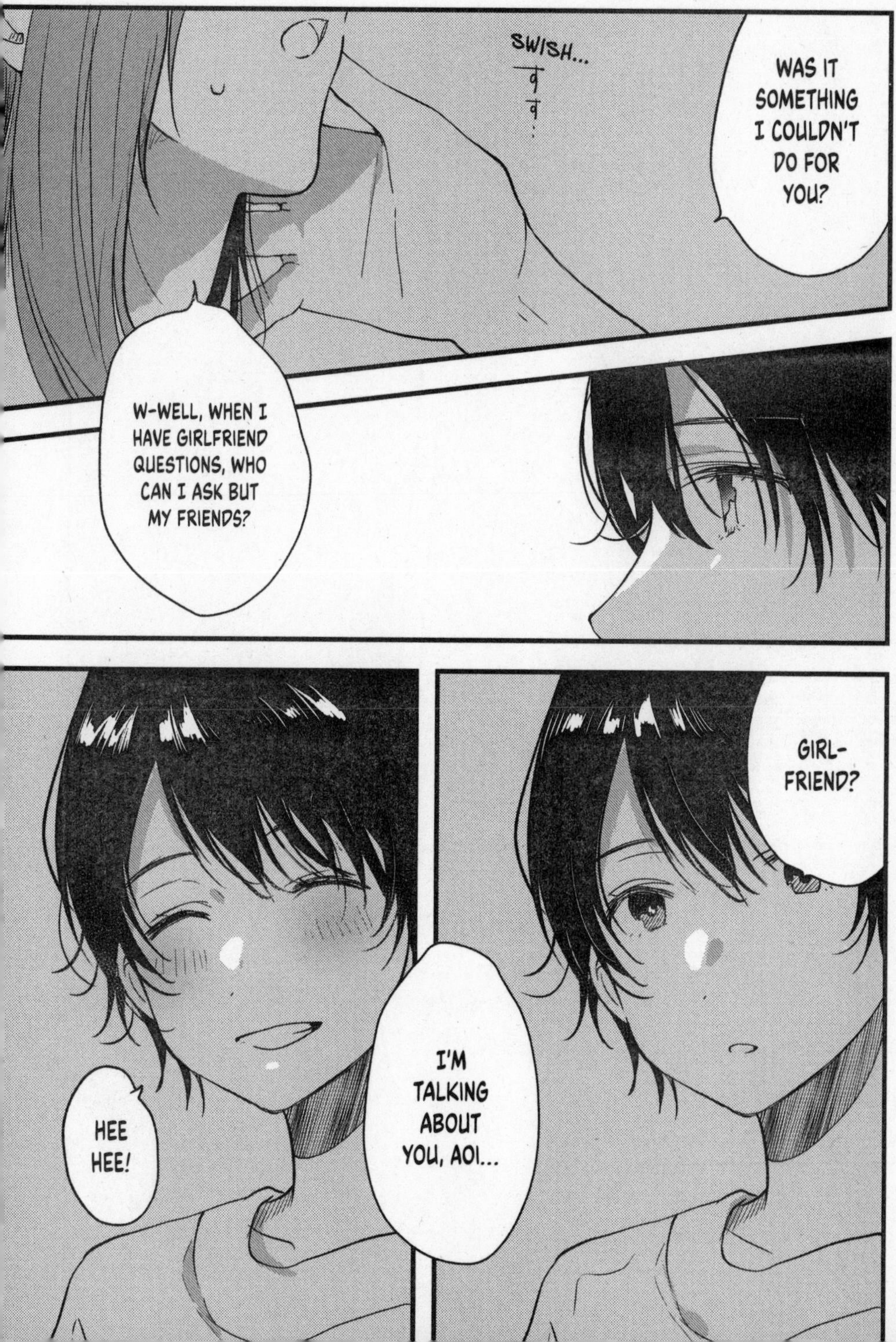
WAS IT SOMETHING I COULDN'T DO FOR YOU?
SWISH...
すす…
W-WELL, WHEN I HAVE GIRLFRIEND QUESTIONS, WHO CAN I ASK BUT MY FRIENDS?
GIRL-FRIEND?
I'M TALKING ABOUT YOU, AOI...
HEE HEE!

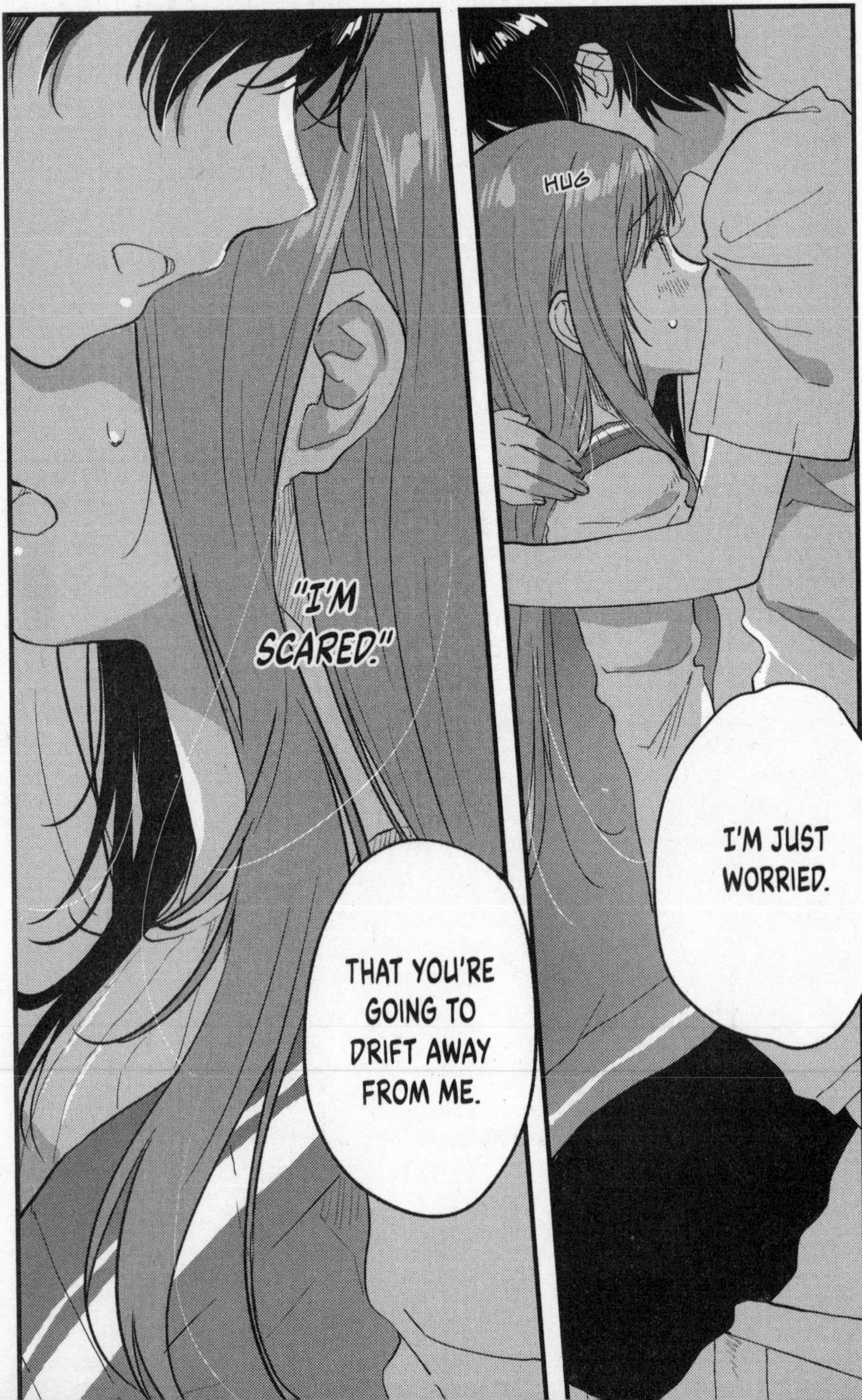
HUG
I'M JUST WORRIED.
"I'M SCARED."
THAT YOU'RE GOING TO DRIFT AWAY FROM ME.

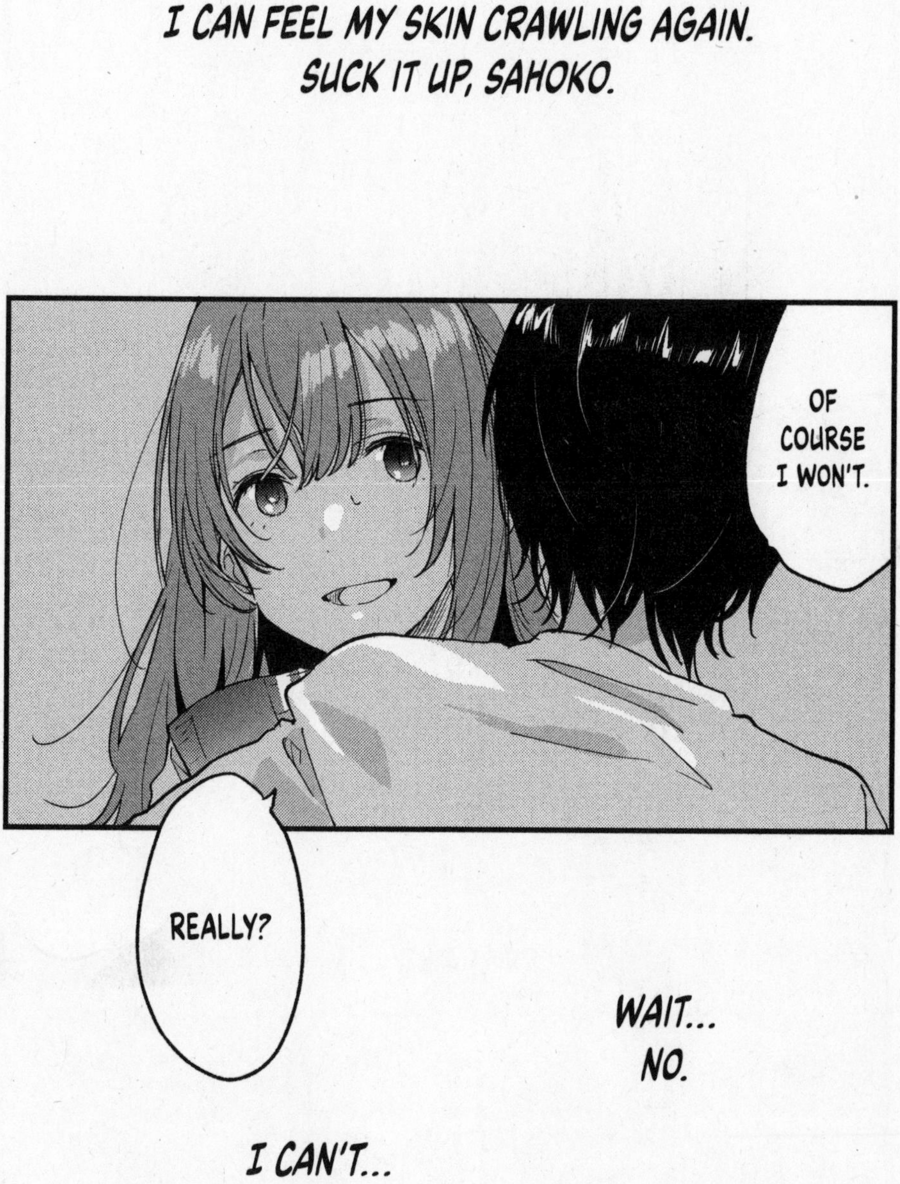
I CAN FEEL MY SKIN CRAWLING AGAIN.
SUCK IT UP, SAHOKO.
OF COURSE I WON'T.
REALLY?
WAIT... NO.
I CAN'T...

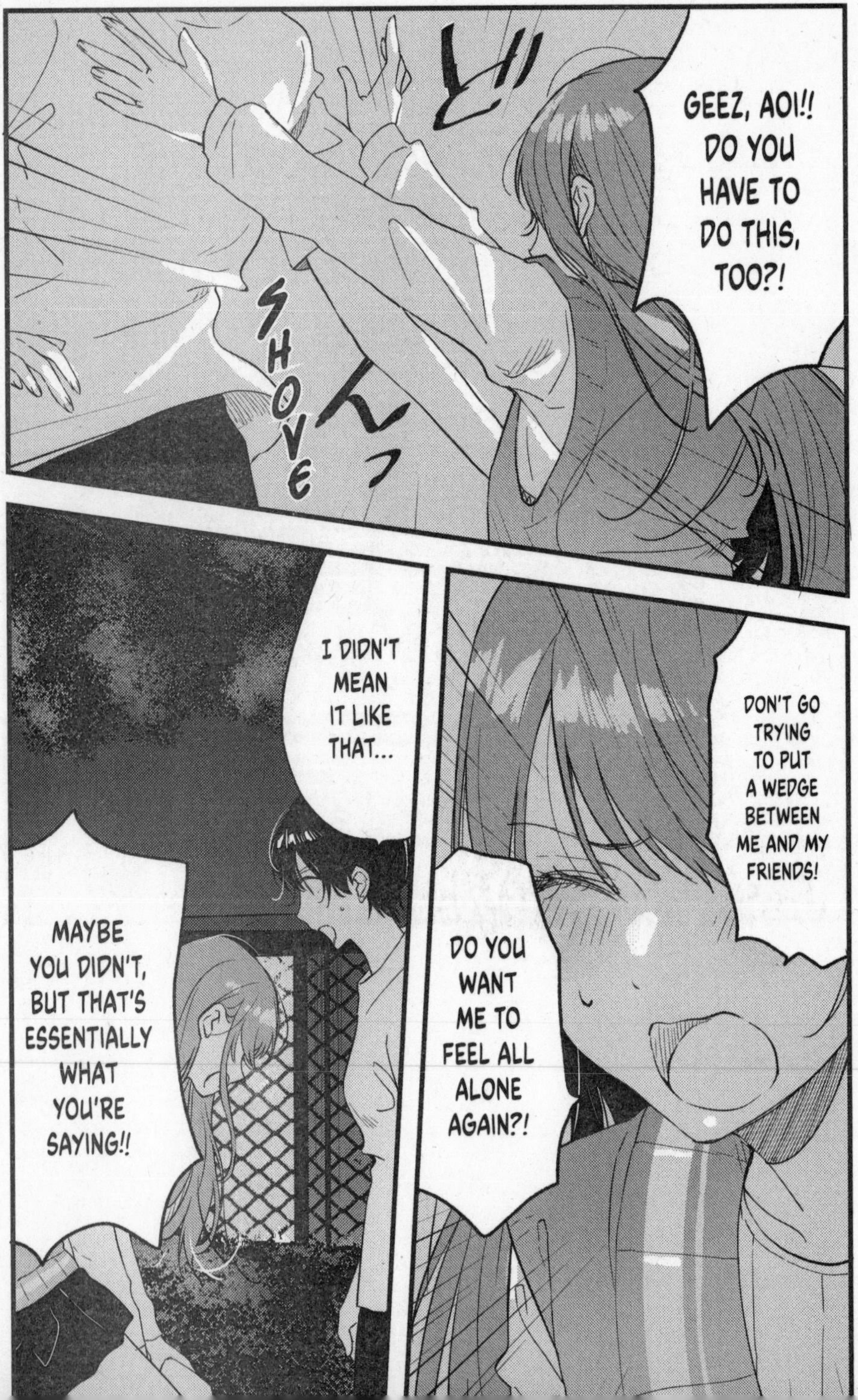
GEEZ, AOI!! DO YOU HAVE TO DO THIS, TOO?!
SHOVE
DON'T GO TRYING TO PUT A WEDGE BETWEEN ME AND MY FRIENDS!
DO YOU WANT ME TO FEEL ALL ALONE AGAIN?!
I DIDN'T MEAN IT LIKE THAT...
MAYBE YOU DIDN'T, BUT THAT'S ESSENTIALLY WHAT YOU'RE SAYING!!

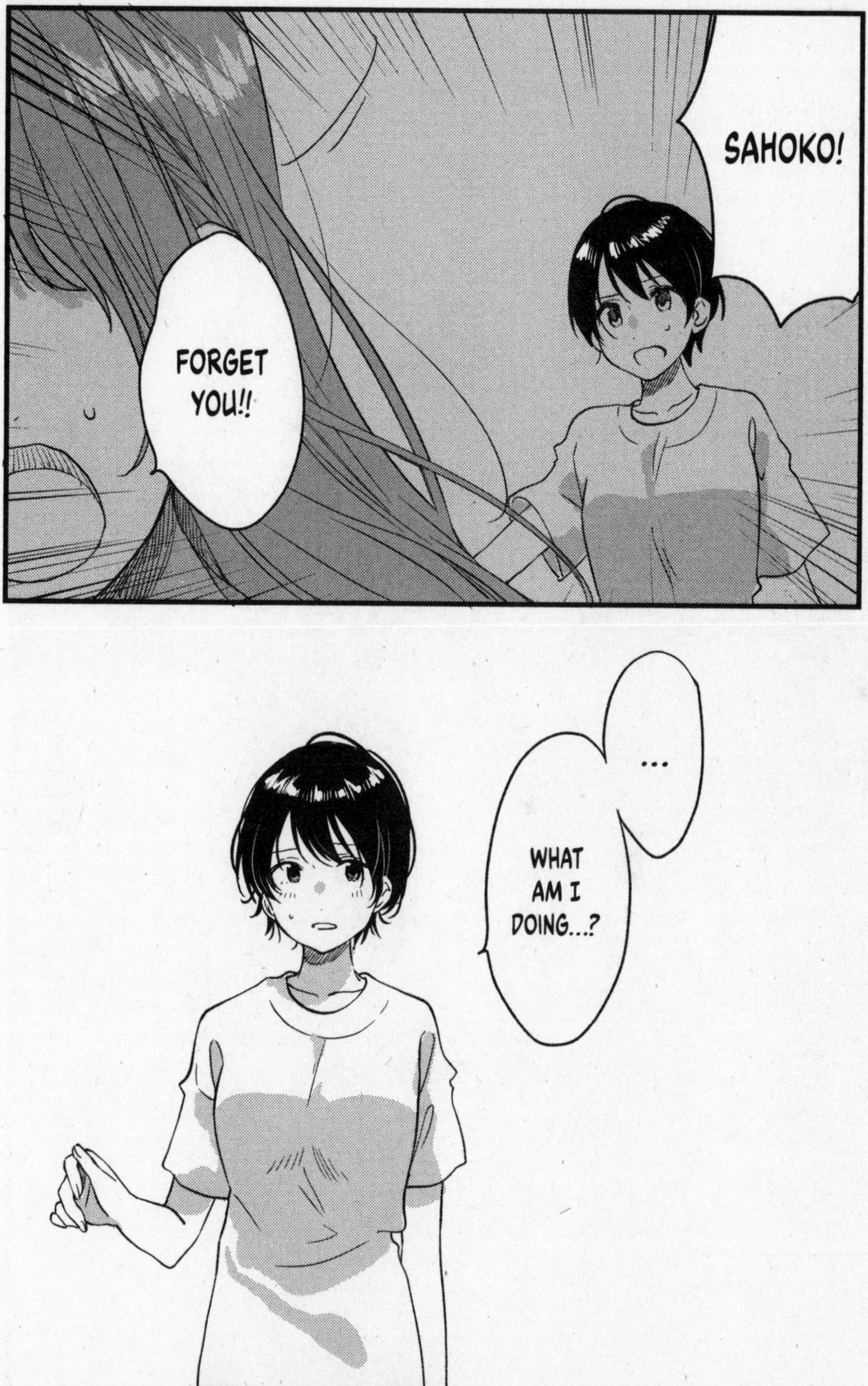
SAHOKO!
FORGET YOU!!
...
WHAT AM I DOING...?

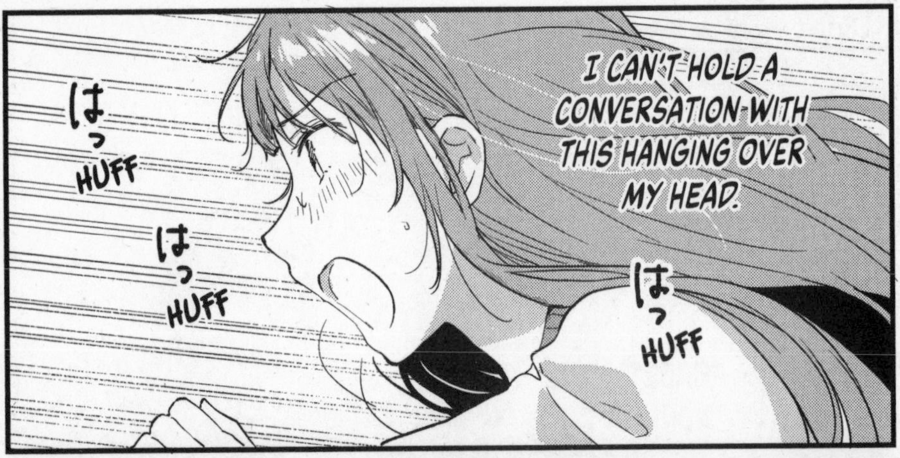
I CAN'T HOLD A CONVERSATION WITH THIS HANGING OVER MY HEAD.
はっ
HUFF
はっ
HUFF
はっ
HUFF
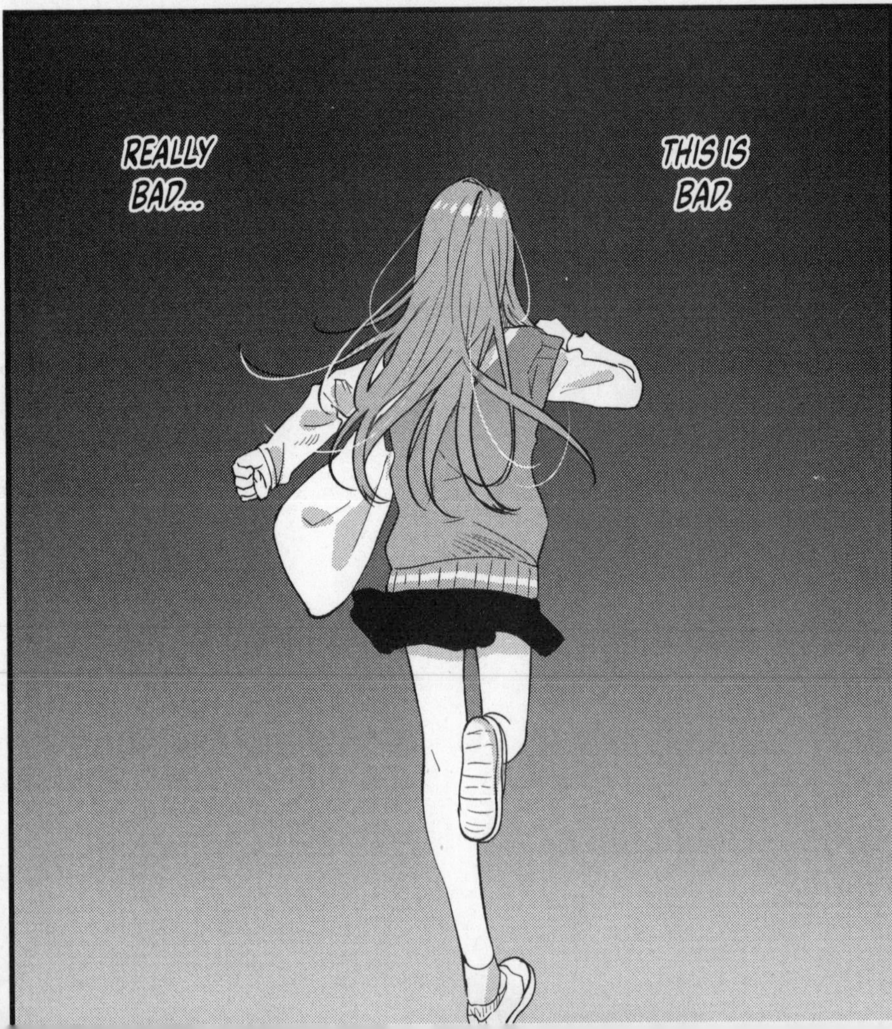
THIS IS BAD.
REALLY BAD...

Chapter 29:
Didn't Want to Know (Part 1)

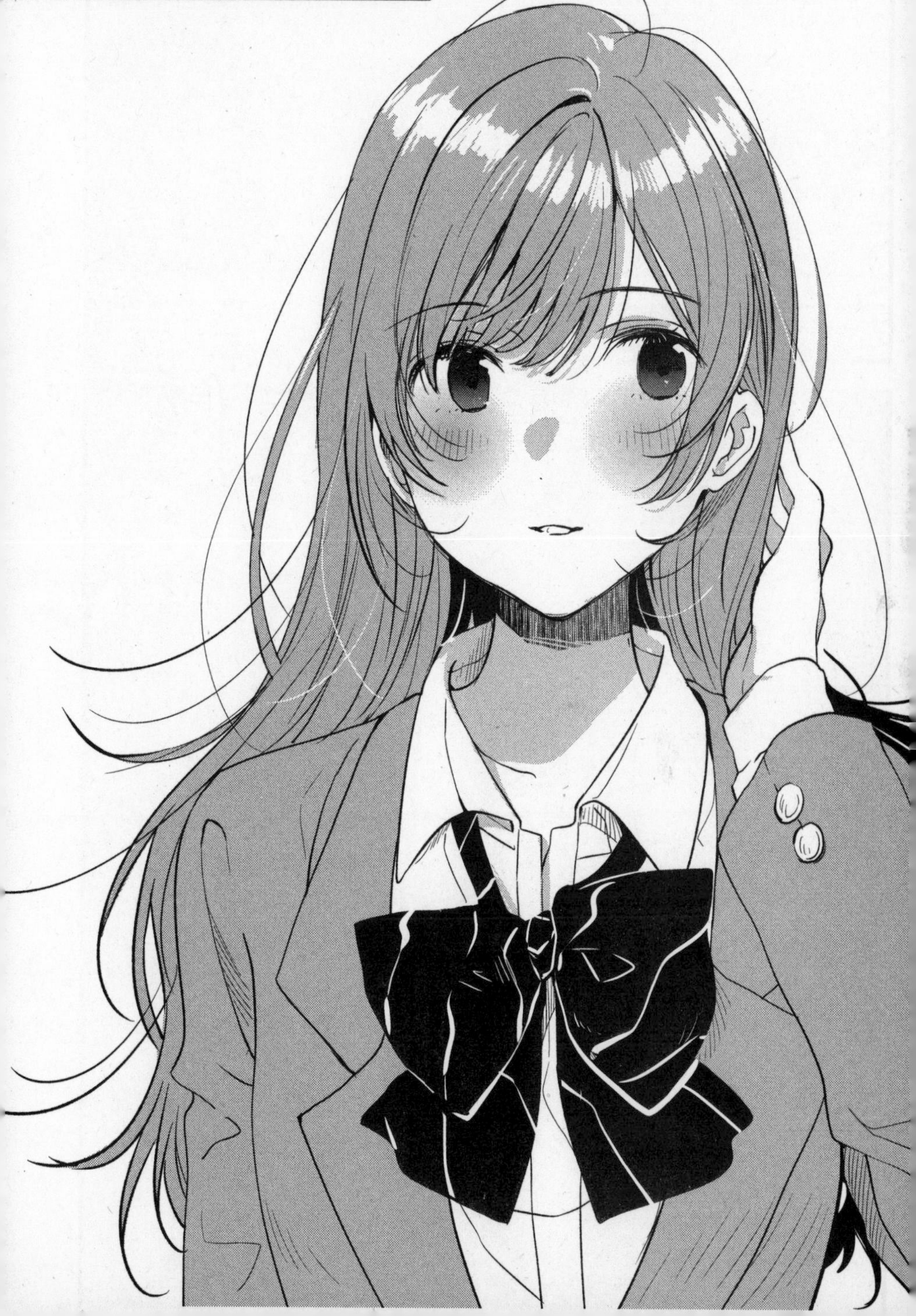

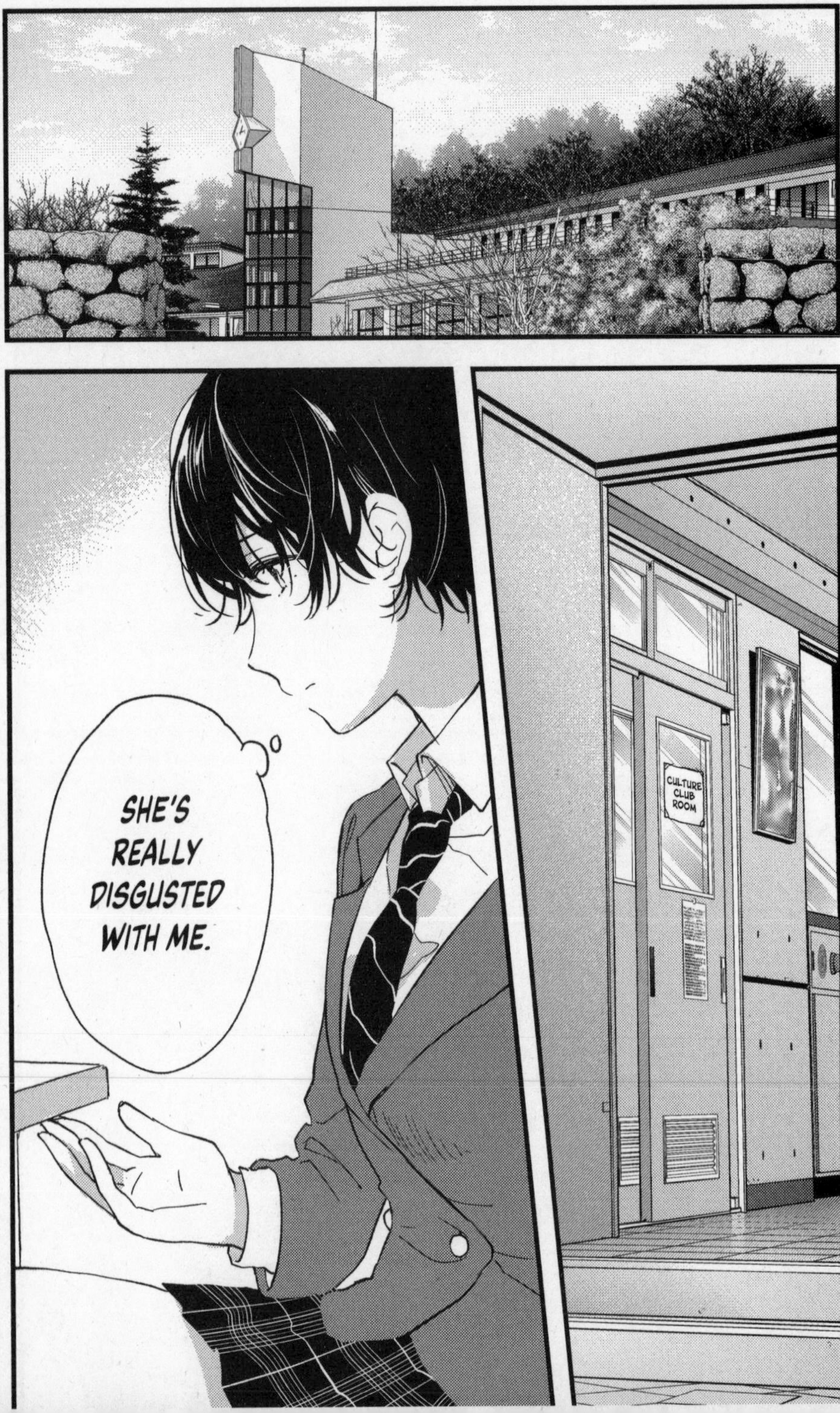
CULTURE CLUB ROOM
SHE'S REALLY DISGUSTED WITH ME.

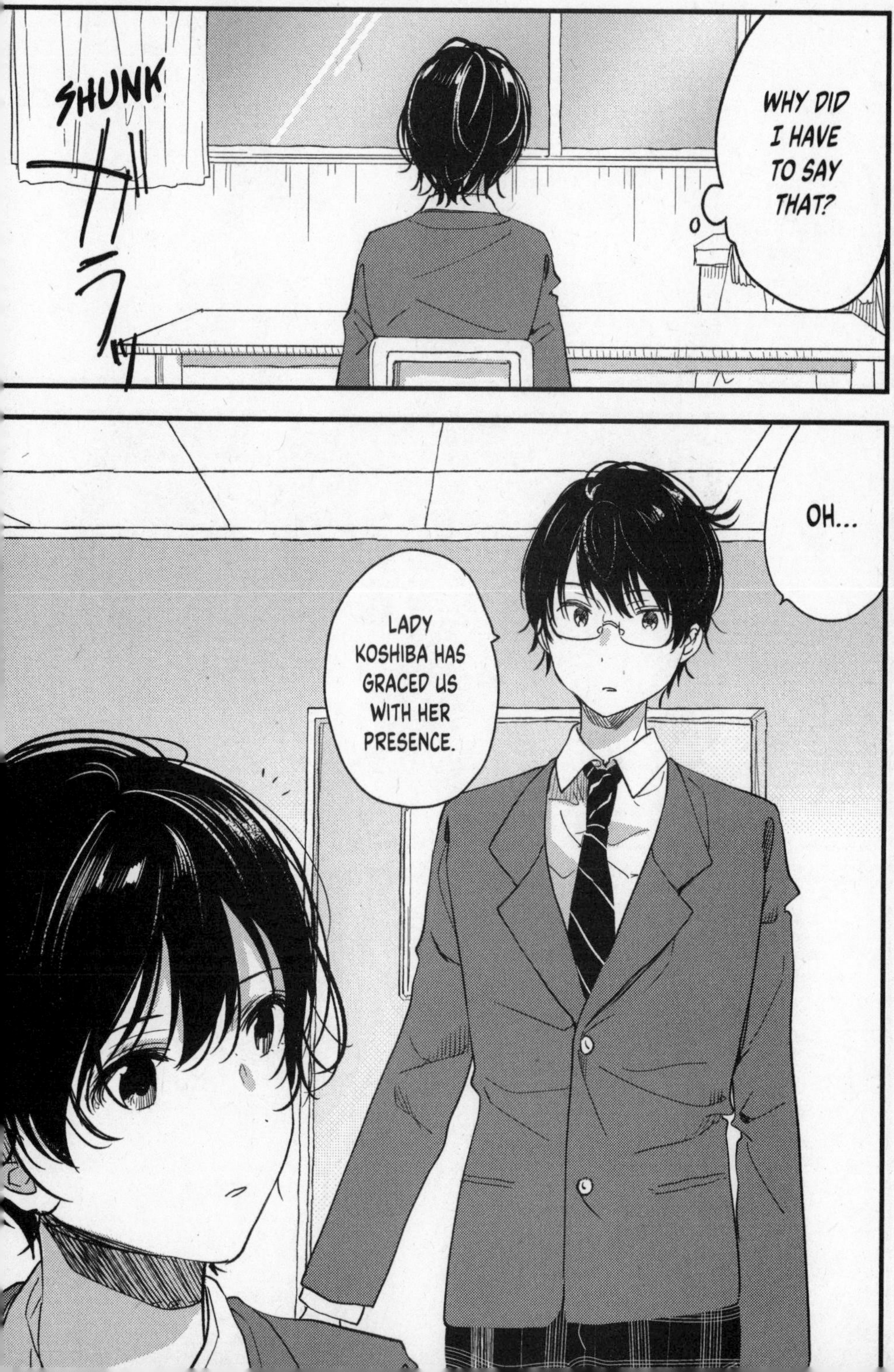
WHY DID I HAVE TO SAY THAT?
SHUNK
OH...
LADY KOSHIBA HAS GRACED US WITH HER PRESENCE.

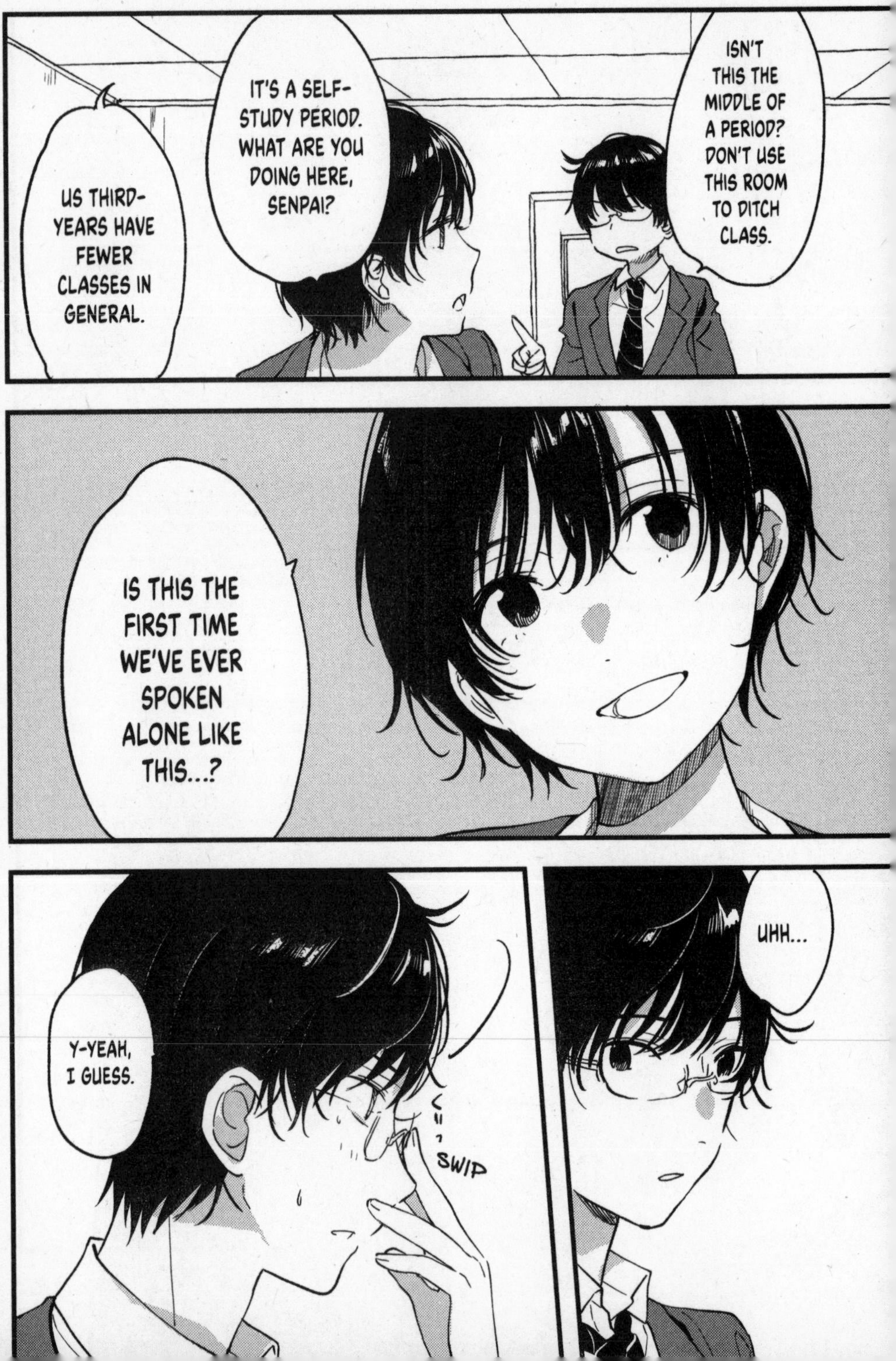
ISN'T THIS THE MIDDLE OF A PERIOD? DON'T USE THIS ROOM TO DITCH CLASS.
IT'S A SELF-STUDY PERIOD. WHAT ARE YOU DOING HERE, SENPAI?
US THIRD-YEARS HAVE FEWER CLASSES IN GENERAL.
IS THIS THE FIRST TIME WE'VE EVER SPOKEN ALONE LIKE THIS...?
UHH...
Y-YEAH, I GUESS.
SWIP

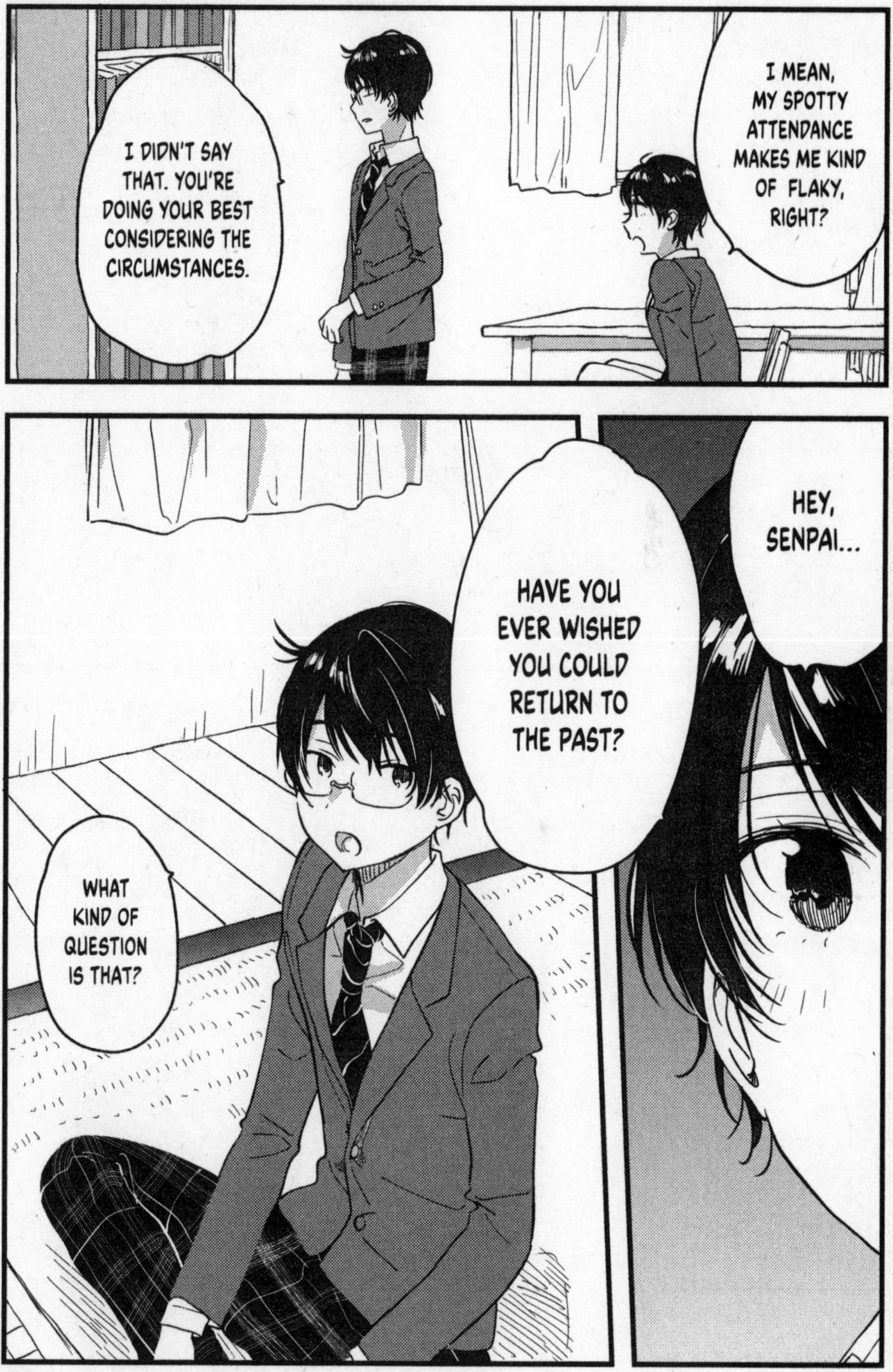
I MEAN, MY SPOTTY ATTENDANCE MAKES ME KIND OF FLAKY, RIGHT?
I DIDN'T SAY THAT. YOU'RE DOING YOUR BEST CONSIDERING THE CIRCUMSTANCES.
HEY, SENPAI...
HAVE YOU EVER WISHED YOU COULD RETURN TO THE PAST?
WHAT KIND OF QUESTION IS THAT?

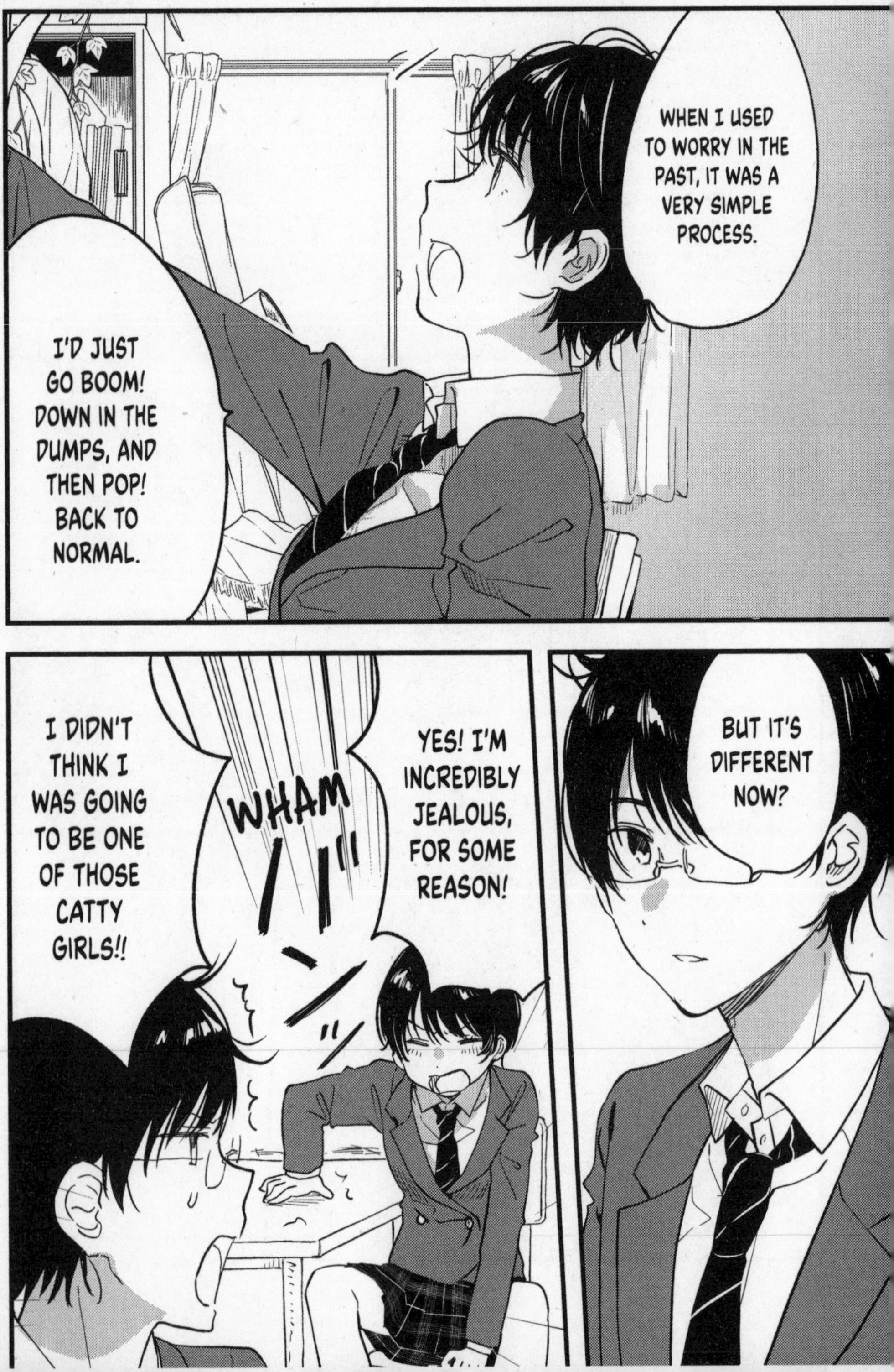
WHEN I USED TO WORRY IN THE PAST, IT WAS A VERY SIMPLE PROCESS.
I'D JUST GO BOOM! DOWN IN THE DUMPS, AND THEN POP! BACK TO NORMAL.
BUT IT'S DIFFERENT NOW?
YES! I'M INCREDIBLY JEALOUS, FOR SOME REASON!
WHAM
I DIDN'T THINK I WAS GOING TO BE ONE OF THOSE CATTY GIRLS!!

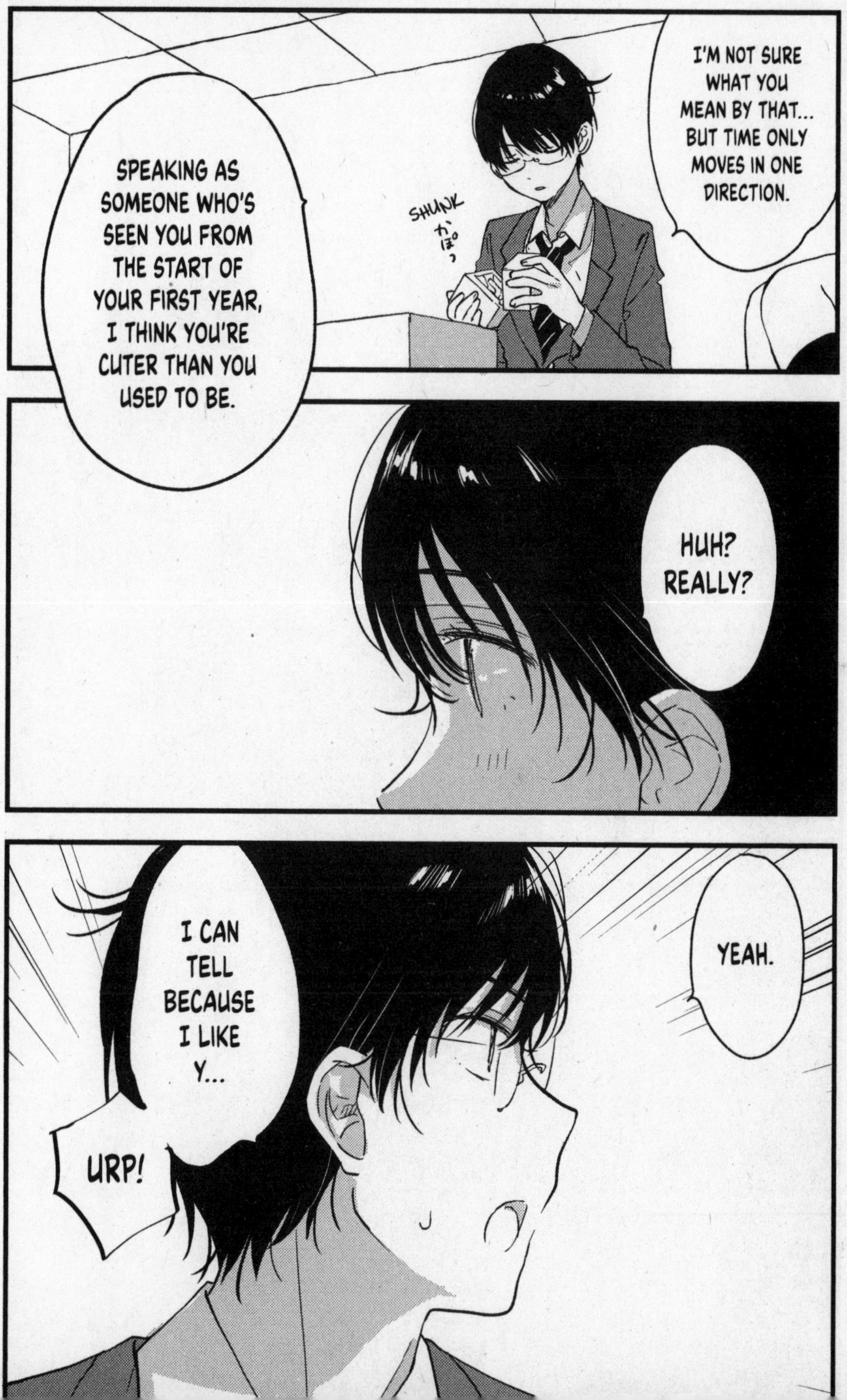
I'M NOT SURE WHAT YOU MEAN BY THAT... BUT TIME ONLY MOVES IN ONE DIRECTION.
SHUNK
かぽっ
SPEAKING AS SOMEONE WHO'S SEEN YOU FROM THE START OF YOUR FIRST YEAR, I THINK YOU'RE CUTER THAN YOU USED TO BE.
HUH? REALLY?
YEAH.
I CAN TELL BECAUSE I LIKE Y...
URP!

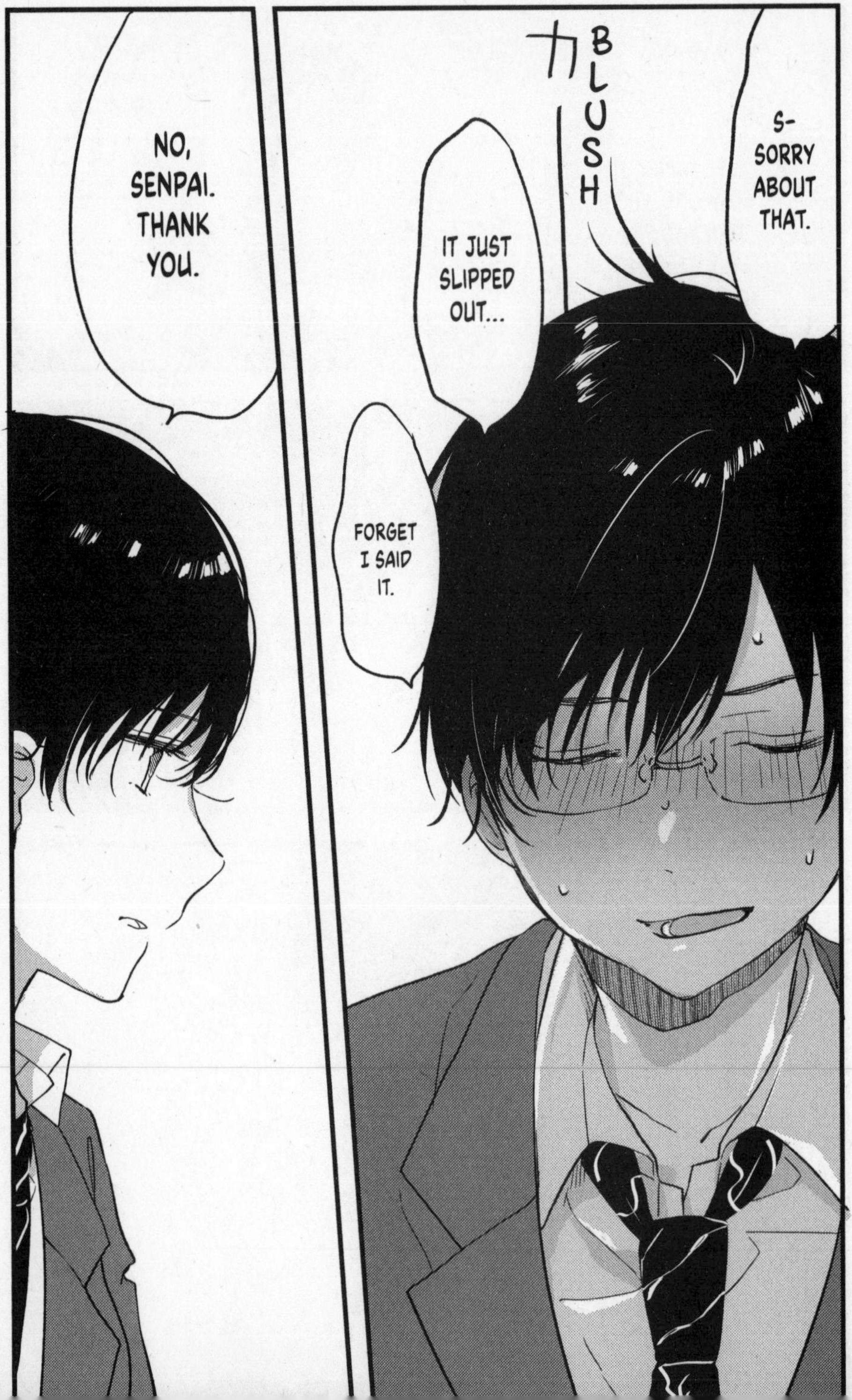
S-SORRY ABOUT THAT.
カ
BLUSH
IT JUST SLIPPED OUT...
FORGET I SAID IT.
NO, SENPAI. THANK YOU.

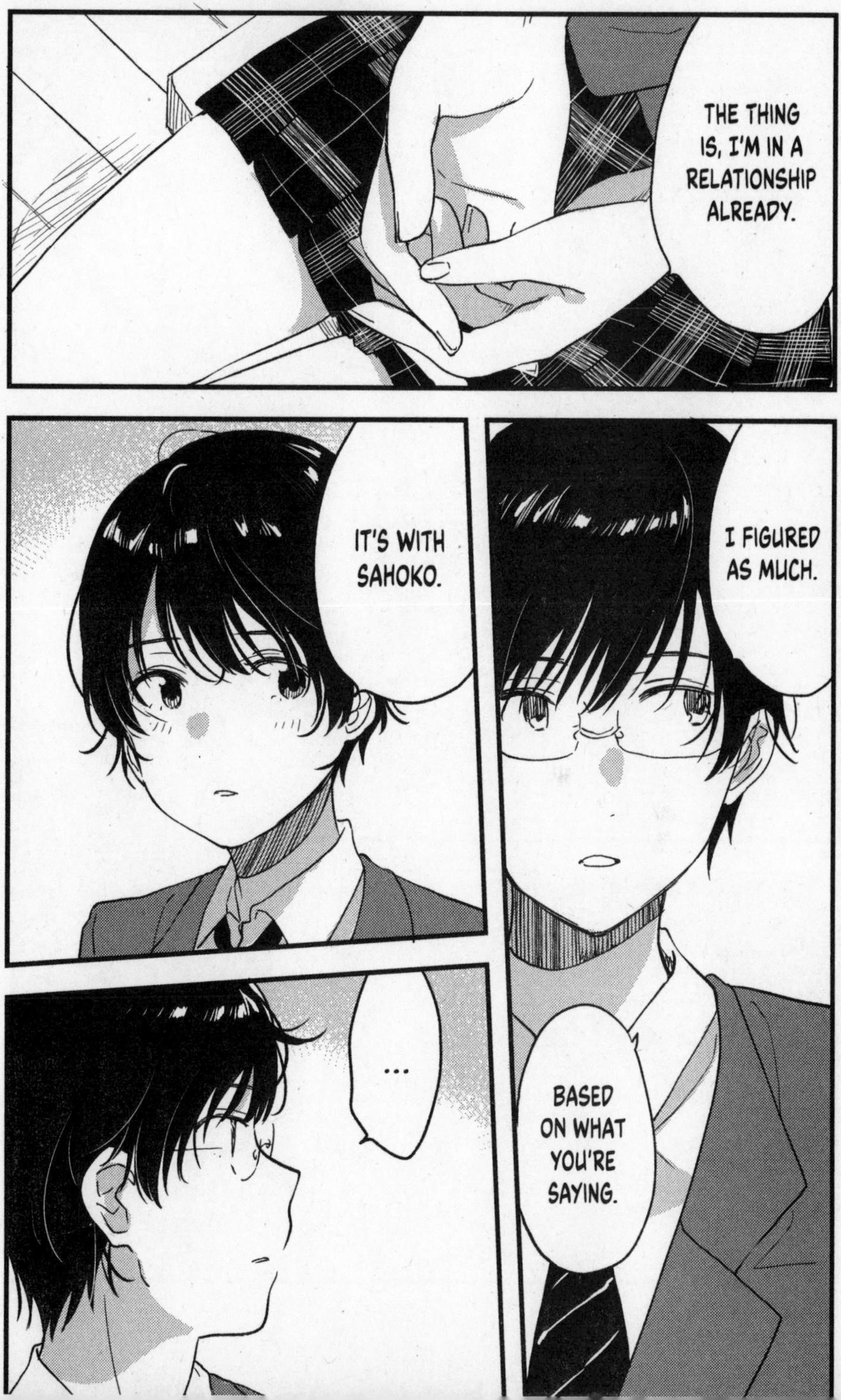
THE THING IS, I'M IN A RELATIONSHIP ALREADY.
I FIGURED AS MUCH.
BASED ON WHAT YOU'RE SAYING.
IT'S WITH SAHOKO.
...

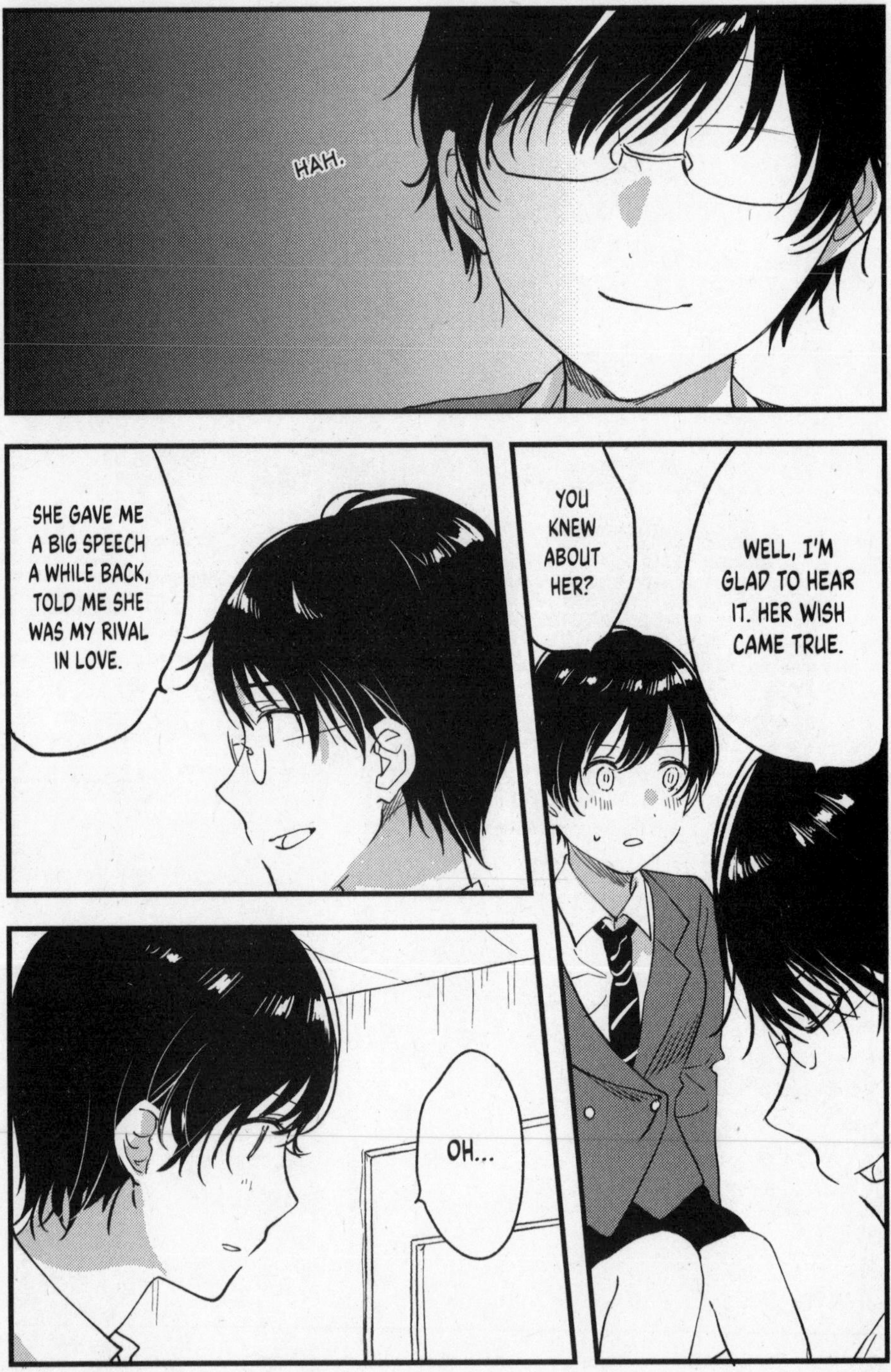
HAH.
WELL, I'M GLAD TO HEAR IT. HER WISH CAME TRUE.
YOU KNEW ABOUT HER?
SHE GAVE ME A BIG SPEECH A WHILE BACK, TOLD ME SHE WAS MY RIVAL IN LOVE.
OH...

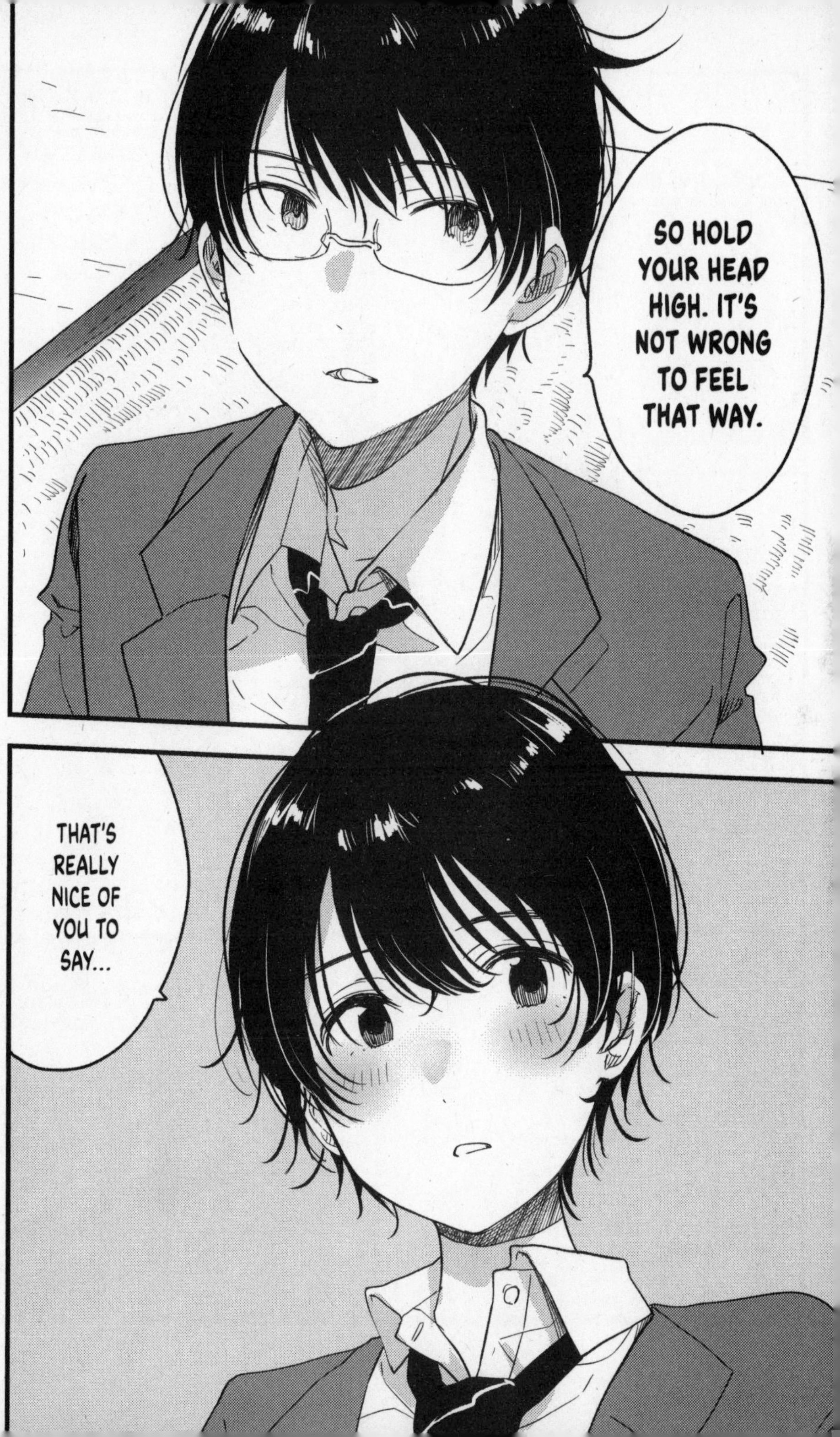
SO HOLD YOUR HEAD HIGH. IT'S NOT WRONG TO FEEL THAT WAY.
THAT'S REALLY NICE OF YOU TO SAY...

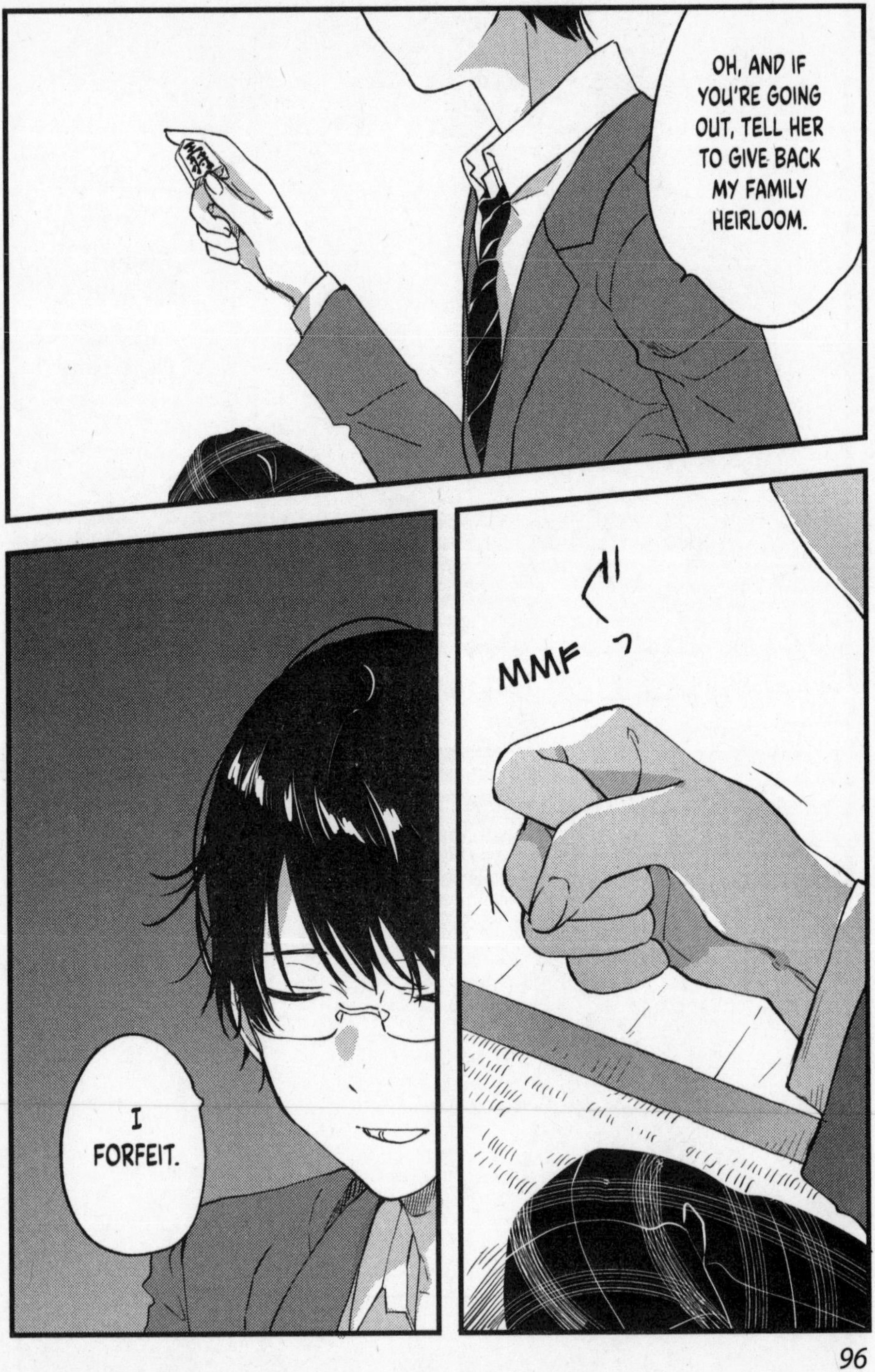
OH, AND IF YOU'RE GOING OUT, TELL HER TO GIVE BACK MY FAMILY HEIRLOOM.
MMF
I FORFEIT.

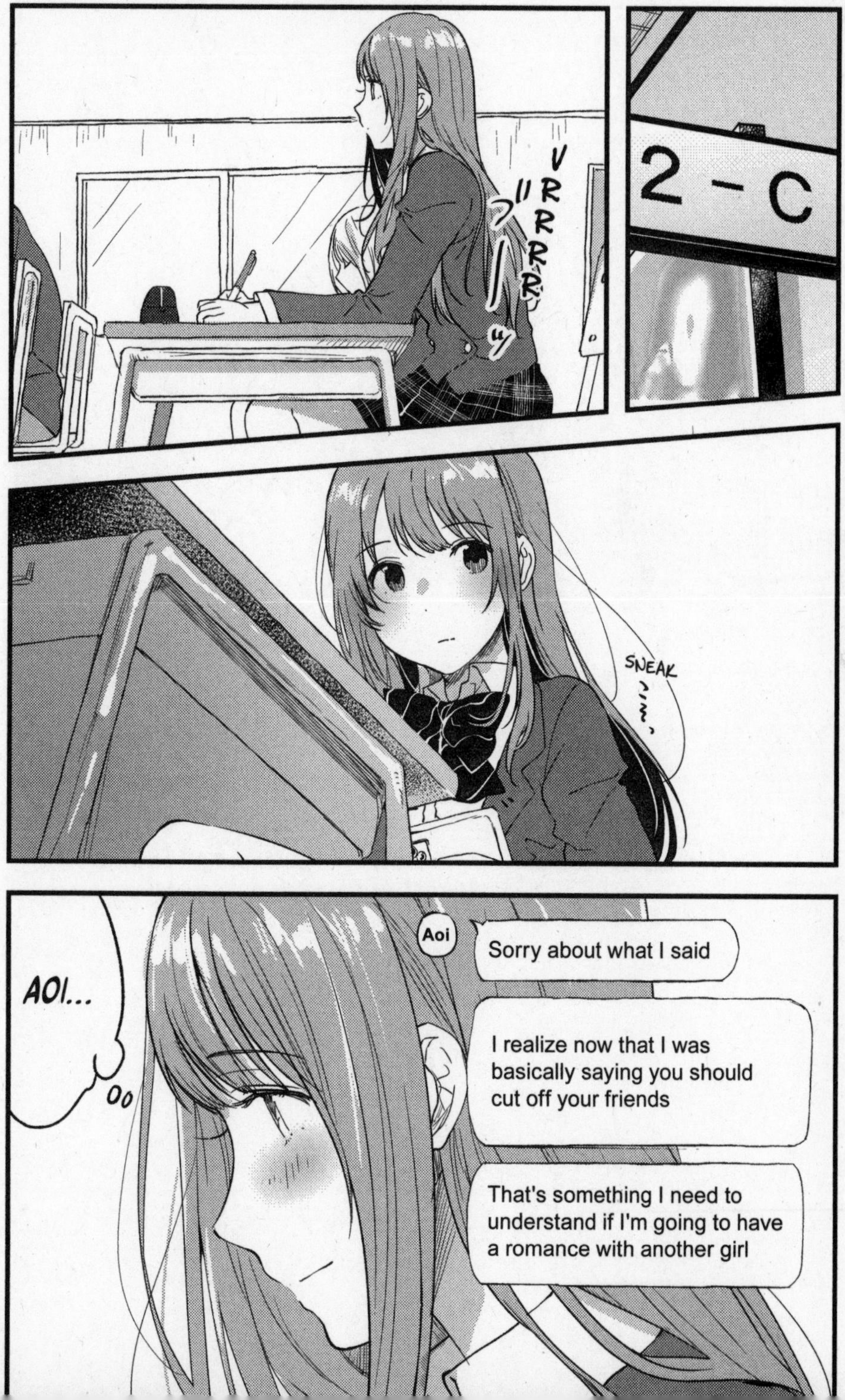
2-C
VRRRRR
SNEAK
AOI...
Aoi
Sorry about what I said
I realize now that I was basically saying you should cut off your friends
That's something I need to understand if I'm going to have a romance with another girl

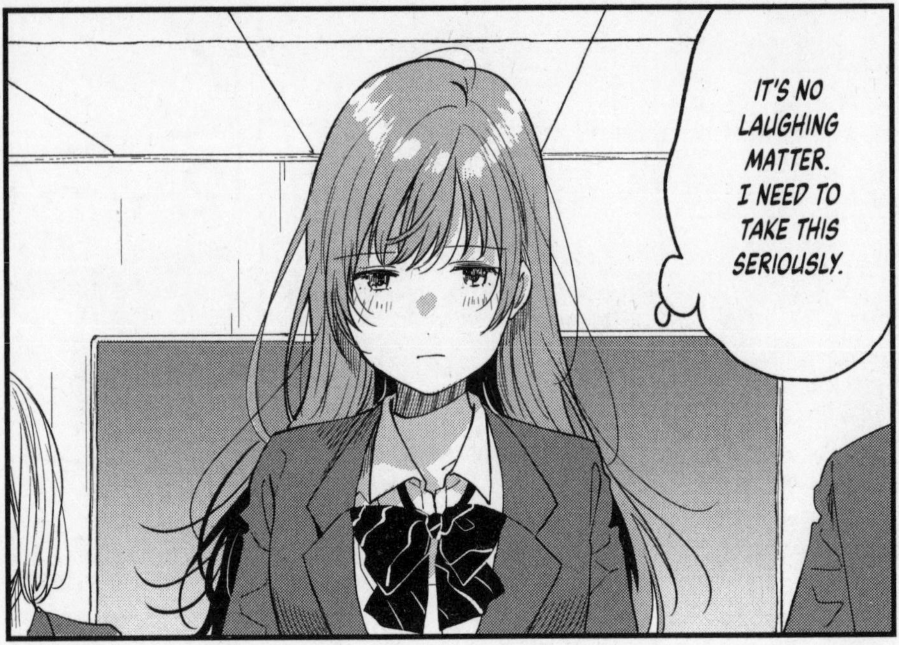
IT'S NO LAUGHING MATTER. I NEED TO TAKE THIS SERIOUSLY.

I LIKE AOI.

AND BECAUSE I LIKE HER...

Chapter 30:
Didn't Want to Know (Part 2)

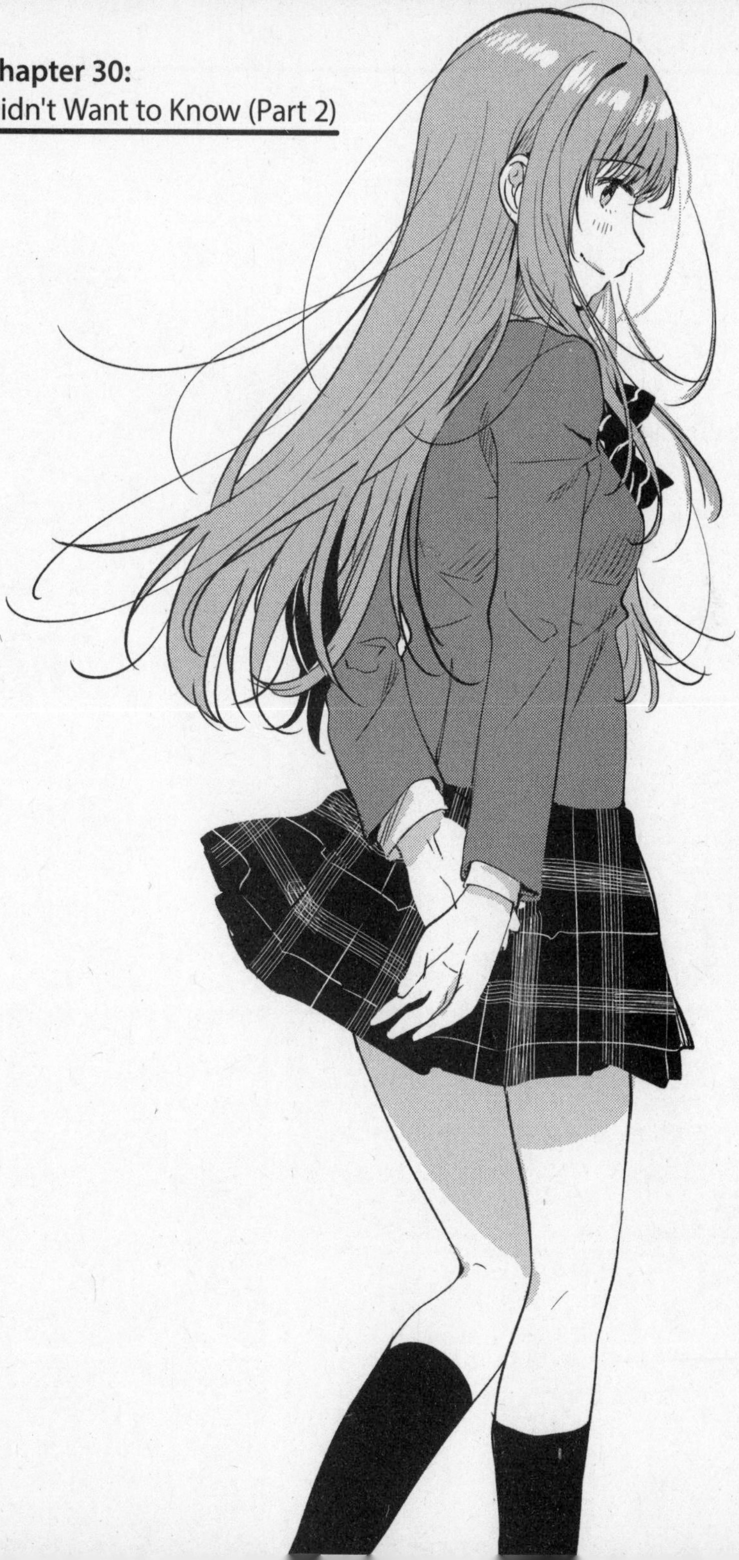

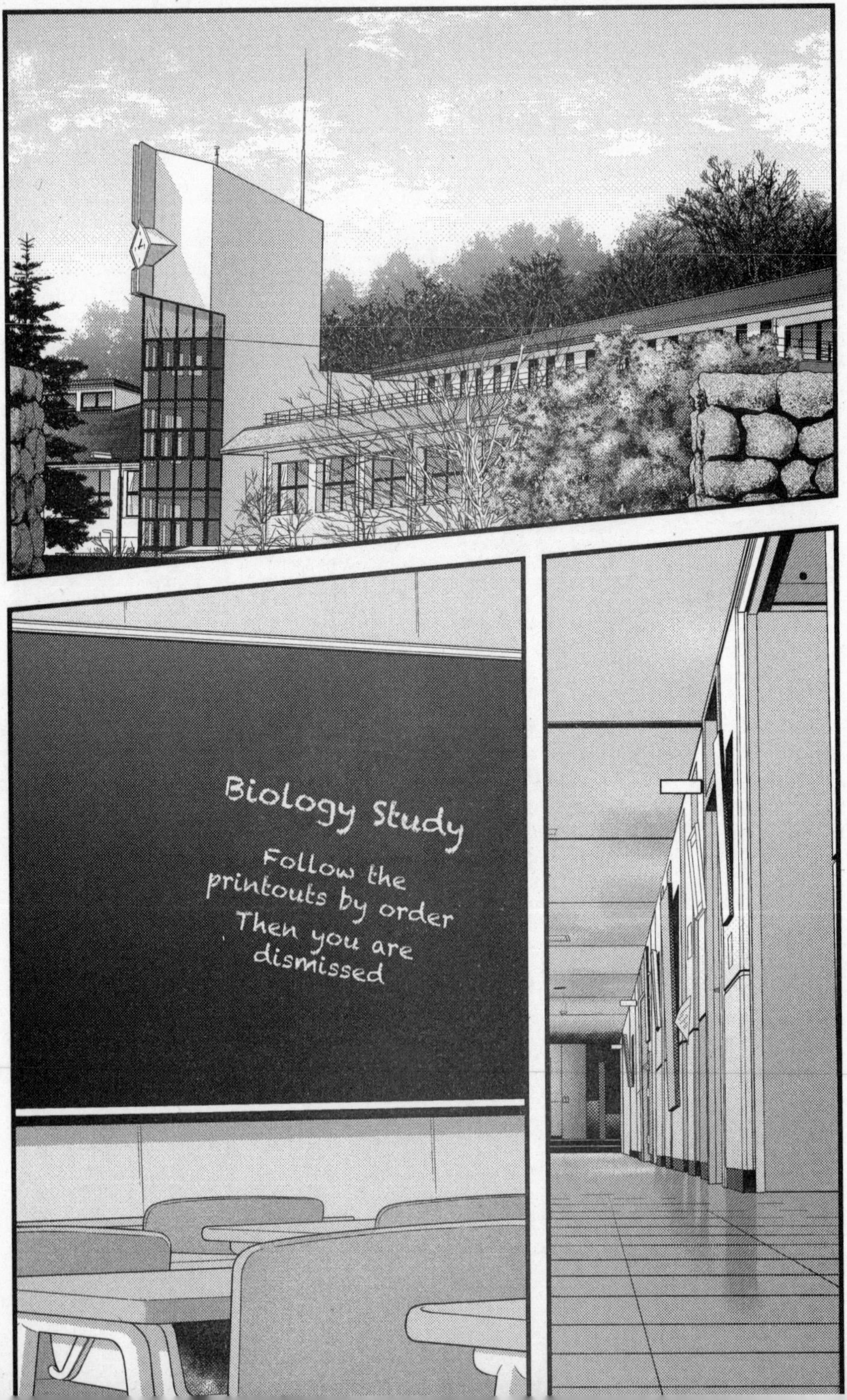
Biology Study
Follow the printouts by order Then you are dismissed

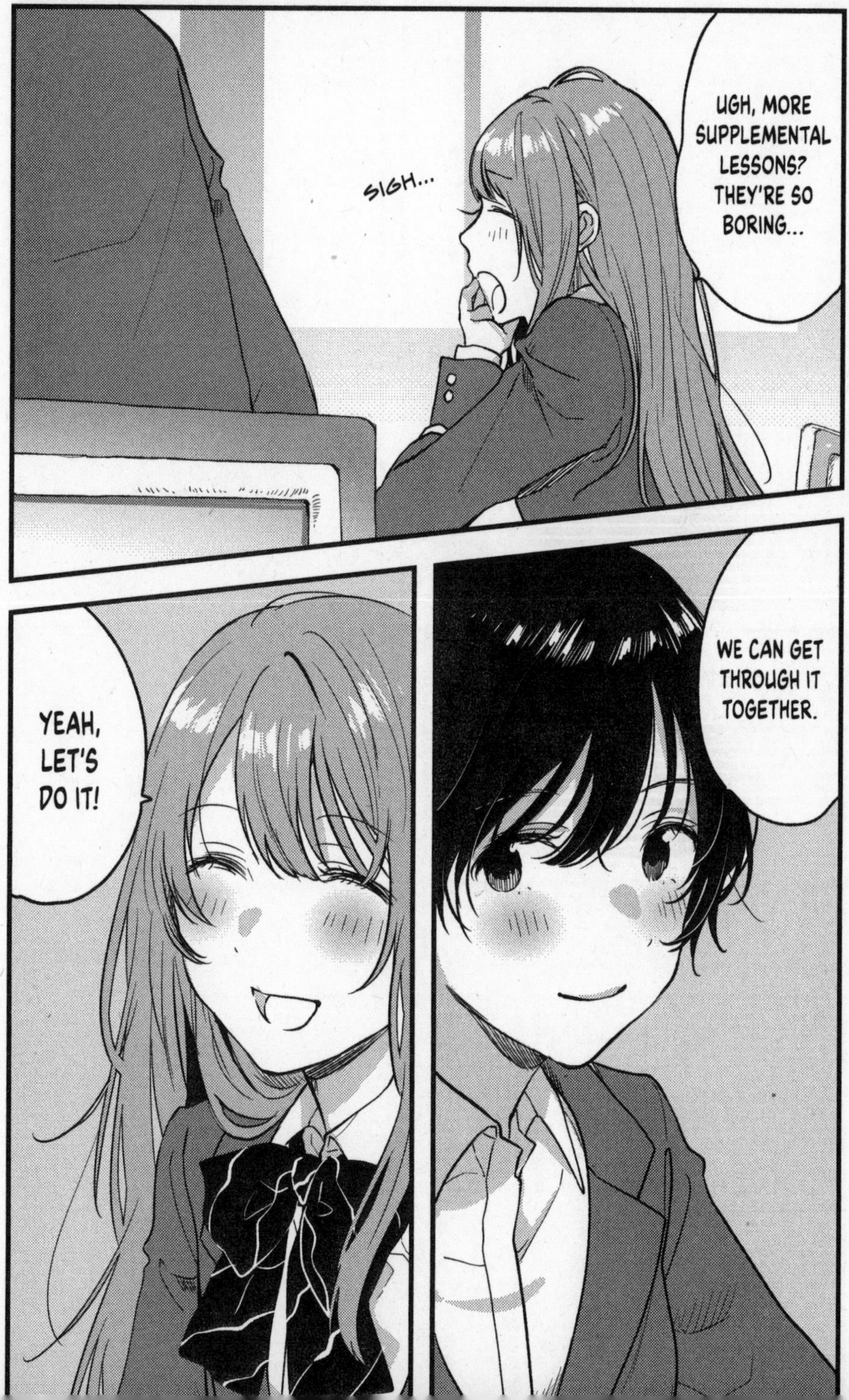
UGH, MORE SUPPLEMENTAL LESSONS? THEY'RE SO BORING...
SIGH...
WE CAN GET THROUGH IT TOGETHER.
YEAH, LET'S DO IT!

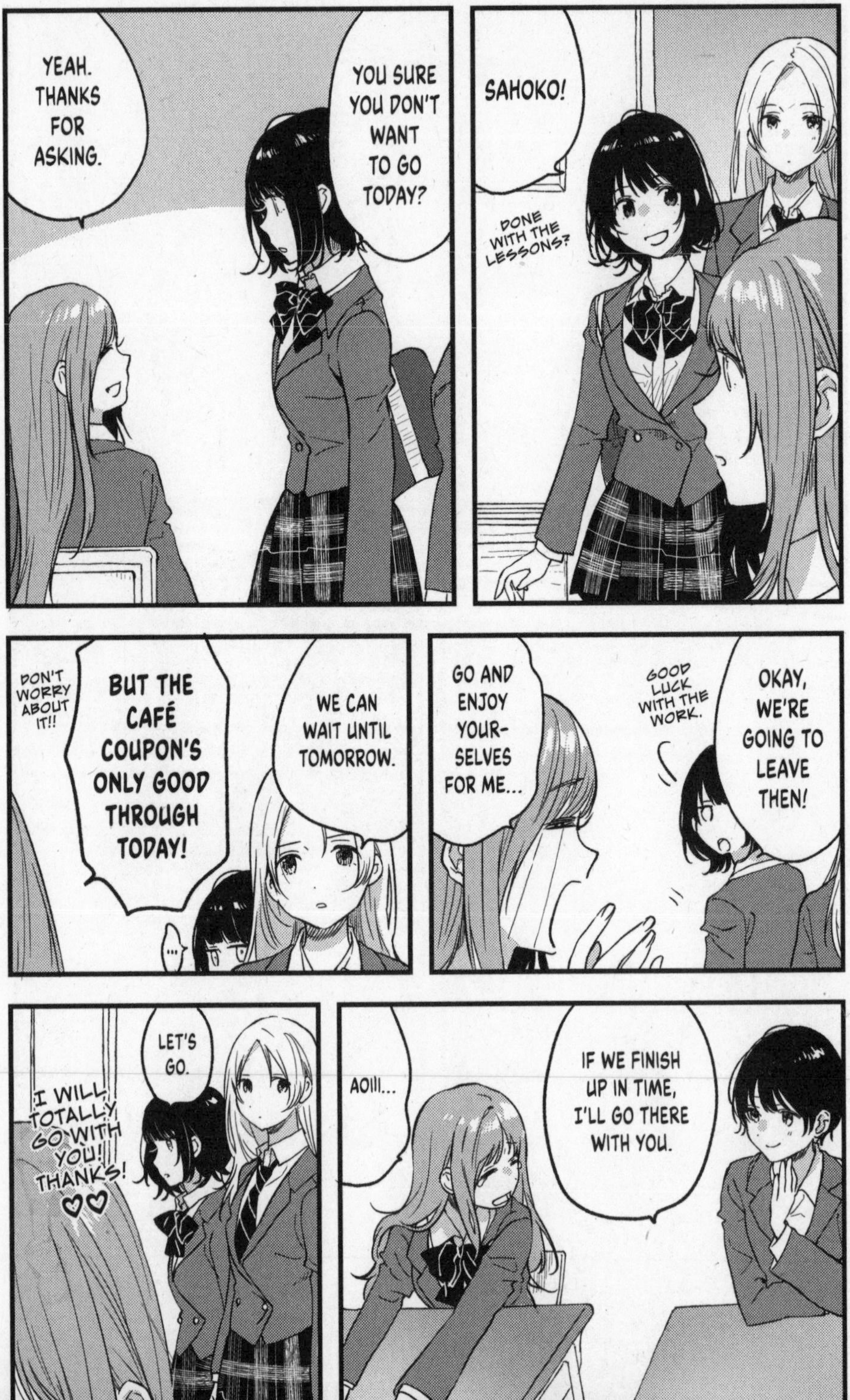
SAHOKO!
DONE WITH THE LESSONS?
YOU SURE YOU DON'T WANT TO GO TODAY?
YEAH. THANKS FOR ASKING.
OKAY, WE'RE GOING TO LEAVE THEN!
GOOD LUCK WITH THE WORK.
GO AND ENJOY YOUR-SELVES FOR ME...
WE CAN WAIT UNTIL TOMORROW.
BUT THE CAFÉ COUPON'S ONLY GOOD THROUGH TODAY!
DON'T WORRY ABOUT IT!!
...
IF WE FINISH UP IN TIME, I'LL GO THERE WITH YOU.
AOIII...
LET'S GO.
I WILL TOTALLY GO WITH YOU! THANKS! ♡♡

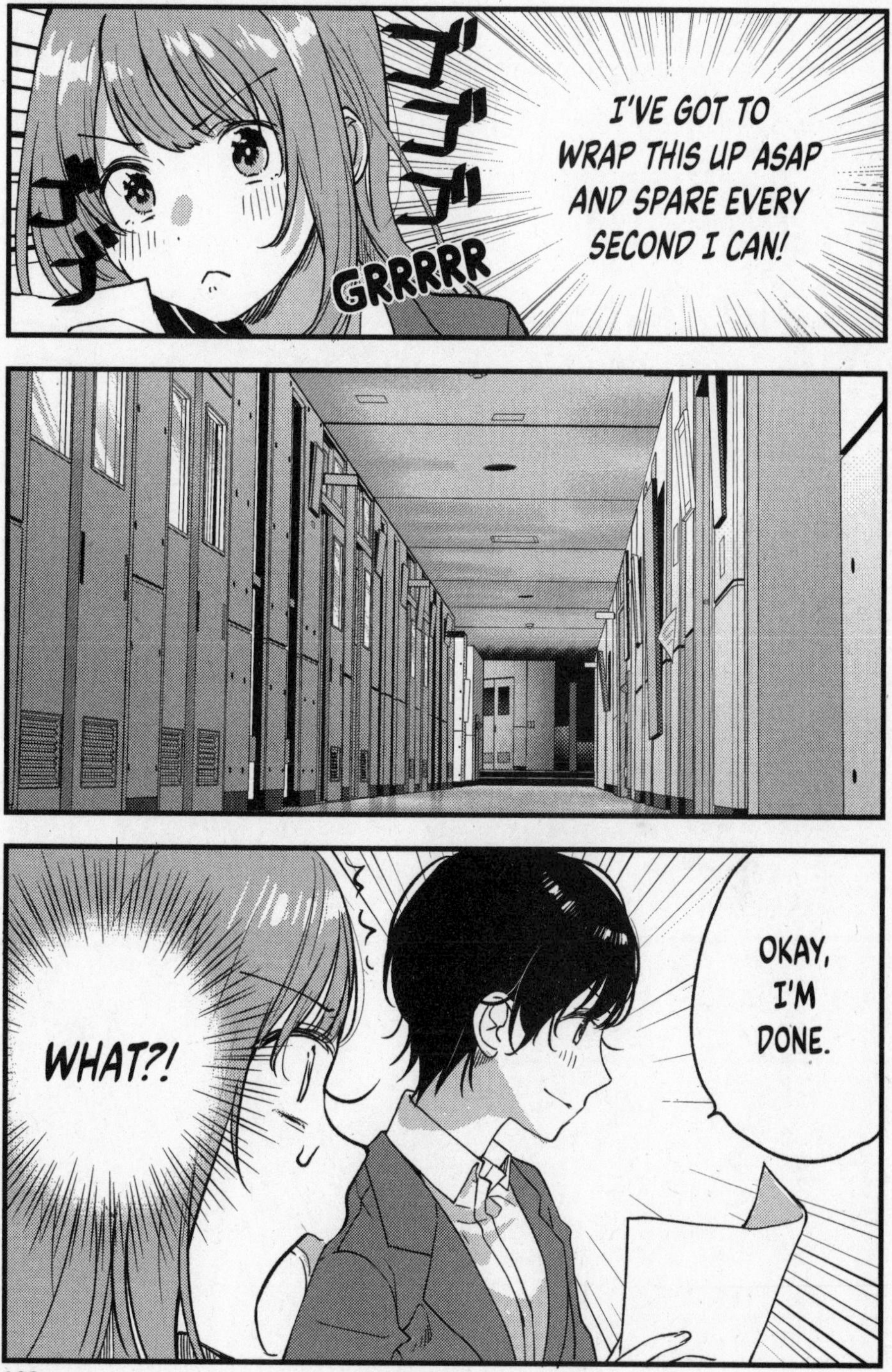
I'VE GOT TO WRAP THIS UP ASAP AND SPARE EVERY SECOND I CAN!
GRRRRR
OKAY, I'M DONE.
WHAT?!

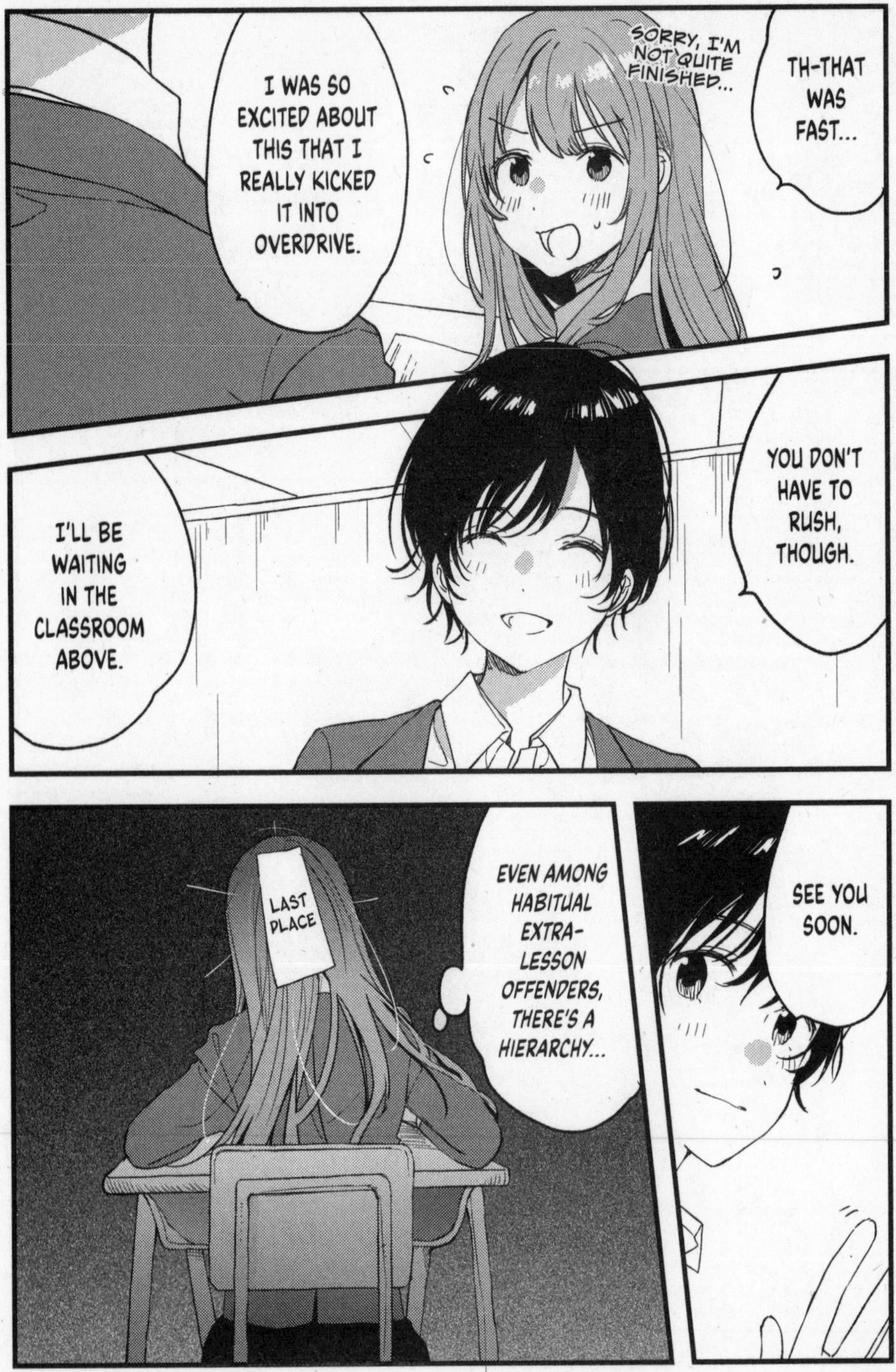
TH-THAT WAS FAST...
SORRY, I'M NOT QUITE FINISHED...
I WAS SO EXCITED ABOUT THIS THAT I REALLY KICKED IT INTO OVERDRIVE.
YOU DON'T HAVE TO RUSH, THOUGH.
I'LL BE WAITING IN THE CLASSROOM ABOVE.
SEE YOU SOON.
EVEN AMONG HABITUAL EXTRA-LESSON OFFENDERS, THERE'S A HIERARCHY...
LAST PLACE

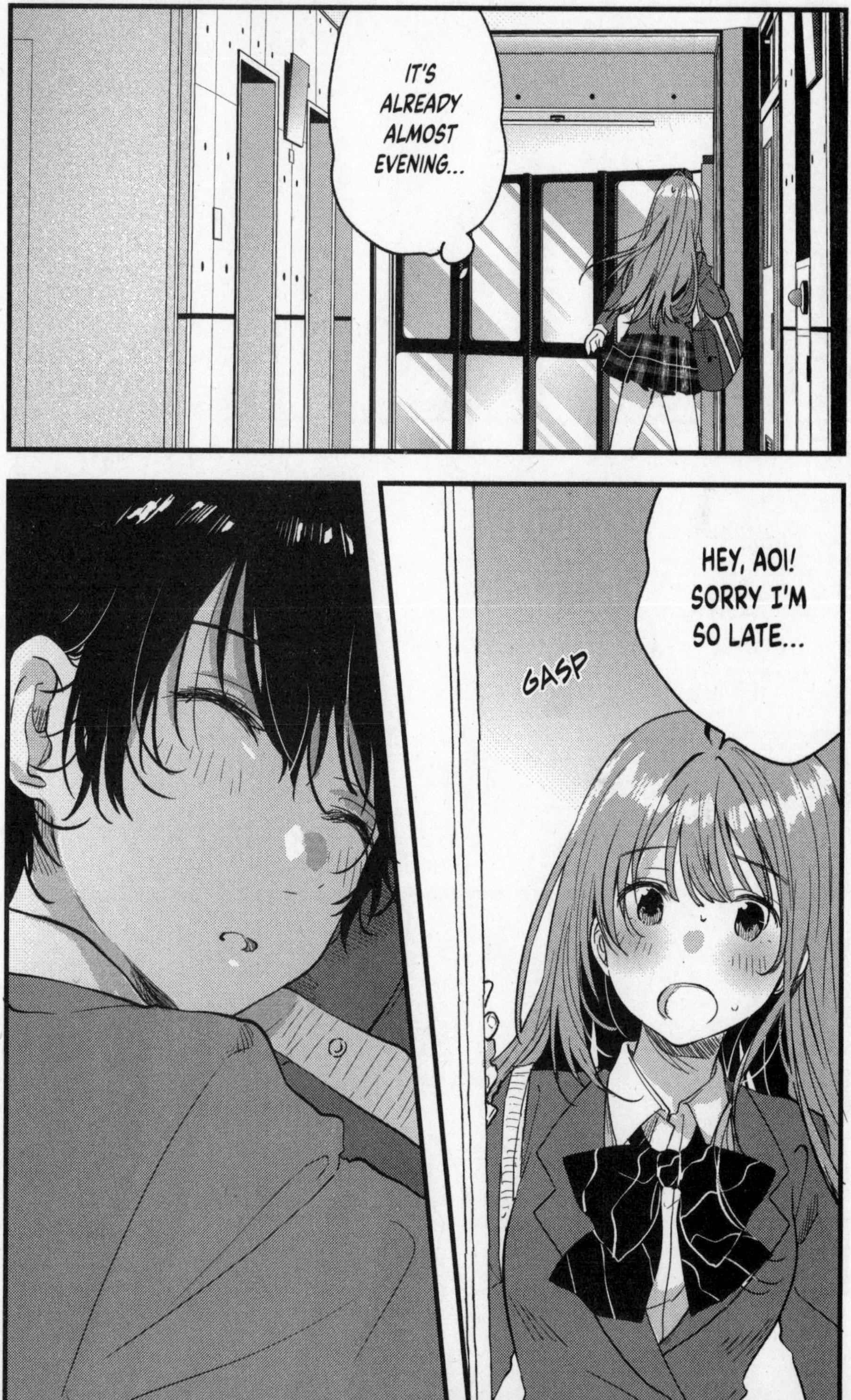
IT'S ALREADY ALMOST EVENING...
HEY, AOI! SORRY I'M SO LATE...
GASP

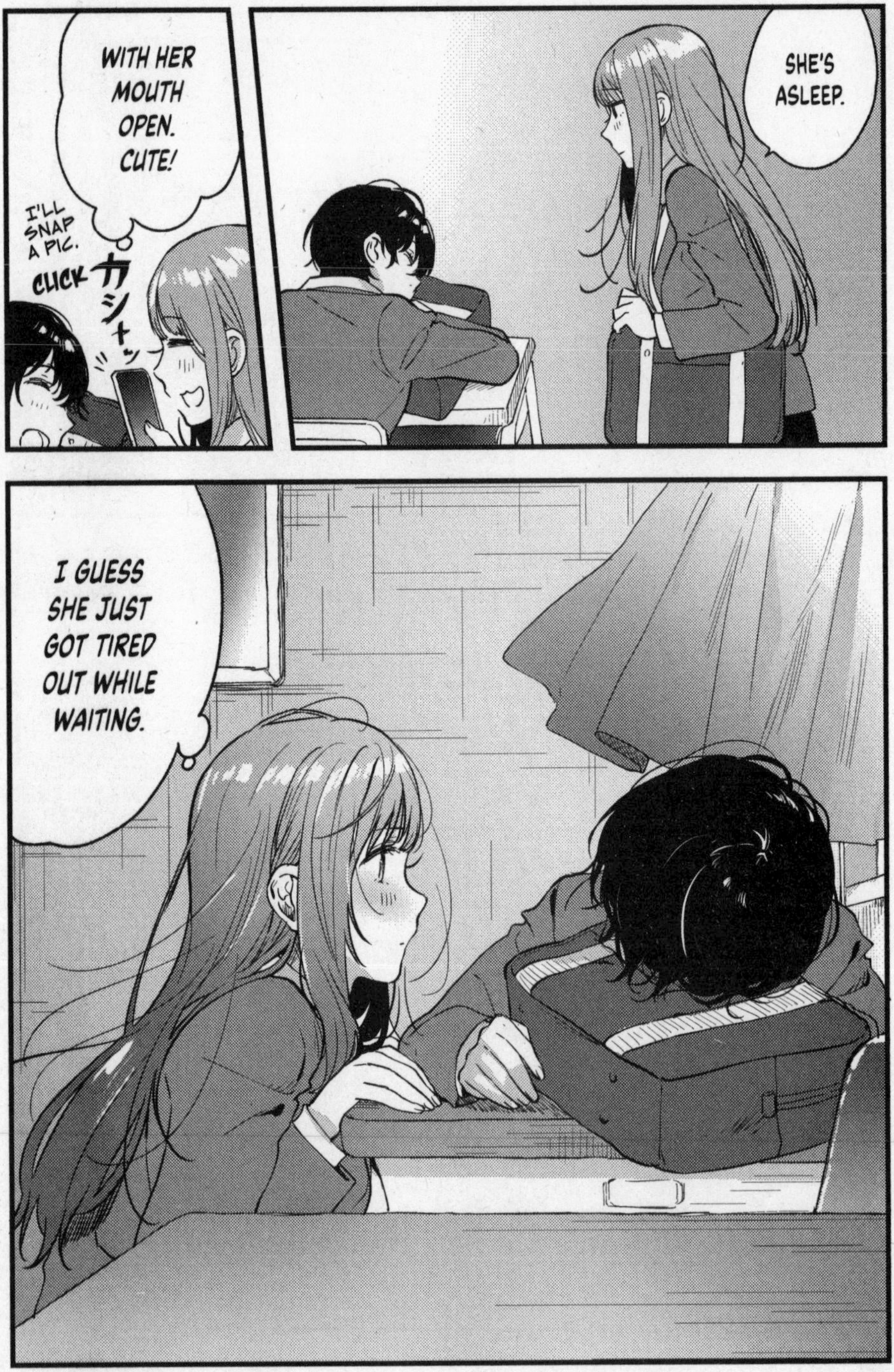
SHE'S ASLEEP.
WITH HER MOUTH OPEN. CUTE!
I'LL SNAP A PIC.
CLICK
カシャッ
I GUESS SHE JUST GOT TIRED OUT WHILE WAITING.

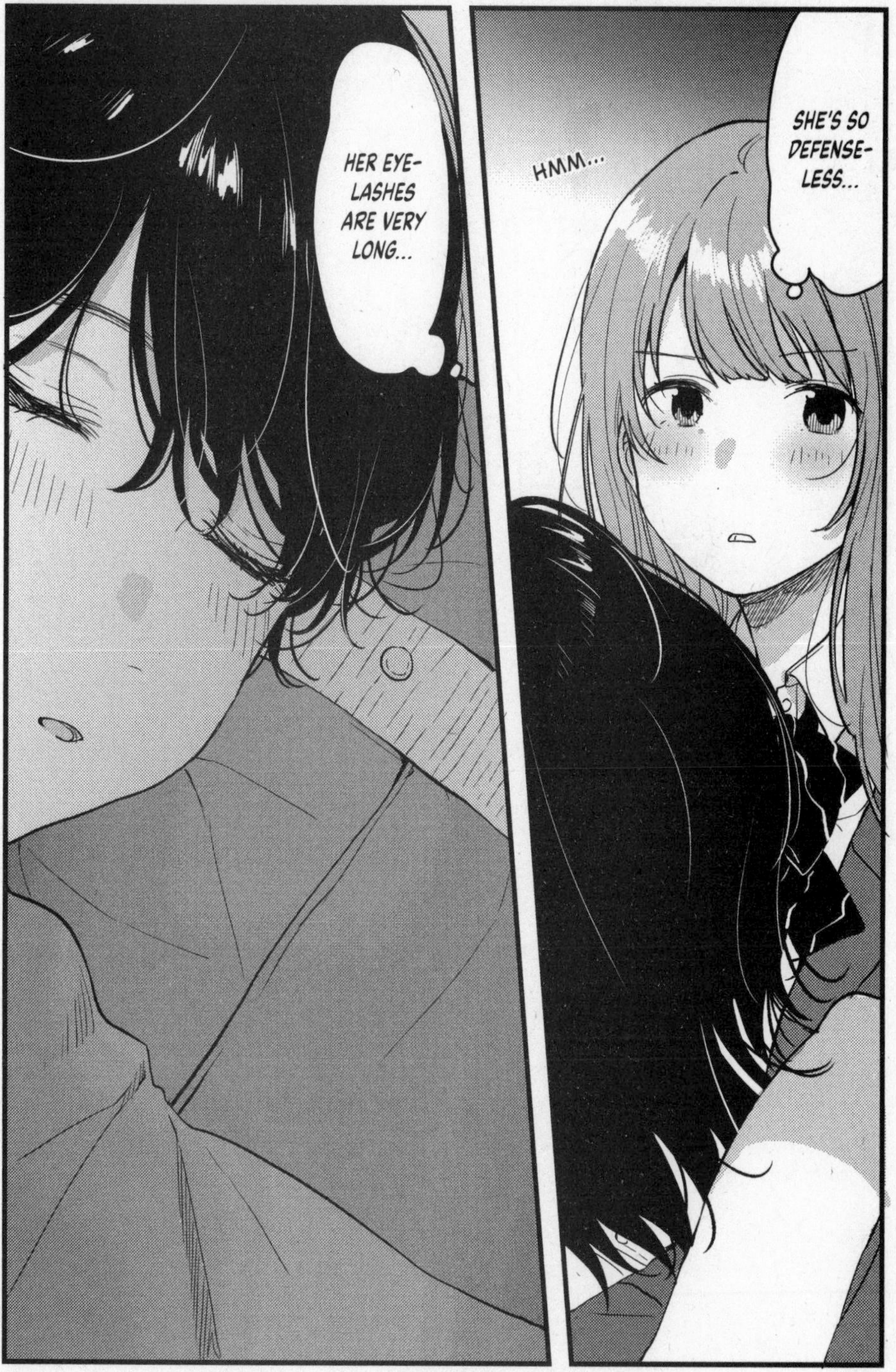
SHE'S SO DEFENSE-LESS...
HMM...
HER EYE-LASHES ARE VERY LONG...

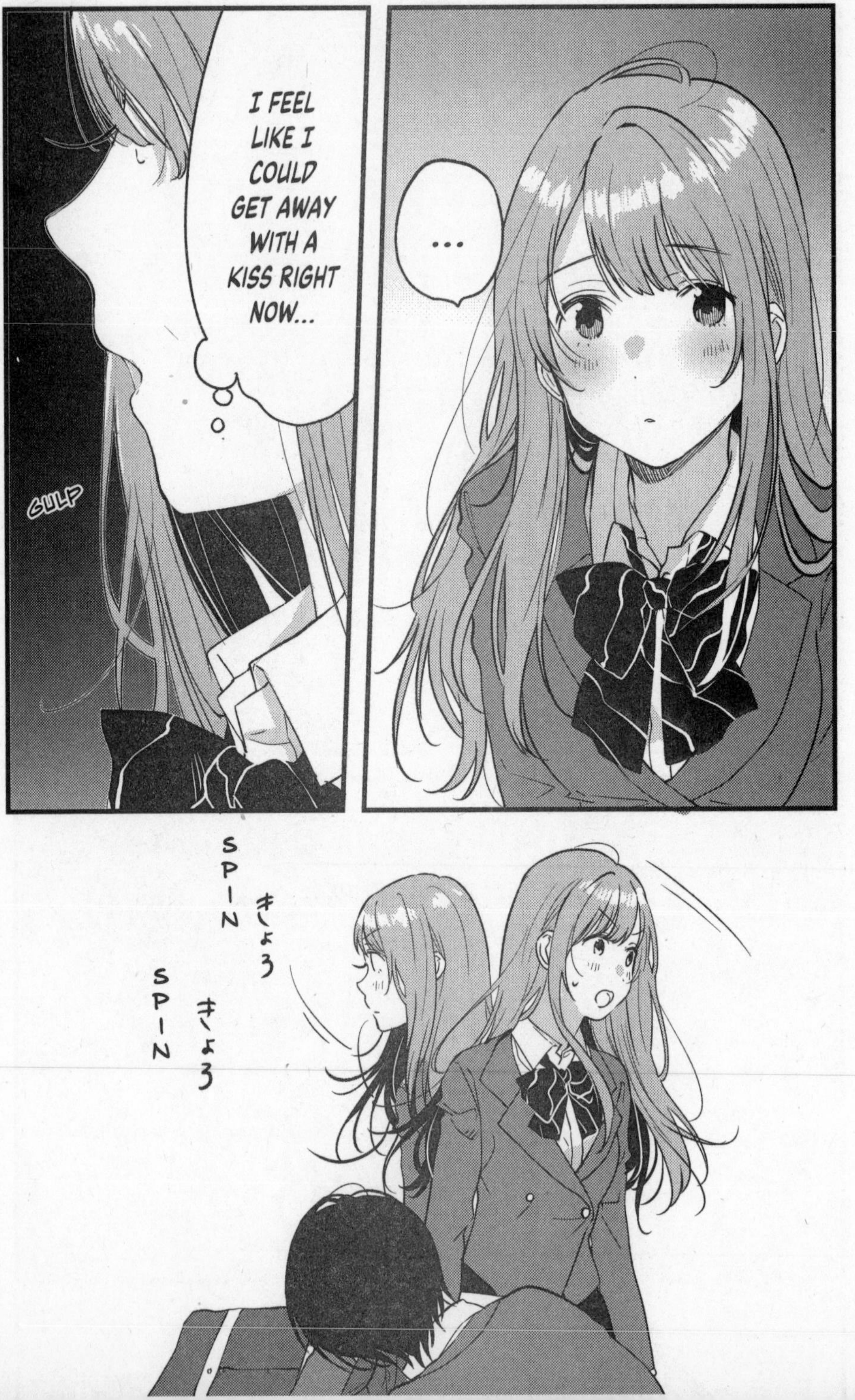
...
I FEEL LIKE I COULD GET AWAY WITH A KISS RIGHT NOW...
GULP
きょろ
SPIN
きょろ
SPIN

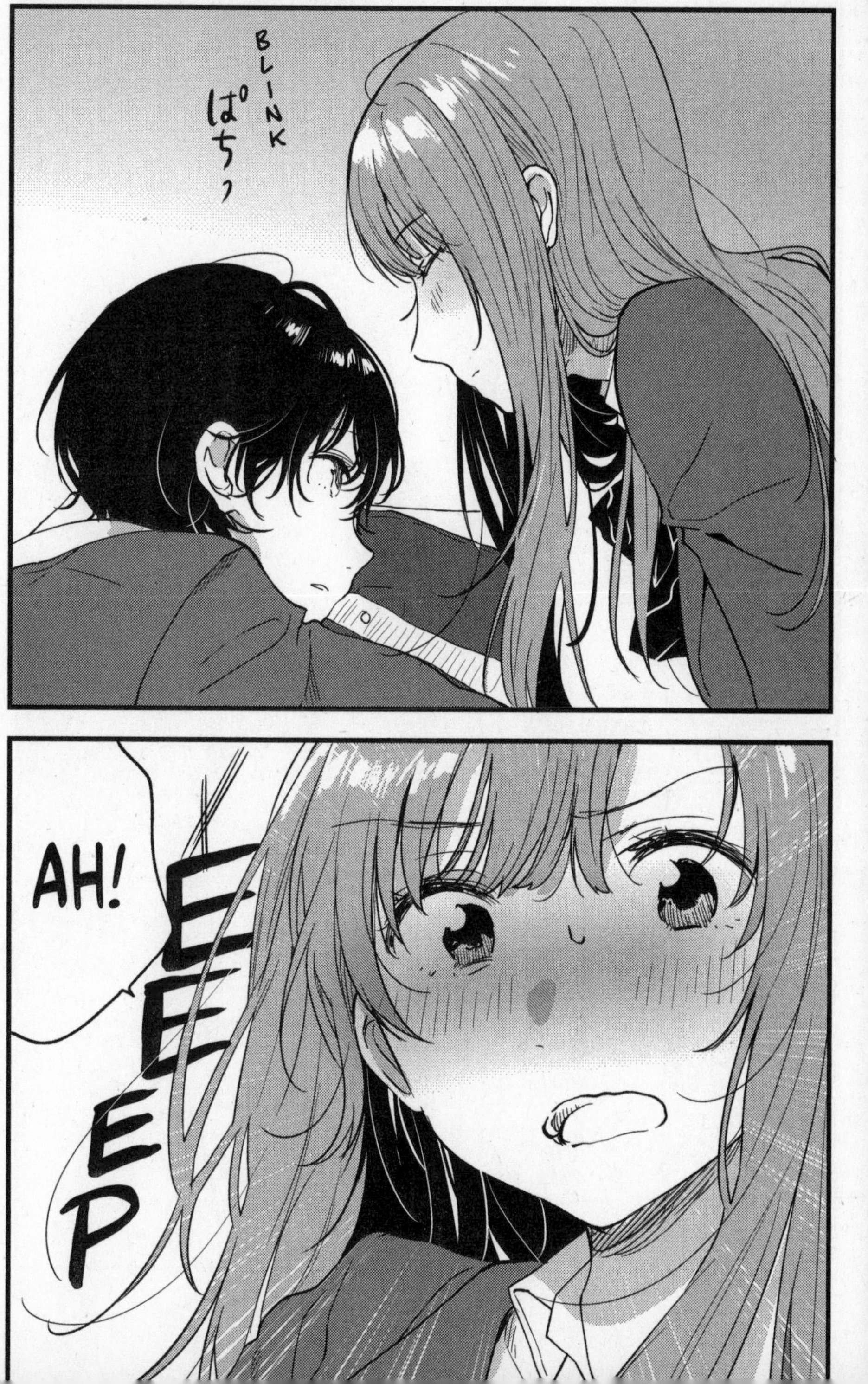
BLINK
ぱちっ
AH!
EEEP

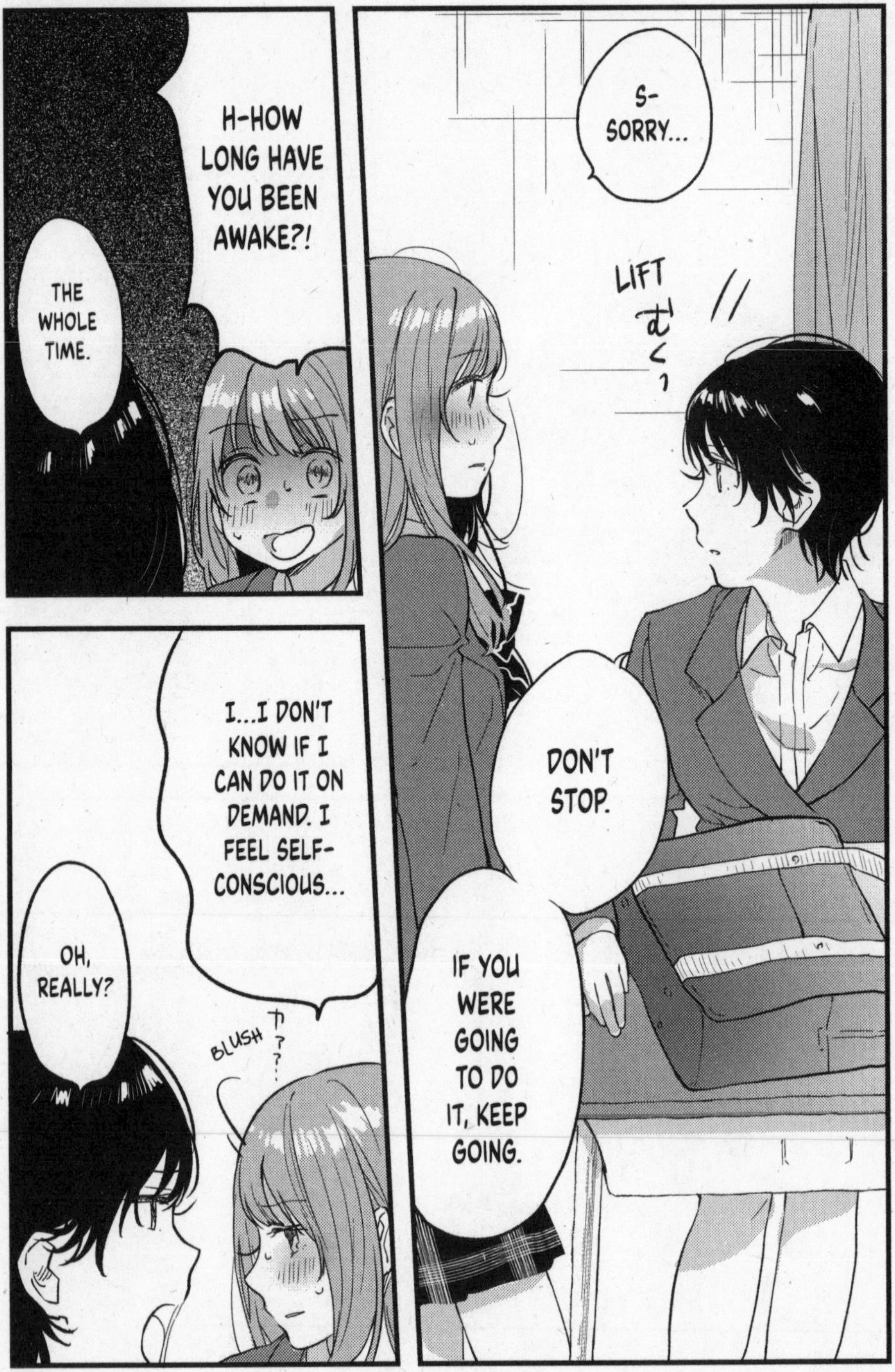
S-SORRY...
LIFT
DON'T STOP.
IF YOU WERE GOING TO DO IT, KEEP GOING.
H-HOW LONG HAVE YOU BEEN AWAKE?!
THE WHOLE TIME.
I...I DON'T KNOW IF I CAN DO IT ON DEMAND. I FEEL SELF-CONSCIOUS...
BLUSH
OH, REALLY?

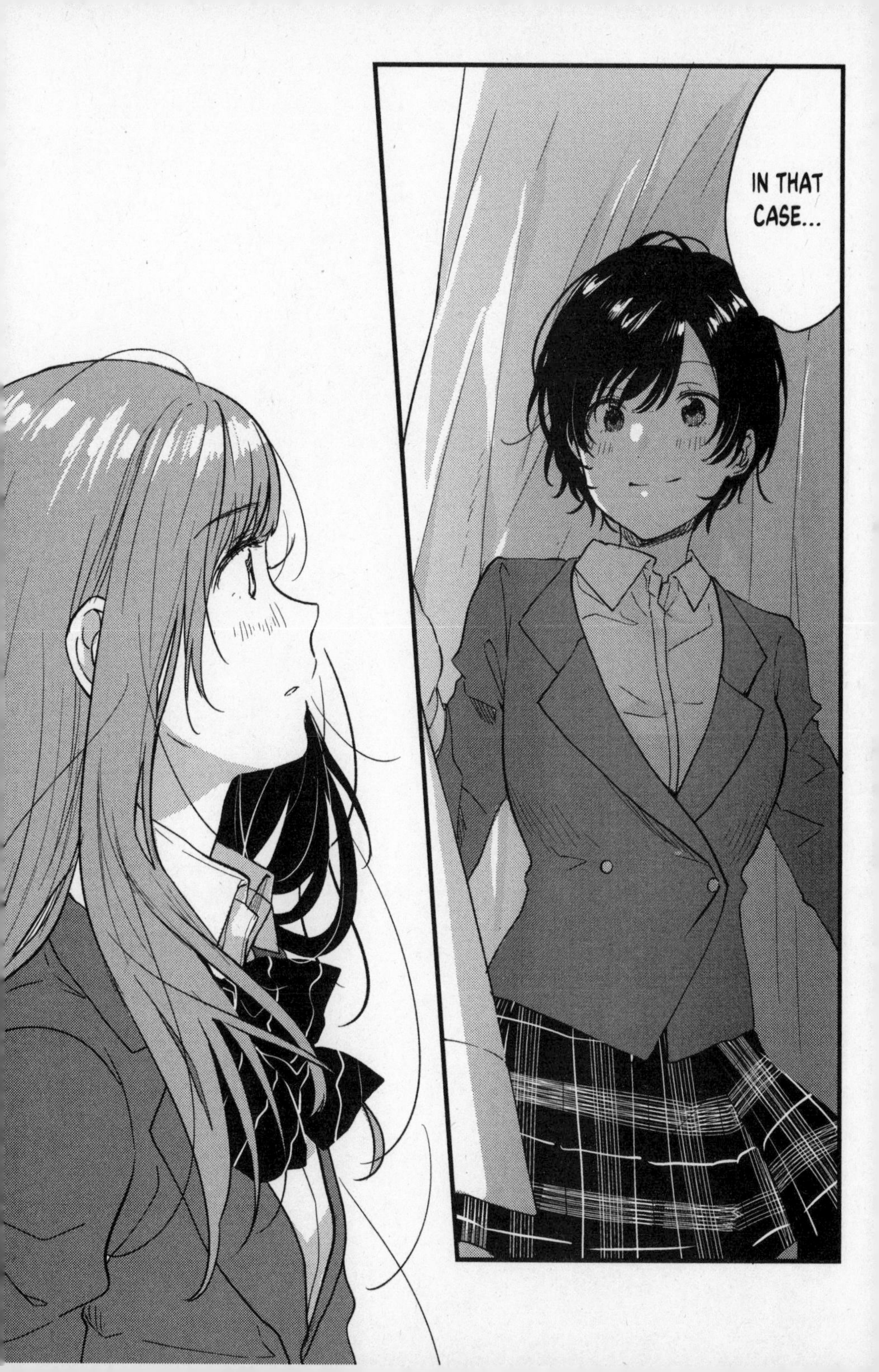
IN THAT CASE...

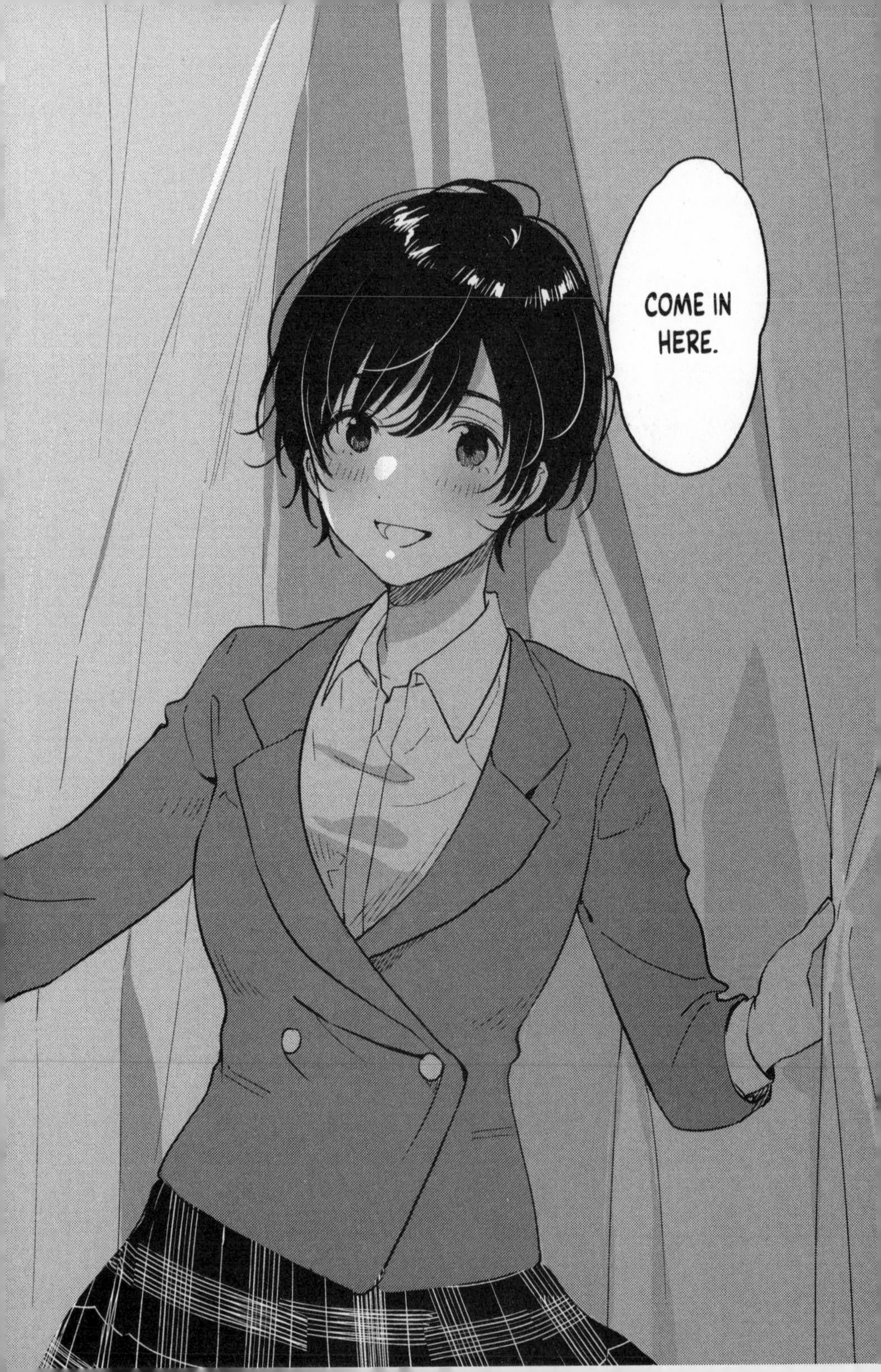
COME IN HERE.

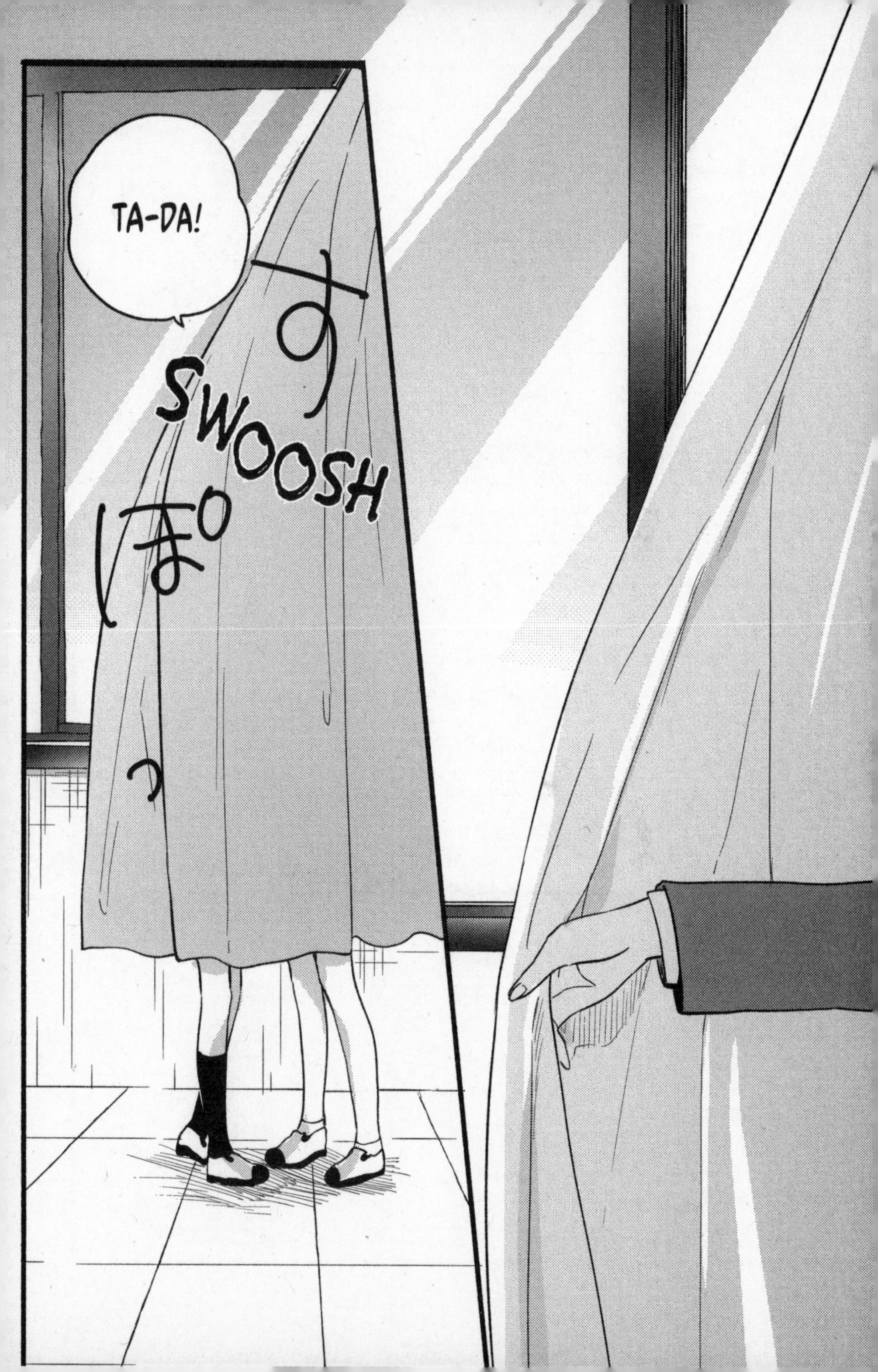

TA-DA!
すっ
SWOOSH
ぽっ

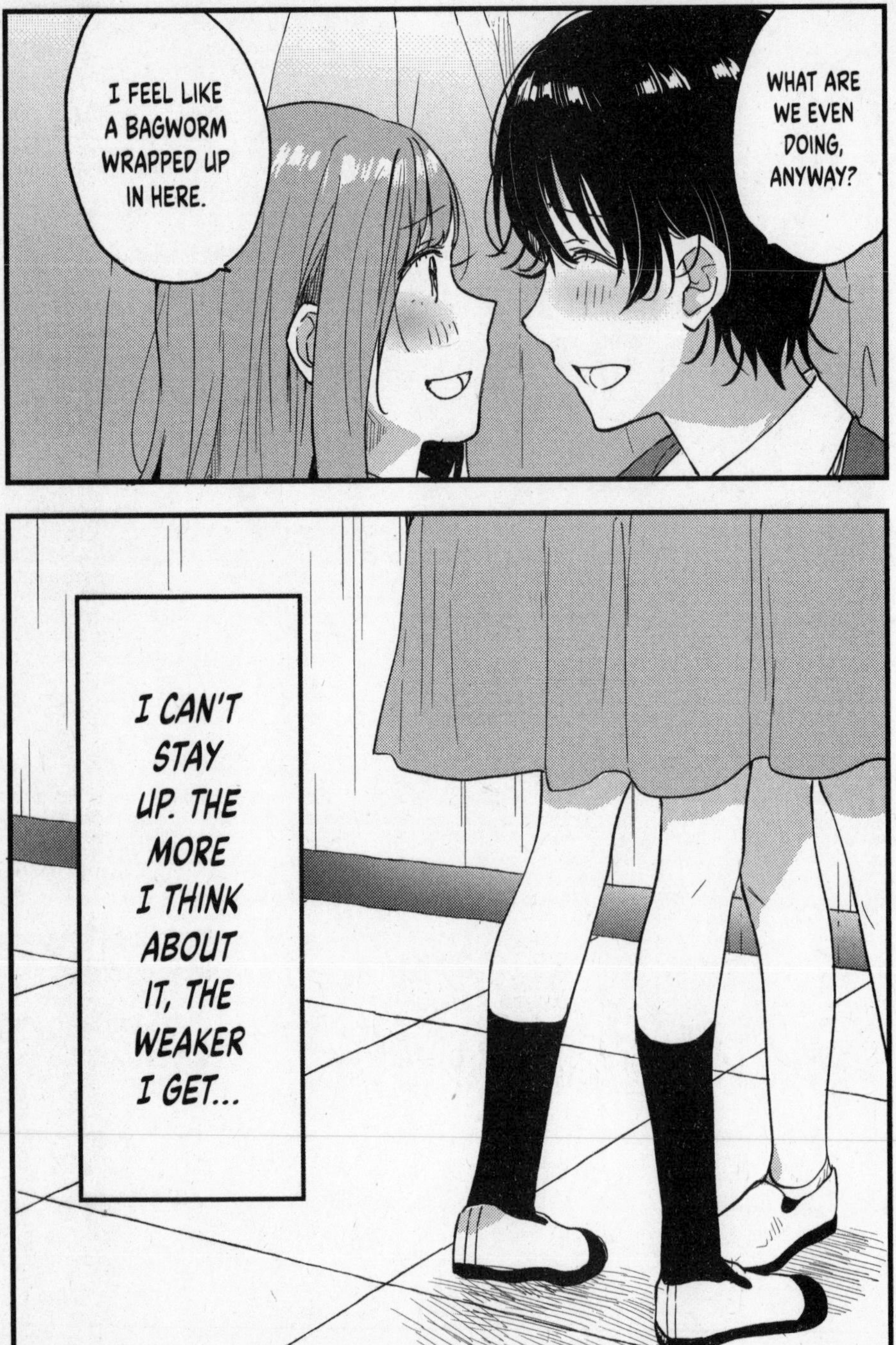
WHAT ARE WE EVEN DOING, ANYWAY?
I FEEL LIKE A BAGWORM WRAPPED UP IN HERE.
I CAN'T STAY UP. THE MORE I THINK ABOUT IT, THE WEAKER I GET...

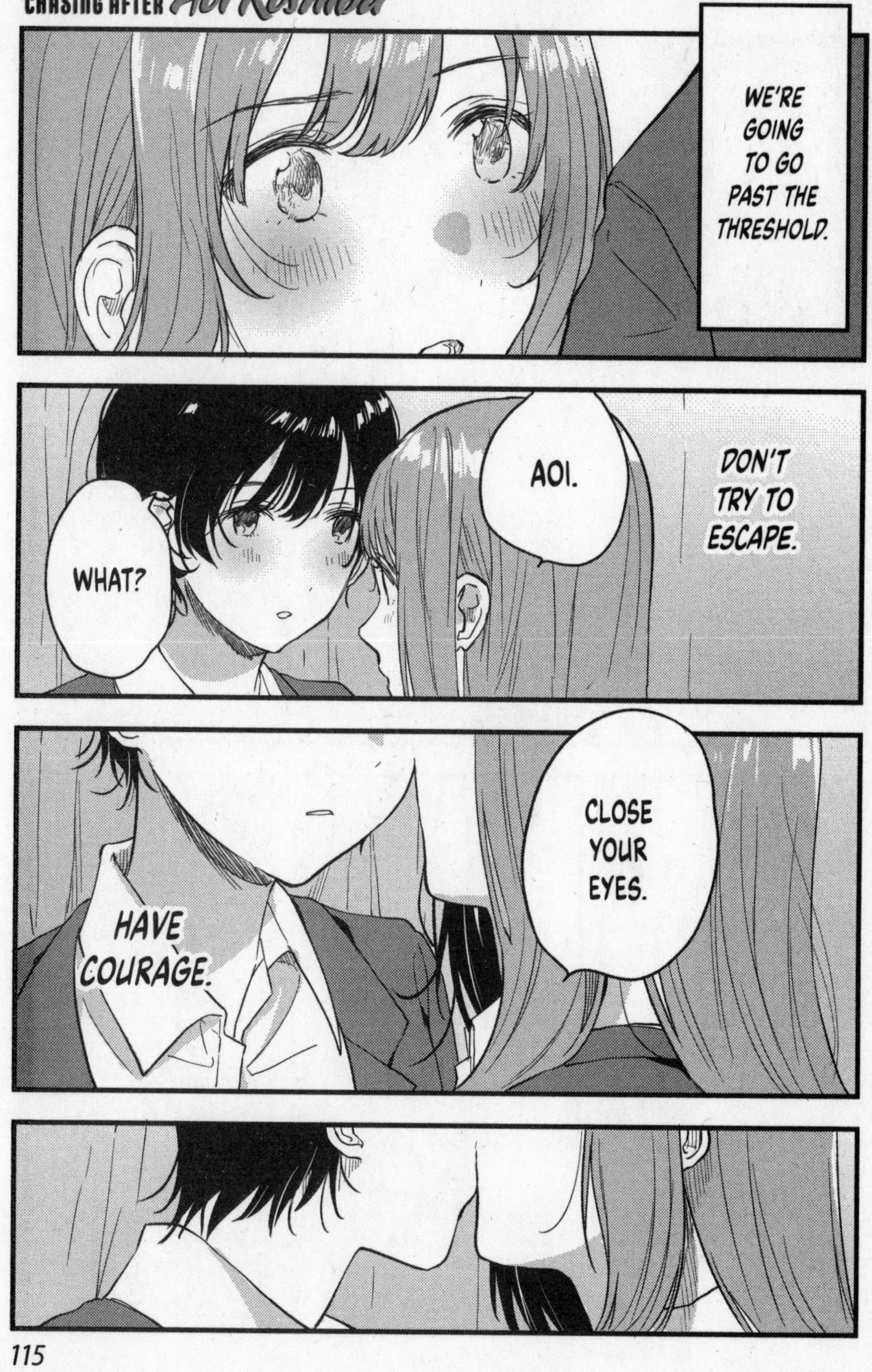
WE'RE GOING TO GO PAST THE THRESHOLD.
DON'T TRY TO ESCAPE.
AOI.
WHAT?
CLOSE YOUR EYES.
HAVE COURAGE.

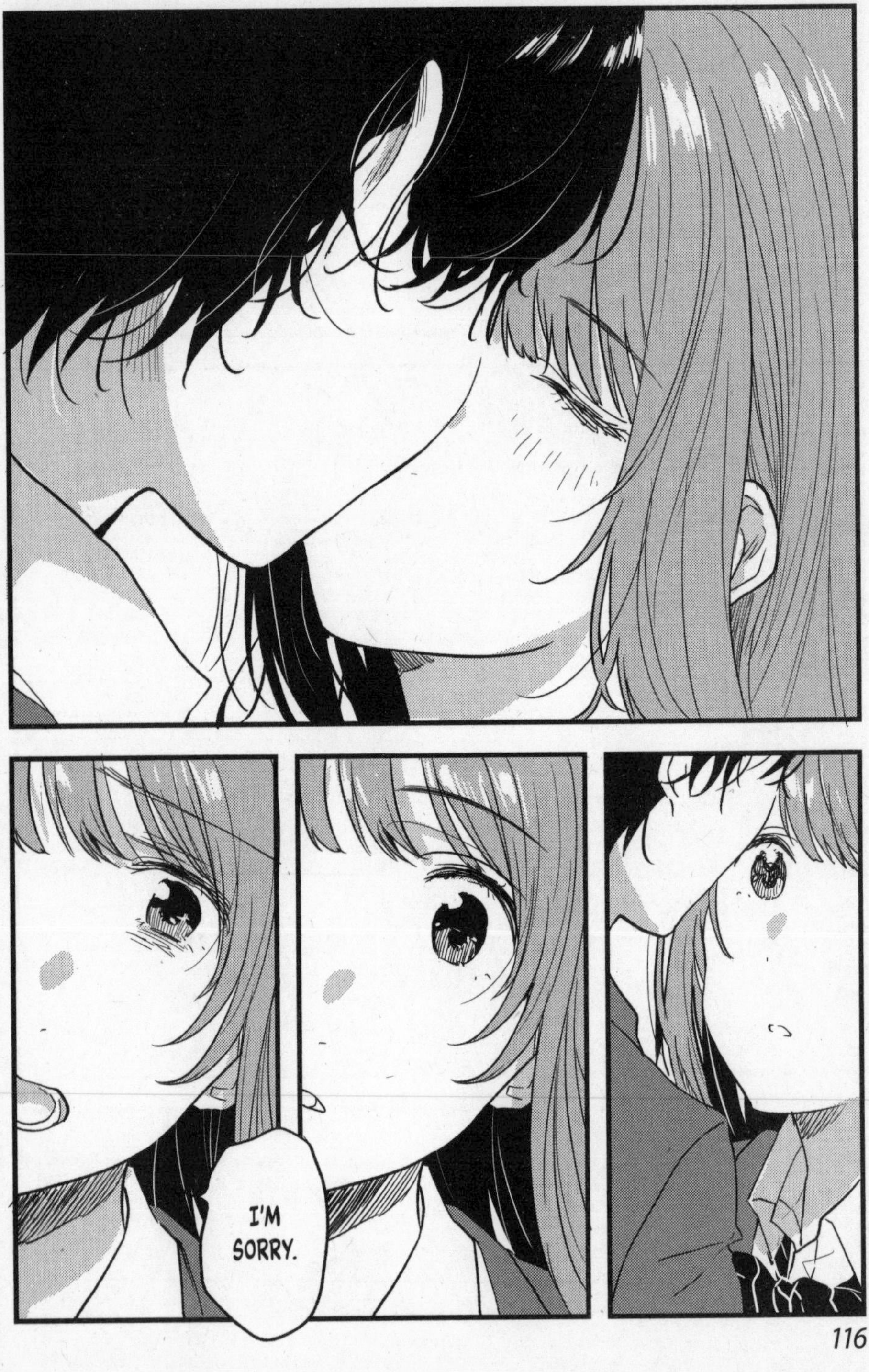
I'M
SORRY.

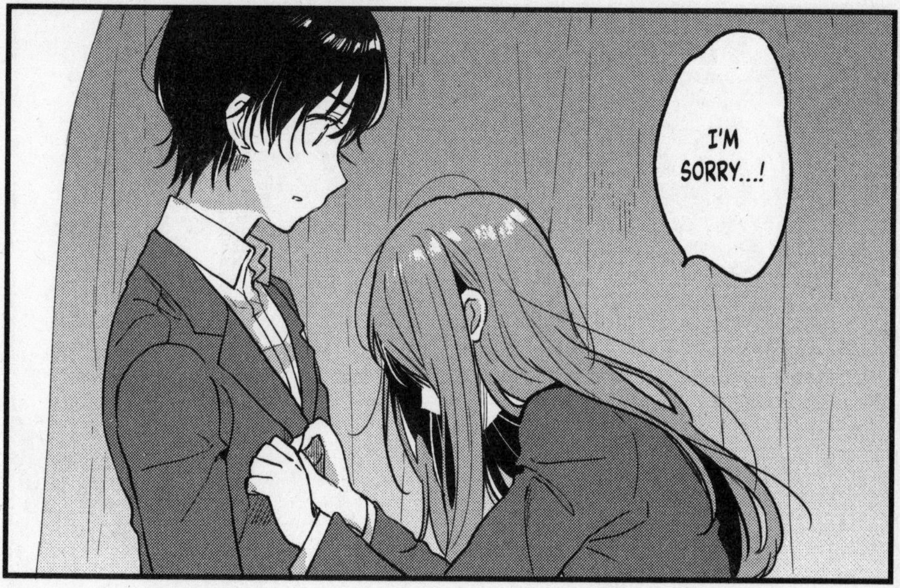
I'M SORRY...!

THE FEELING OF WRONGNESS IS SURGING UP AGAIN.

THE SAME WAY IT DID BEFORE.

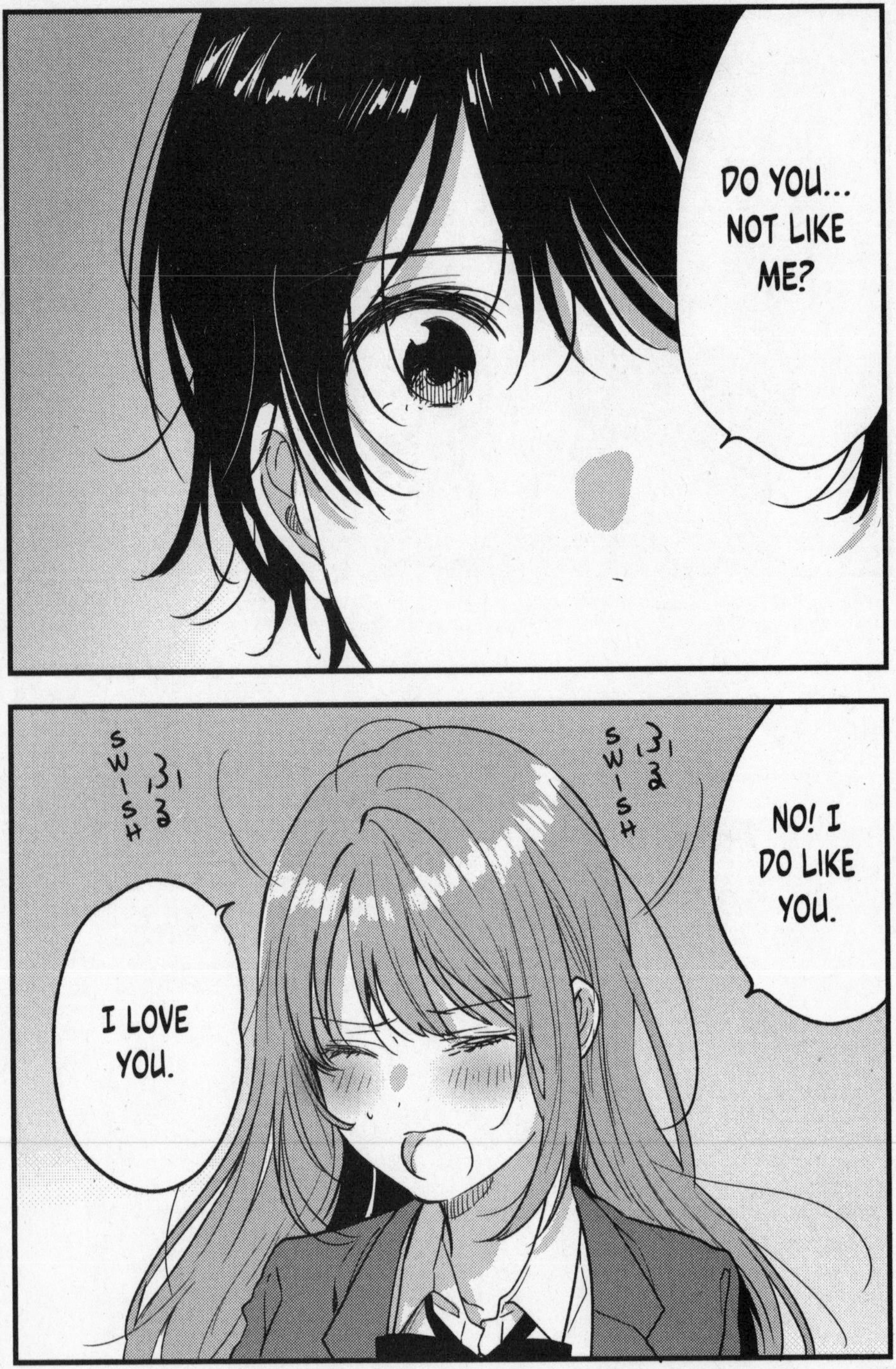
DO YOU... NOT LIKE ME?
NO! I DO LIKE YOU.
ふる
SWISH
ふる
SWISH
I LOVE YOU.

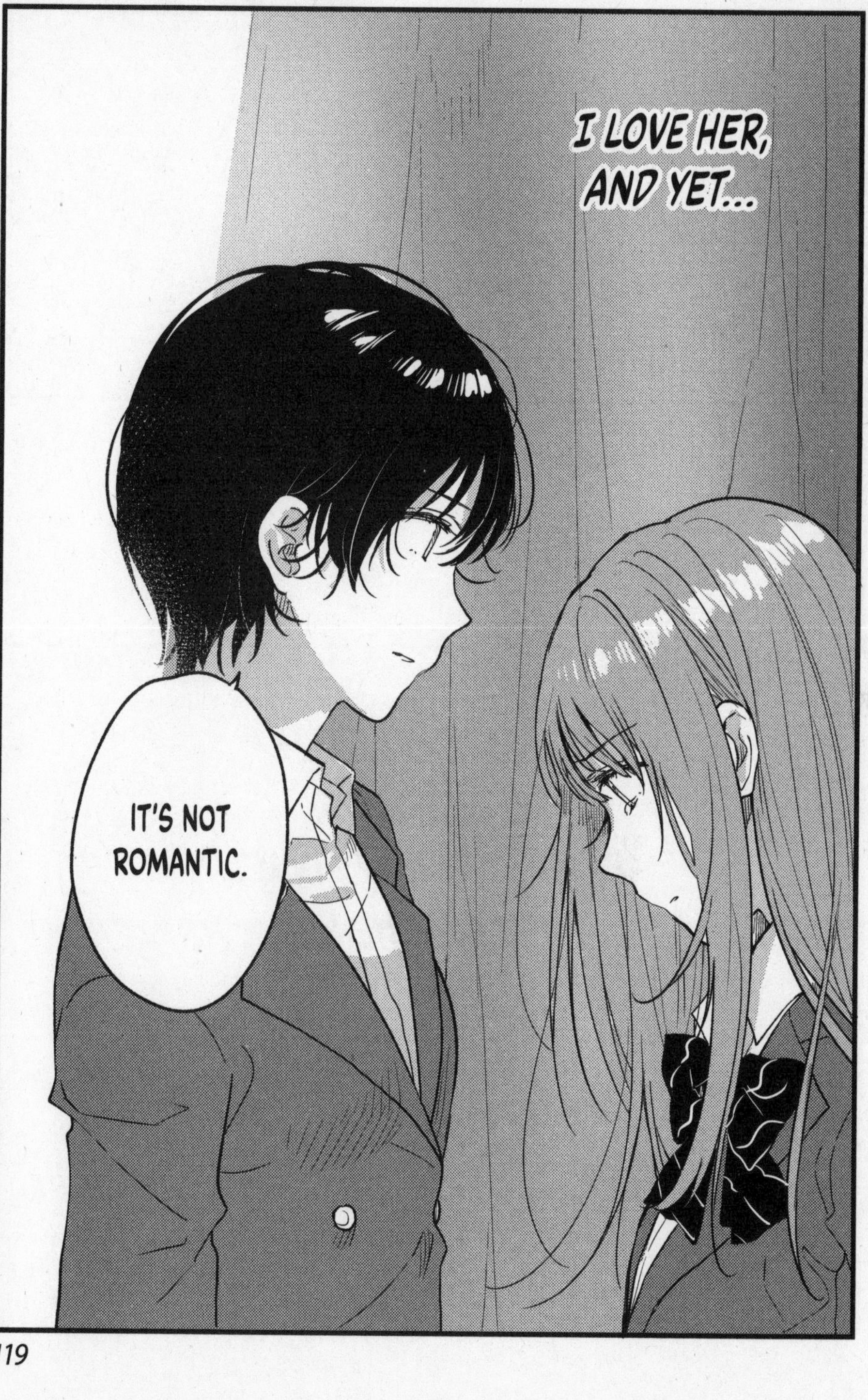
I LOVE HER, AND YET...
IT'S NOT ROMANTIC.

*IT'S LIKE A WEDGE
BETWEEN US,
DEFINITIVE AND FINAL,
SPELLING THE END.*

CHASING AFTER *Aoi Koshiba*

Autumn, Second Year of High School

CHASING AFTER *Aoi Koshiba*

Autumn, Second Year of High School

Chapter 31:
To Aoi Koshiba (Part 1)

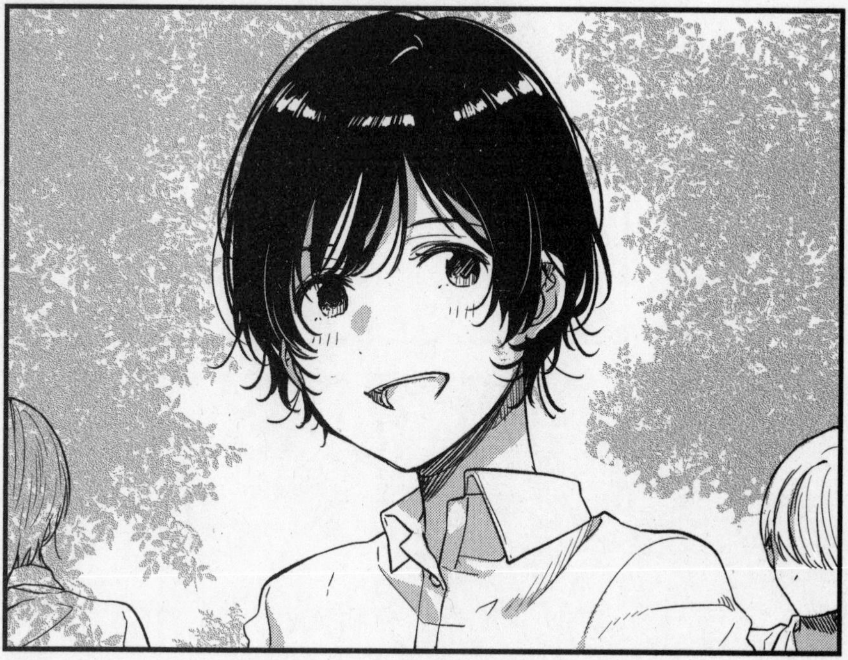

I THINK EVERYONE HAS A VERSION OF THEMSELVES THEY WANT TO BE.

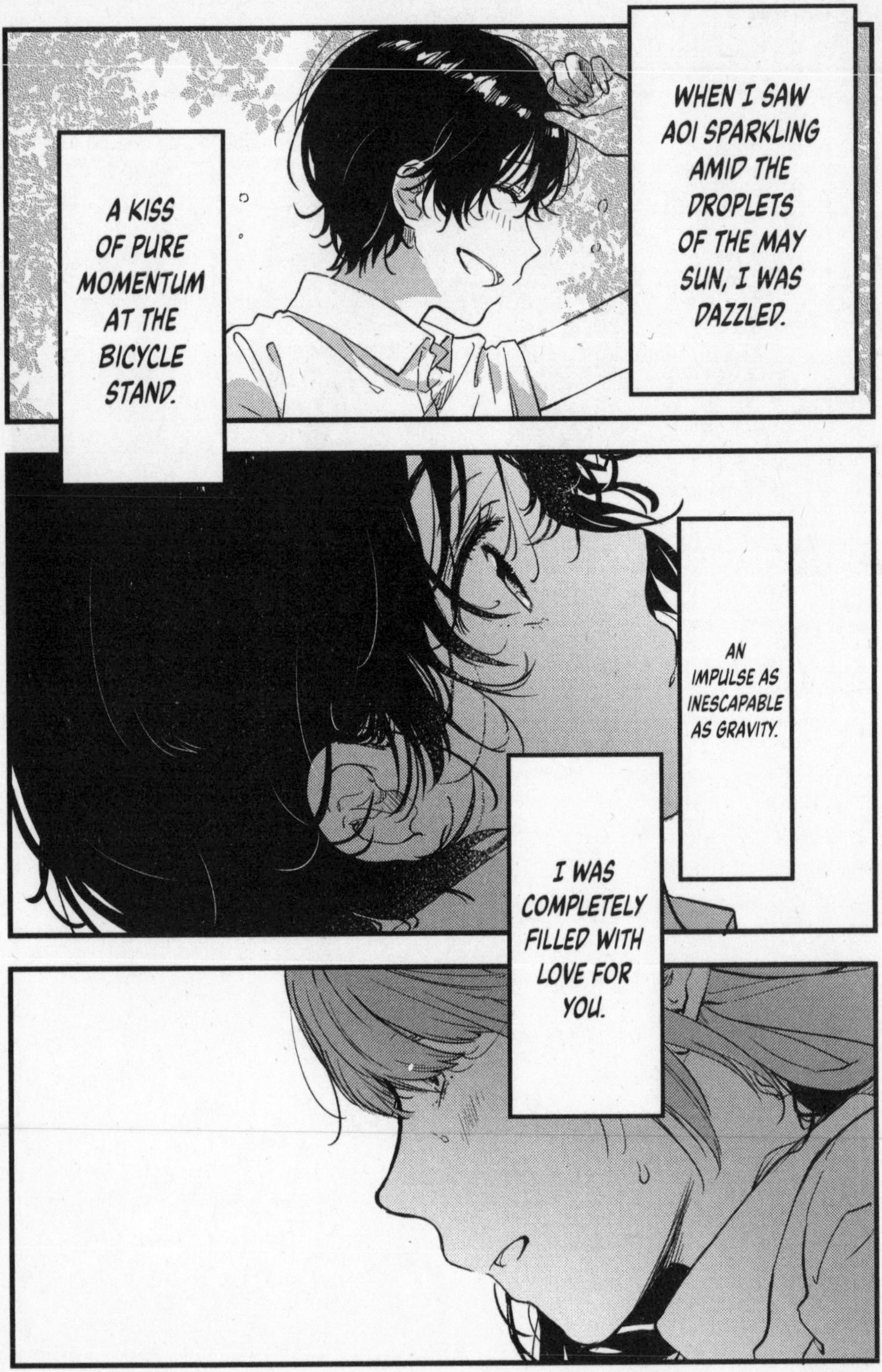
WHEN I SAW AOI SPARKLING AMID THE DROPLETS OF THE MAY SUN, I WAS DAZZLED.
A KISS OF PURE MOMENTUM AT THE BICYCLE STAND.
AN IMPULSE AS INESCAPABLE AS GRAVITY.
I WAS COMPLETELY FILLED WITH LOVE FOR YOU.

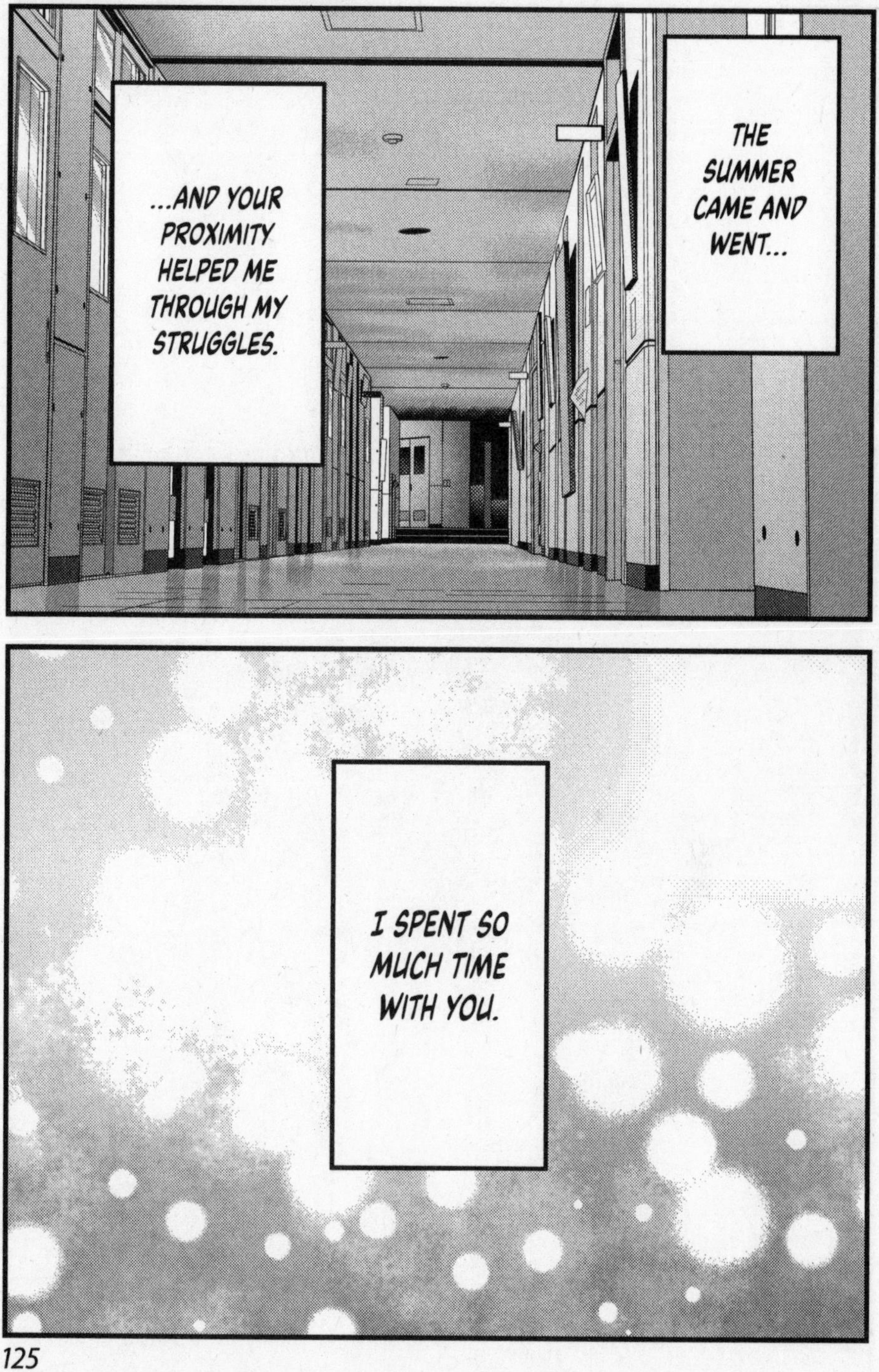
THE SUMMER CAME AND WENT...
...AND YOUR PROXIMITY HELPED ME THROUGH MY STRUGGLES.
I SPENT SO MUCH TIME WITH YOU.

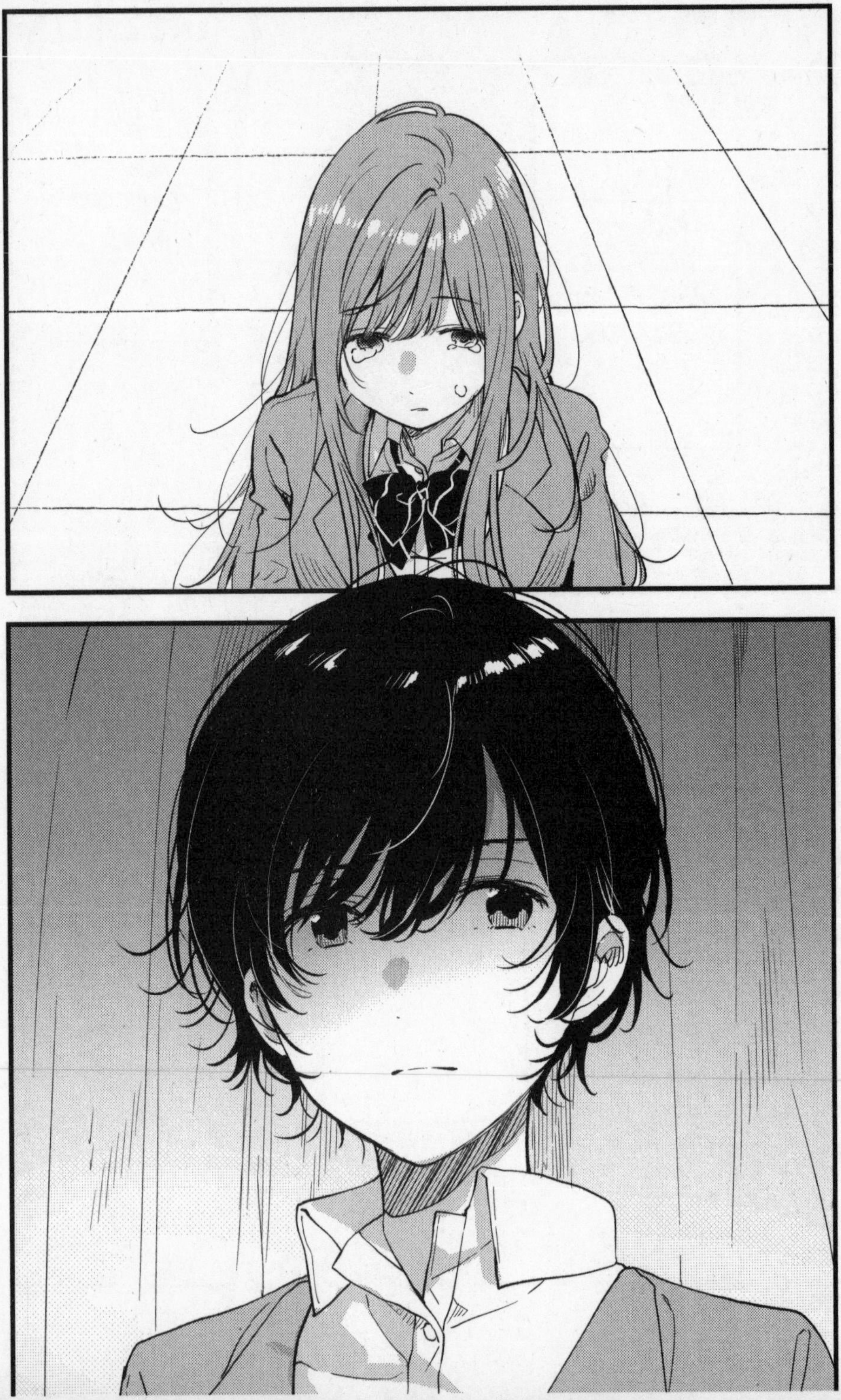

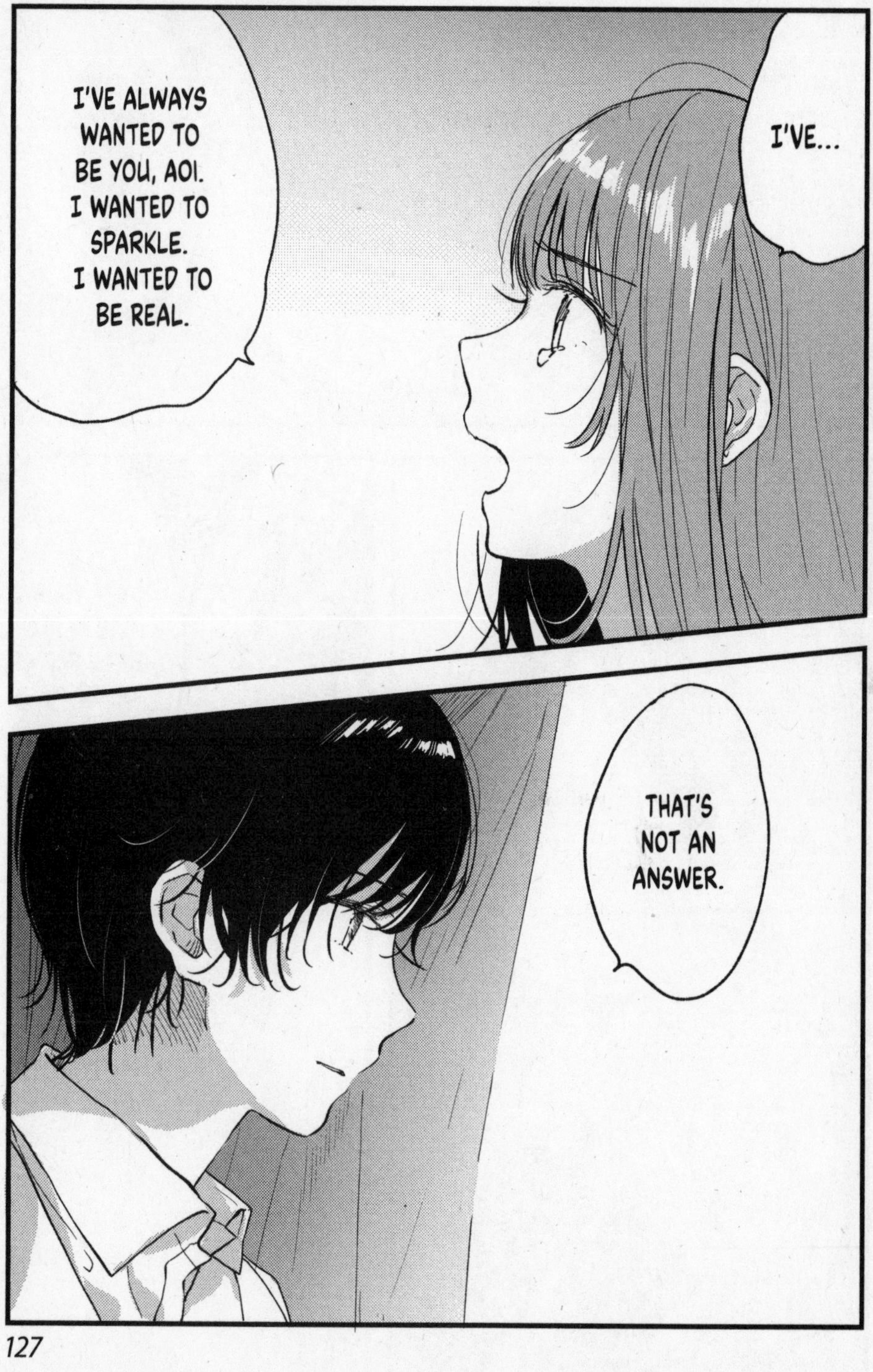
I'VE...
I'VE ALWAYS WANTED TO BE YOU, AOI. I WANTED TO SPARKLE. I WANTED TO BE REAL.
THAT'S NOT AN ANSWER.

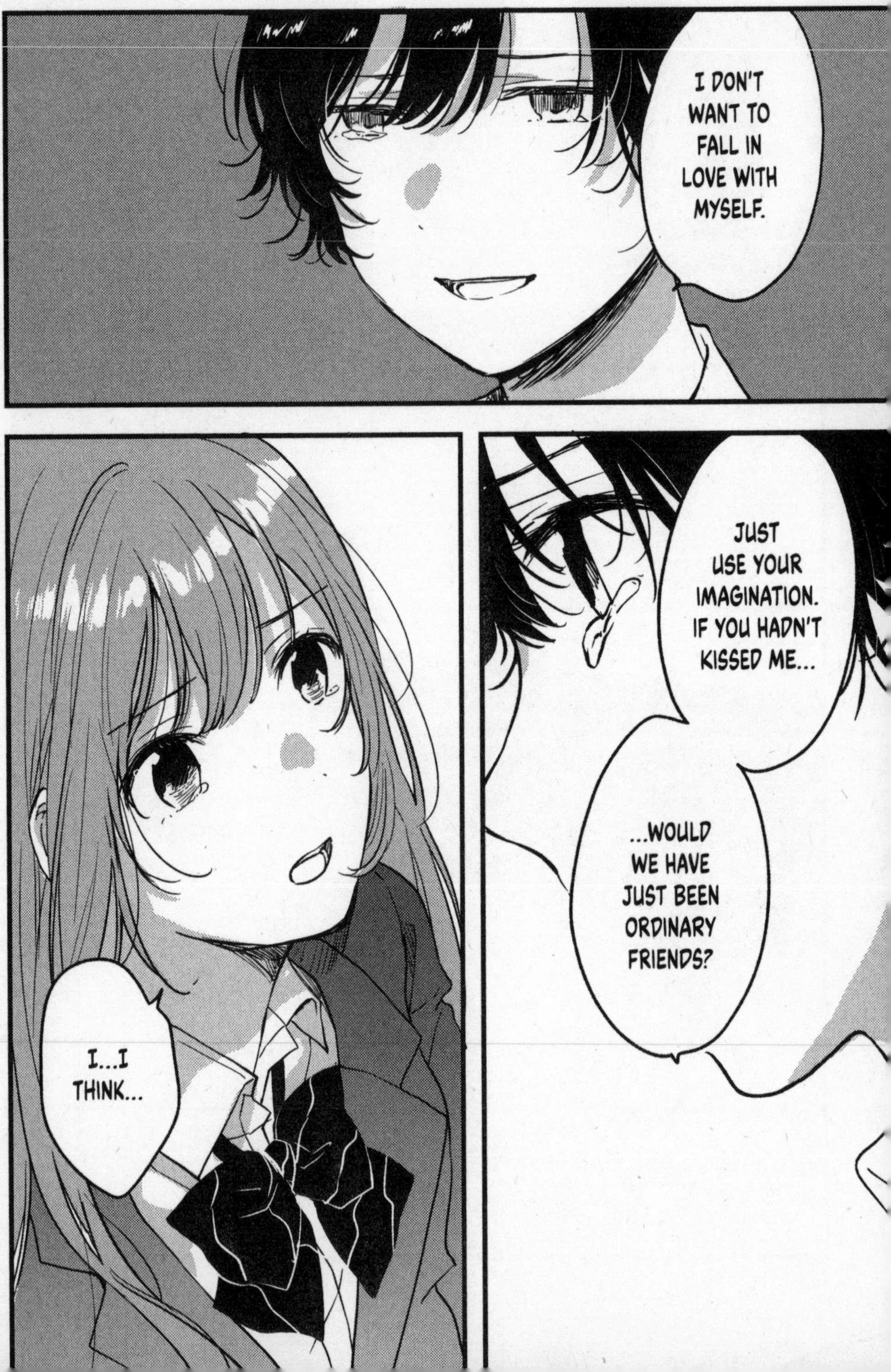
I DON'T WANT TO FALL IN LOVE WITH MYSELF.
JUST USE YOUR IMAGINATION. IF YOU HADN'T KISSED ME...
...WOULD WE HAVE JUST BEEN ORDINARY FRIENDS?
I...I THINK...

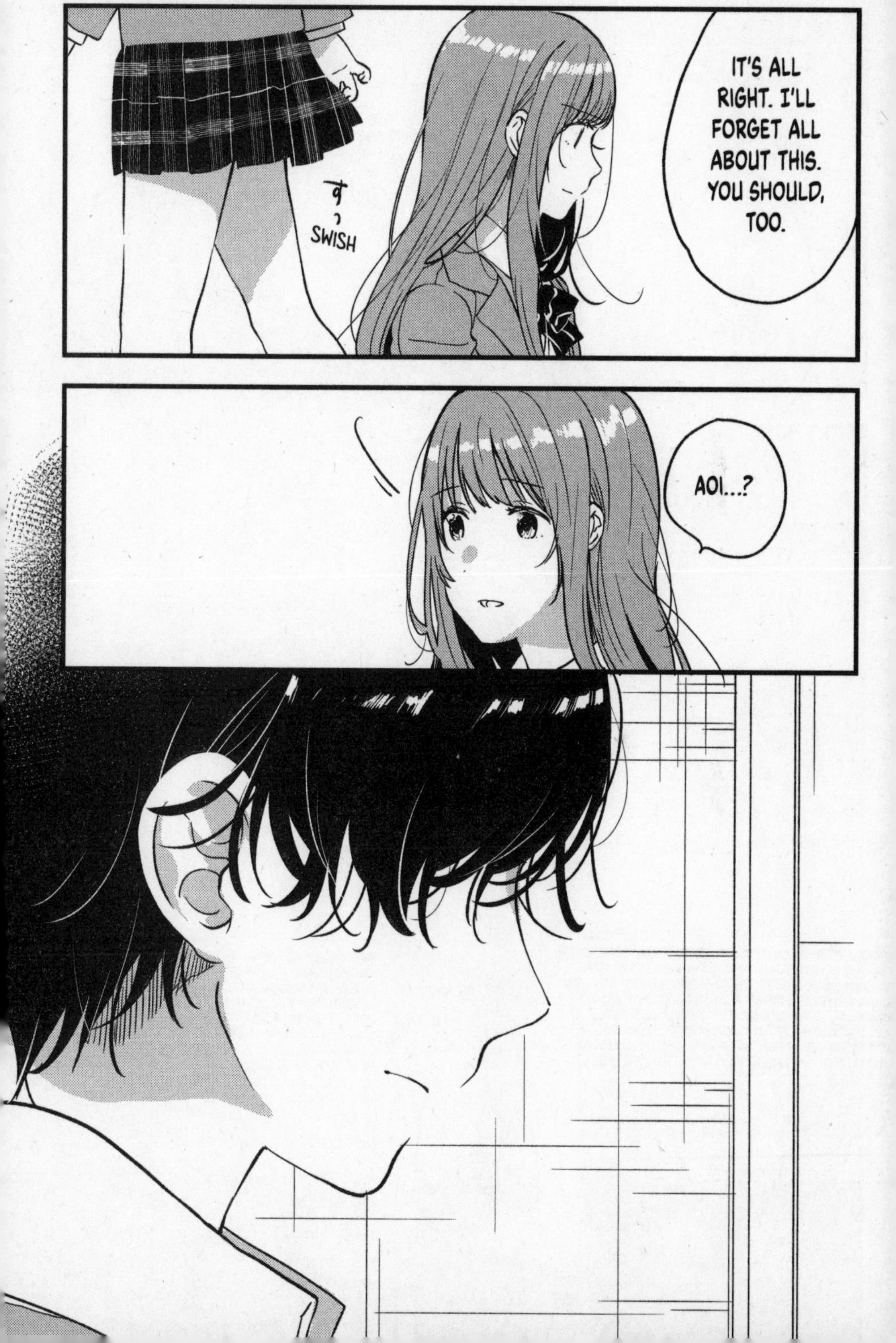
IT'S ALL RIGHT. I'LL FORGET ALL ABOUT THIS. YOU SHOULD, TOO.
す
SWISH
AOI...?

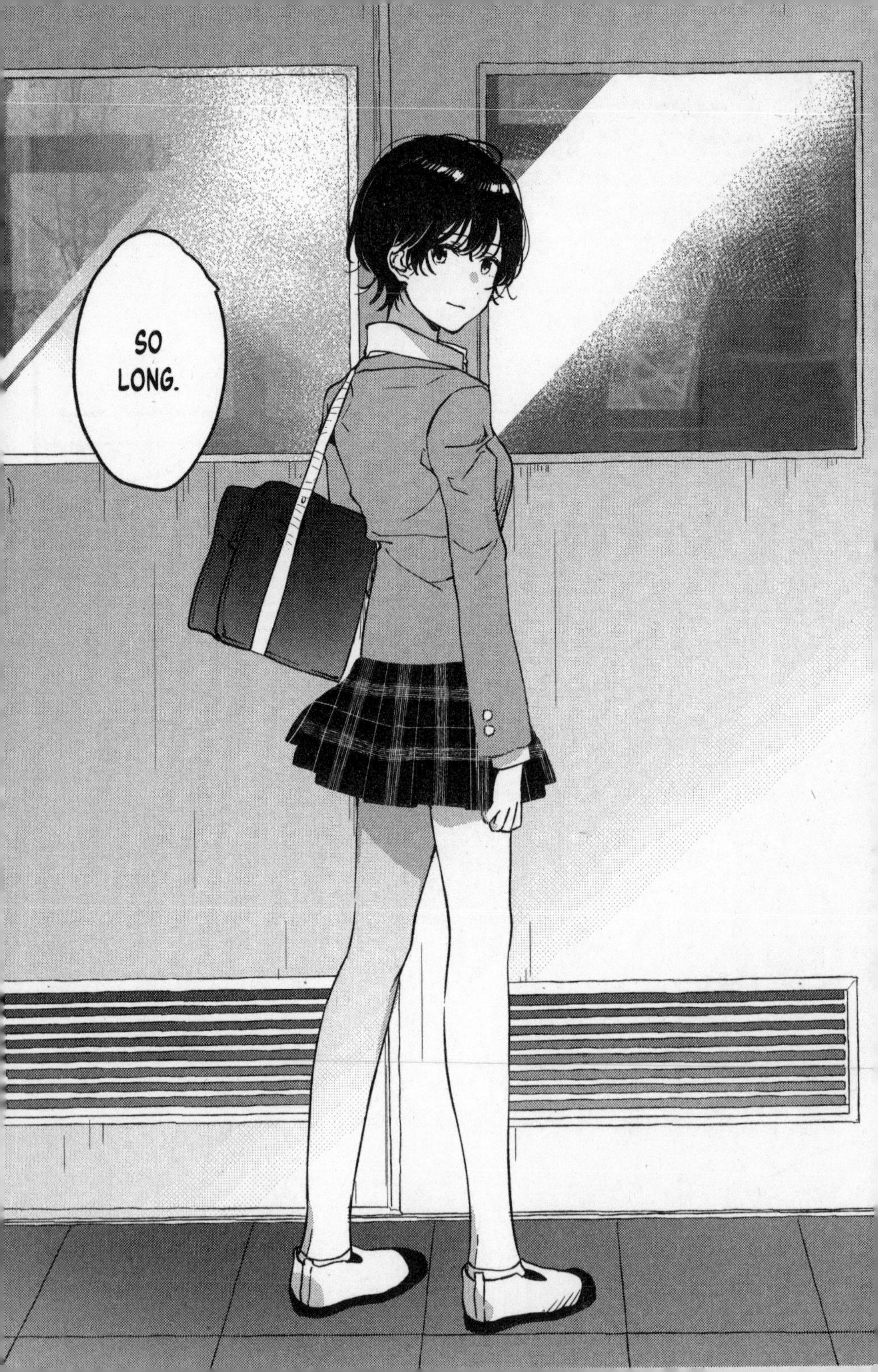
SO LONG.

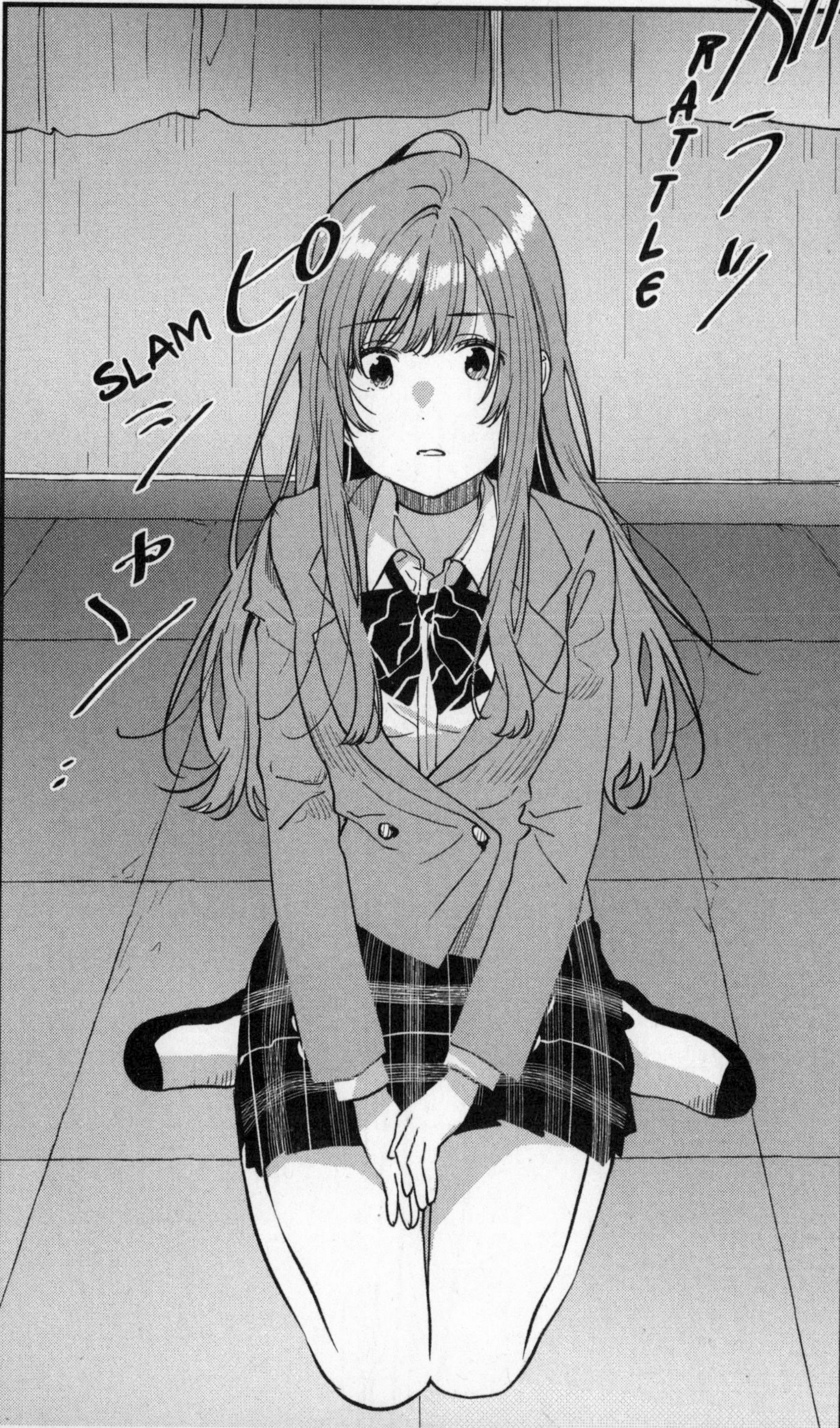
RATTLE
SLAM

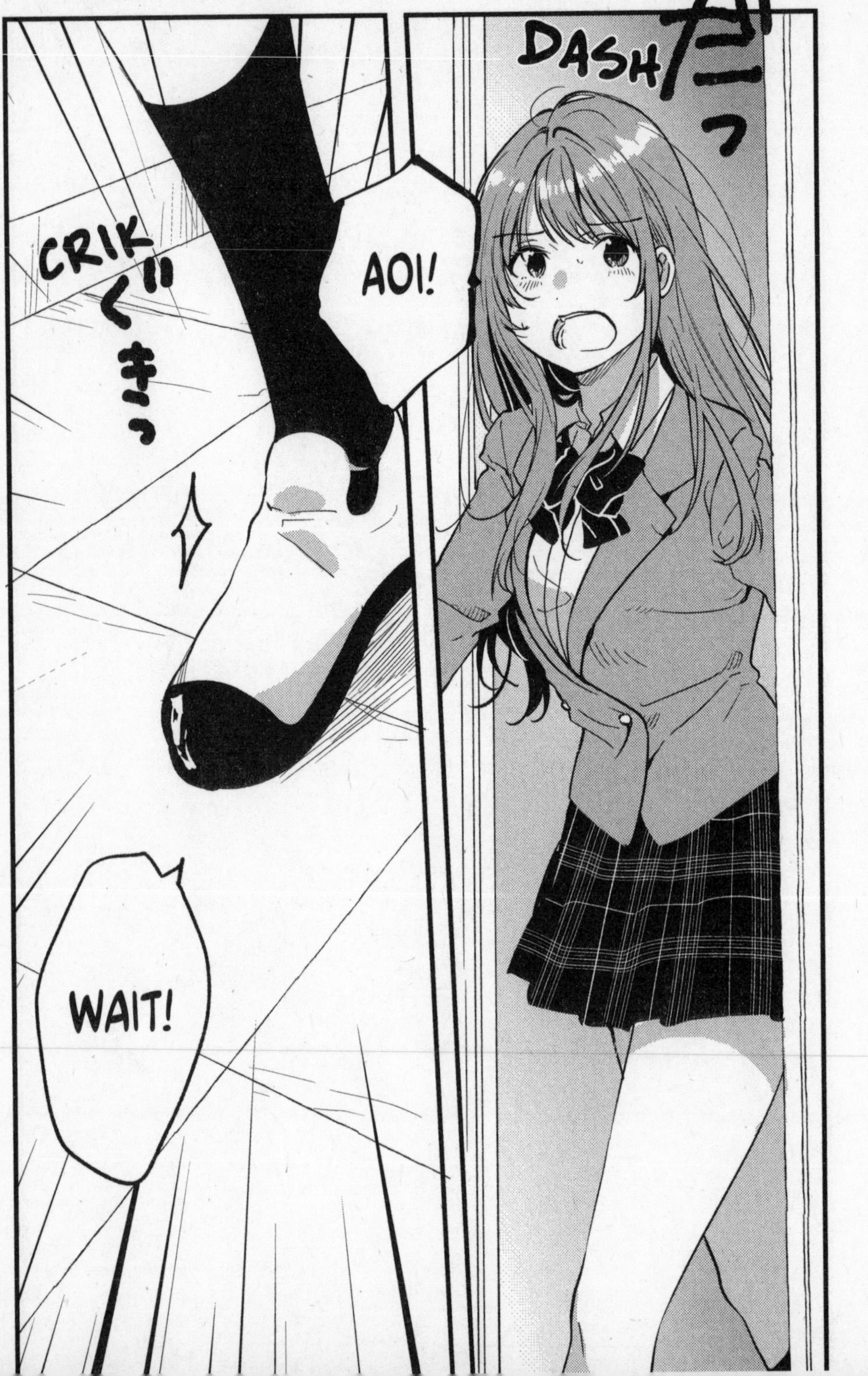
DASH
だーっ
AOI!
CRIK
ぐきっ
WAIT!

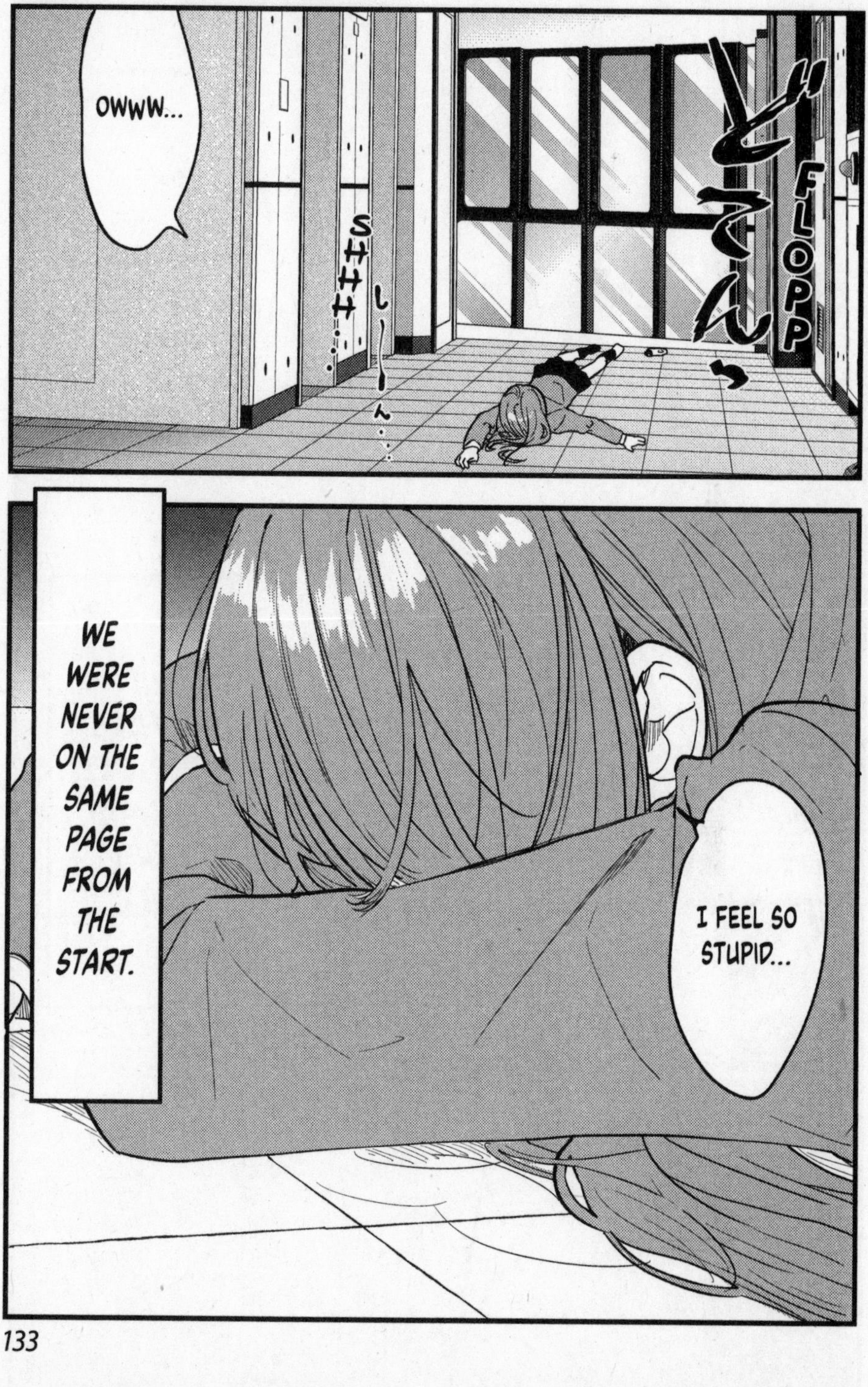
どてん
FLOPP
しーん…
SHHHH…
OWWW…
WE WERE NEVER ON THE SAME PAGE FROM THE START.
I FEEL SO STUPID…

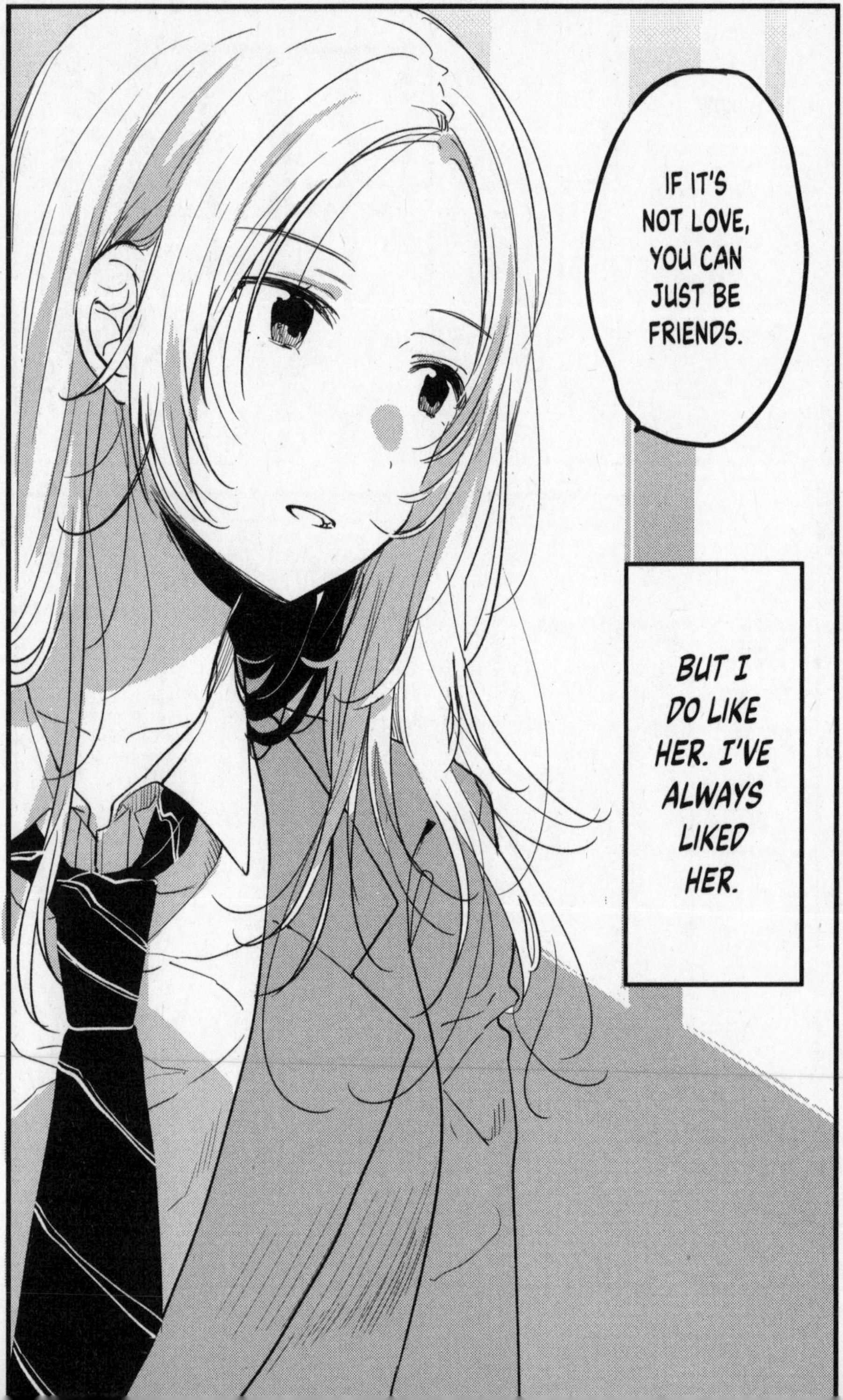
IF IT'S NOT LOVE, YOU CAN JUST BE FRIENDS.
BUT I DO LIKE HER. I'VE ALWAYS LIKED HER.

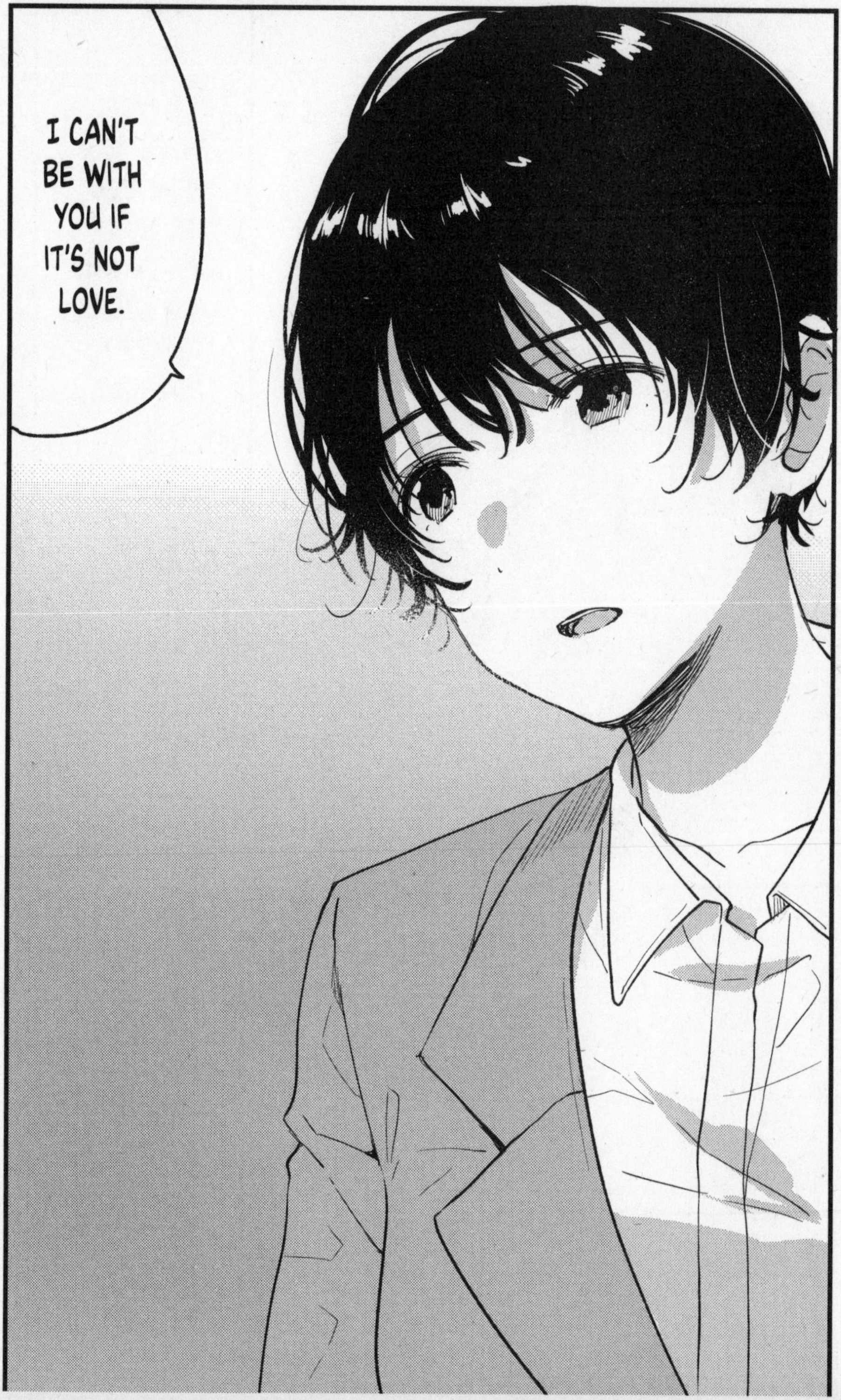
I CAN'T BE WITH YOU IF IT'S NOT LOVE.

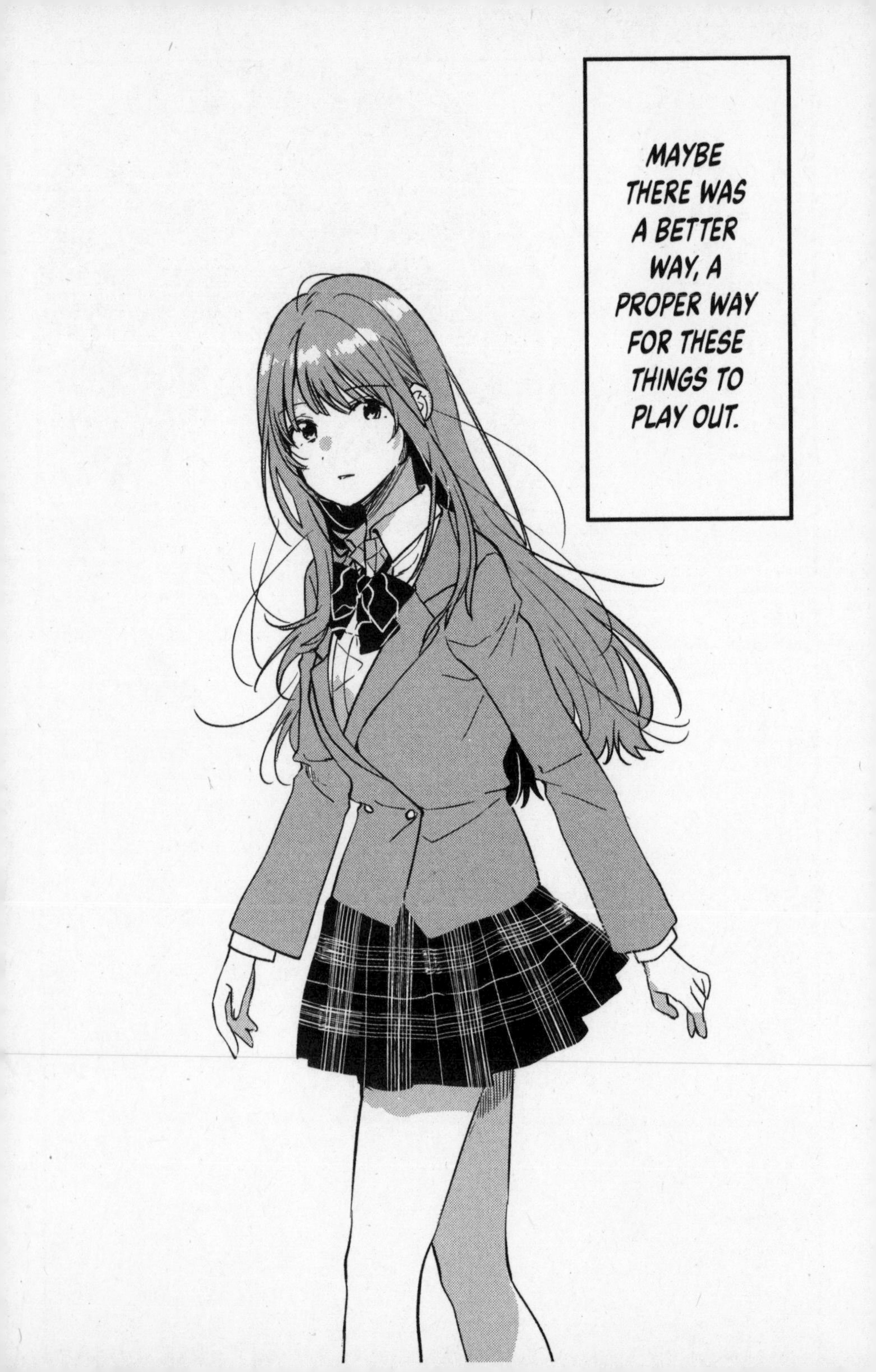
MAYBE THERE WAS A BETTER WAY, A PROPER WAY FOR THESE THINGS TO PLAY OUT.

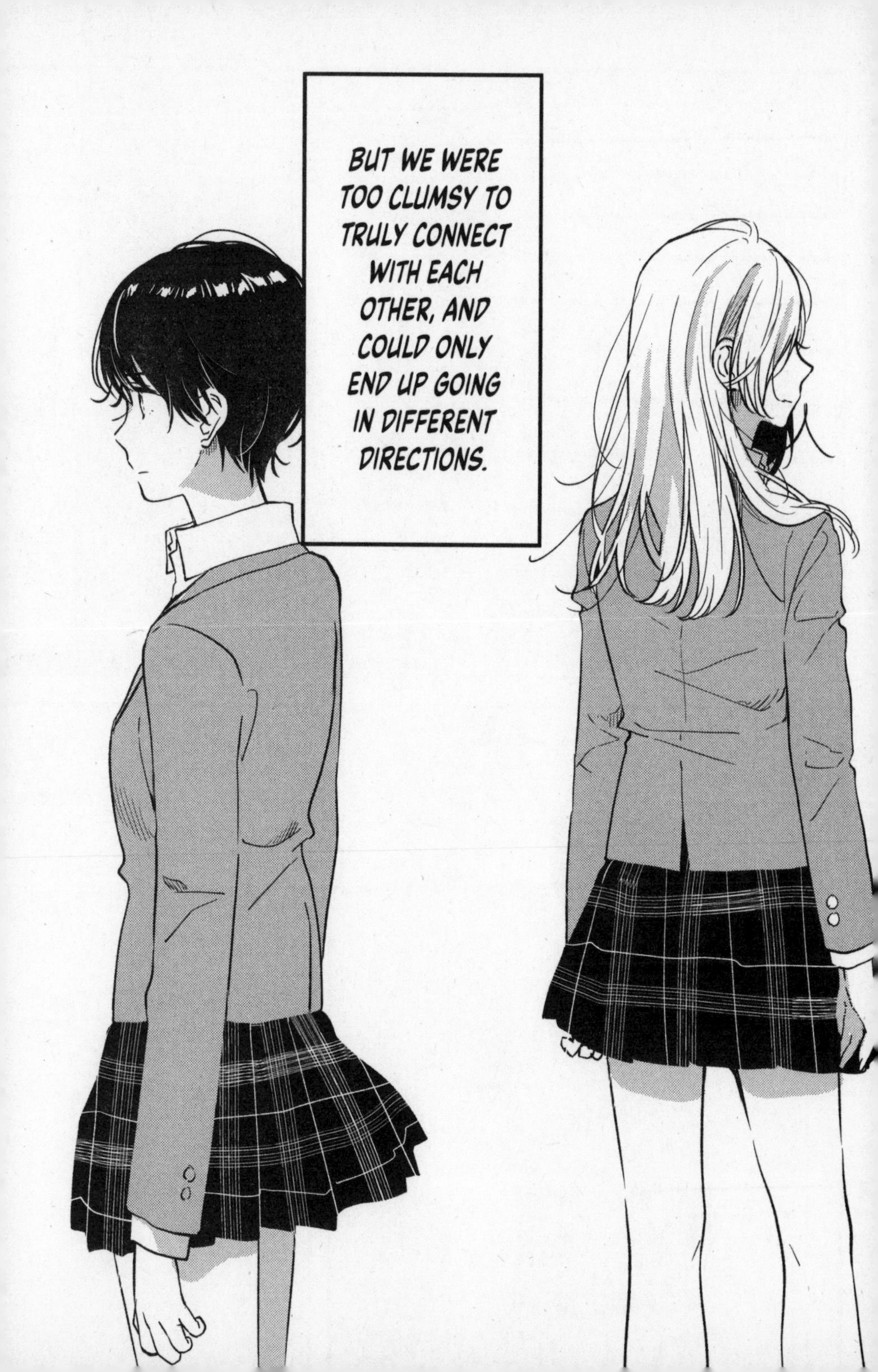
BUT WE WERE TOO CLUMSY TO TRULY CONNECT WITH EACH OTHER, AND COULD ONLY END UP GOING IN DIFFERENT DIRECTIONS.

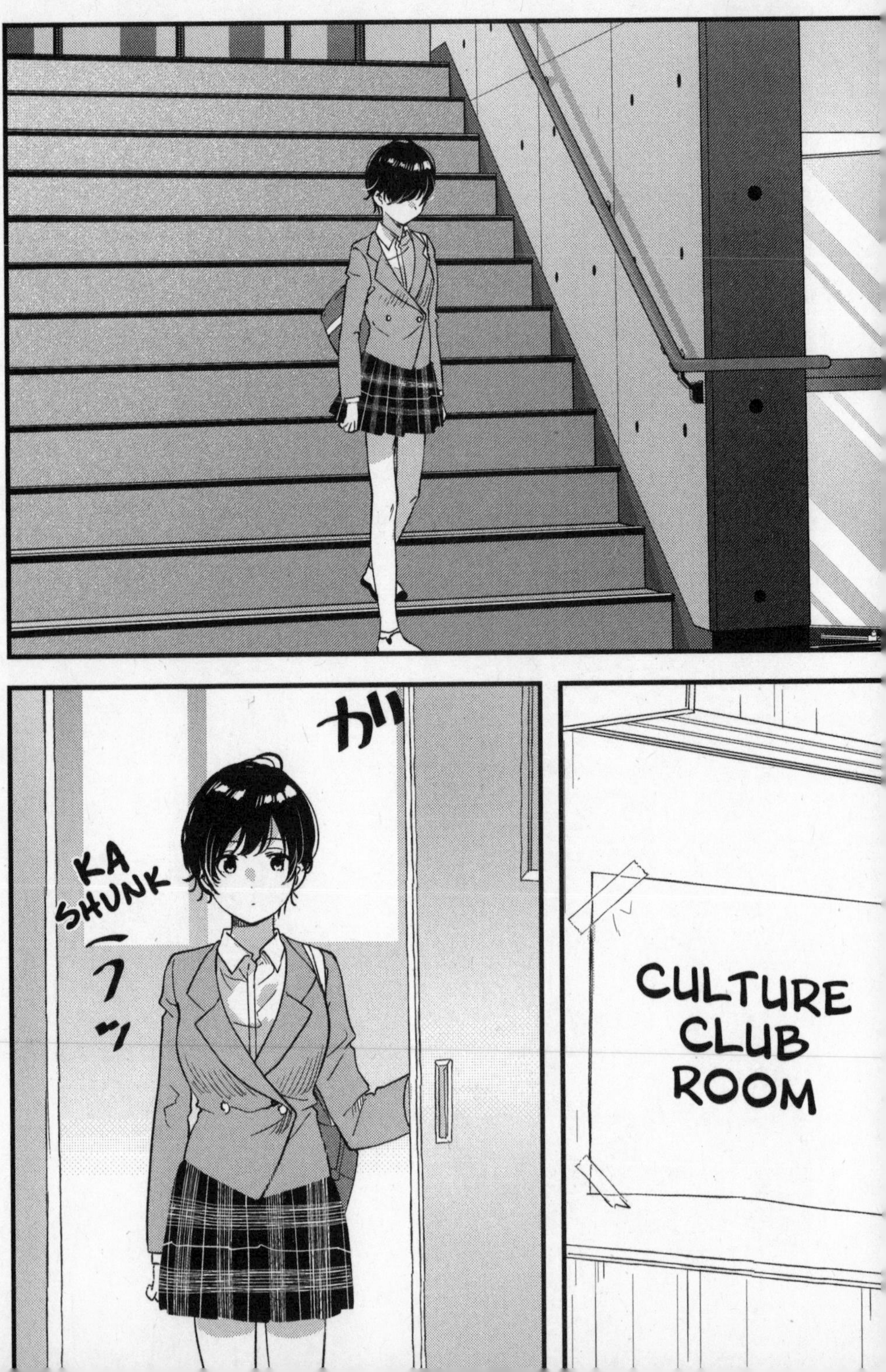
CULTURE CLUB ROOM
ガラッ
KA SHUNK

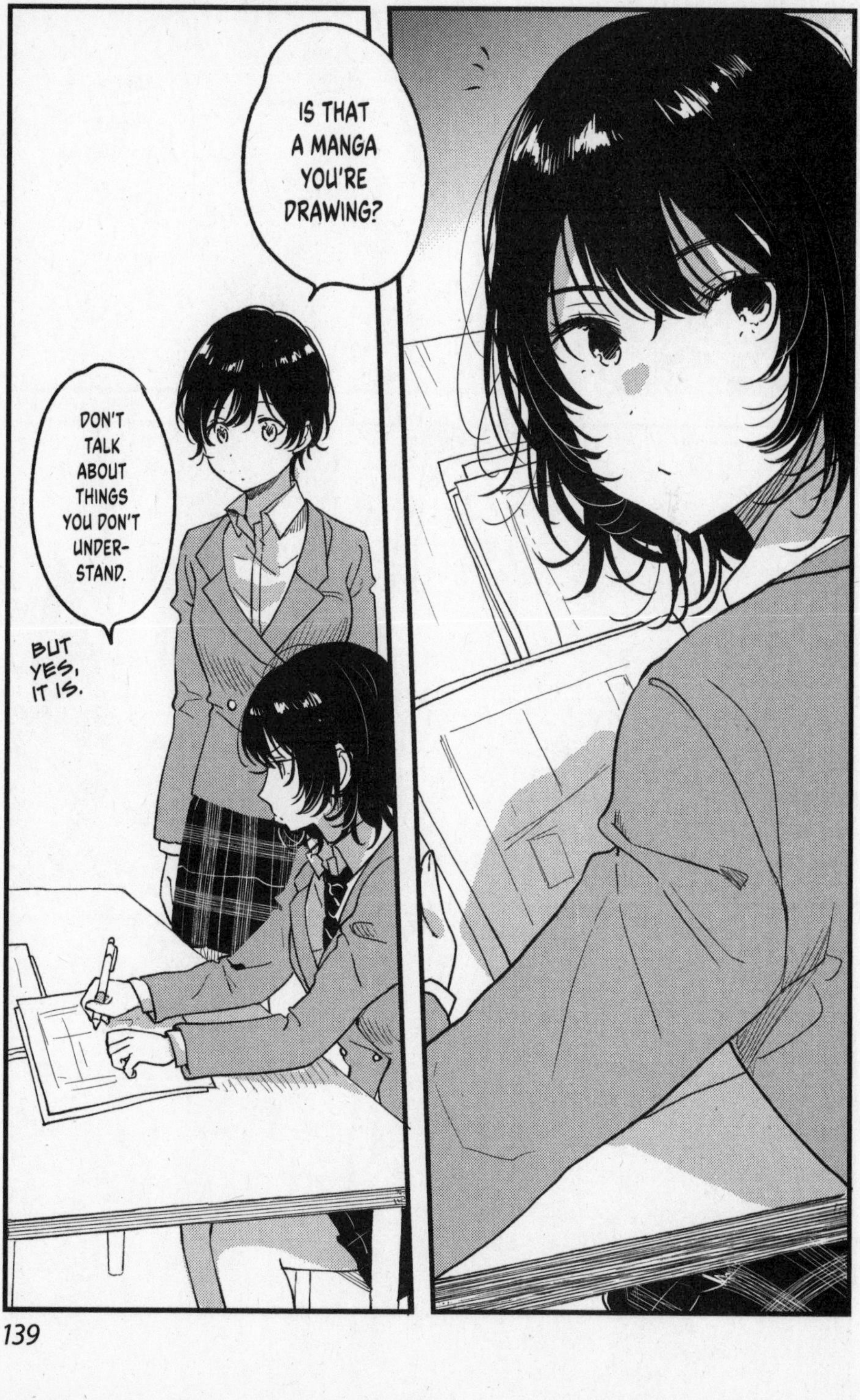
IS THAT A MANGA YOU'RE DRAWING?
DON'T TALK ABOUT THINGS YOU DON'T UNDER-STAND.
BUT YES, IT IS.

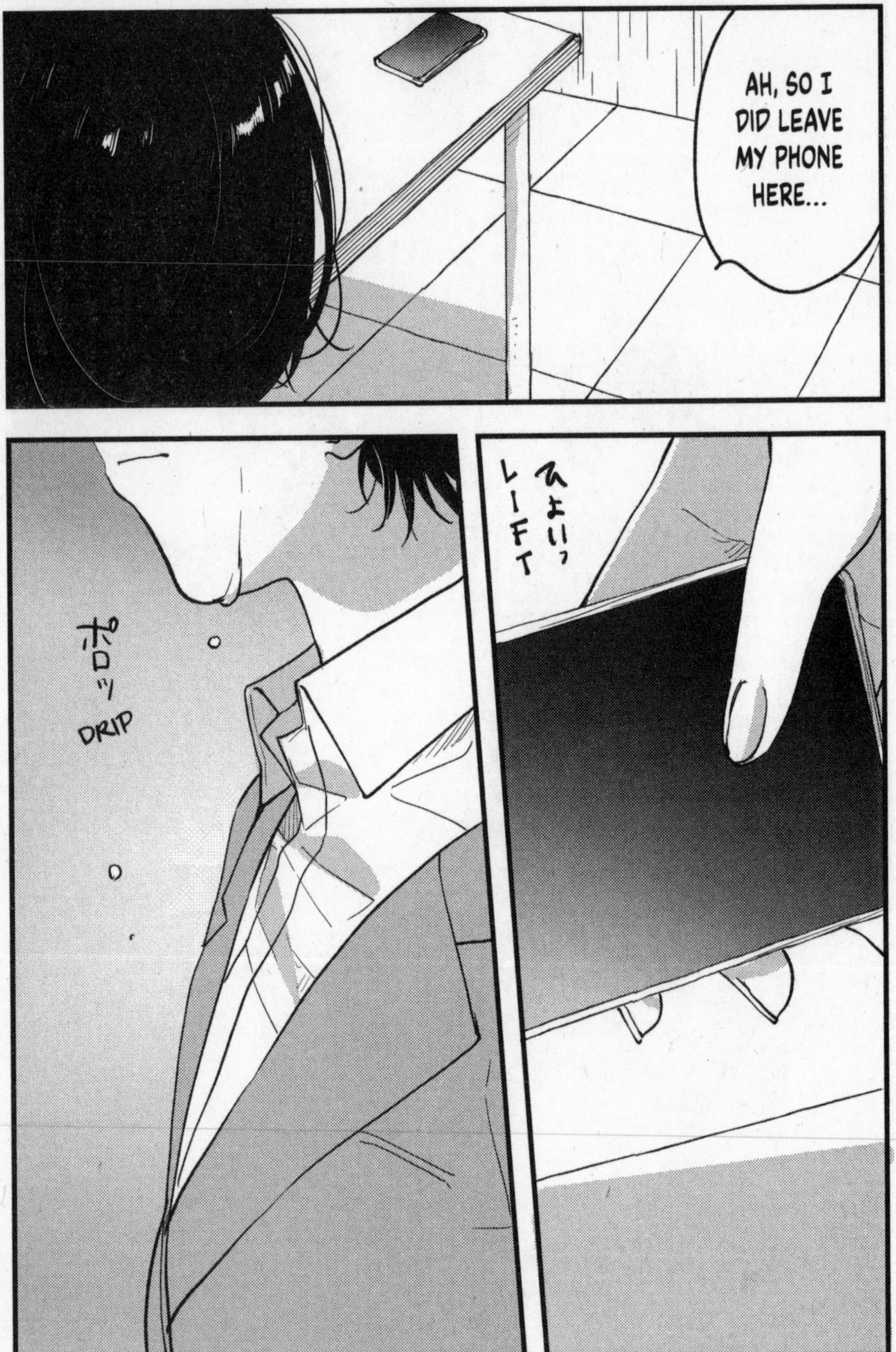
AH, SO I DID LEAVE MY PHONE HERE...
ひょいっ
LIFT
ポロッ
DRIP

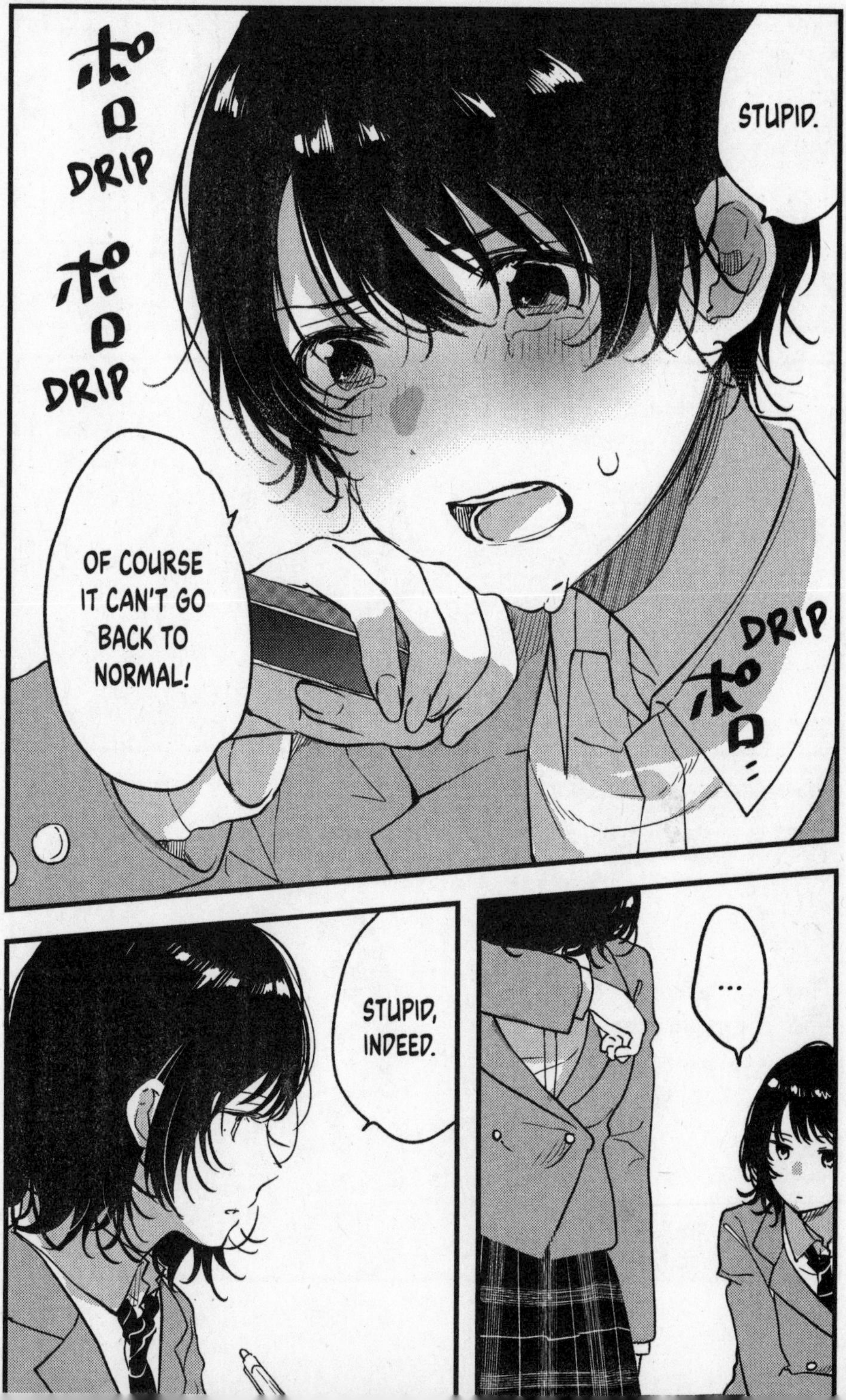
STUPID.
ポロ DRIP
ポロ DRIP
OF COURSE IT CAN'T GO BACK TO NORMAL!
DRIP ポロ
...
STUPID, INDEED.

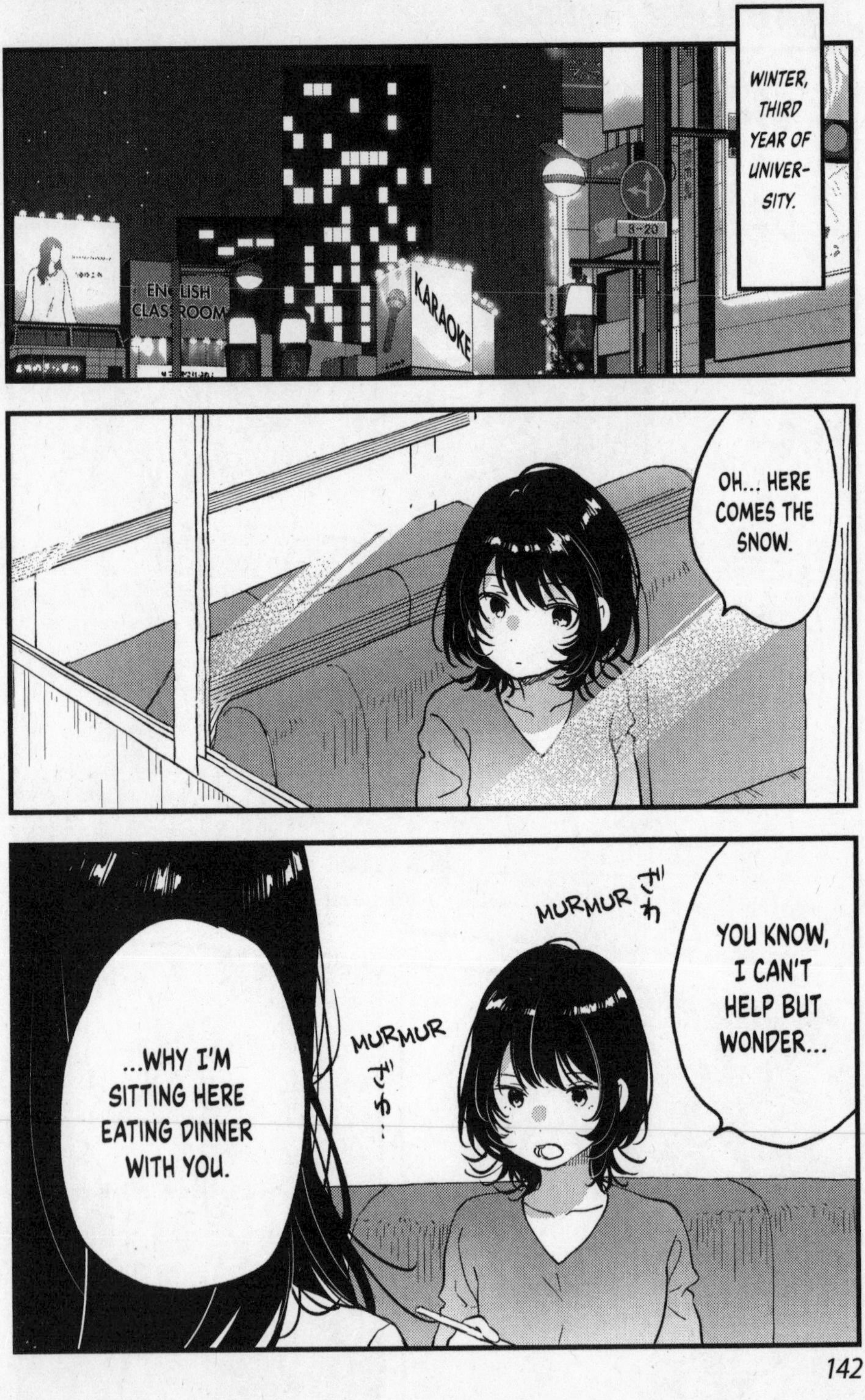
WINTER, THIRD YEAR OF UNIVER-SITY.
ENGLISH CLASSROOM
KARAOKE
8-20
OH... HERE COMES THE SNOW.
YOU KNOW, I CAN'T HELP BUT WONDER...
MURMUR ざわ
MURMUR ざわ…
...WHY I'M SITTING HERE EATING DINNER WITH YOU.

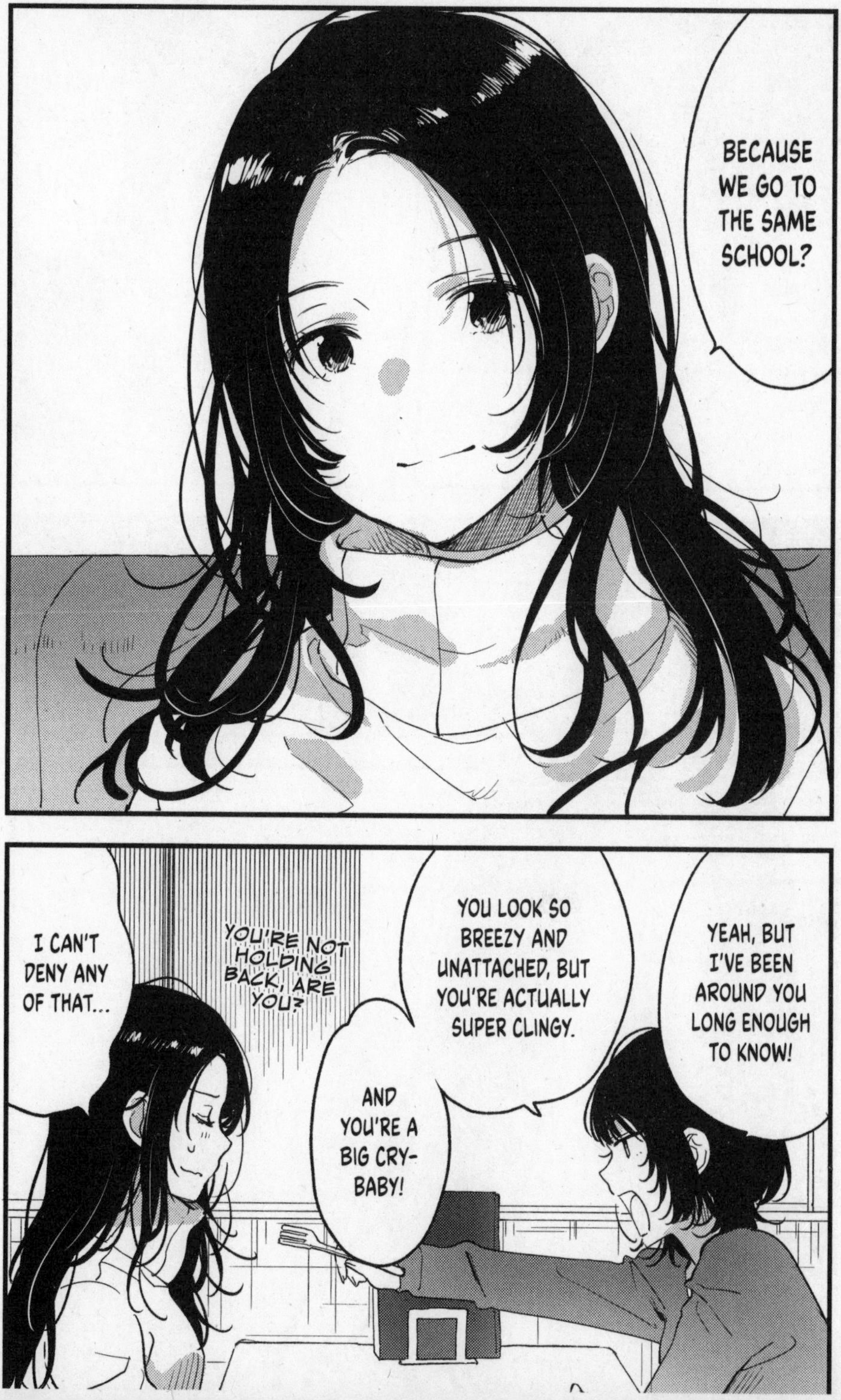
BECAUSE WE GO TO THE SAME SCHOOL?
YEAH, BUT I'VE BEEN AROUND YOU LONG ENOUGH TO KNOW!
YOU LOOK SO BREEZY AND UNATTACHED, BUT YOU'RE ACTUALLY SUPER CLINGY.
AND YOU'RE A BIG CRY-BABY!
YOU'RE NOT HOLDING BACK, ARE YOU?
I CAN'T DENY ANY OF THAT...

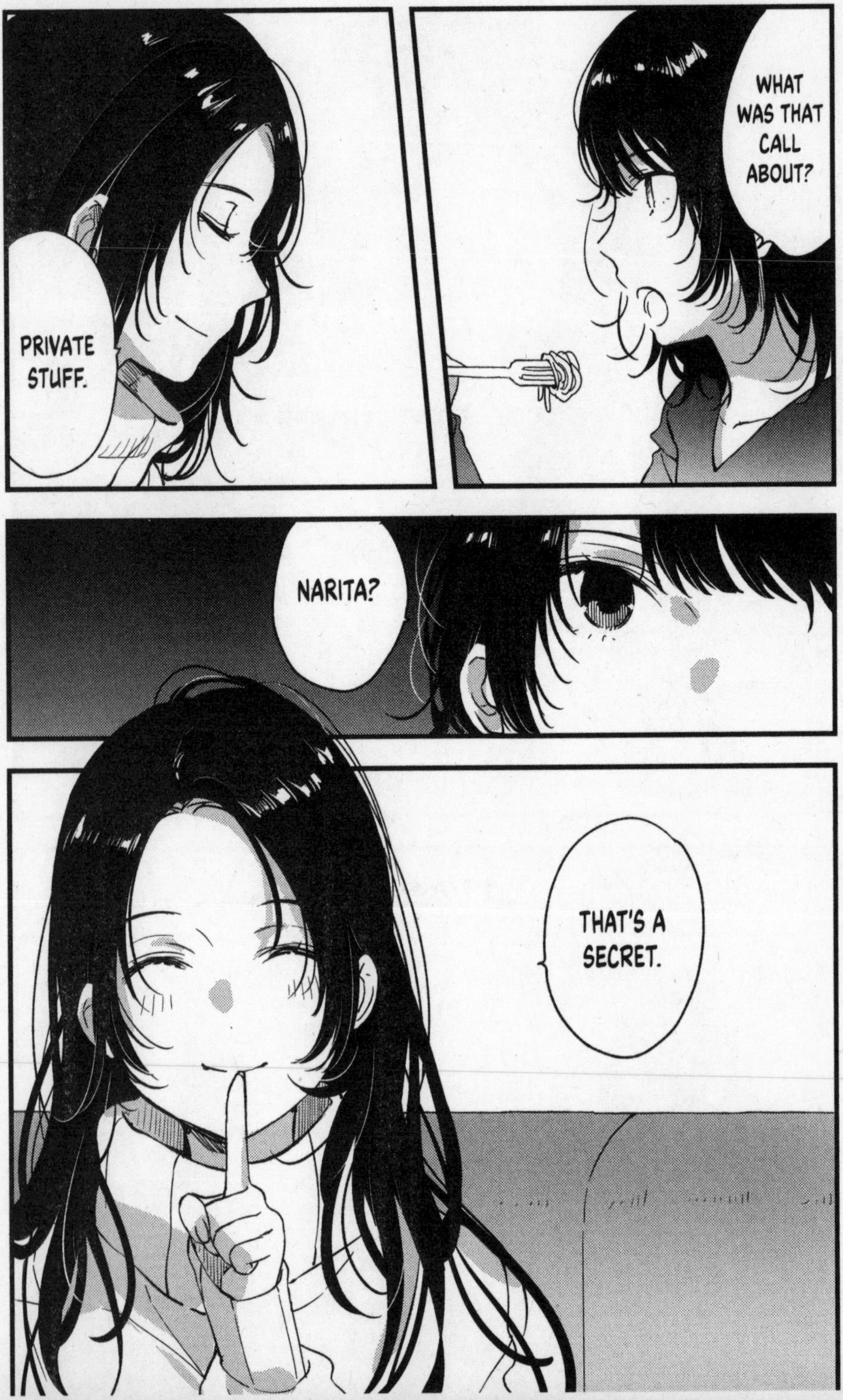
WHAT WAS THAT CALL ABOUT?
PRIVATE STUFF.
NARITA?
THAT'S A SECRET.

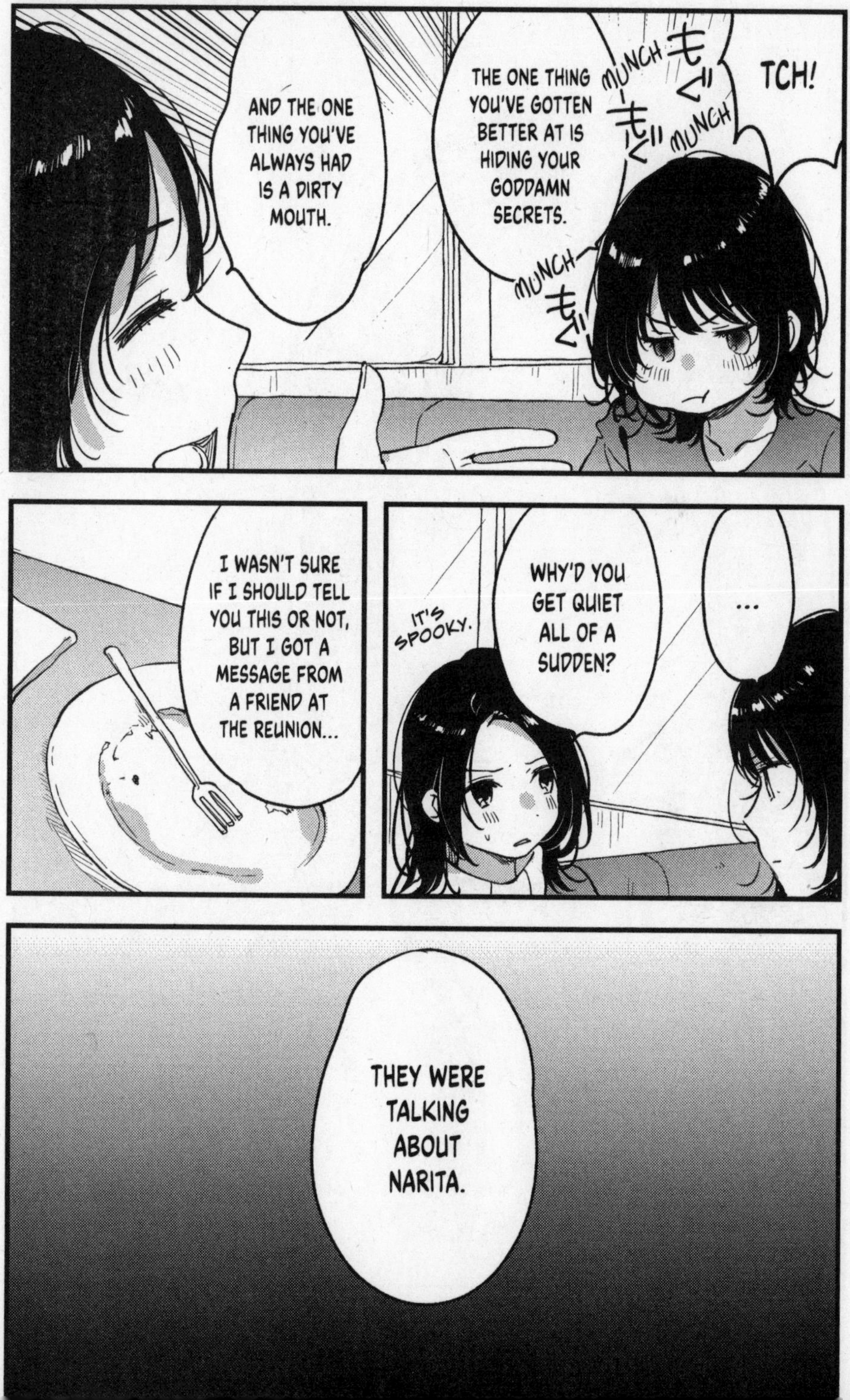
TCH!
MUNCH MUNCH
THE ONE THING YOU'VE GOTTEN BETTER AT IS HIDING YOUR GODDAMN SECRETS.
MUNCH
AND THE ONE THING YOU'VE ALWAYS HAD IS A DIRTY MOUTH.
...
WHY'D YOU GET QUIET ALL OF A SUDDEN?
IT'S SPOOKY.
I WASN'T SURE IF I SHOULD TELL YOU THIS OR NOT, BUT I GOT A MESSAGE FROM A FRIEND AT THE REUNION...
THEY WERE TALKING ABOUT NARITA.

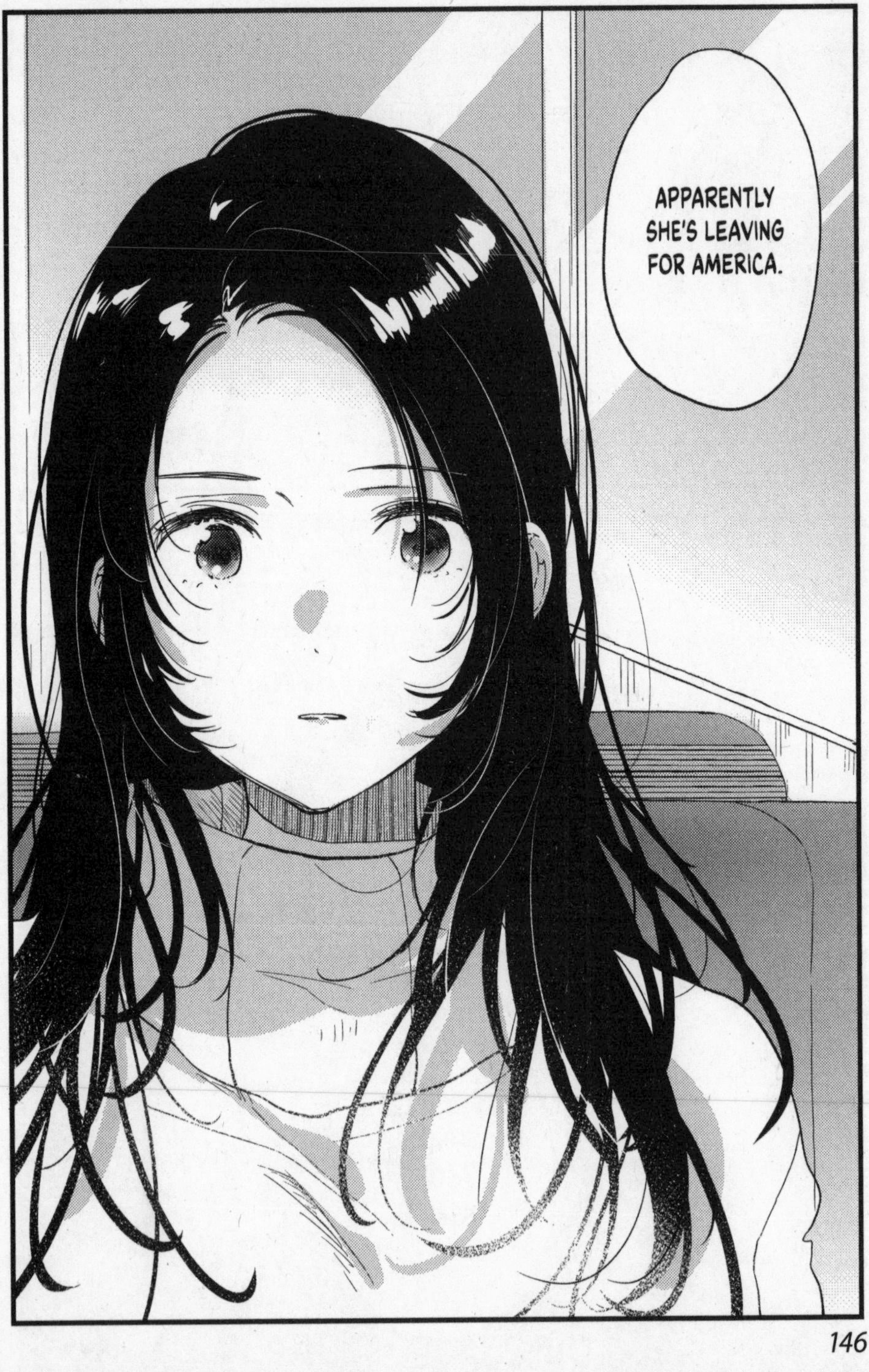
APPARENTLY SHE'S LEAVING FOR AMERICA.

Chapter 32:
To Aoi Koshiba (Part 2)

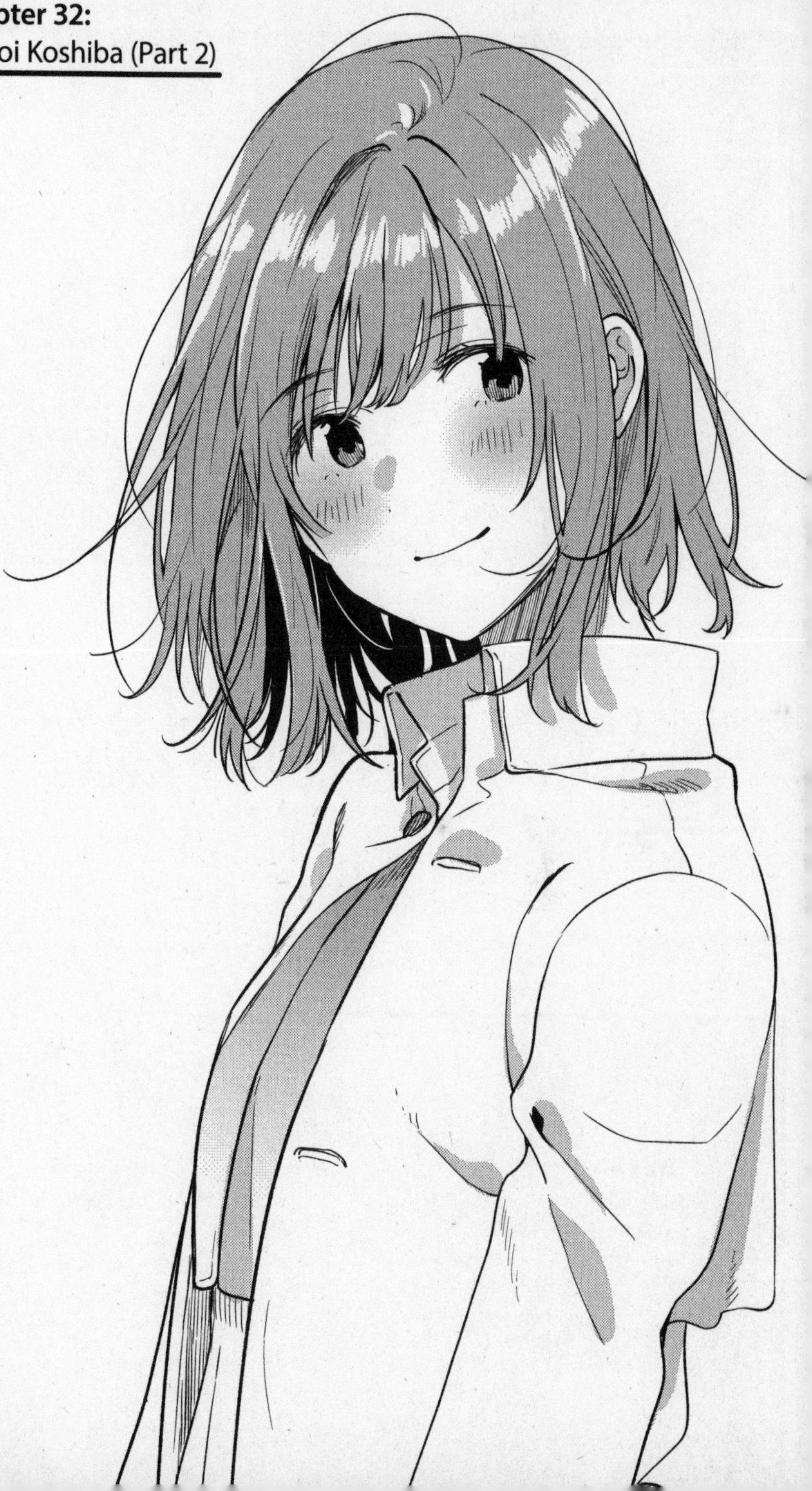

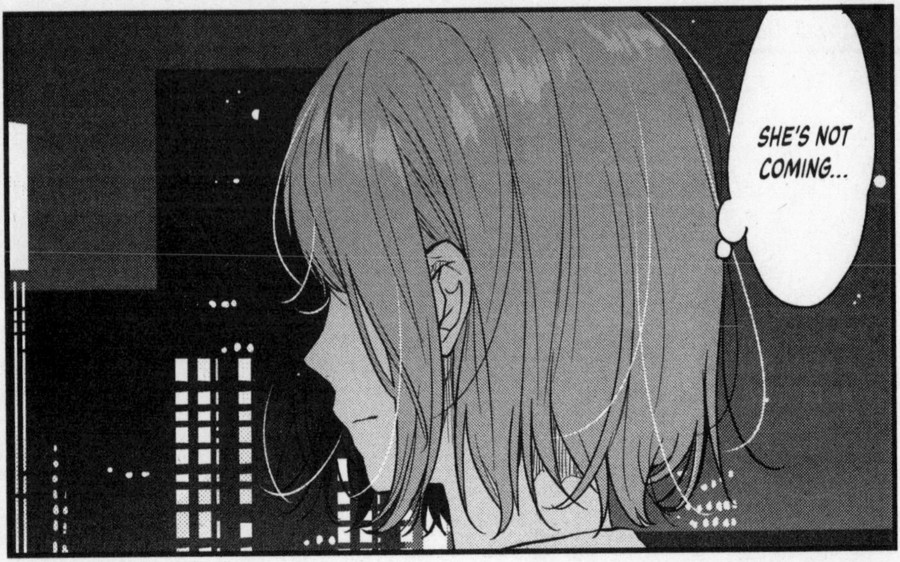
SHE'S NOT COMING...

AOI'S NOT COMING.

I WON'T GET TO SEE HER.

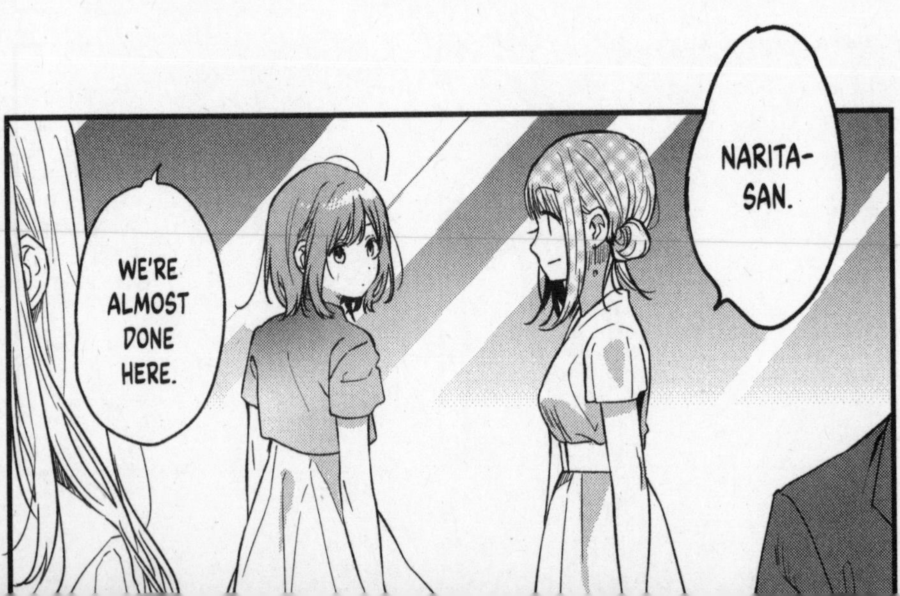
NARITA-SAN.
WE'RE ALMOST DONE HERE.

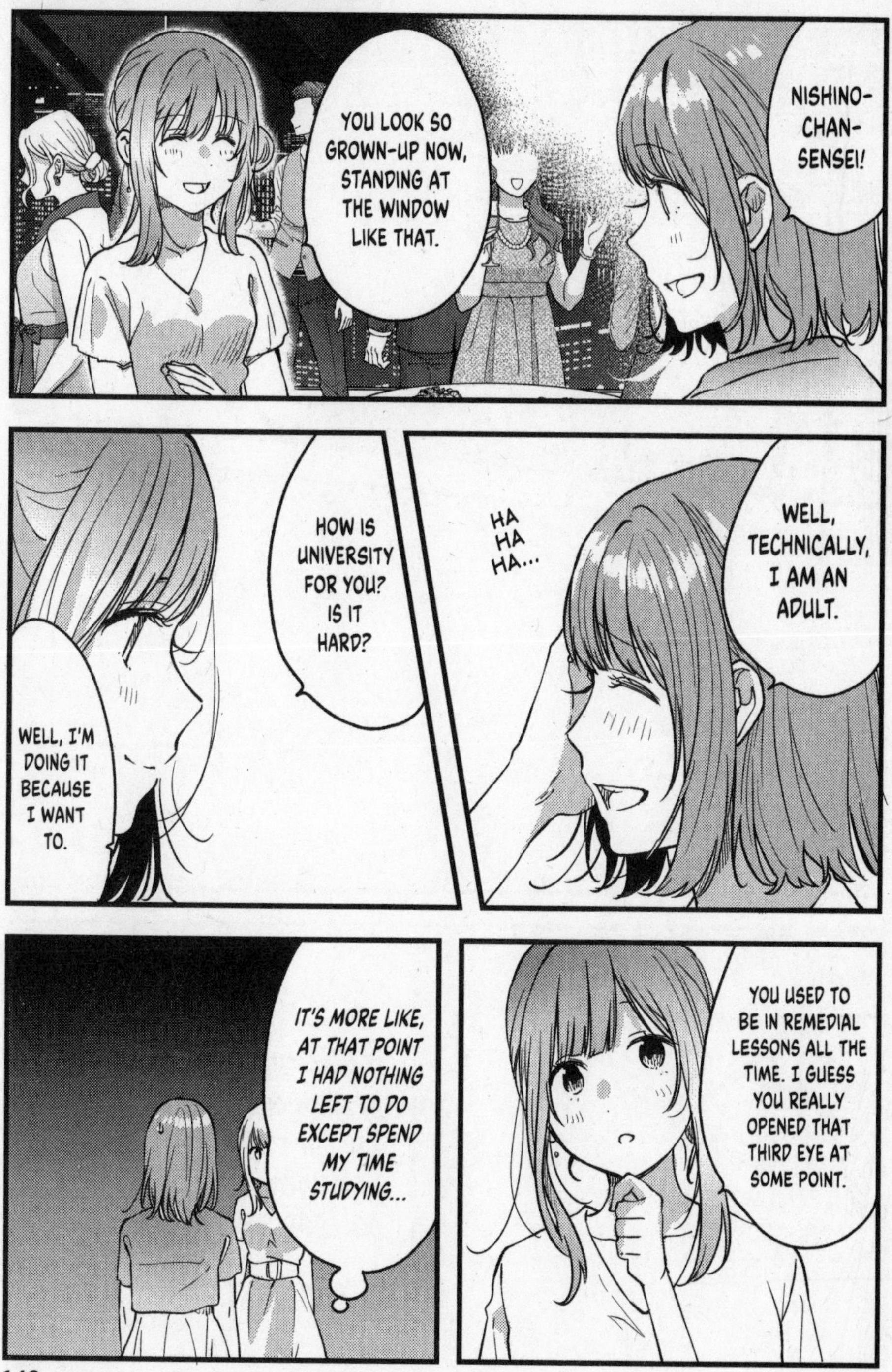
NISHINO-CHAN-SENSEI!
YOU LOOK SO GROWN-UP NOW, STANDING AT THE WINDOW LIKE THAT.
WELL, TECHNICALLY, I AM AN ADULT.
HA HA HA...
HOW IS UNIVERSITY FOR YOU? IS IT HARD?
WELL, I'M DOING IT BECAUSE I WANT TO.
YOU USED TO BE IN REMEDIAL LESSONS ALL THE TIME. I GUESS YOU REALLY OPENED THAT THIRD EYE AT SOME POINT.
IT'S MORE LIKE, AT THAT POINT I HAD NOTHING LEFT TO DO EXCEPT SPEND MY TIME STUDYING...

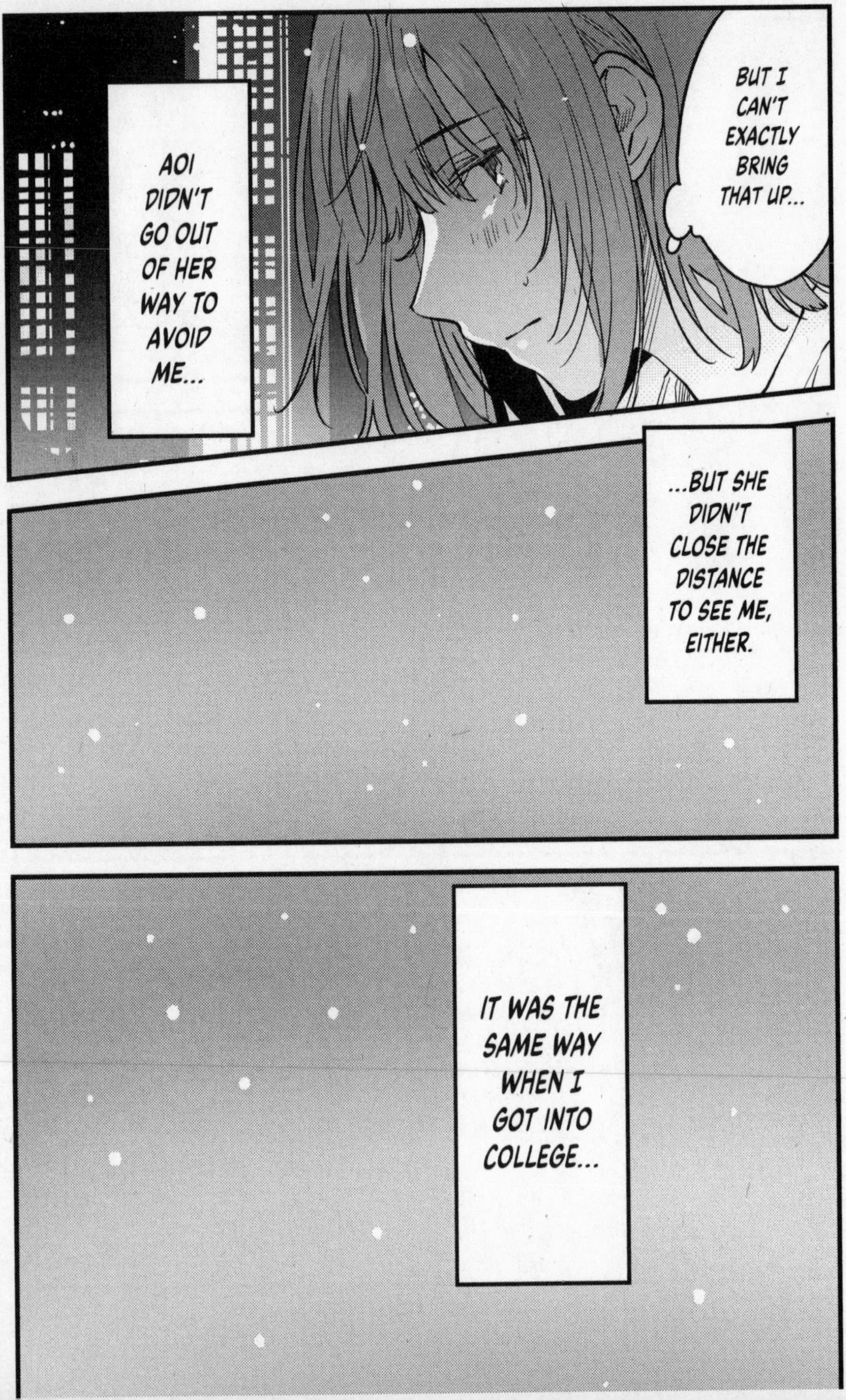
BUT I CAN'T EXACTLY BRING THAT UP...
AOI DIDN'T GO OUT OF HER WAY TO AVOID ME...
...BUT SHE DIDN'T CLOSE THE DISTANCE TO SEE ME, EITHER.
IT WAS THE SAME WAY WHEN I GOT INTO COLLEGE...

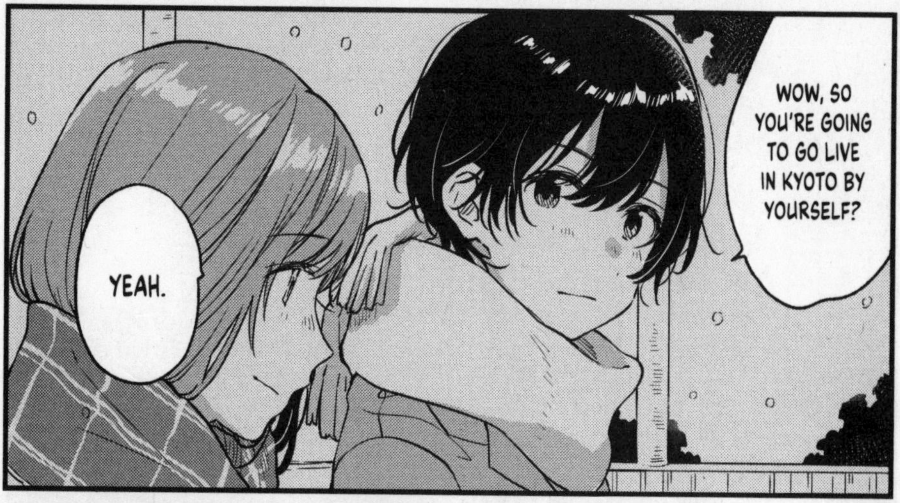
WOW, SO YOU'RE GOING TO GO LIVE IN KYOTO BY YOURSELF?
YEAH.

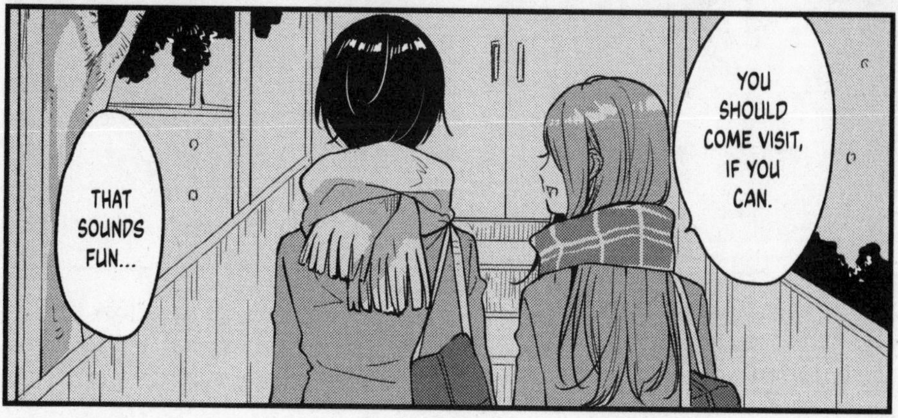
YOU SHOULD COME VISIT, IF YOU CAN.
THAT SOUNDS FUN...

THAT DAY NEVER DID COME, THOUGH.

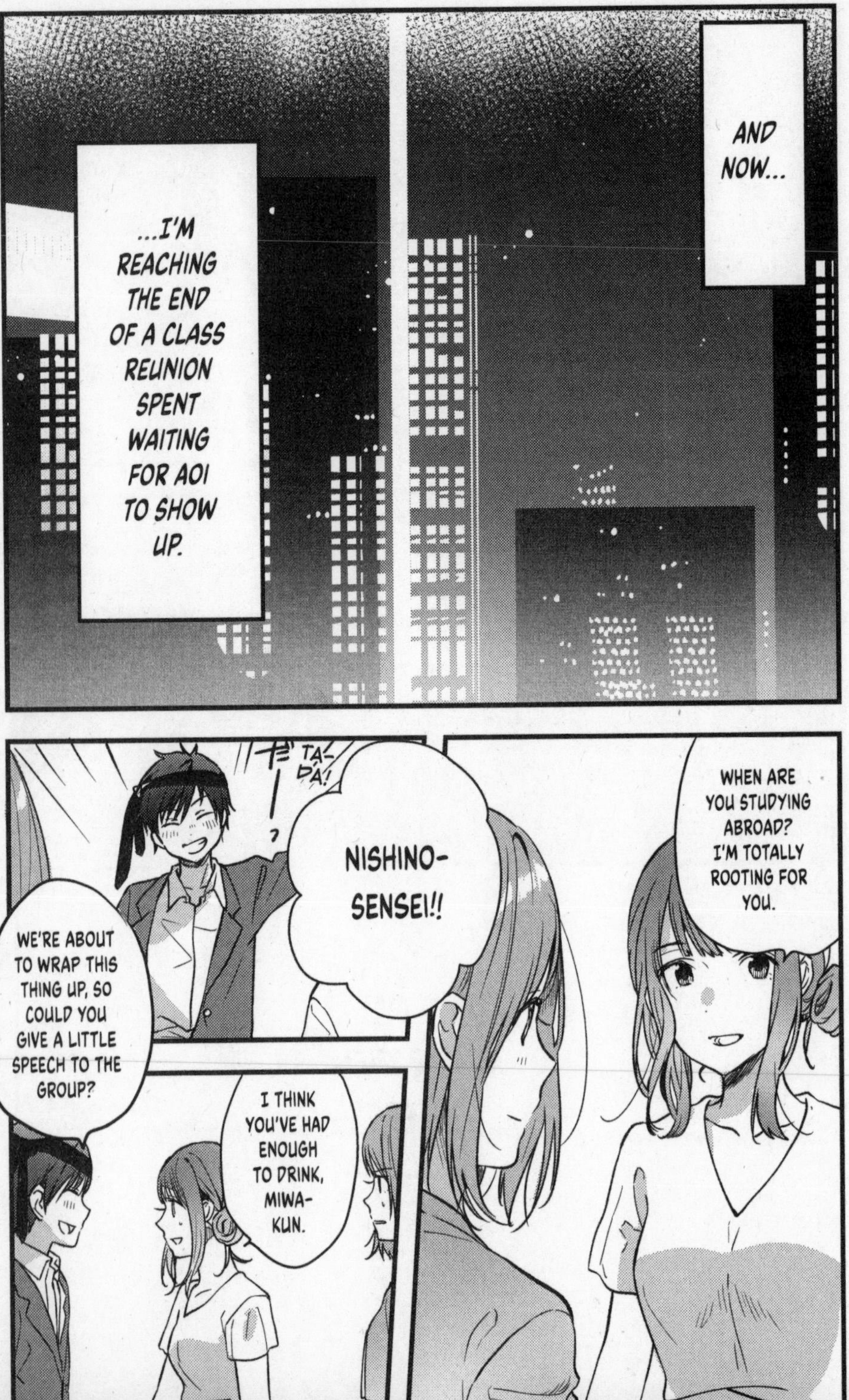
AND NOW...
...I'M REACHING THE END OF A CLASS REUNION SPENT WAITING FOR AOI TO SHOW UP.
WHEN ARE YOU STUDYING ABROAD? I'M TOTALLY ROOTING FOR YOU.
TA-DA!
NISHINO-SENSEI!!
WE'RE ABOUT TO WRAP THIS THING UP, SO COULD YOU GIVE A LITTLE SPEECH TO THE GROUP?
I THINK YOU'VE HAD ENOUGH TO DRINK, MIWA-KUN.

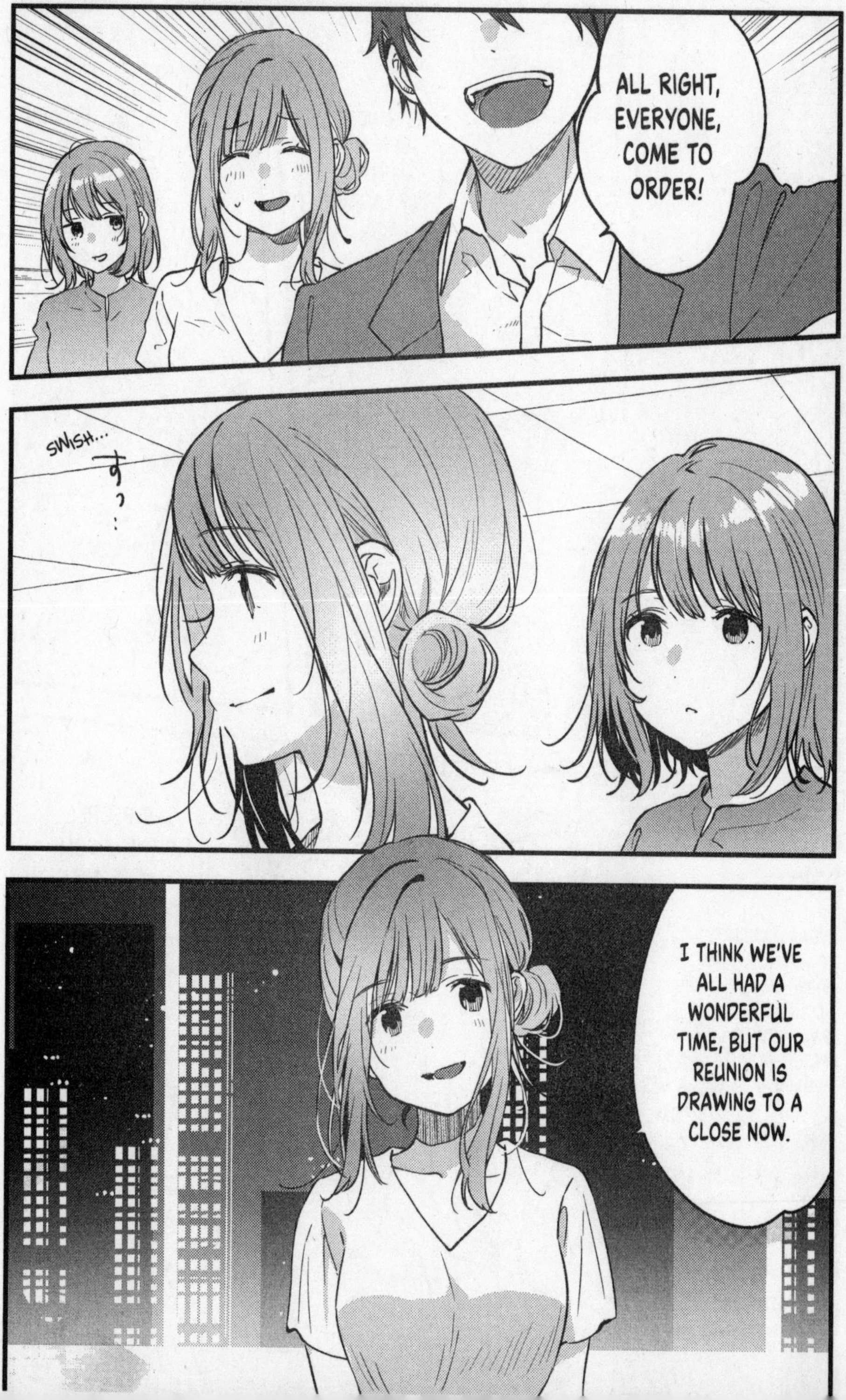
ALL RIGHT, EVERYONE, COME TO ORDER!
SWISH...
すっ…
I THINK WE'VE ALL HAD A WONDERFUL TIME, BUT OUR REUNION IS DRAWING TO A CLOSE NOW.

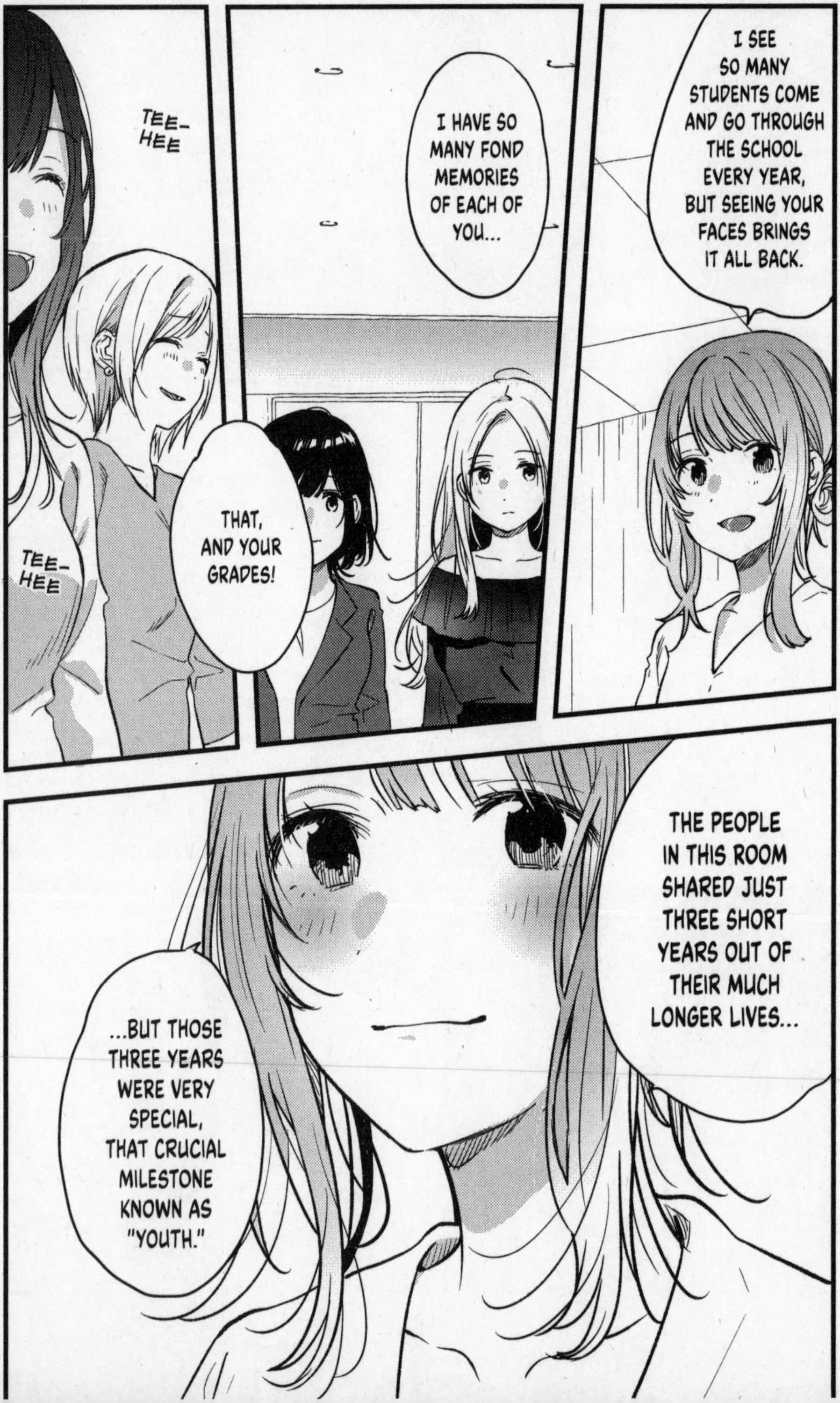
I SEE SO MANY STUDENTS COME AND GO THROUGH THE SCHOOL EVERY YEAR, BUT SEEING YOUR FACES BRINGS IT ALL BACK.
I HAVE SO MANY FOND MEMORIES OF EACH OF YOU...
TEE-HEE
THAT, AND YOUR GRADES!
TEE-HEE
THE PEOPLE IN THIS ROOM SHARED JUST THREE SHORT YEARS OUT OF THEIR MUCH LONGER LIVES...
...BUT THOSE THREE YEARS WERE VERY SPECIAL, THAT CRUCIAL MILESTONE KNOWN AS "YOUTH."

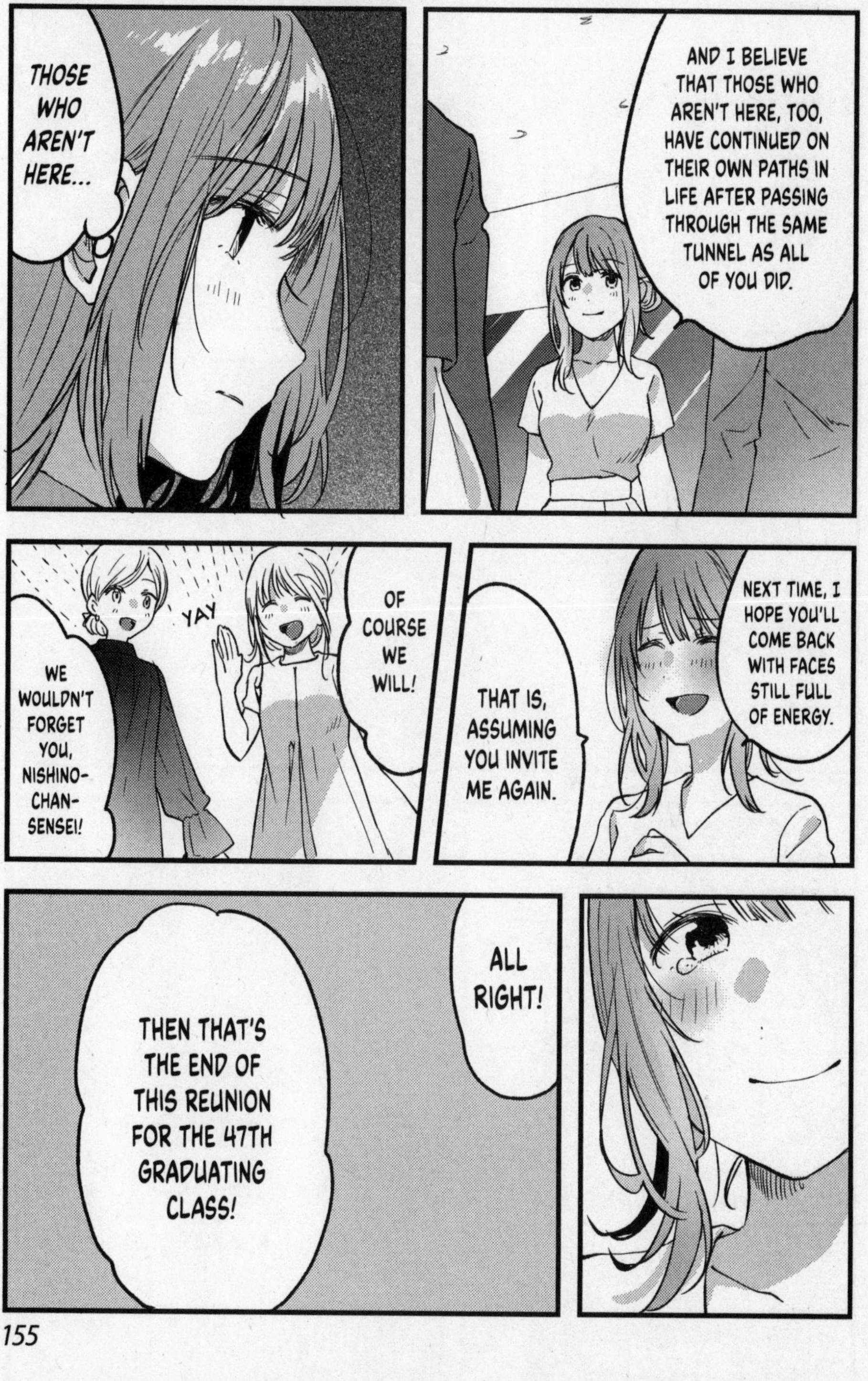
AND I BELIEVE THAT THOSE WHO AREN'T HERE, TOO, HAVE CONTINUED ON THEIR OWN PATHS IN LIFE AFTER PASSING THROUGH THE SAME TUNNEL AS ALL OF YOU DID.
THOSE WHO AREN'T HERE...
NEXT TIME, I HOPE YOU'LL COME BACK WITH FACES STILL FULL OF ENERGY.
THAT IS, ASSUMING YOU INVITE ME AGAIN.
OF COURSE WE WILL!
YAY
WE WOULDN'T FORGET YOU, NISHINO-CHAN-SENSEI!
ALL RIGHT!
THEN THAT'S THE END OF THIS REUNION FOR THE 47TH GRADUATING CLASS!

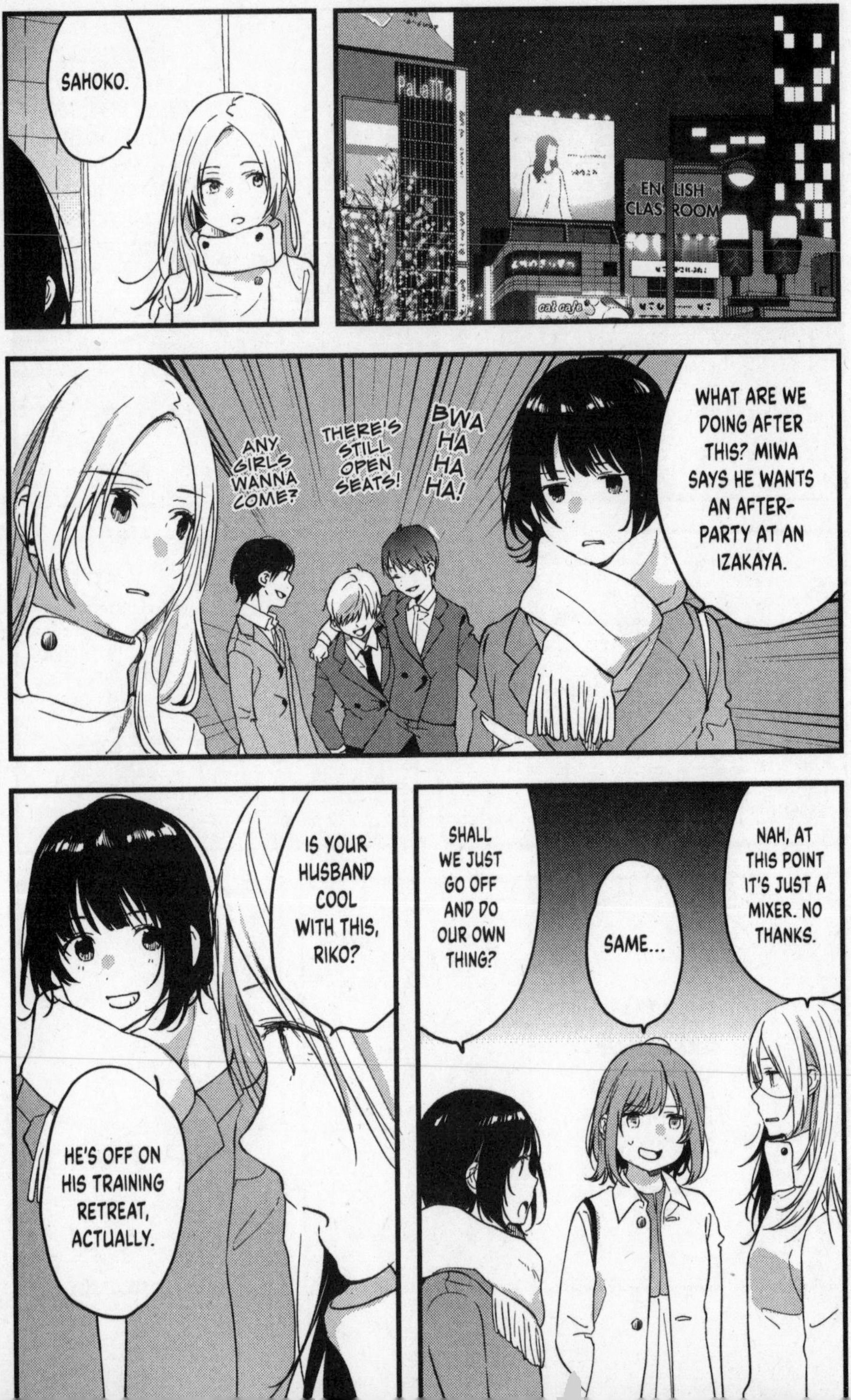
PaLaTTa
ENGLISH CLASSROOM
cat cafe
SAHOKO.
WHAT ARE WE DOING AFTER THIS? MIWA SAYS HE WANTS AN AFTER-PARTY AT AN IZAKAYA.
BWA HA HA HA!
THERE'S STILL OPEN SEATS!
ANY GIRLS WANNA COME?
NAH, AT THIS POINT IT'S JUST A MIXER. NO THANKS.
SAME...
SHALL WE JUST GO OFF AND DO OUR OWN THING?
IS YOUR HUSBAND COOL WITH THIS, RIKO?
HE'S OFF ON HIS TRAINING RETREAT, ACTUALLY.

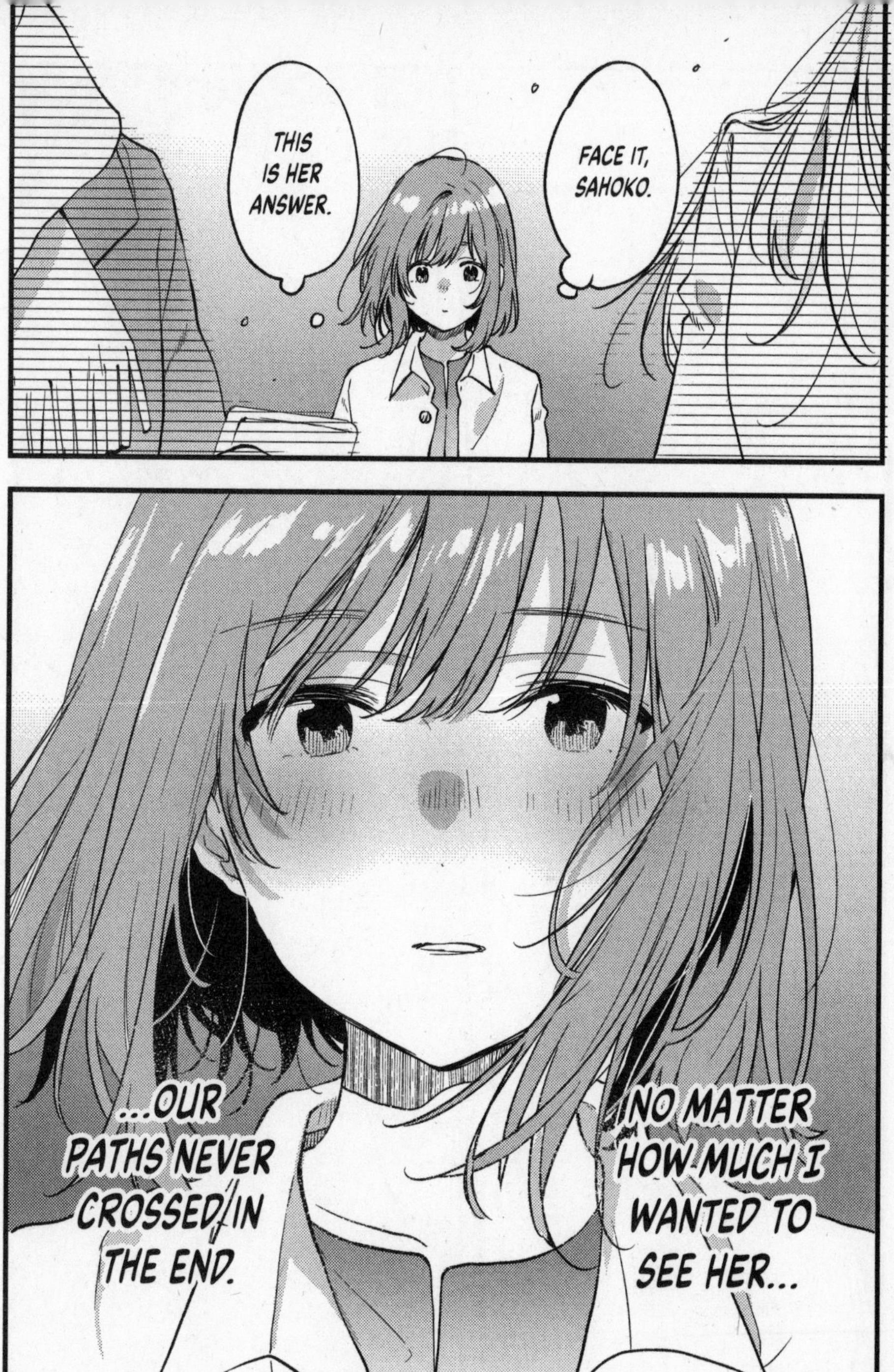
FACE IT, SAHOKO.
THIS IS HER ANSWER.
NO MATTER HOW MUCH I WANTED TO SEE HER...
...OUR PATHS NEVER CROSSED IN THE END.

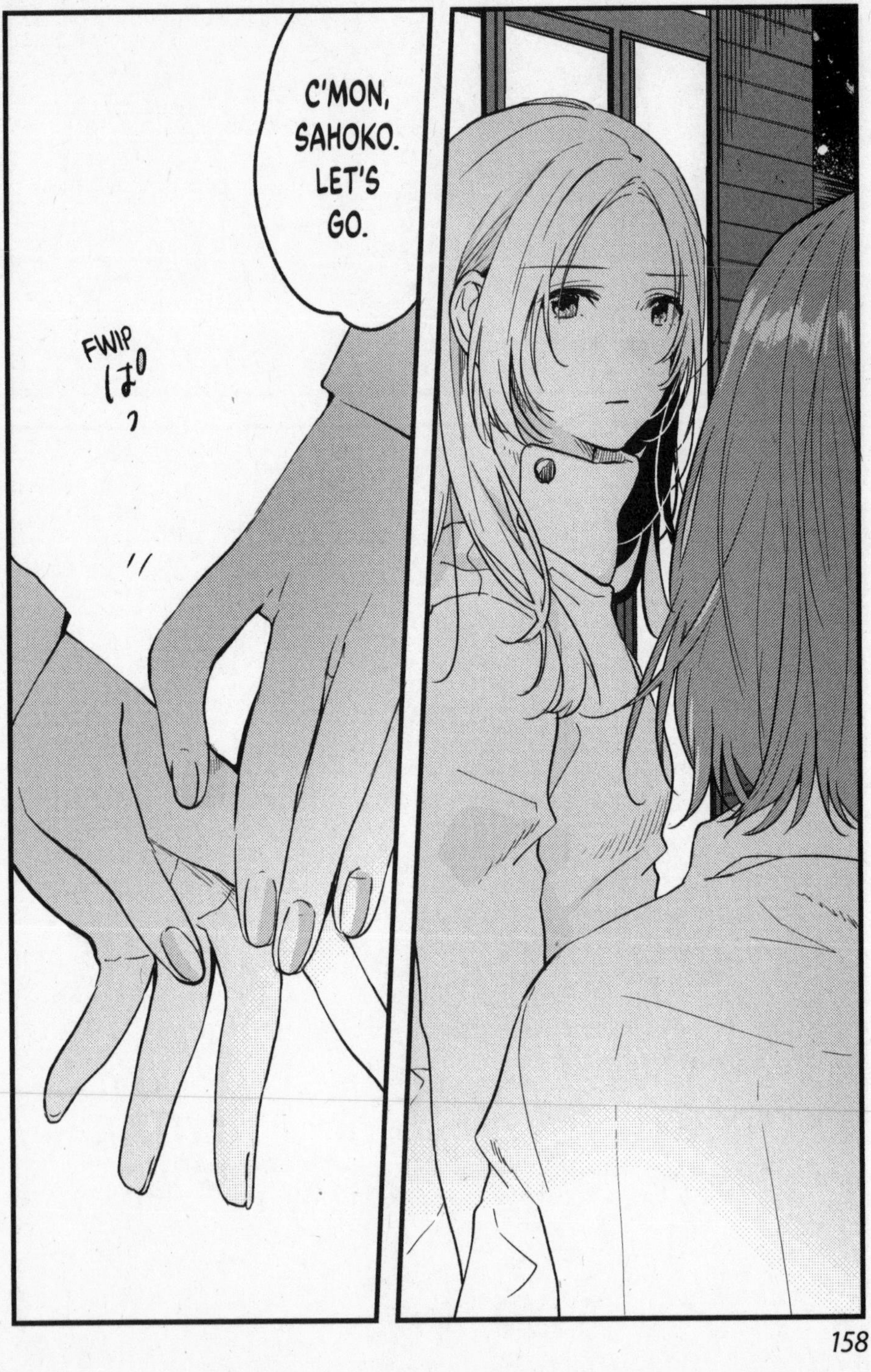
C'MON, SAHOKO. LET'S GO.
FWIP
はっ

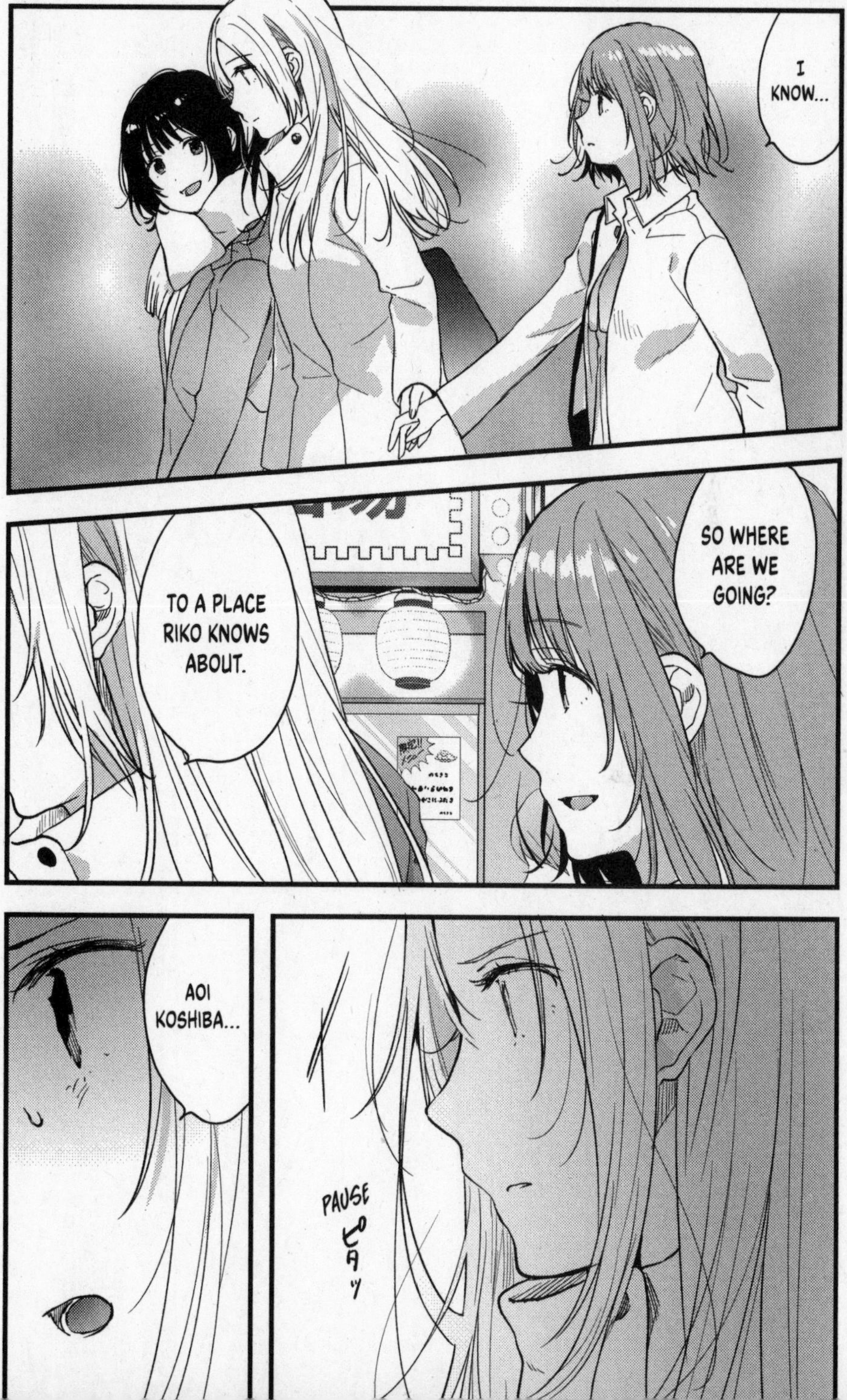
I KNOW...
SO WHERE ARE WE GOING?
TO A PLACE RIKO KNOWS ABOUT.
PAUSE
ピタッ
AOI KOSHIBA...

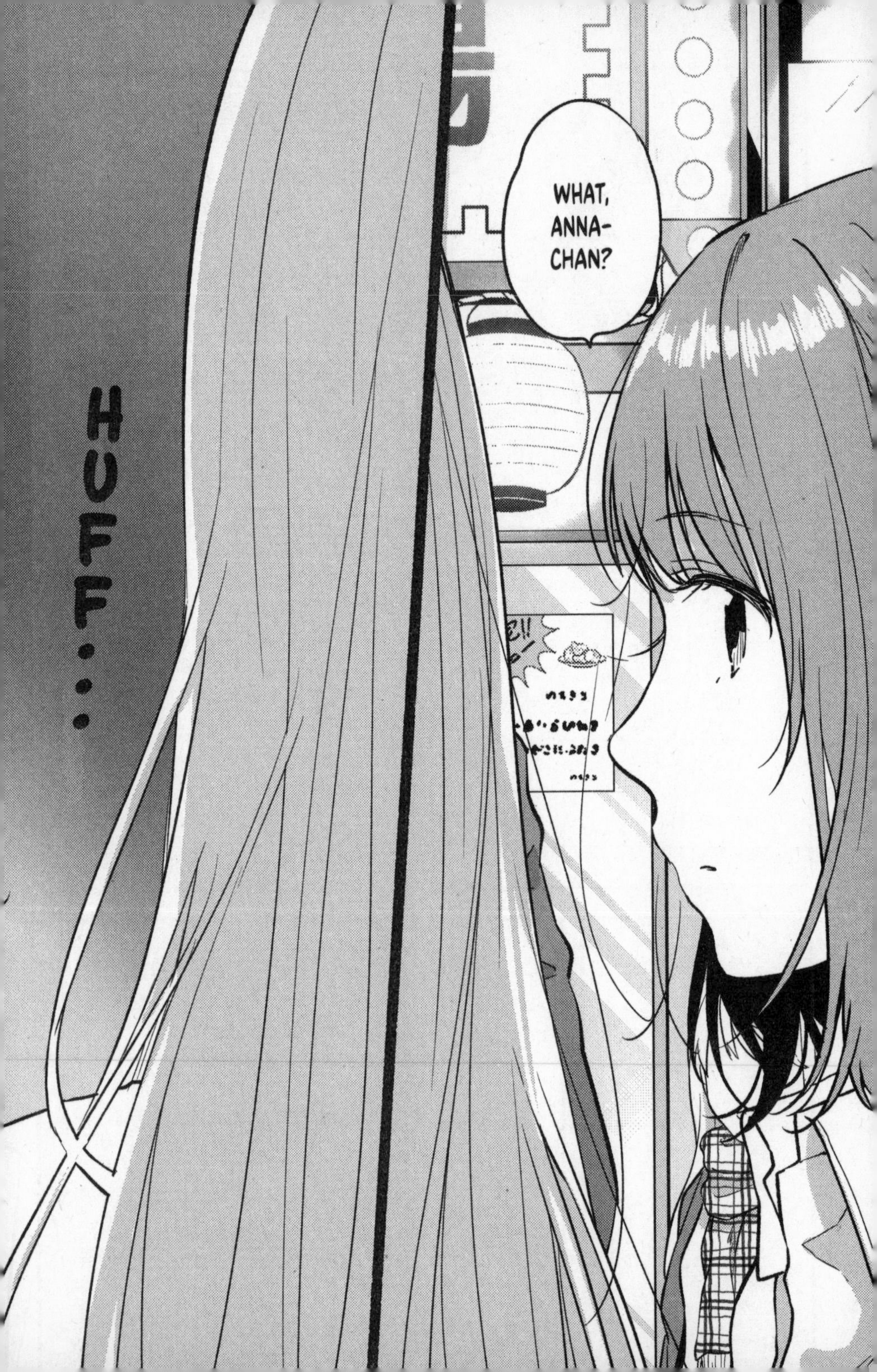
WHAT, ANNA-CHAN?
HUFF...

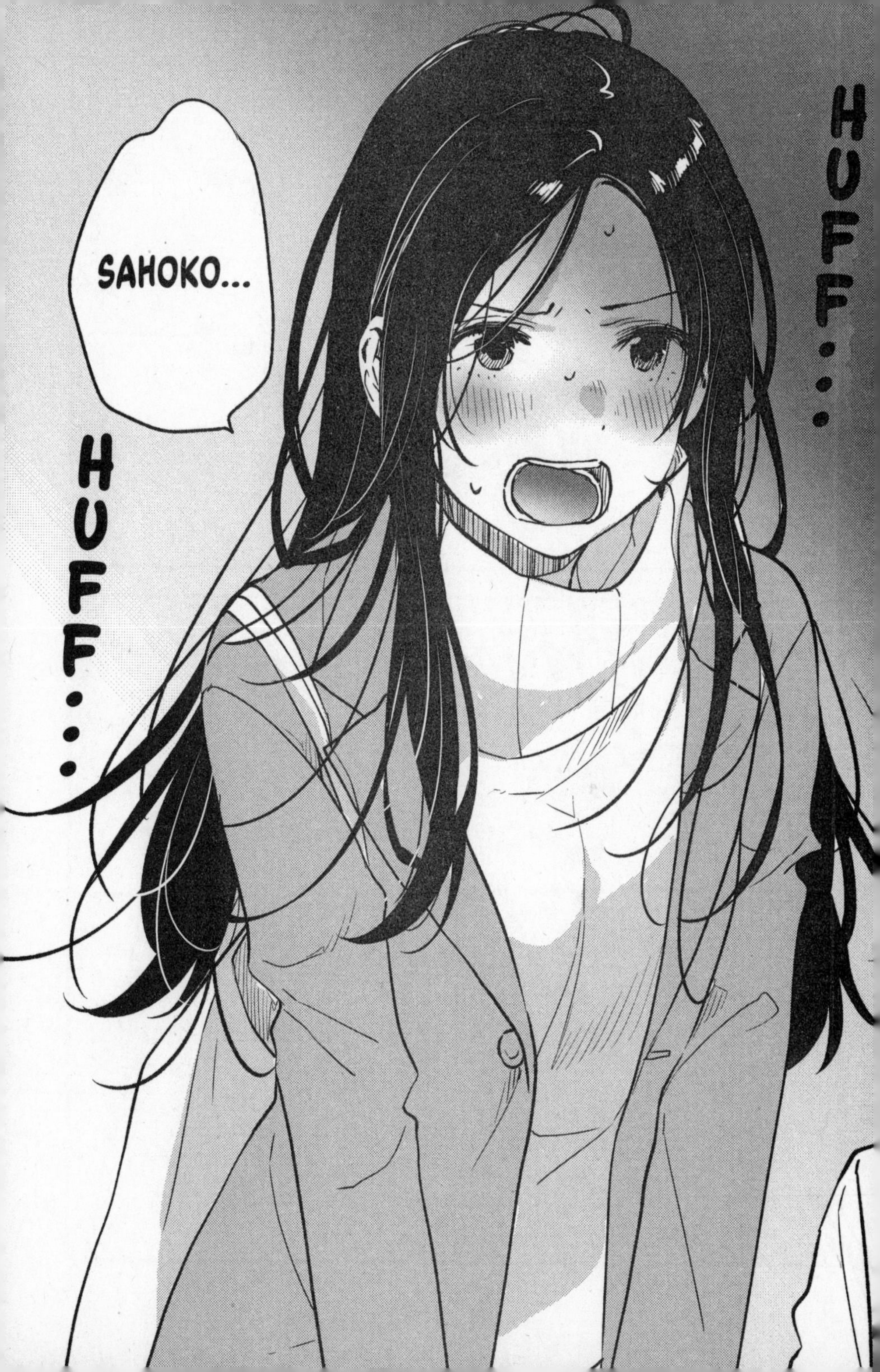
HUFF...
SAHOKO...
HUFF...

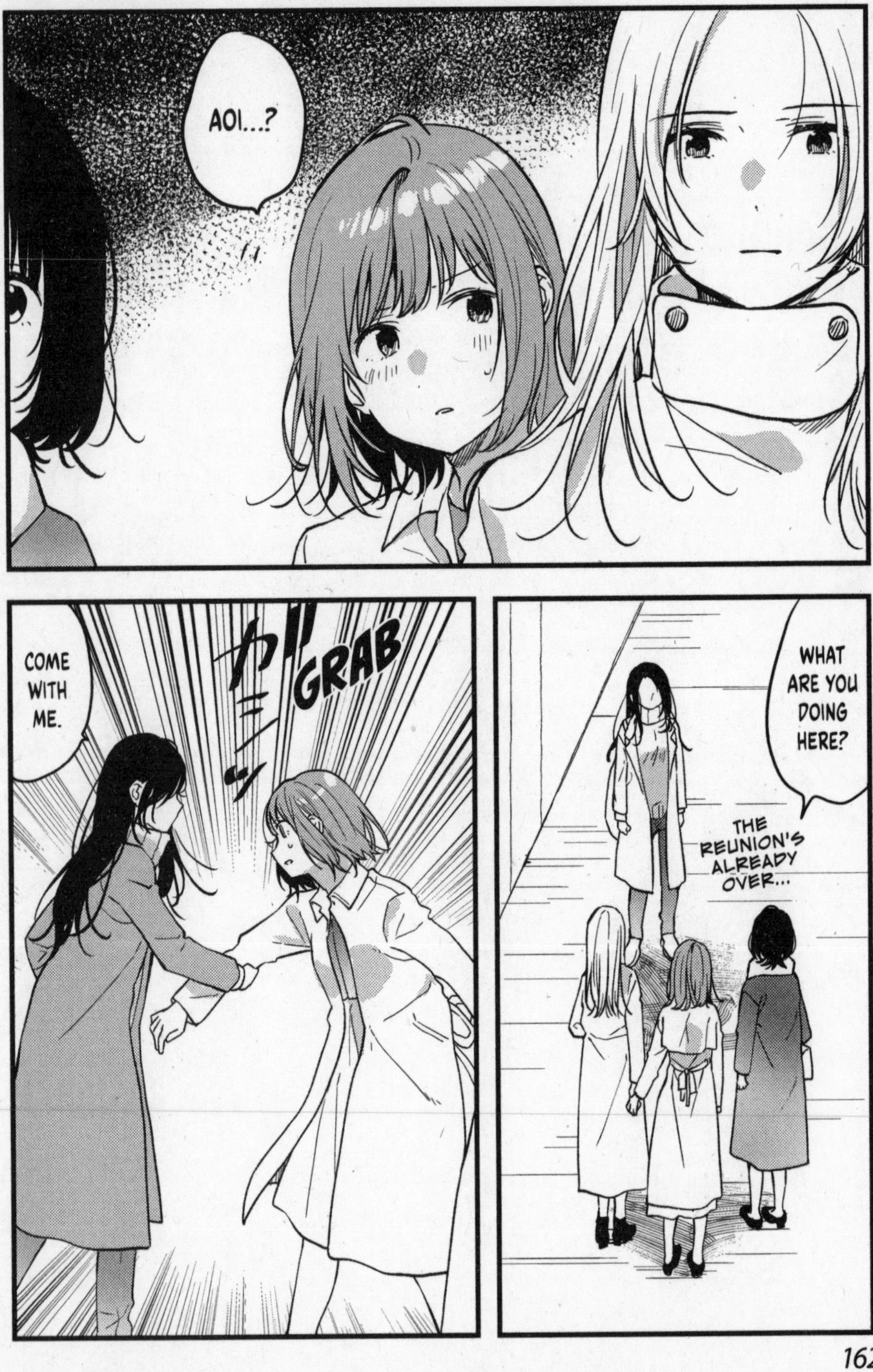
AOI...?
WHAT ARE YOU DOING HERE?
THE REUNION'S ALREADY OVER...
GRAB
COME WITH ME.

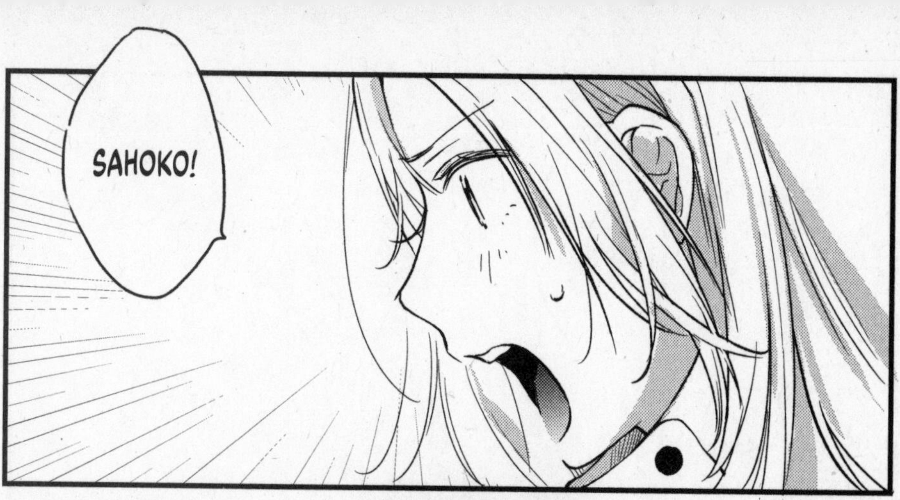
SAHOKO!
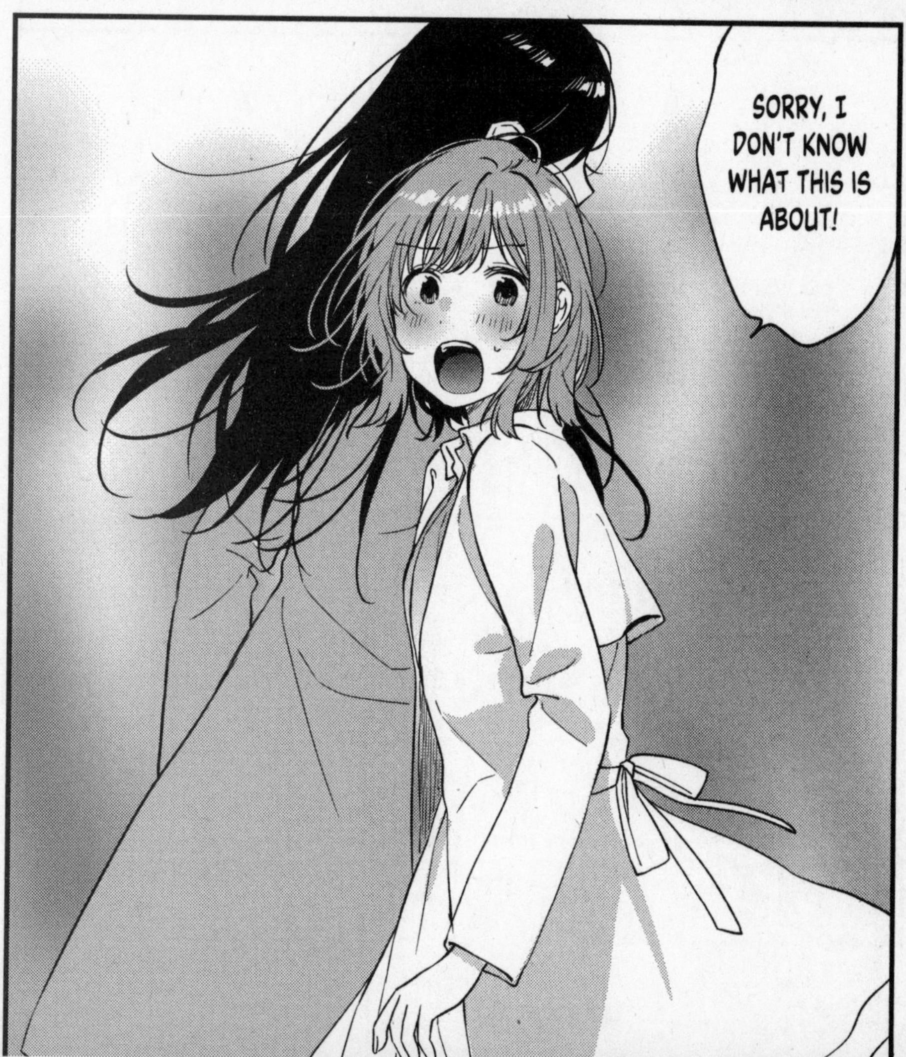
SORRY, I DON'T KNOW WHAT THIS IS ABOUT!

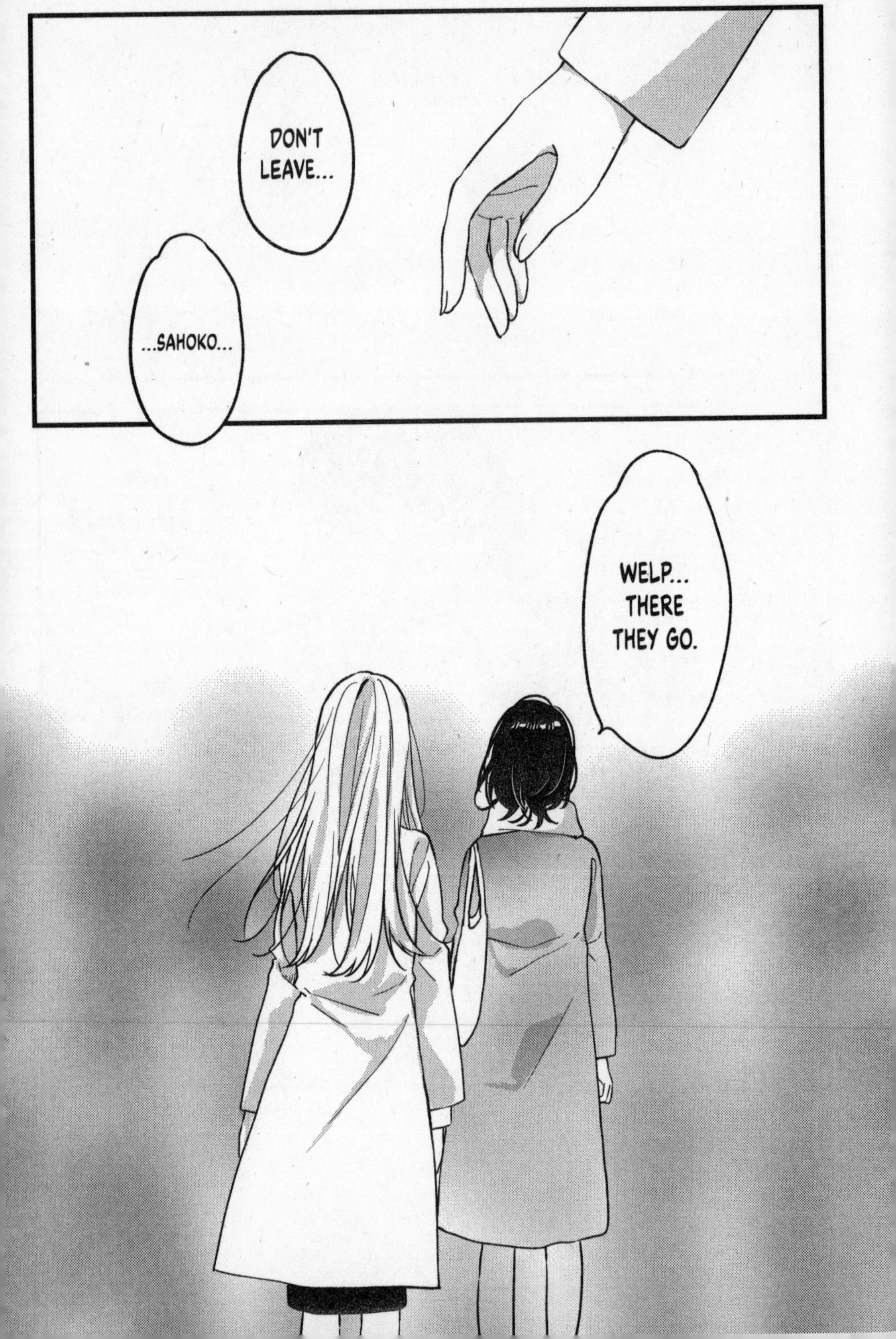
DON'T LEAVE...
...SAHOKO...
WELP... THERE THEY GO.

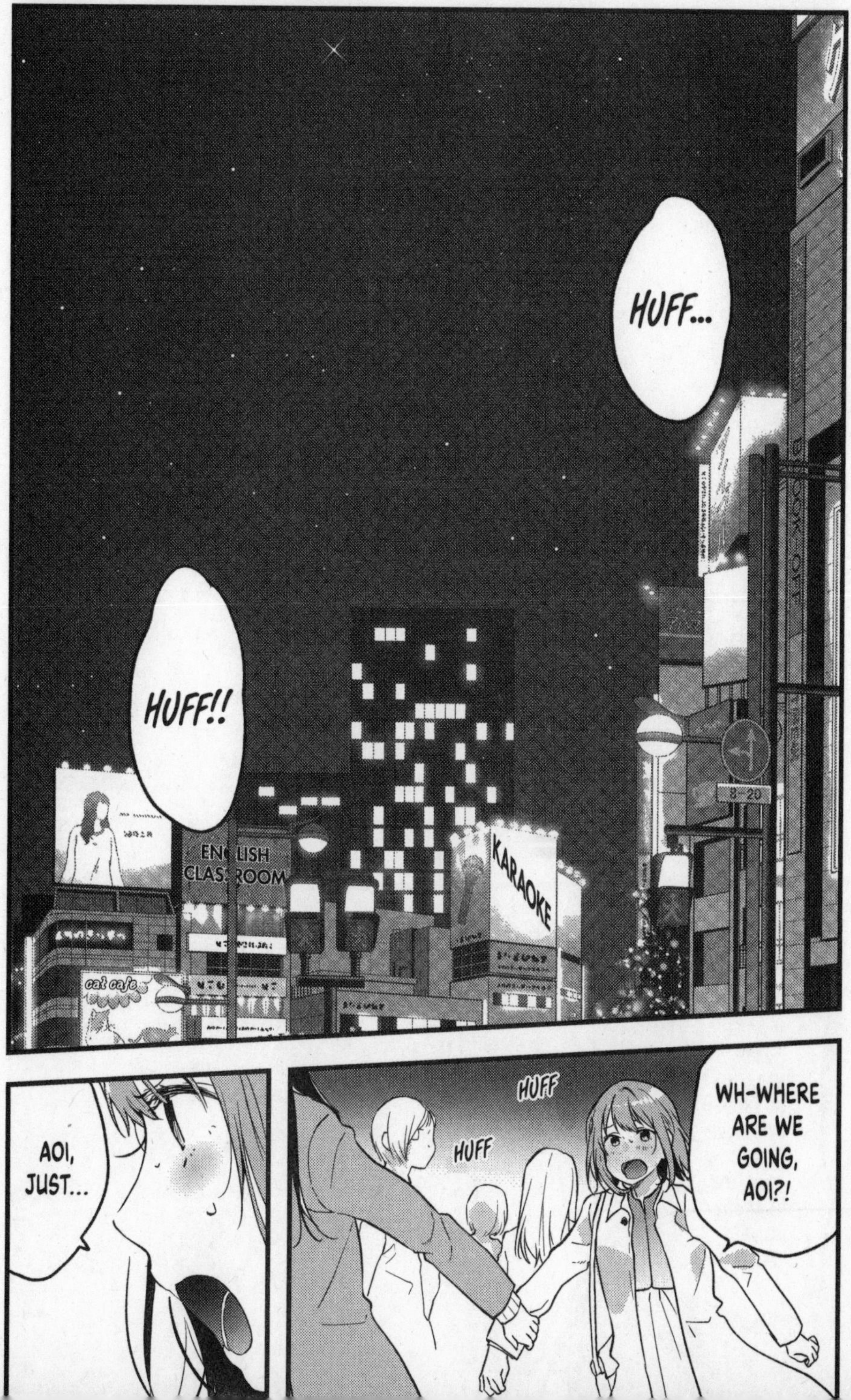
HUFF...
HUFF!!
KARAOKE
ENGLISH CLASSROOM
8-20
cat cafe
WH-WHERE ARE WE GOING, AOI?!
HUFF
HUFF
AOI, JUST...

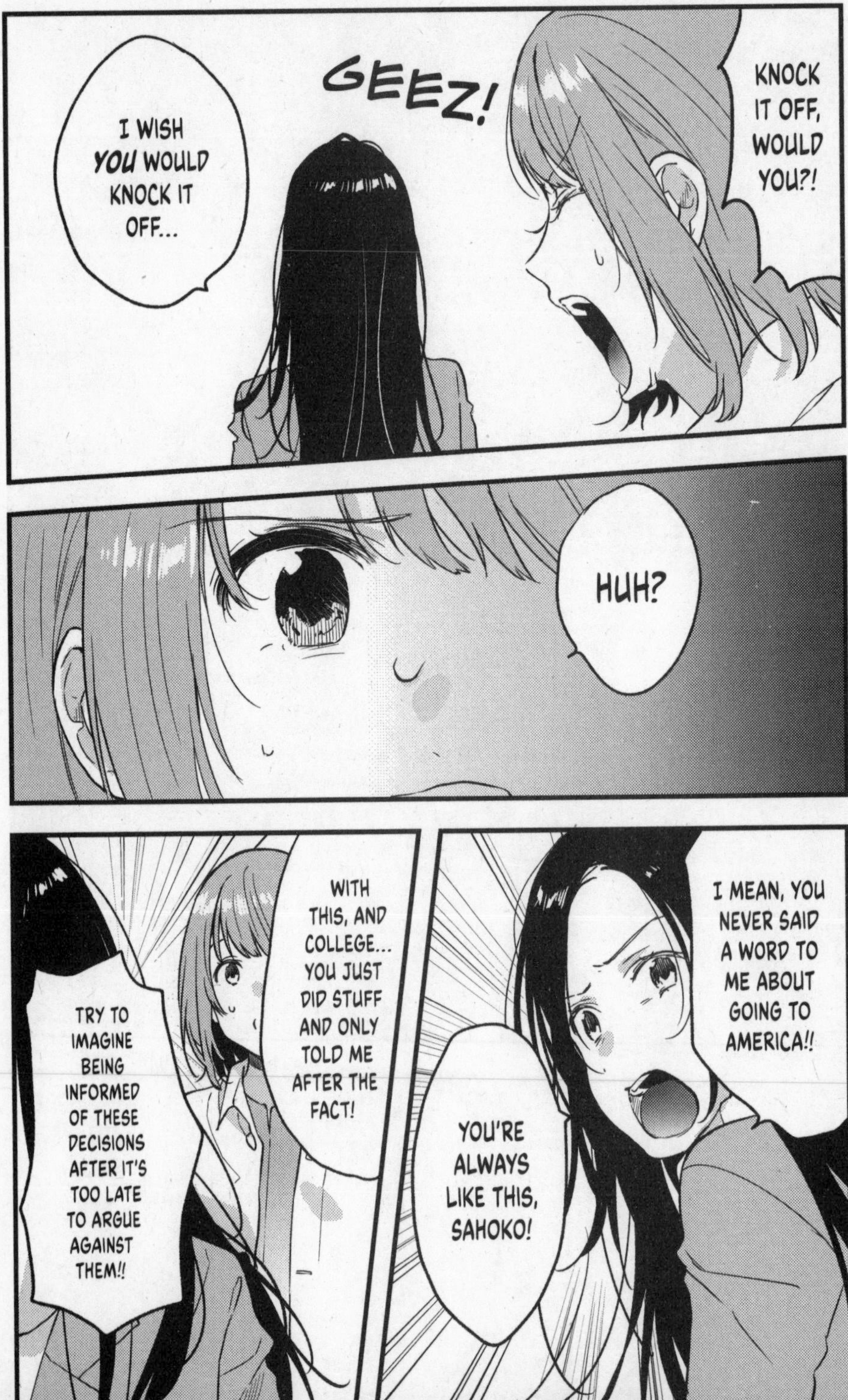
KNOCK IT OFF, WOULD YOU?!
GEEZ!
I WISH *YOU* WOULD KNOCK IT OFF...
HUH?
I MEAN, YOU NEVER SAID A WORD TO ME ABOUT GOING TO AMERICA!!
YOU'RE ALWAYS LIKE THIS, SAHOKO!
WITH THIS, AND COLLEGE... YOU JUST DID STUFF AND ONLY TOLD ME AFTER THE FACT!
TRY TO IMAGINE BEING INFORMED OF THESE DECISIONS AFTER IT'S TOO LATE TO ARGUE AGAINST THEM!!

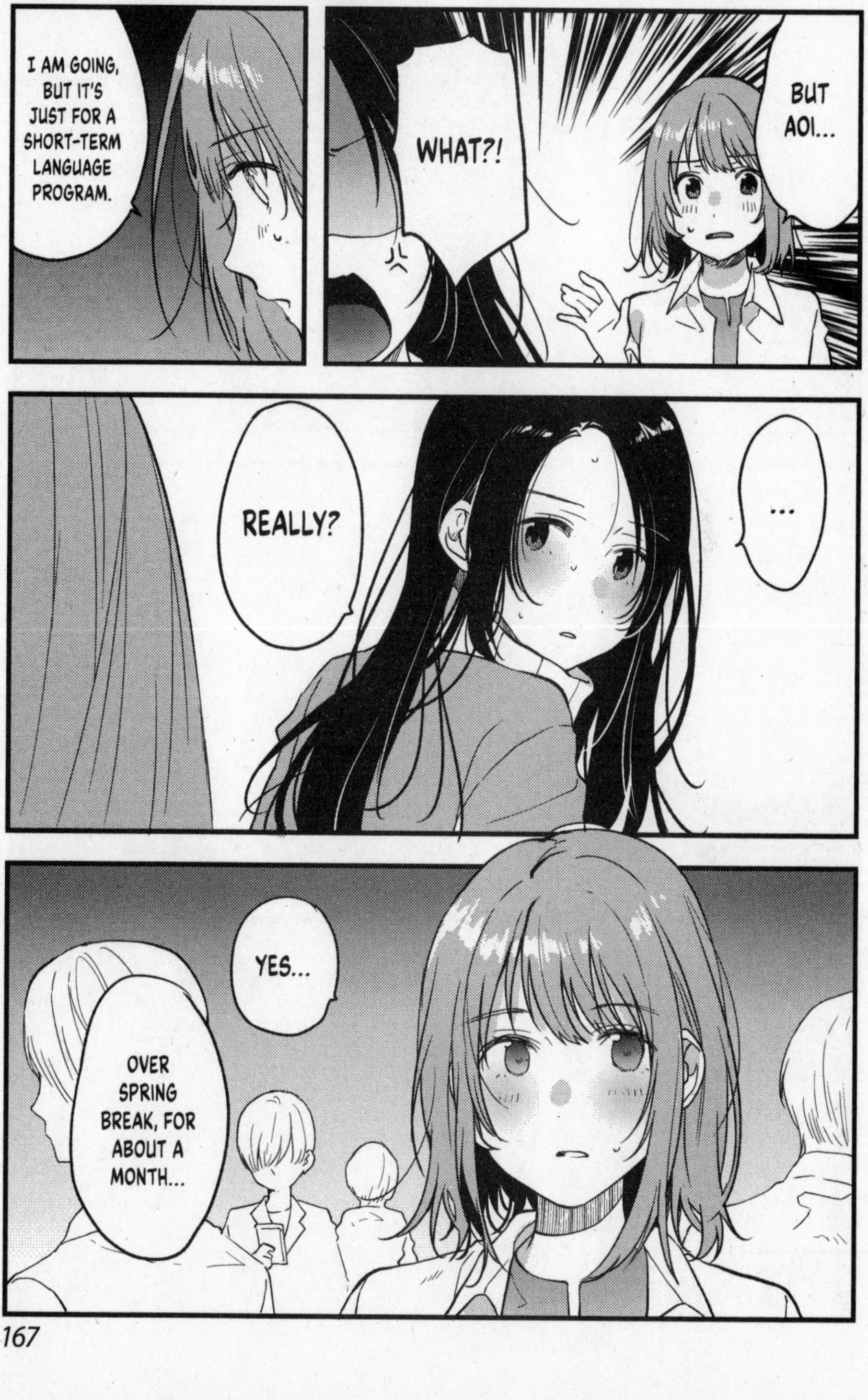
BUT AOI...
WHAT?!
I AM GOING, BUT IT'S JUST FOR A SHORT-TERM LANGUAGE PROGRAM.
...
REALLY?
YES...
OVER SPRING BREAK, FOR ABOUT A MONTH...

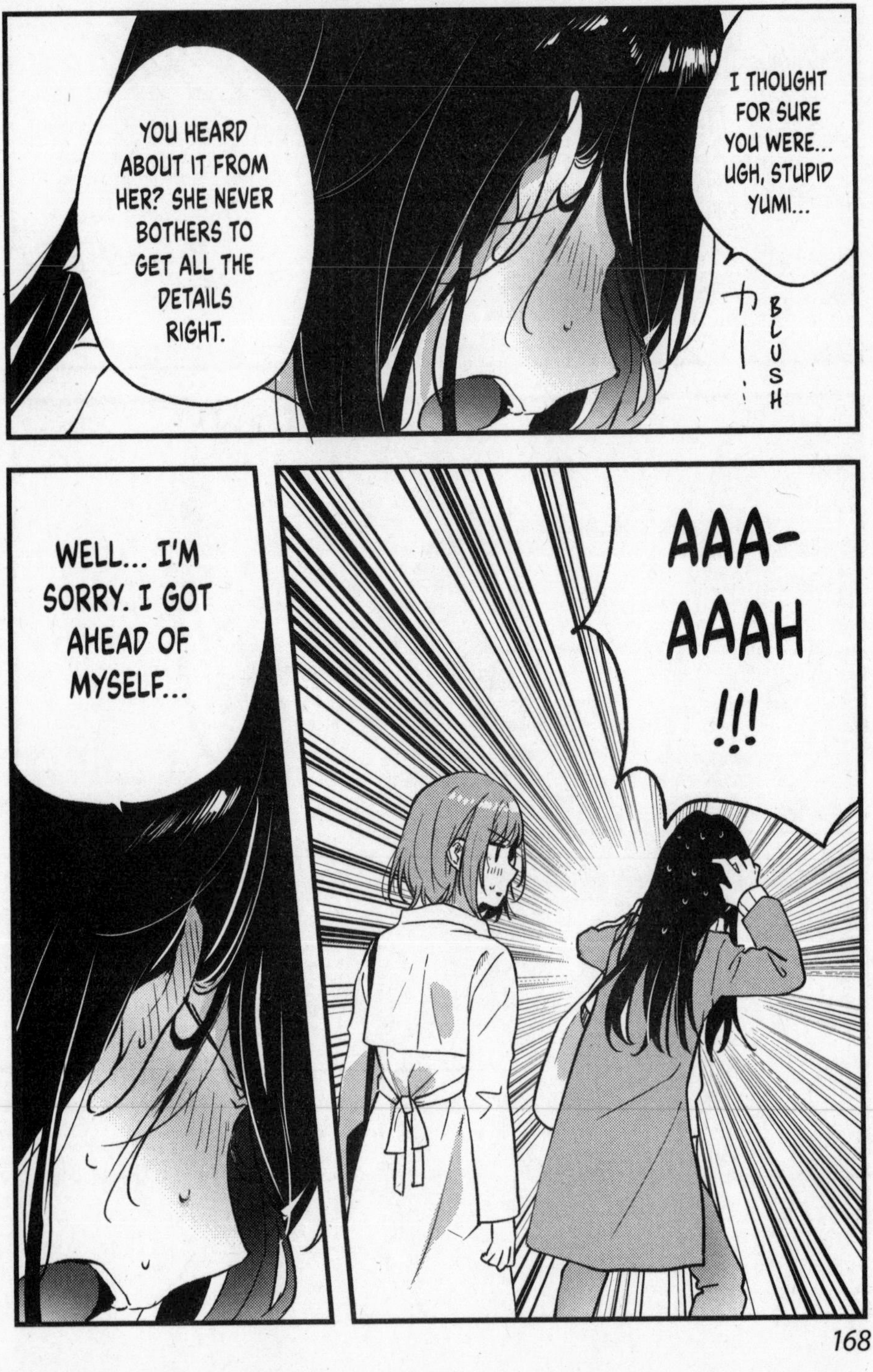
I THOUGHT FOR SURE YOU WERE... UGH, STUPID YUMI...
カー…
BLUSH
YOU HEARD ABOUT IT FROM HER? SHE NEVER BOTHERS TO GET ALL THE DETAILS RIGHT.
AAA-AAAH!!!
WELL... I'M SORRY. I GOT AHEAD OF MYSELF...

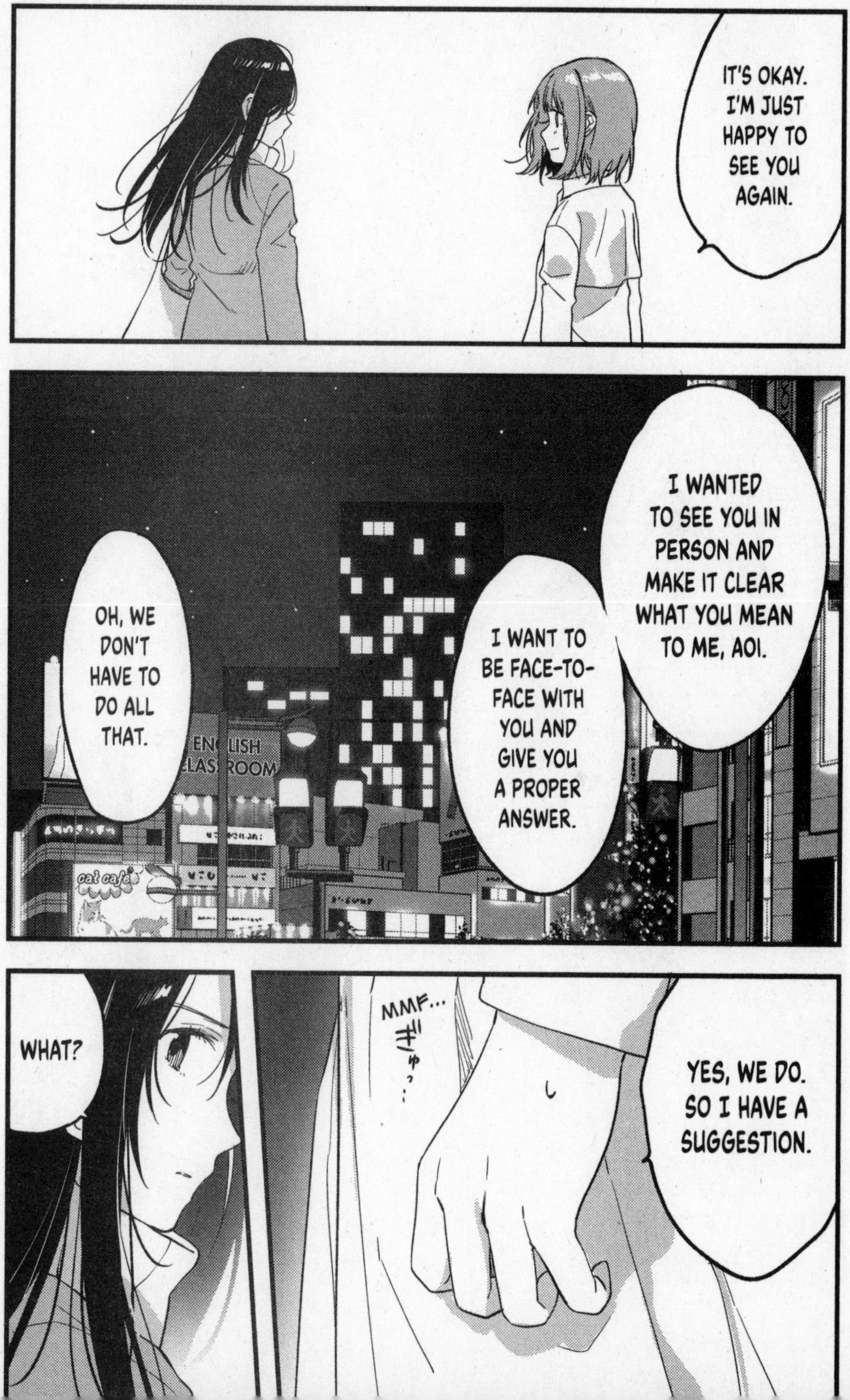
IT'S OKAY. I'M JUST HAPPY TO SEE YOU AGAIN.
I WANTED TO SEE YOU IN PERSON AND MAKE IT CLEAR WHAT YOU MEAN TO ME, AOI.
I WANT TO BE FACE-TO-FACE WITH YOU AND GIVE YOU A PROPER ANSWER.
OH, WE DON'T HAVE TO DO ALL THAT.
ENGLISH CLASSROOM
cat cafe
MMF...
ぎゅっ
YES, WE DO. SO I HAVE A SUGGESTION.
WHAT?

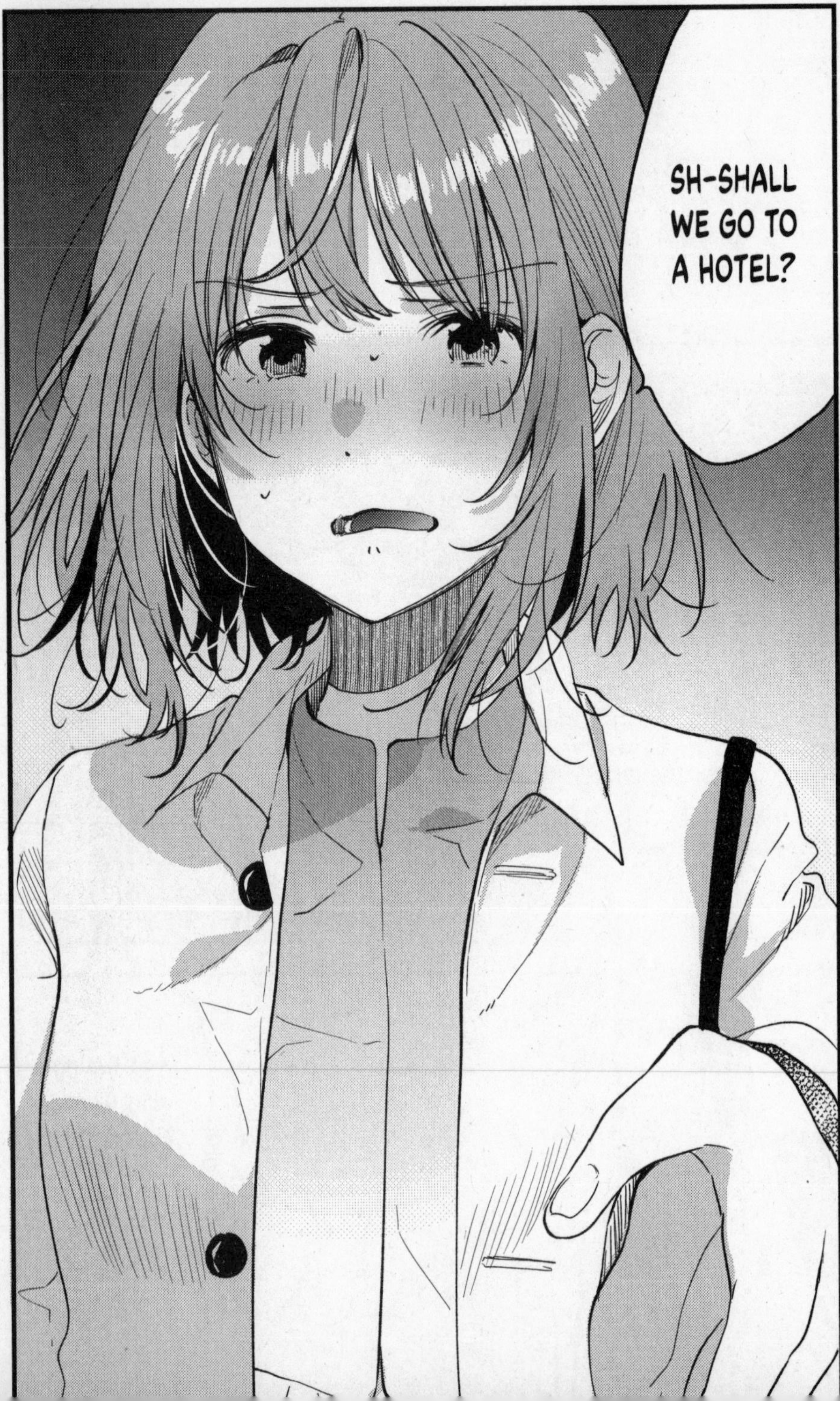
SH-SHALL WE GO TO A HOTEL?

Chapter 33:
To the One I Love

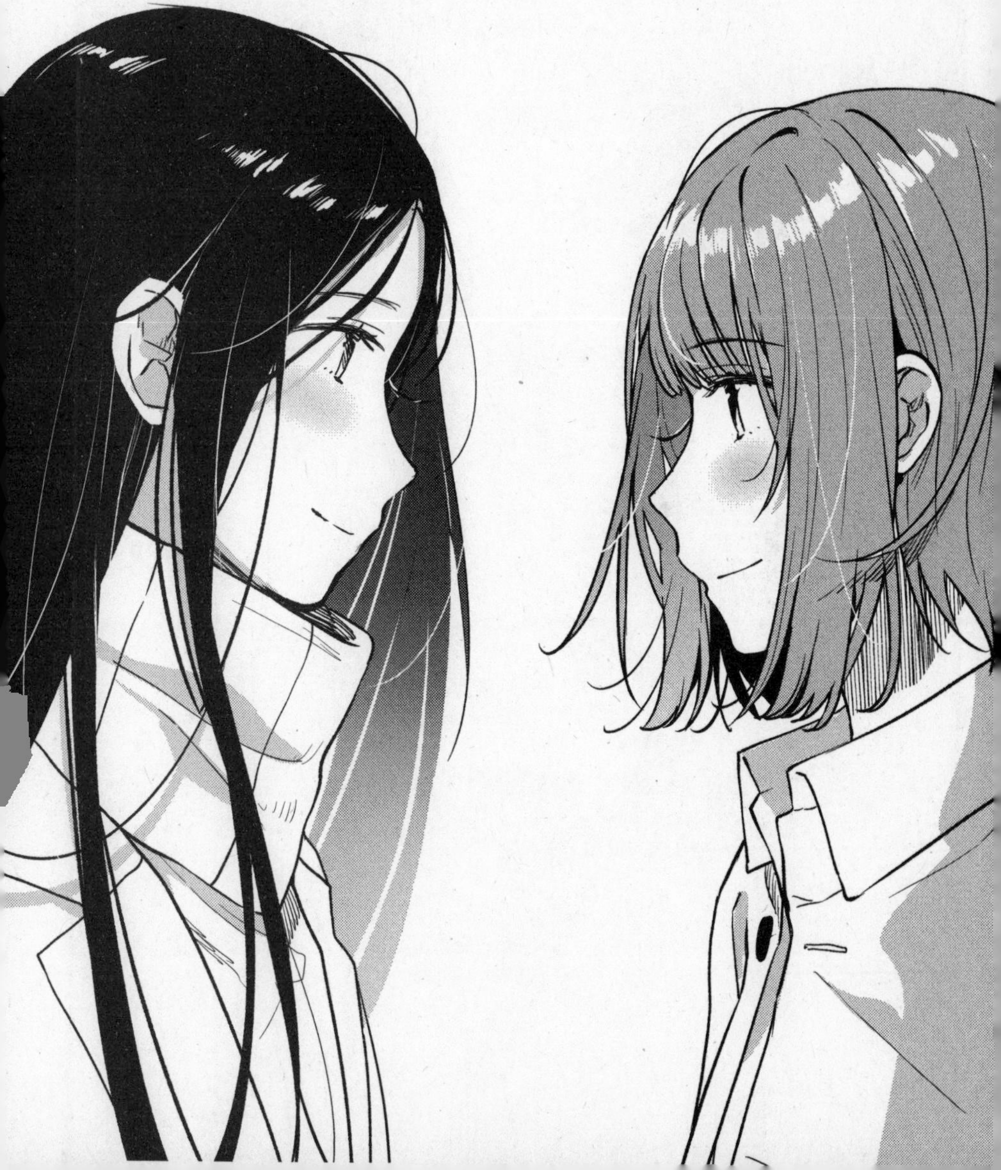

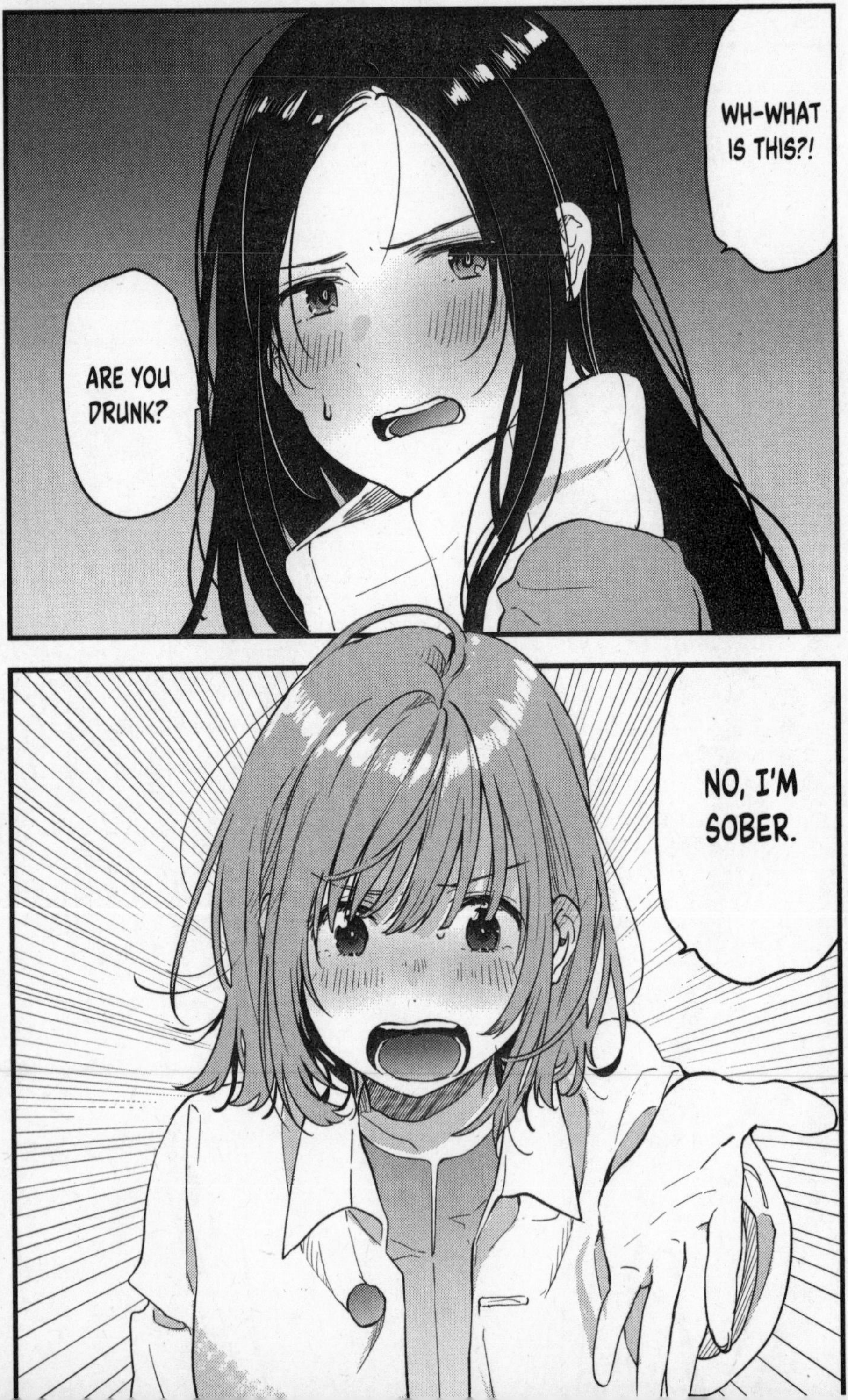
WH-WHAT IS THIS?!
ARE YOU DRUNK?
NO, I'M SOBER.

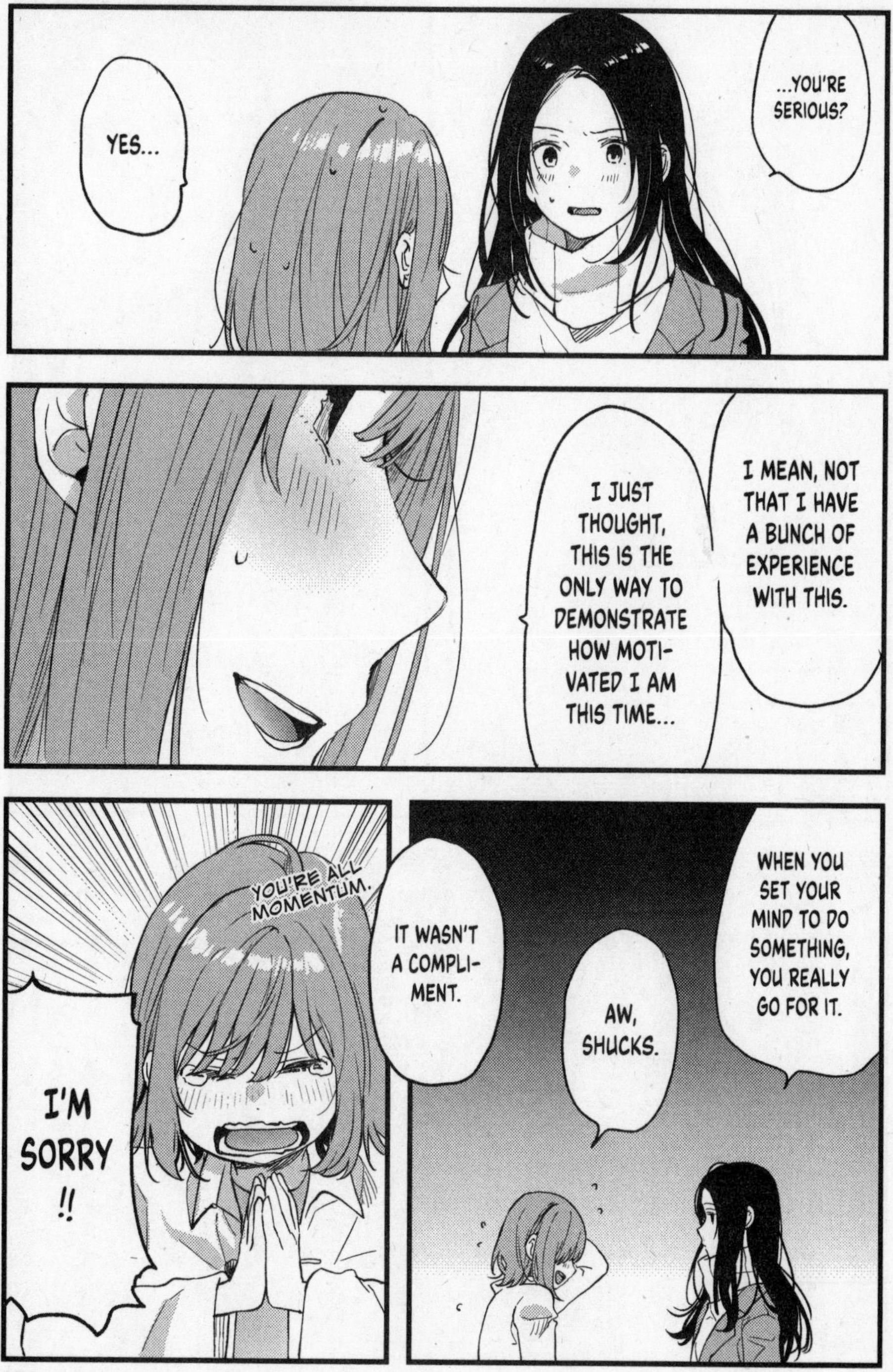
...YOU'RE SERIOUS?
YES...
I MEAN, NOT THAT I HAVE A BUNCH OF EXPERIENCE WITH THIS.
I JUST THOUGHT, THIS IS THE ONLY WAY TO DEMONSTRATE HOW MOTI-VATED I AM THIS TIME...
WHEN YOU SET YOUR MIND TO DO SOMETHING, YOU REALLY GO FOR IT.
AW, SHUCKS.
IT WASN'T A COMPLI-MENT.
YOU'RE ALL MOMENTUM.
I'M SORRY !!

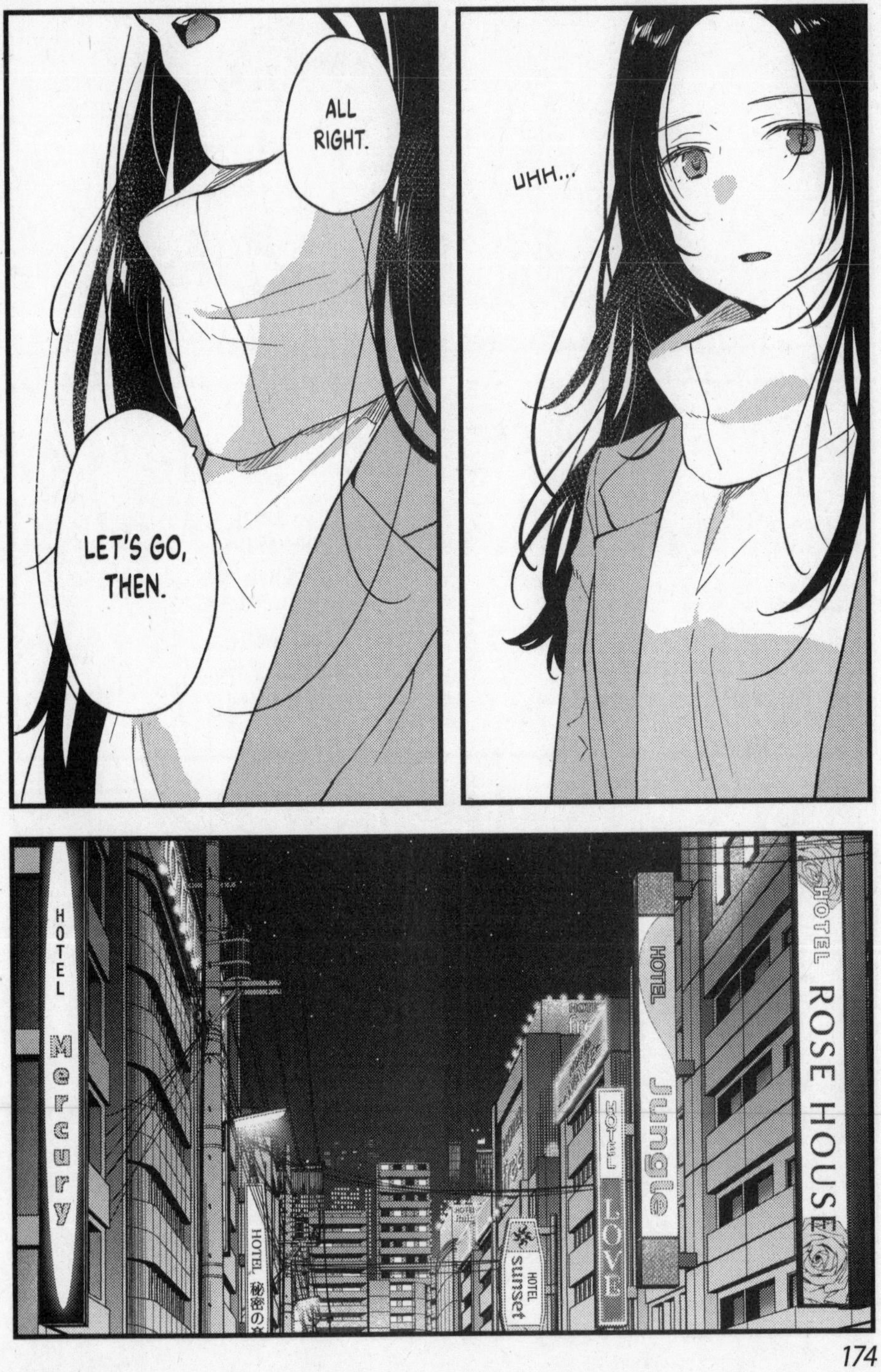
UHH...
ALL RIGHT.
LET'S GO, THEN.
HOTEL ROSE HOUSE
HOTEL Jungle
HOTEL LOVE
HOTEL sunset
HOTEL 秘密の
HOTEL Mercury

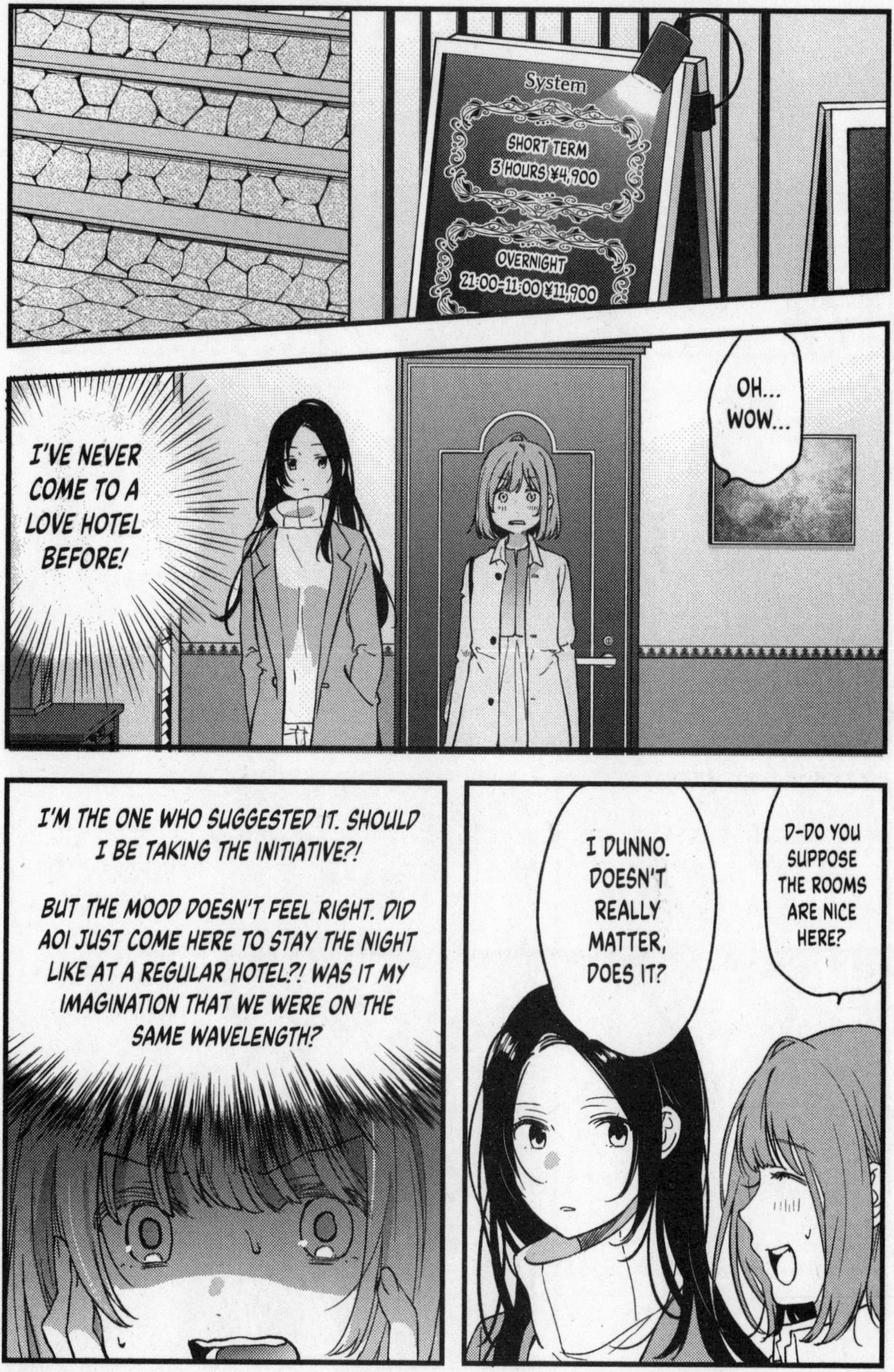
System
SHORT TERM
3 HOURS ¥4,900
OVERNIGHT
21:00-11:00 ¥11,900
OH... WOW...
I'VE NEVER COME TO A LOVE HOTEL BEFORE!
D-DO YOU SUPPOSE THE ROOMS ARE NICE HERE?
I DUNNO. DOESN'T REALLY MATTER, DOES IT?
I'M THE ONE WHO SUGGESTED IT. SHOULD I BE TAKING THE INITIATIVE?!
BUT THE MOOD DOESN'T FEEL RIGHT. DID AOI JUST COME HERE TO STAY THE NIGHT LIKE AT A REGULAR HOTEL?! WAS IT MY IMAGINATION THAT WE WERE ON THE SAME WAVELENGTH?

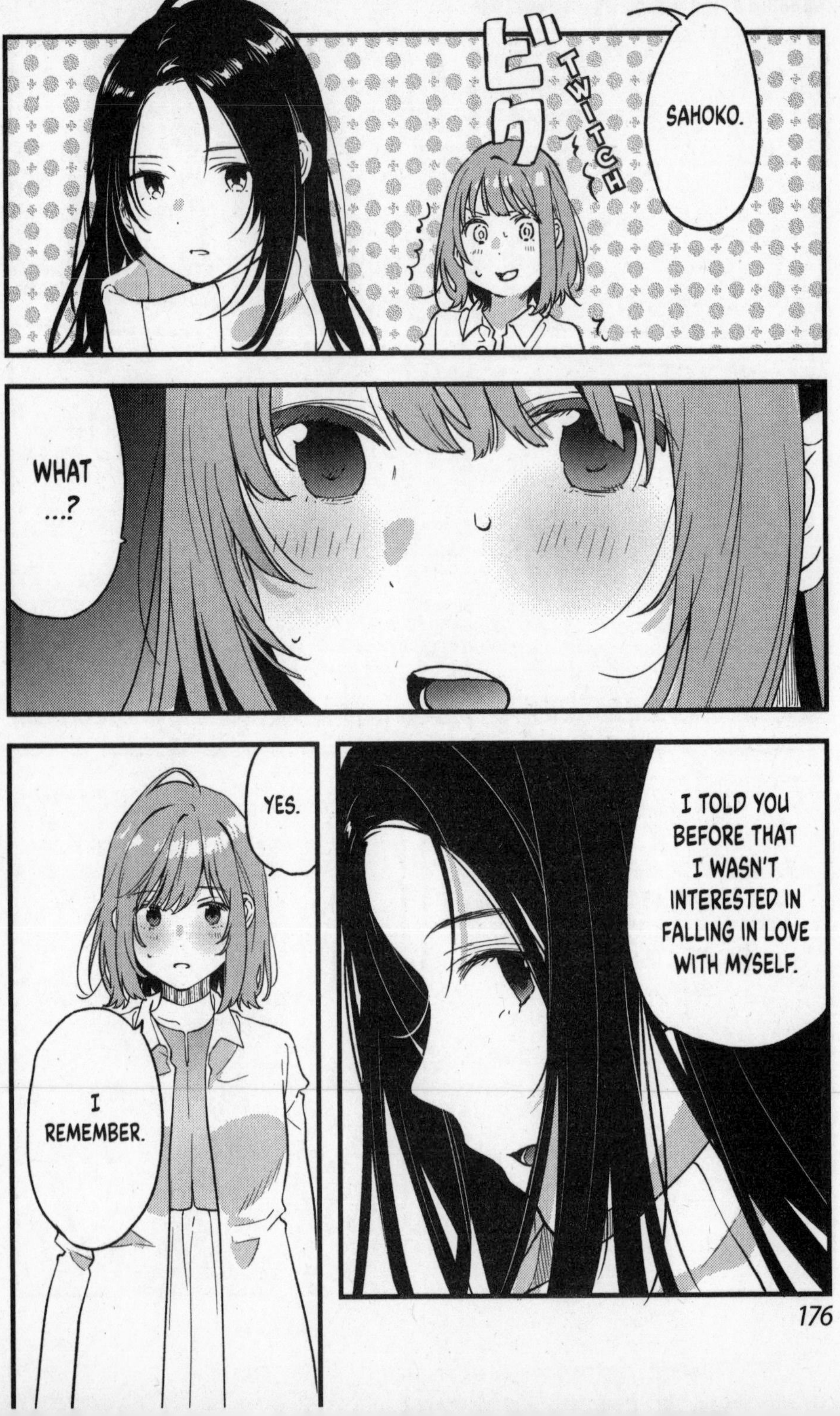
SAHOKO.
ビク
TWITCH
WHAT ...?
I TOLD YOU BEFORE THAT I WASN'T INTERESTED IN FALLING IN LOVE WITH MYSELF.
YES.
I REMEMBER.

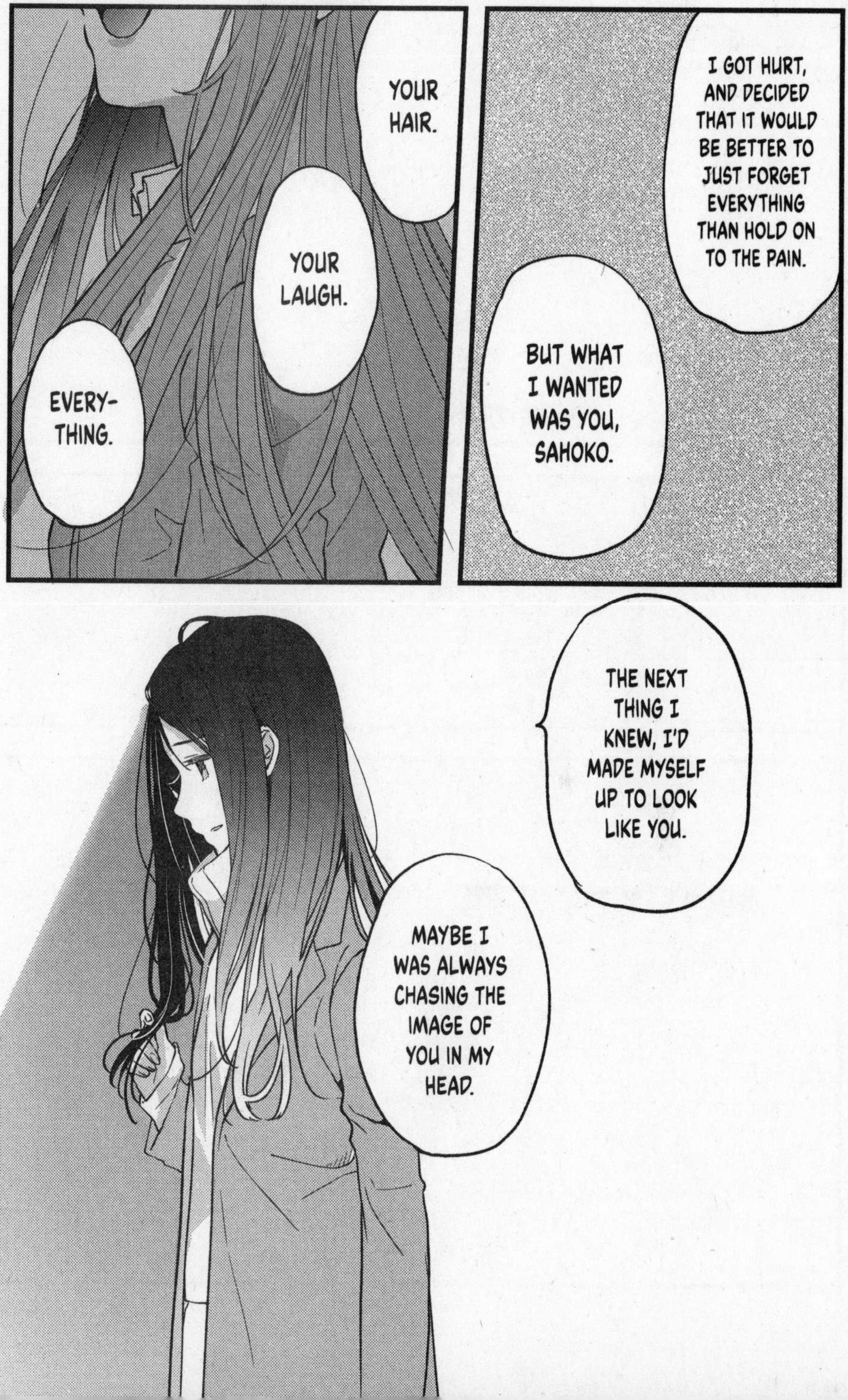
I GOT HURT, AND DECIDED THAT IT WOULD BE BETTER TO JUST FORGET EVERYTHING THAN HOLD ON TO THE PAIN.
BUT WHAT I WANTED WAS YOU, SAHOKO.
YOUR HAIR.
YOUR LAUGH.
EVERY-THING.
THE NEXT THING I KNEW, I'D MADE MYSELF UP TO LOOK LIKE YOU.
MAYBE I WAS ALWAYS CHASING THE IMAGE OF YOU IN MY HEAD.

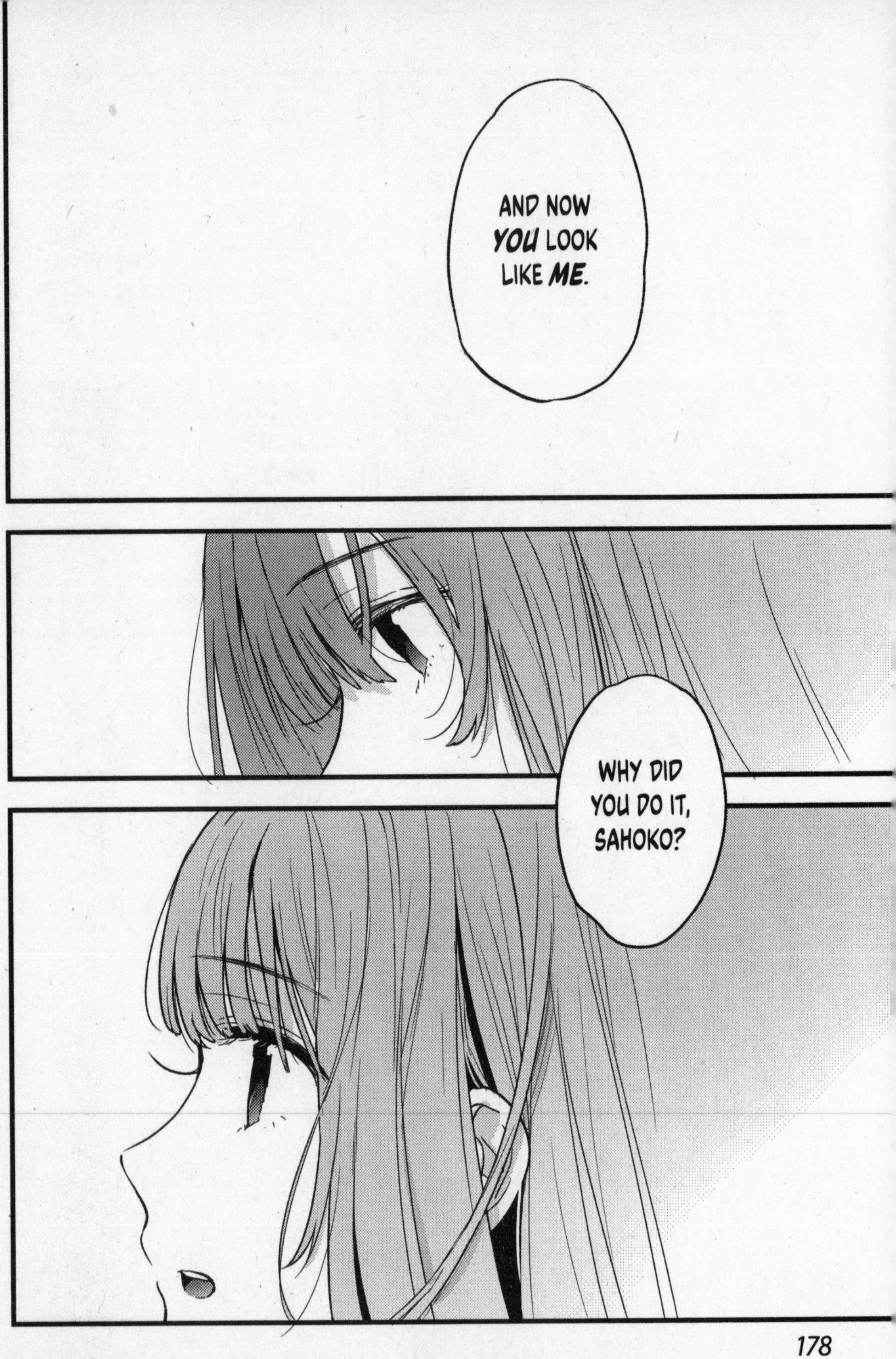
AND NOW YOU LOOK LIKE ME.
WHY DID YOU DO IT, SAHOKO?

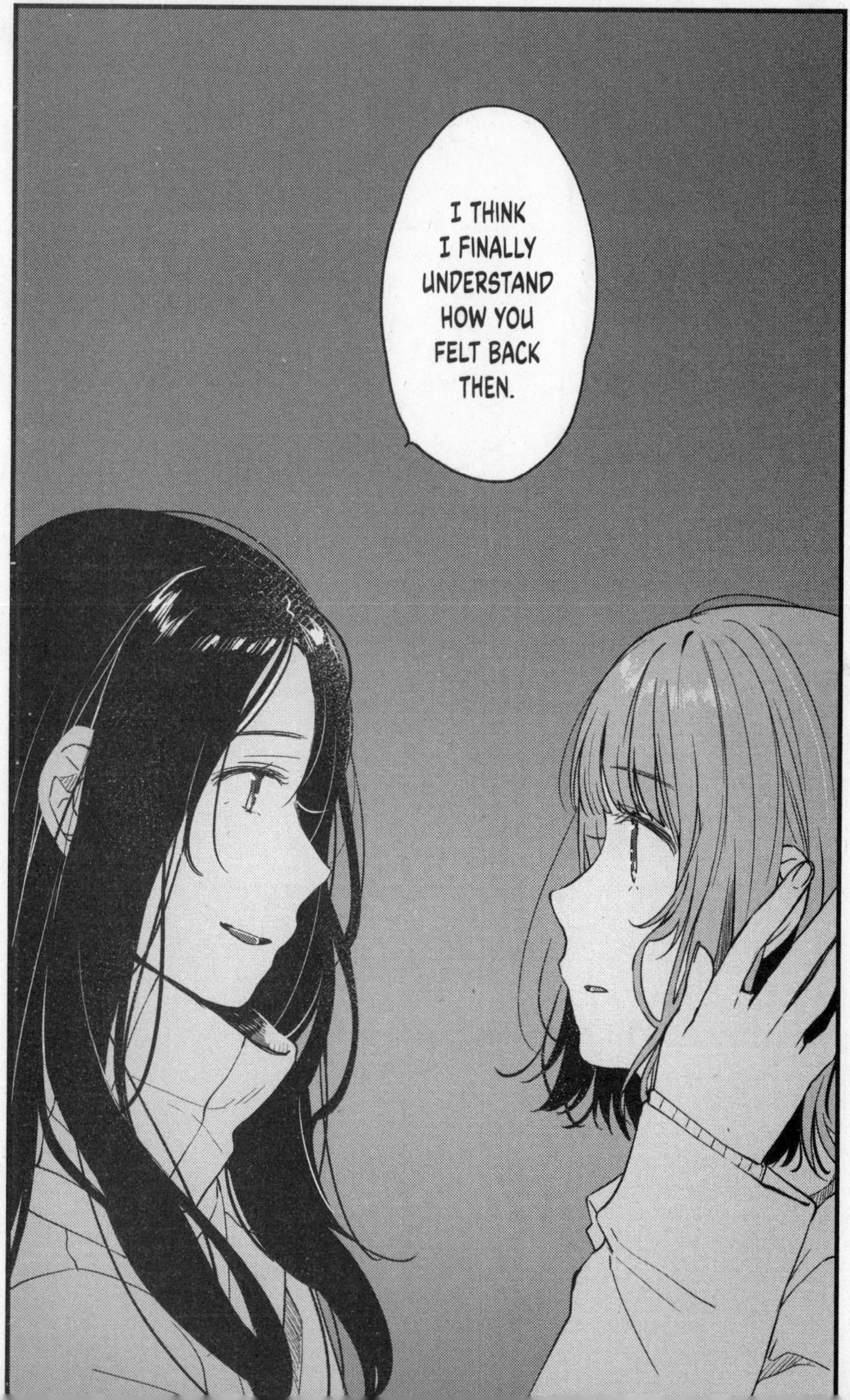
I THINK I FINALLY UNDERSTAND HOW YOU FELT BACK THEN.

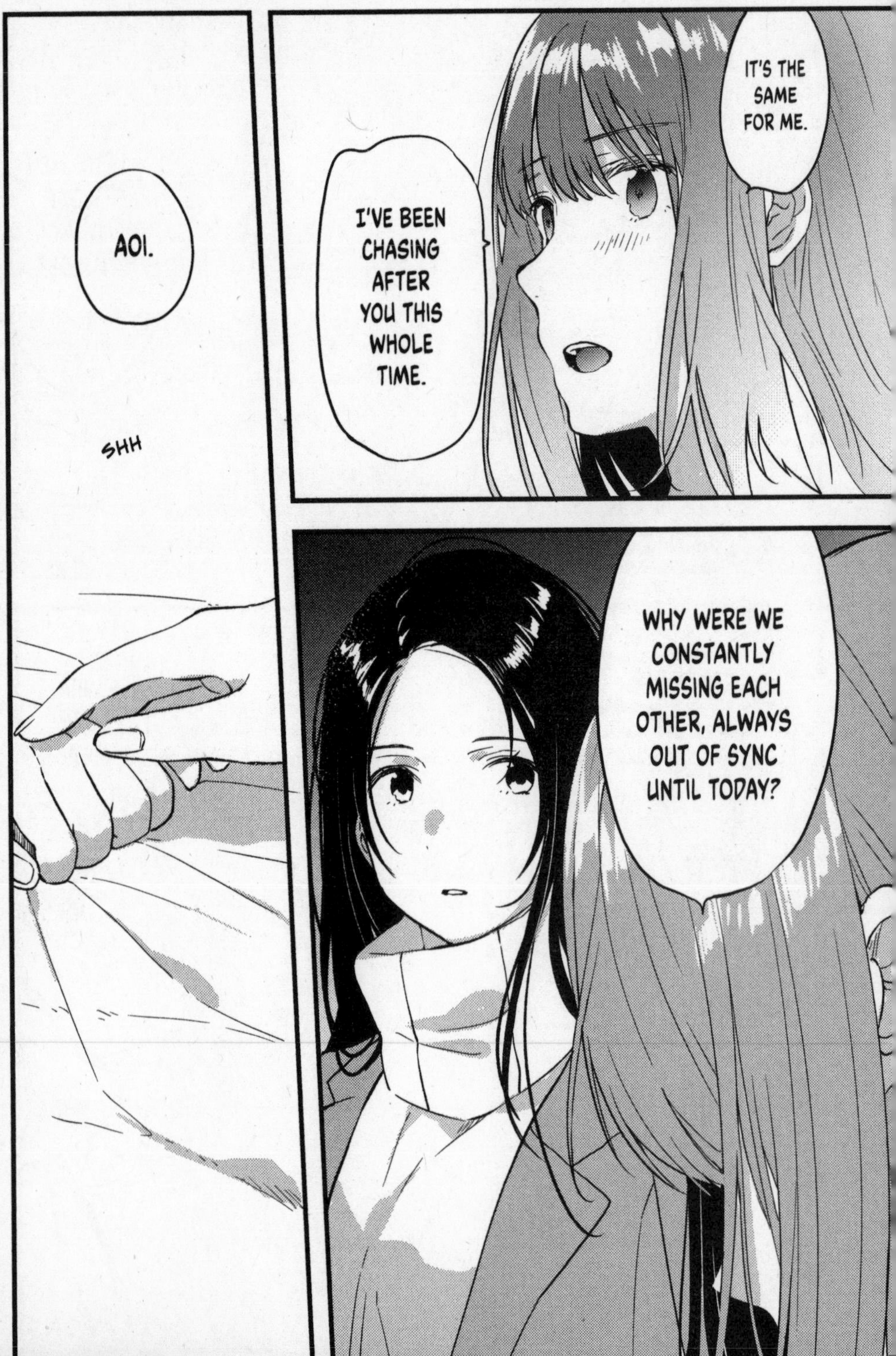
IT'S THE SAME FOR ME.
I'VE BEEN CHASING AFTER YOU THIS WHOLE TIME.
WHY WERE WE CONSTANTLY MISSING EACH OTHER, ALWAYS OUT OF SYNC UNTIL TODAY?
AOI.
SHH

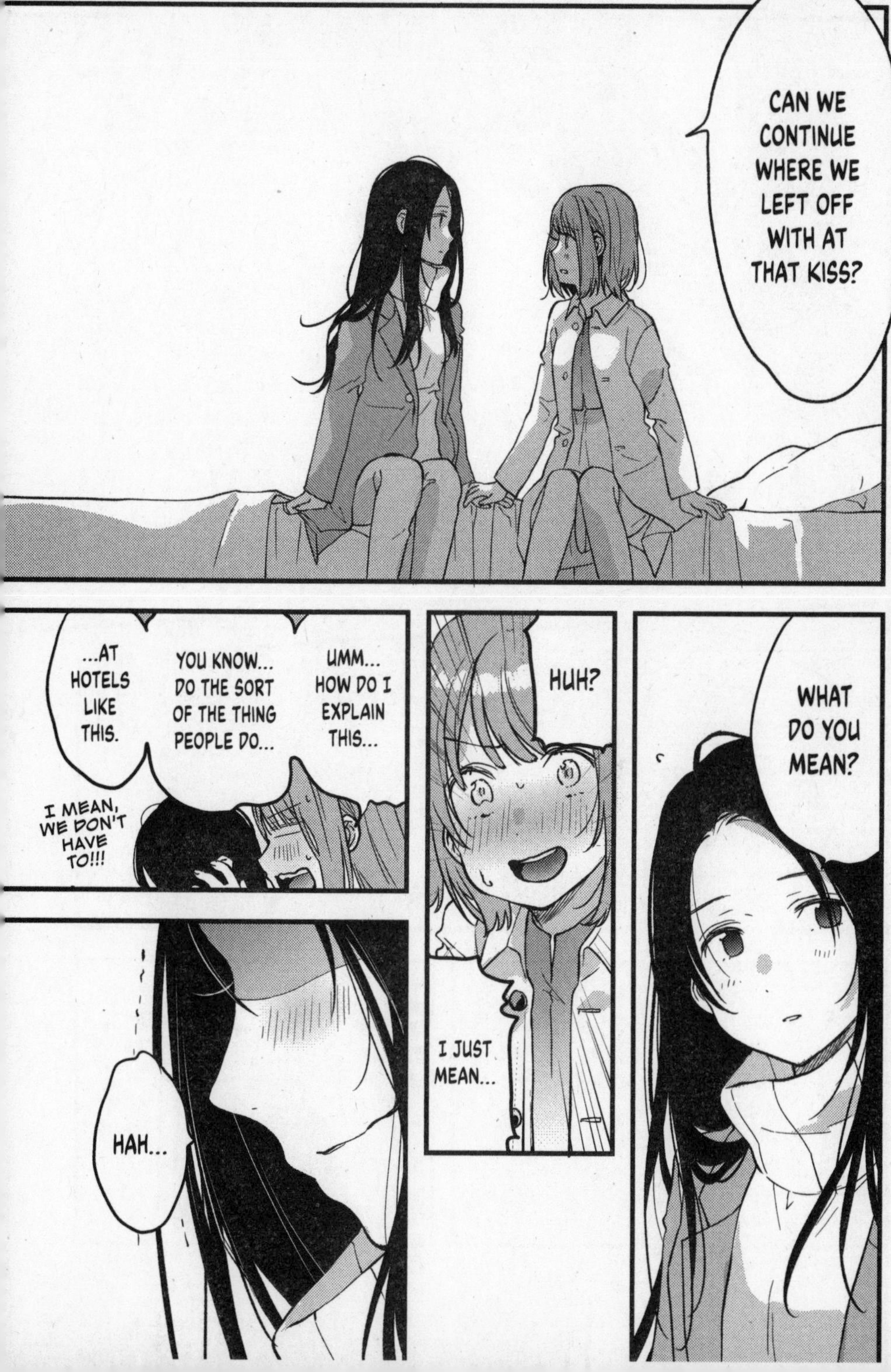
CAN WE CONTINUE WHERE WE LEFT OFF WITH AT THAT KISS?
WHAT DO YOU MEAN?
HUH?
I JUST MEAN...
UMM... HOW DO I EXPLAIN THIS...
YOU KNOW... DO THE SORT OF THE THING PEOPLE DO...
...AT HOTELS LIKE THIS.
I MEAN, WE DON'T HAVE TO!!!
HAH...

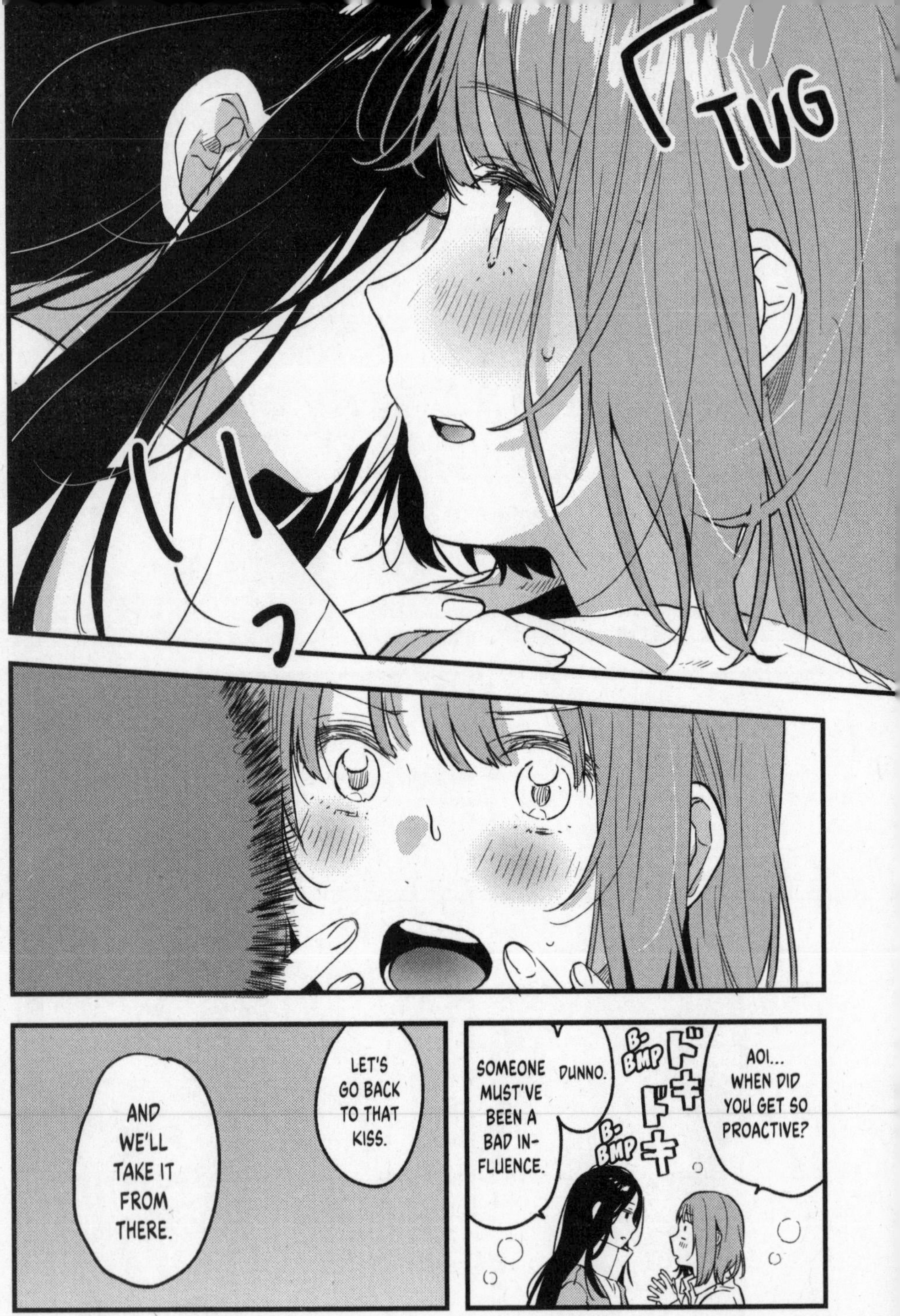
TUG
AOI... WHEN DID YOU GET SO PROACTIVE?
B-BMP ドキ
B-BMP ドキ
DUNNO.
SOMEONE MUST'VE BEEN A BAD IN-FLUENCE.
LET'S GO BACK TO THAT KISS.
AND WE'LL TAKE IT FROM THERE.

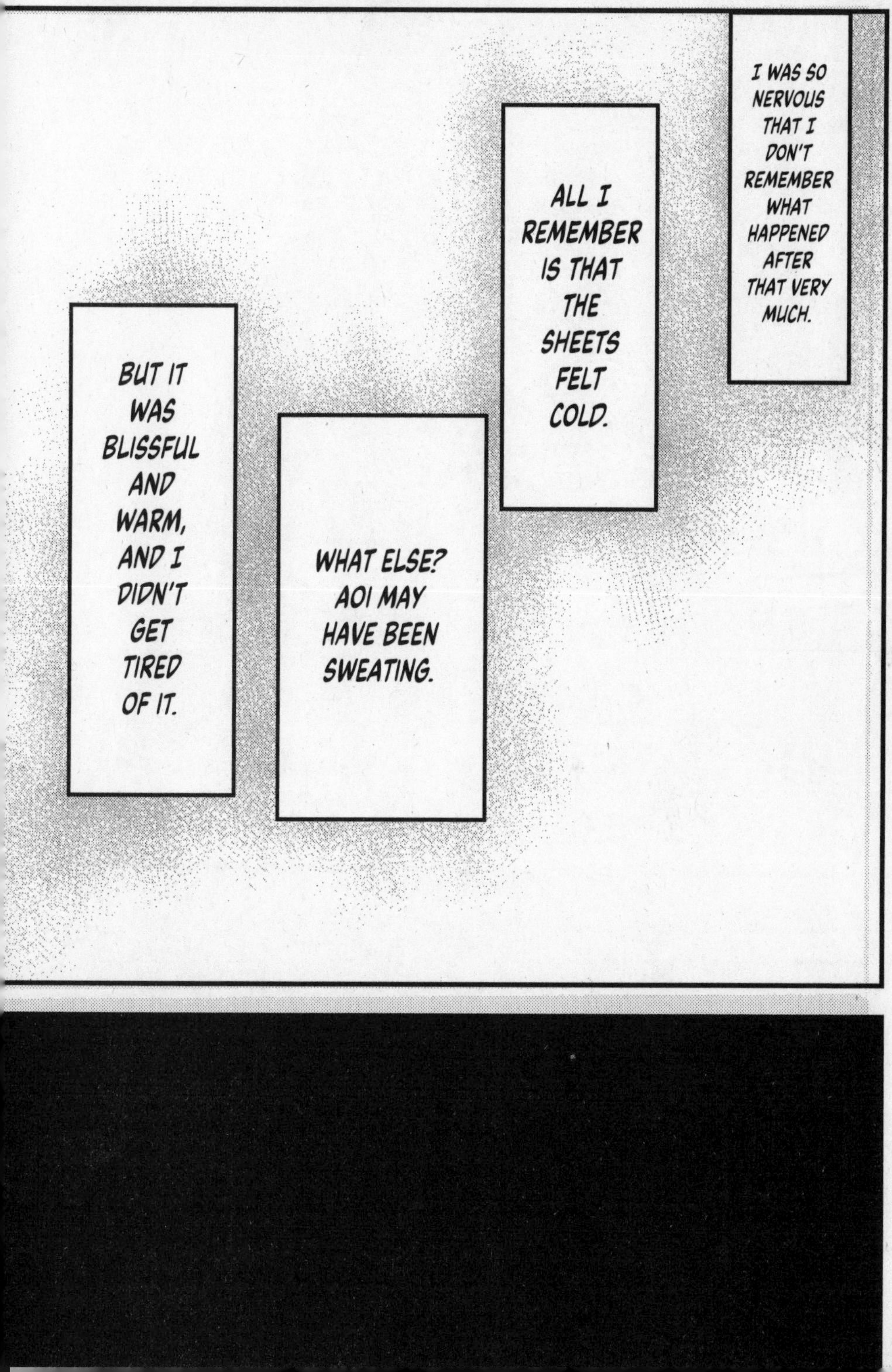
I WAS SO NERVOUS THAT I DON'T REMEMBER WHAT HAPPENED AFTER THAT VERY MUCH.
ALL I REMEMBER IS THAT THE SHEETS FELT COLD.
WHAT ELSE? AOI MAY HAVE BEEN SWEATING.
BUT IT WAS BLISSFUL AND WARM, AND I DIDN'T GET TIRED OF IT.

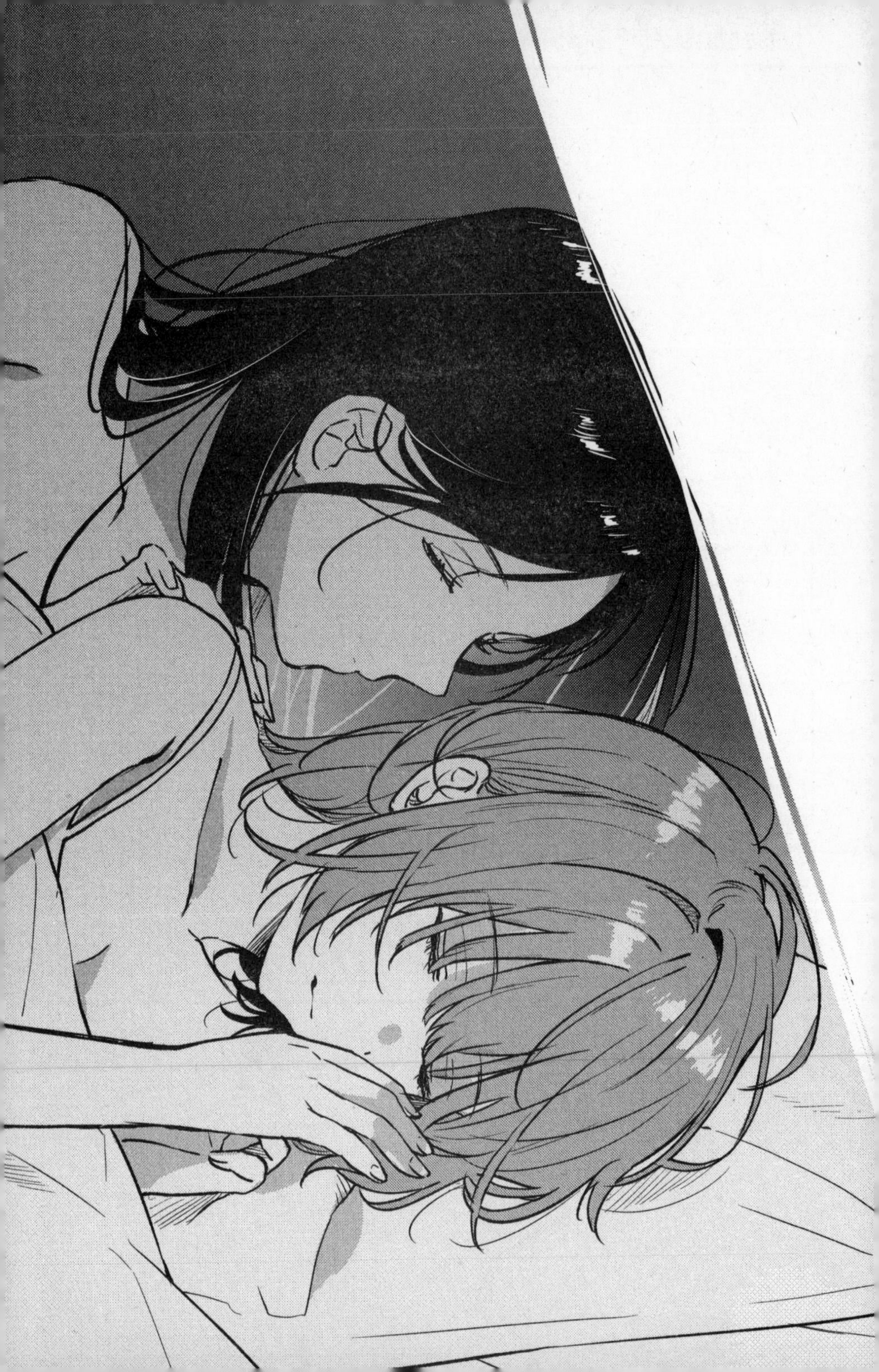

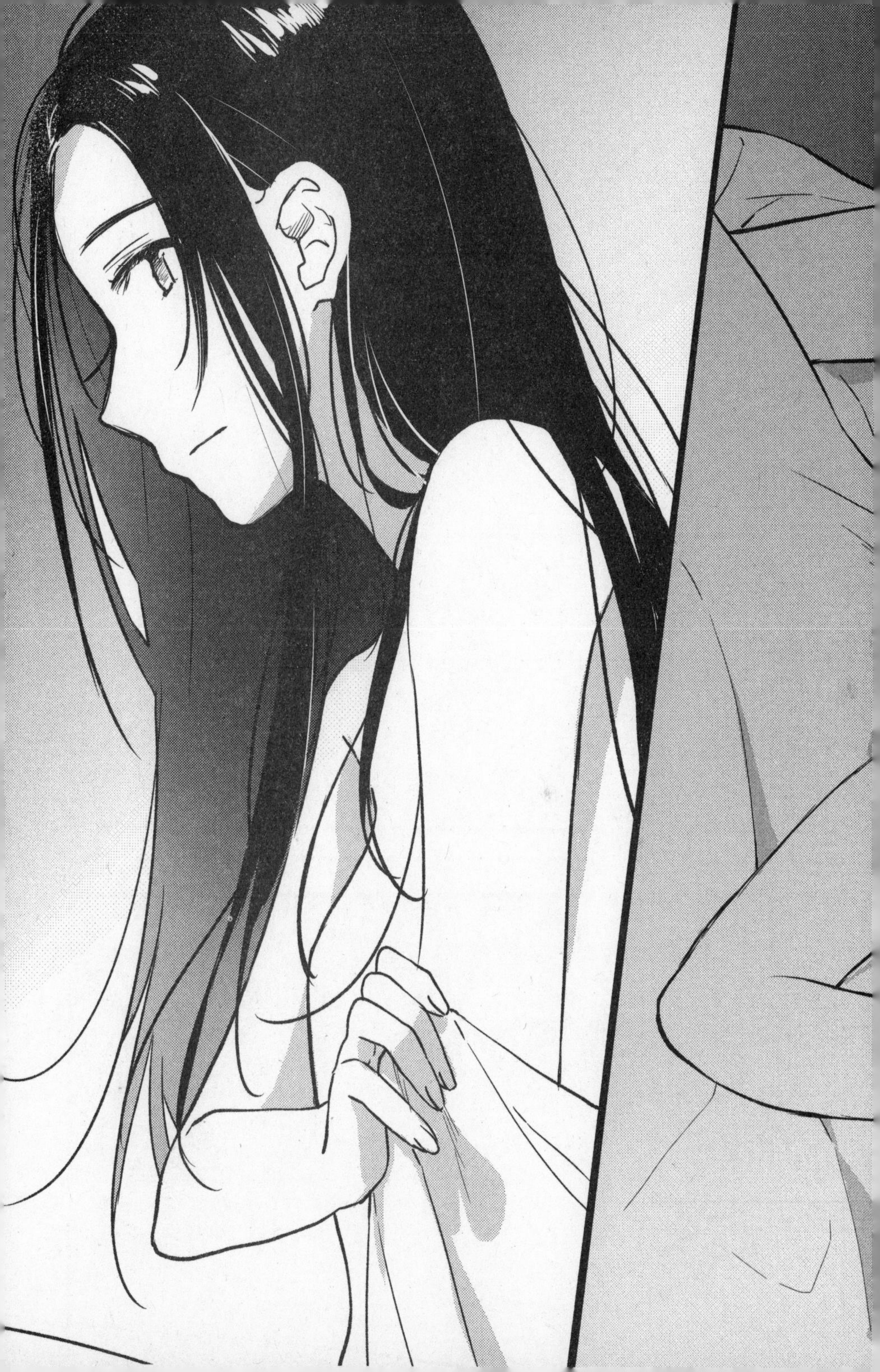

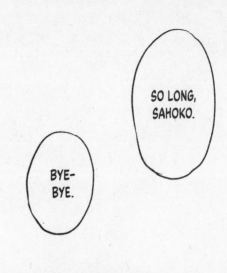

SO LONG, SAHOKO.

BYE-BYE.

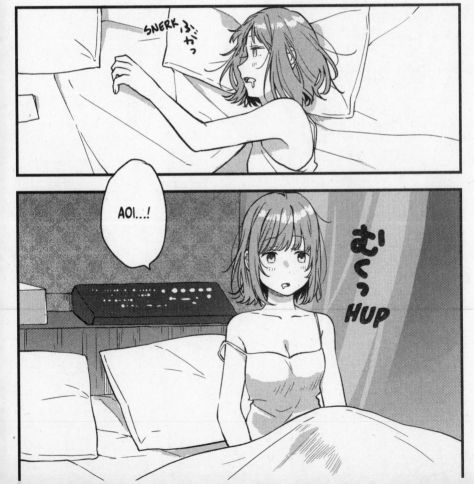

SNERK

AOI...!

HUP

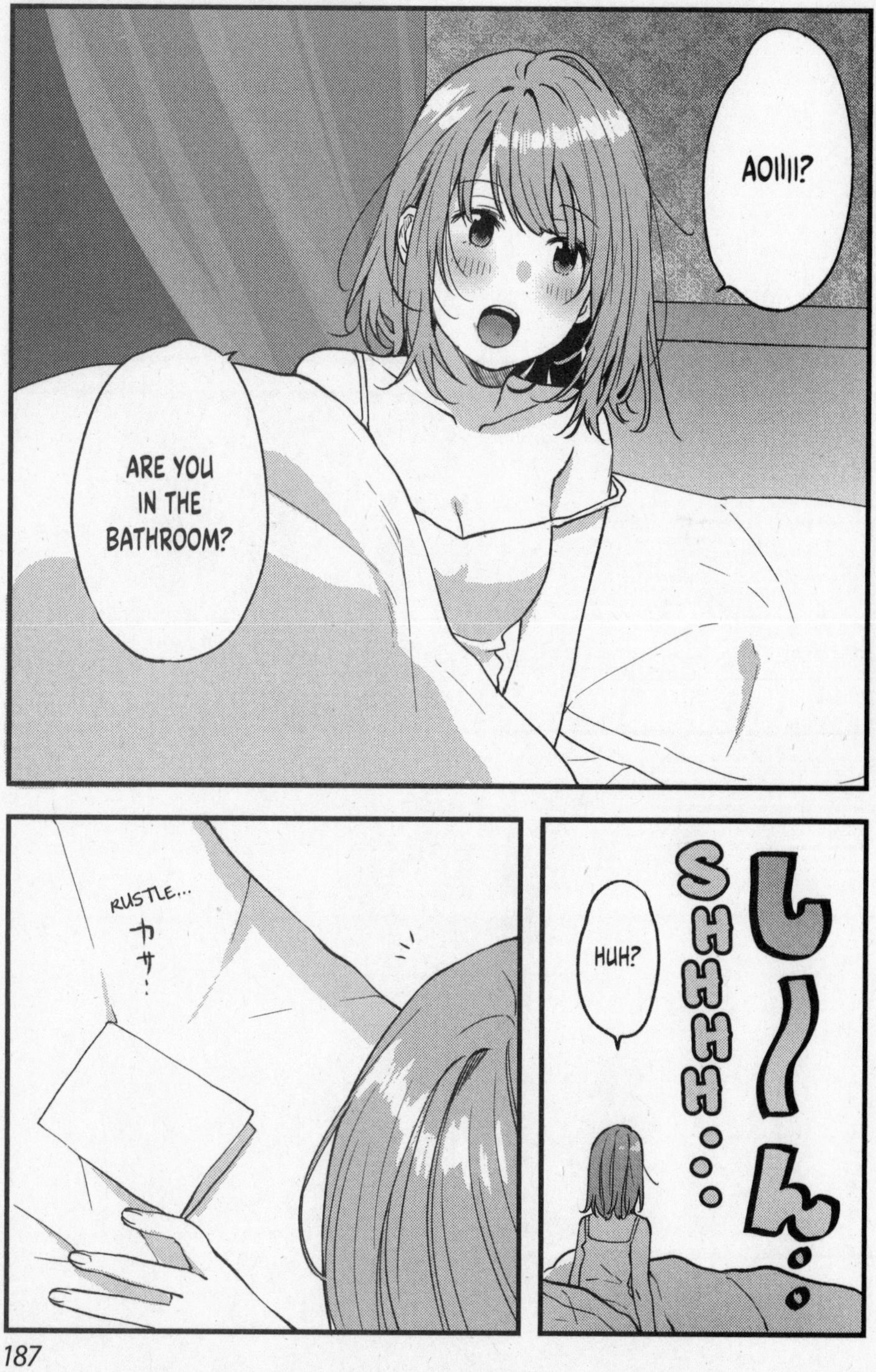
AOIIII?
ARE YOU IN THE BATHROOM?
しーん…
SHHHH...
HUH?
RUSTLE...
カサ

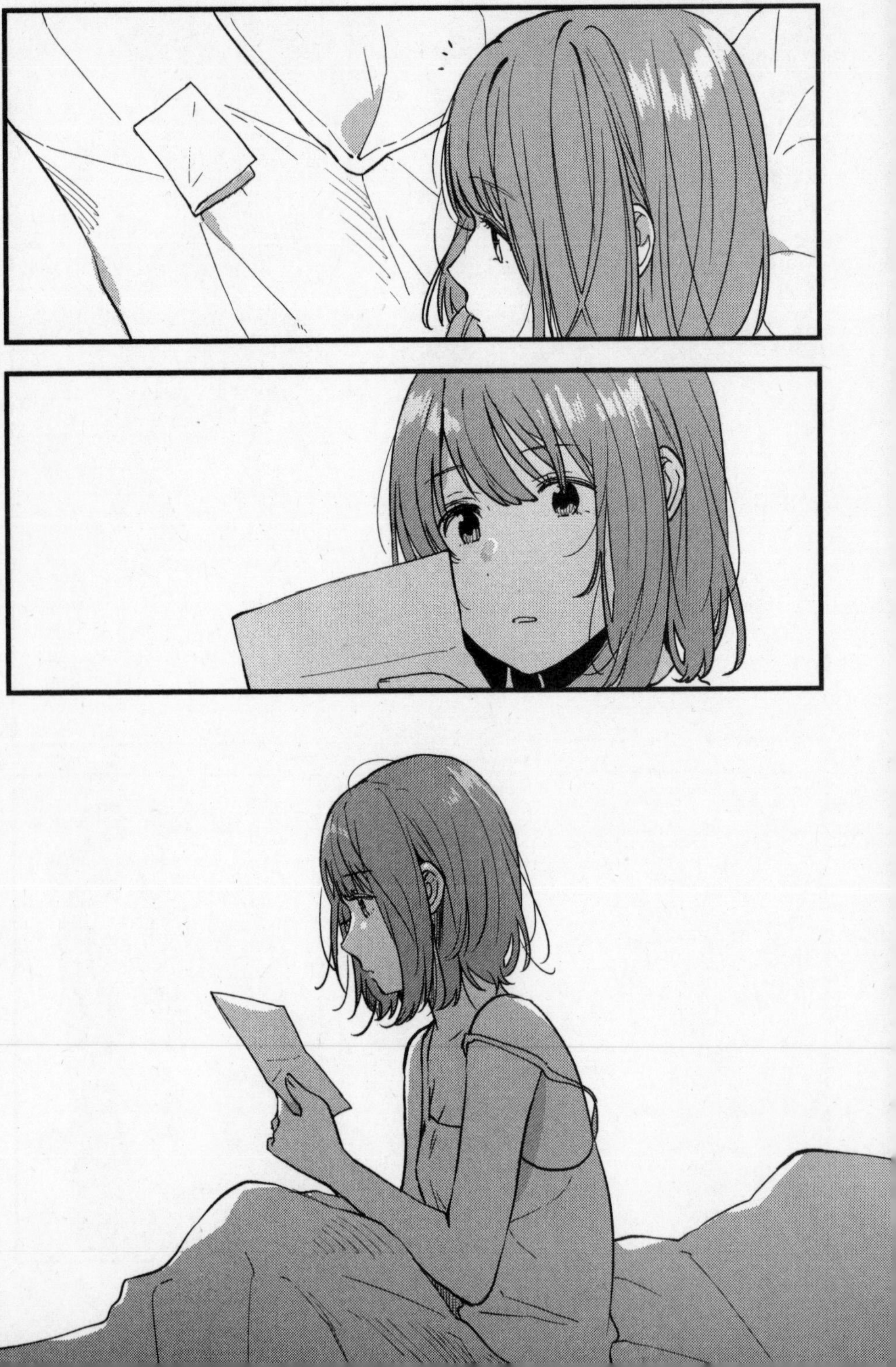

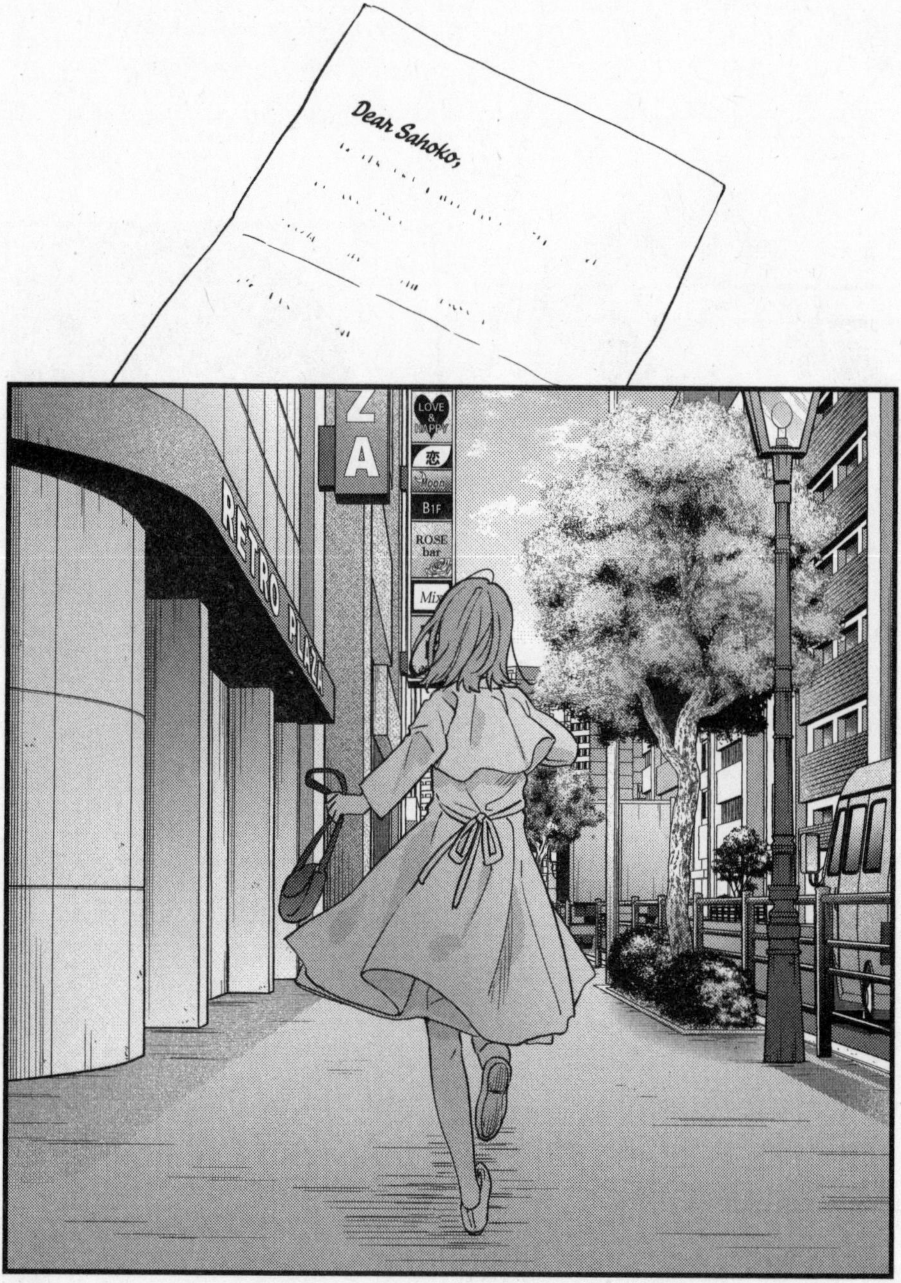
Dear Sahoko,
RETRO PLAZA
ZA
LOVE & HAPPY
恋
Moon
B1F
ROSE bar
Mix

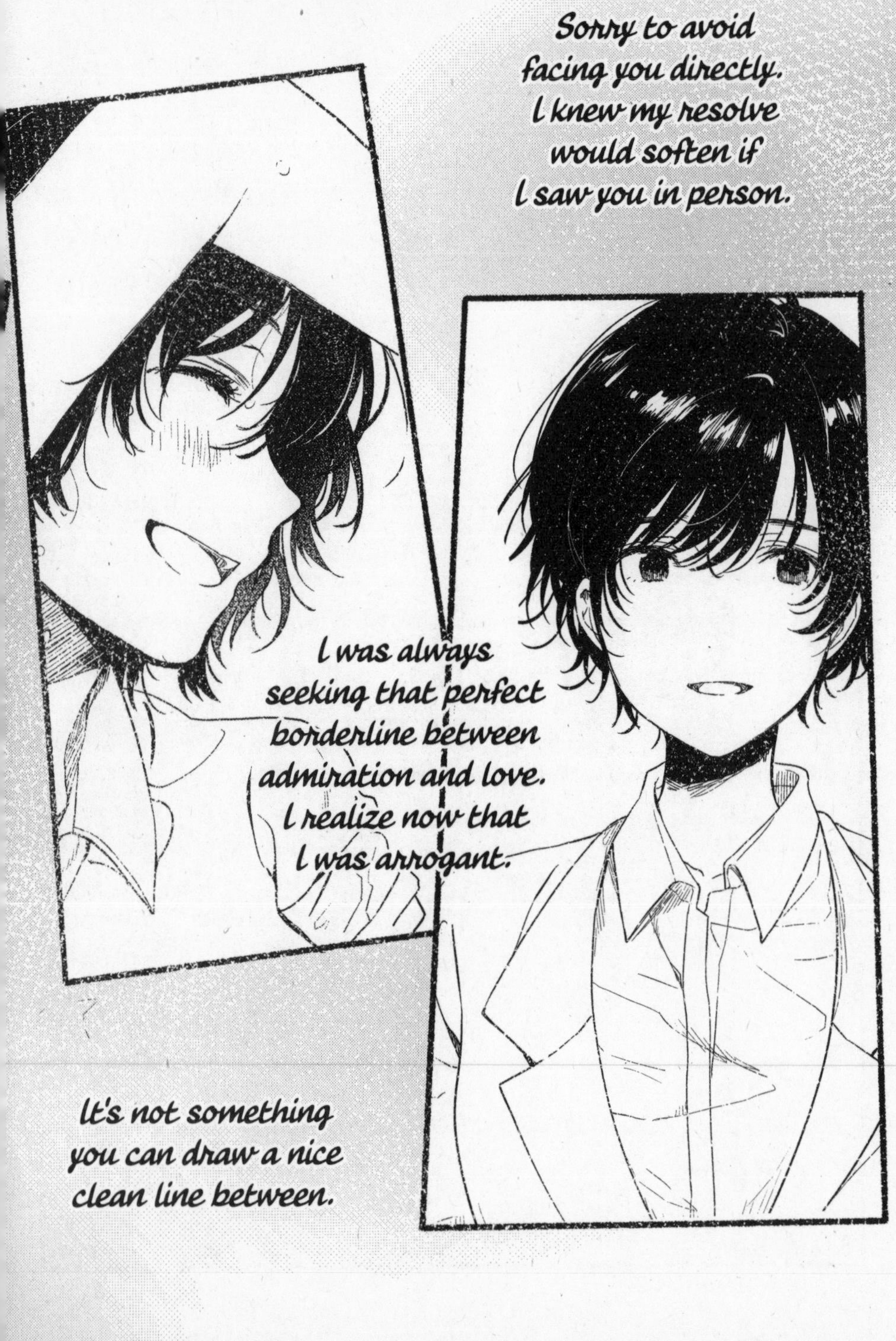
Sorry to avoid facing you directly. I knew my resolve would soften if I saw you in person.
I was always seeking that perfect borderline between admiration and love. I realize now that I was arrogant.
It's not something you can draw a nice clean line between.

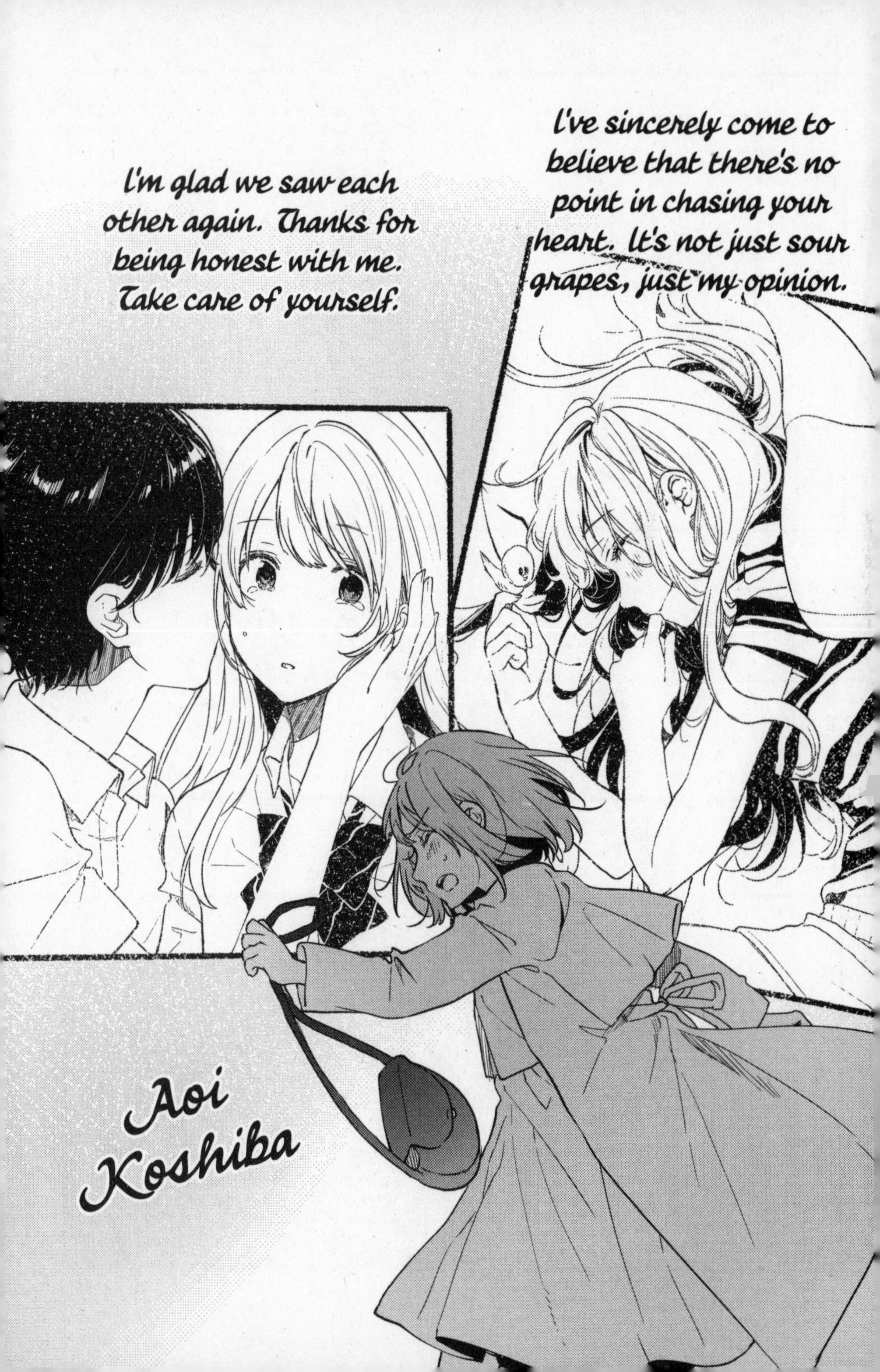
I've sincerely come to believe that there's no point in chasing your heart. It's not just sour grapes, just my opinion.
I'm glad we saw each other again. Thanks for being honest with me. Take care of yourself.
Aoi Koshiba

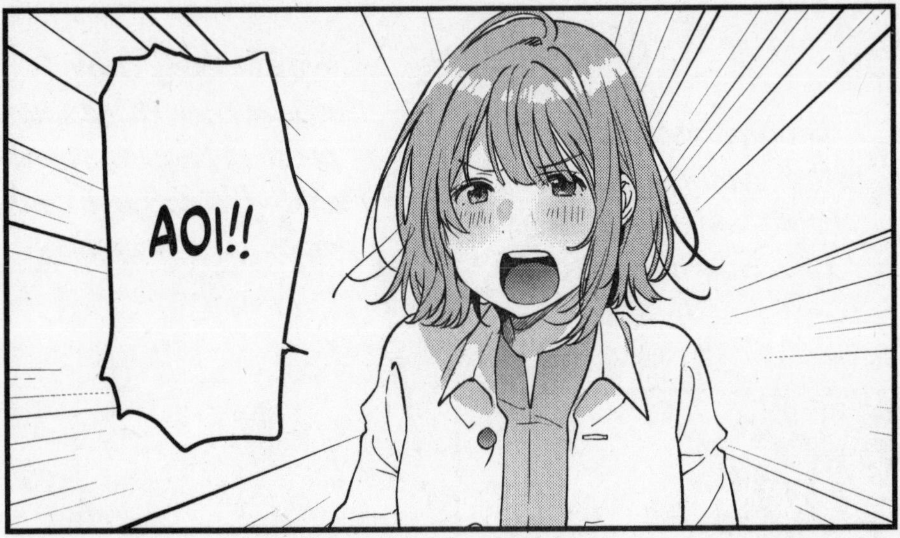
AOI!!

WHAT AM I SUPPOSED TO SAY IN A
SITUATION LIKE THIS?

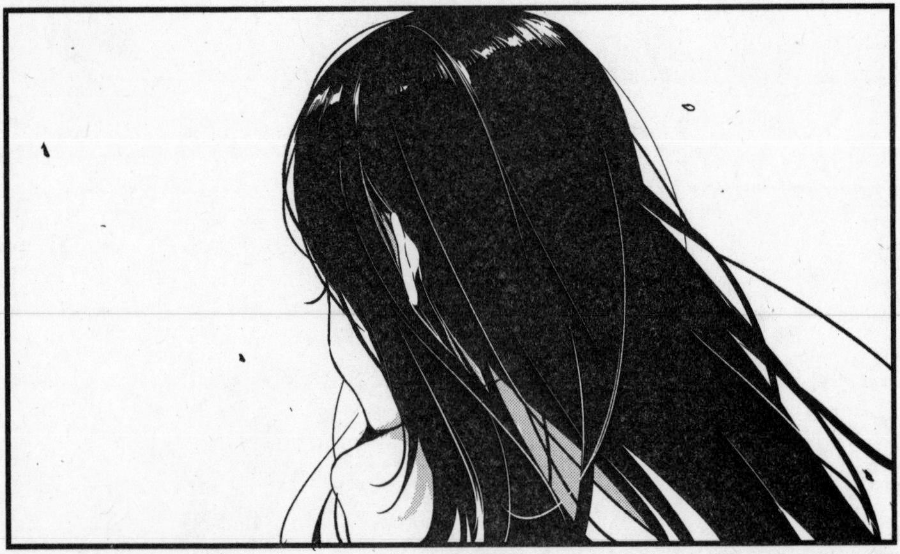

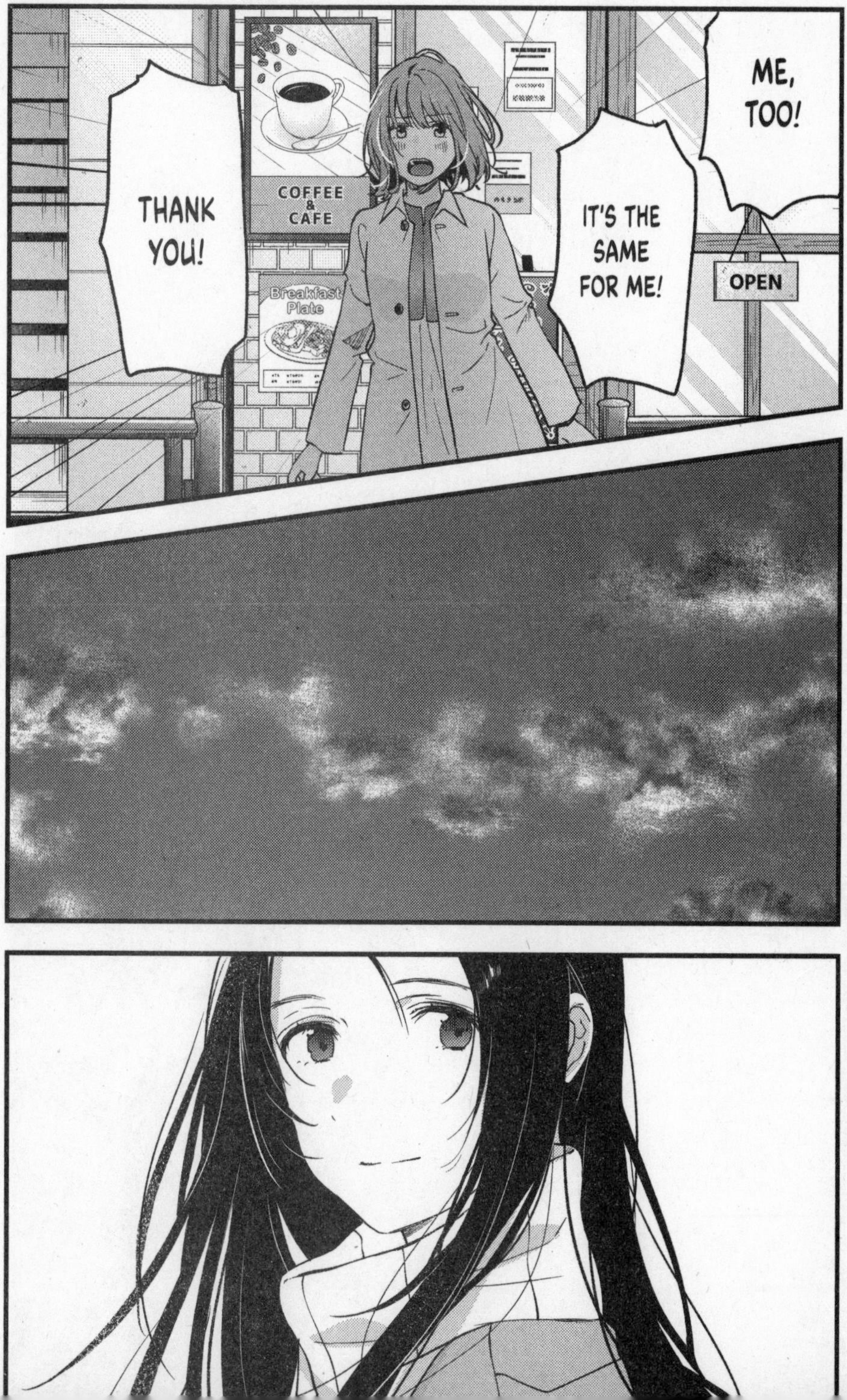
ME, TOO!
OPEN
IT'S THE SAME FOR ME!
COFFEE & CAFE
Breakfast Plate
THANK YOU!

THAT WAS IT.
THAT WAS EVERYTHING.

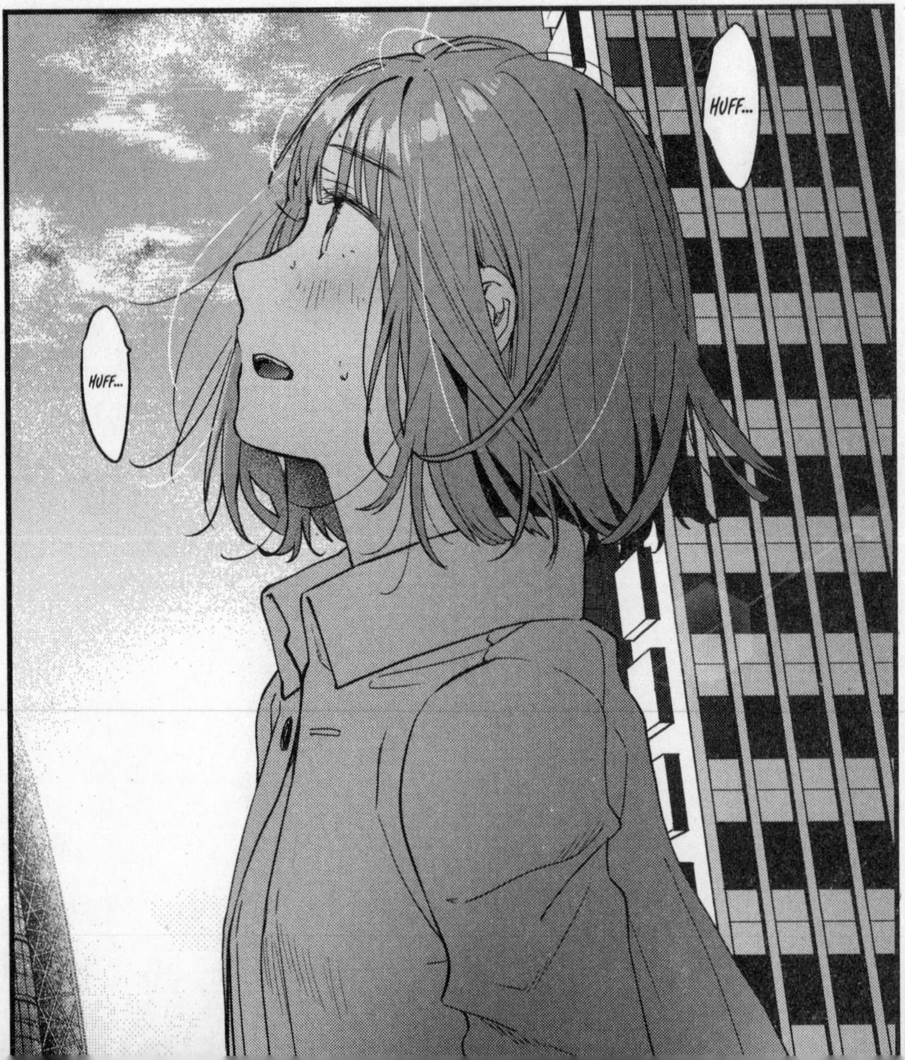
HUFF...
HUFF...

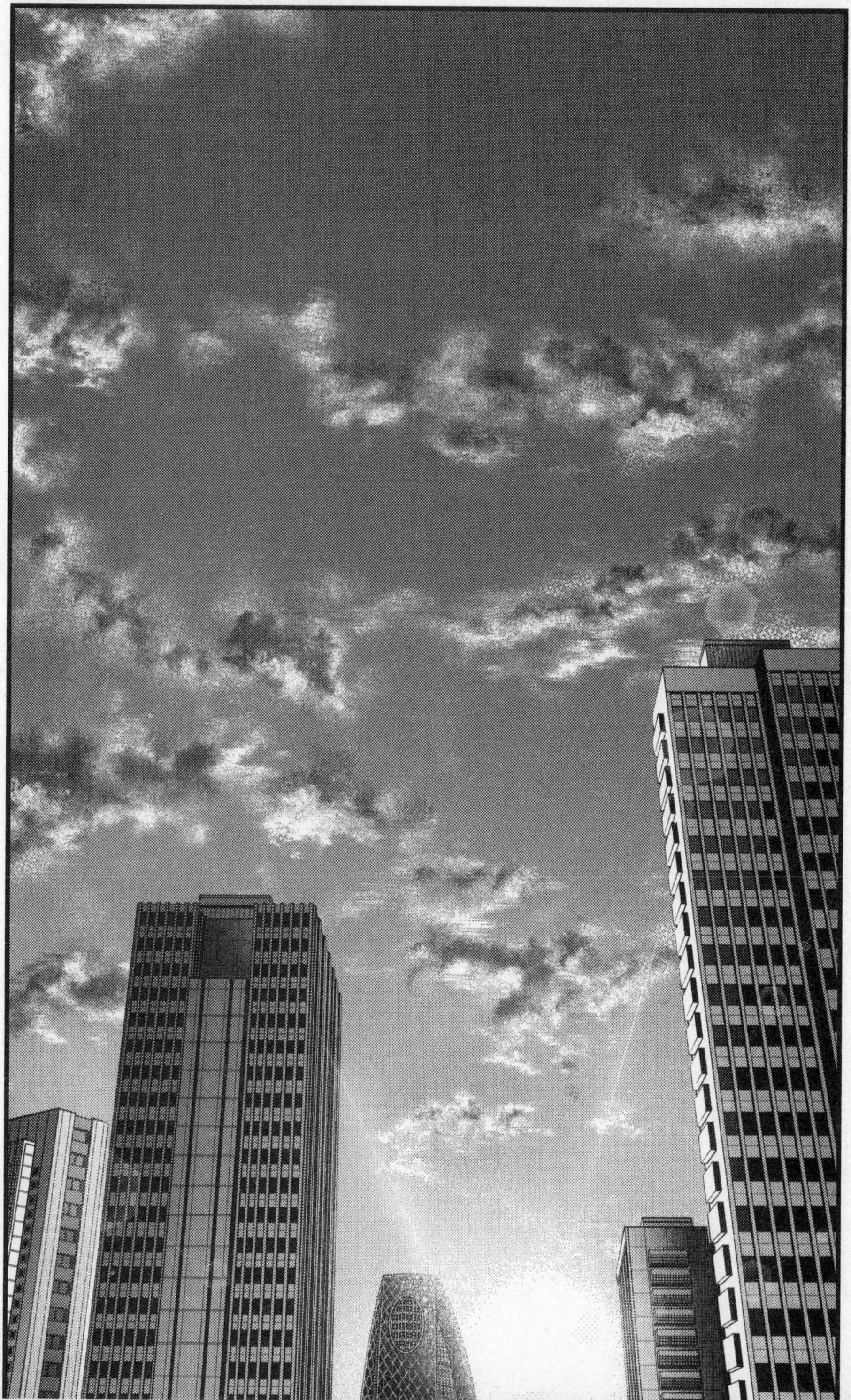

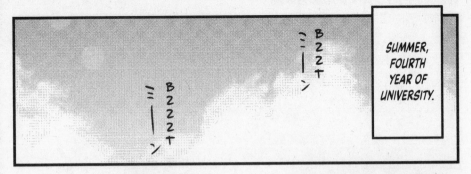

SUMMER, FOURTH YEAR OF UNIVERSITY.

GONNA BE ANOTHER HOT ONE...

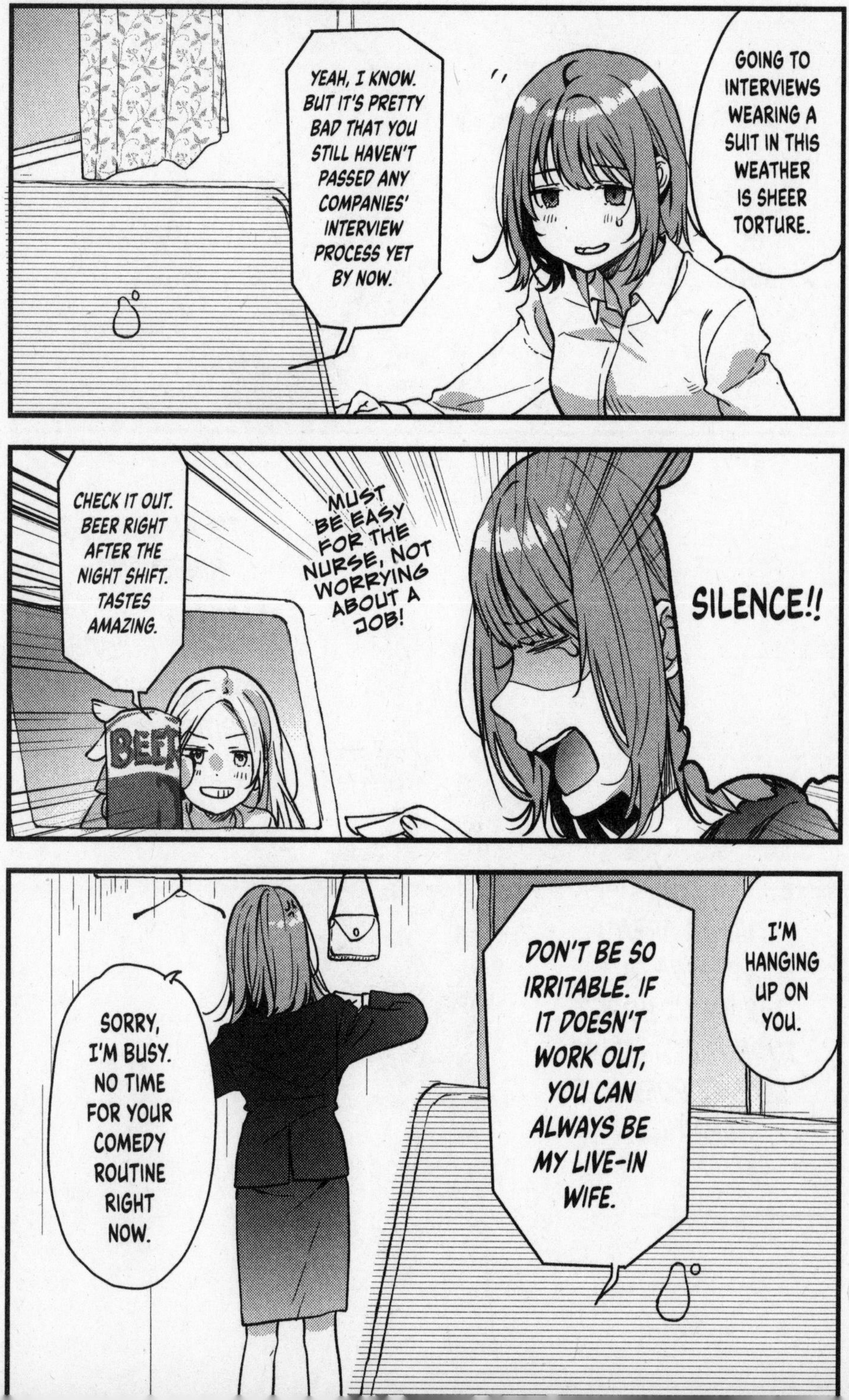
GOING TO INTERVIEWS WEARING A SUIT IN THIS WEATHER IS SHEER TORTURE.
YEAH, I KNOW. BUT IT'S PRETTY BAD THAT YOU STILL HAVEN'T PASSED ANY COMPANIES' INTERVIEW PROCESS YET BY NOW.
SILENCE!!
MUST BE EASY FOR THE NURSE, NOT WORRYING ABOUT A JOB!
CHECK IT OUT. BEER RIGHT AFTER THE NIGHT SHIFT. TASTES AMAZING.
BEER
I'M HANGING UP ON YOU.
DON'T BE SO IRRITABLE. IF IT DOESN'T WORK OUT, YOU CAN ALWAYS BE MY LIVE-IN WIFE.
SORRY, I'M BUSY. NO TIME FOR YOUR COMEDY ROUTINE RIGHT NOW.

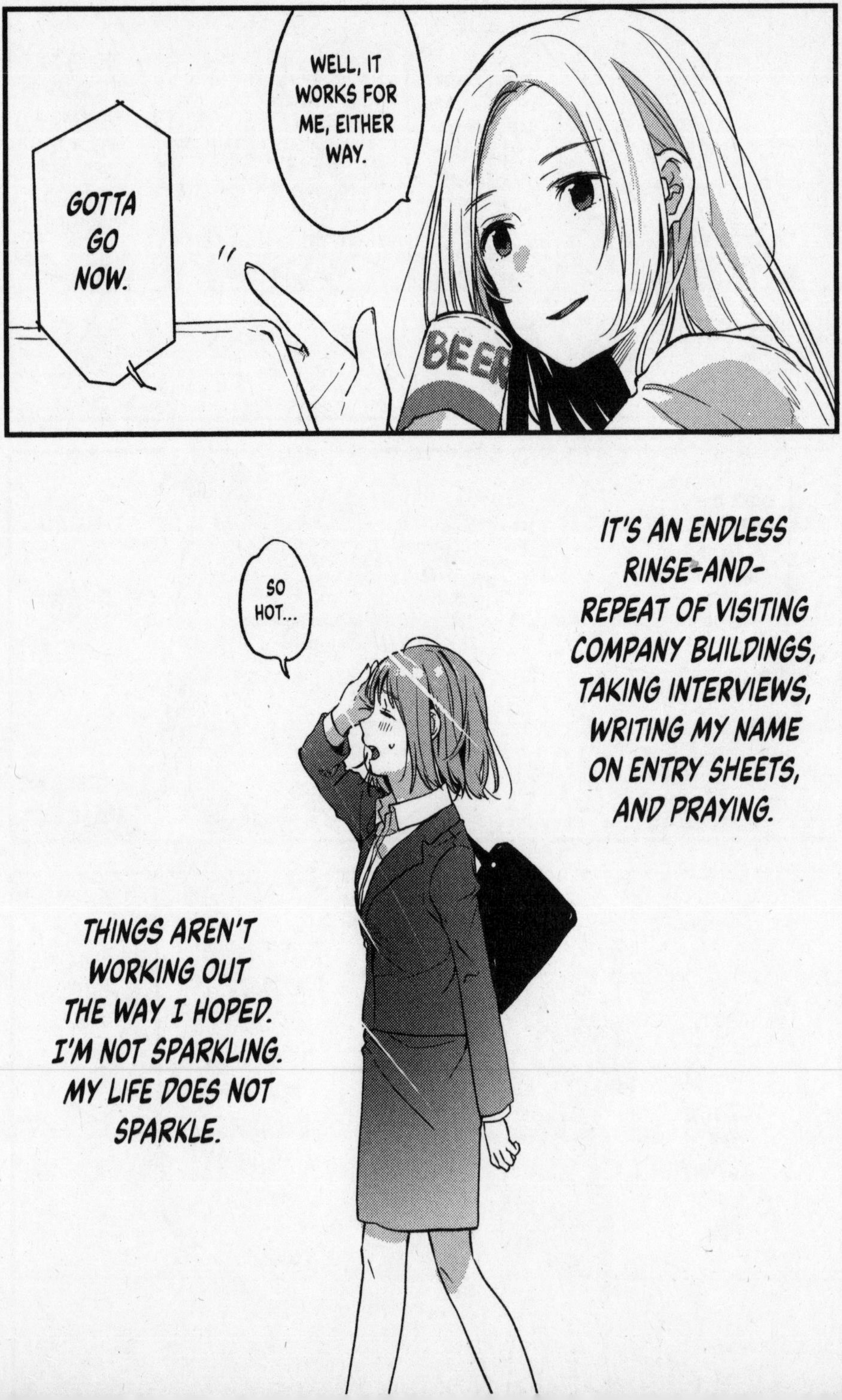
WELL, IT WORKS FOR ME, EITHER WAY.
GOTTA GO NOW.
IT'S AN ENDLESS RINSE-AND-REPEAT OF VISITING COMPANY BUILDINGS, TAKING INTERVIEWS, WRITING MY NAME ON ENTRY SHEETS, AND PRAYING.
SO HOT...
THINGS AREN'T WORKING OUT THE WAY I HOPED. I'M NOT SPARKLING. MY LIFE DOES NOT SPARKLE.

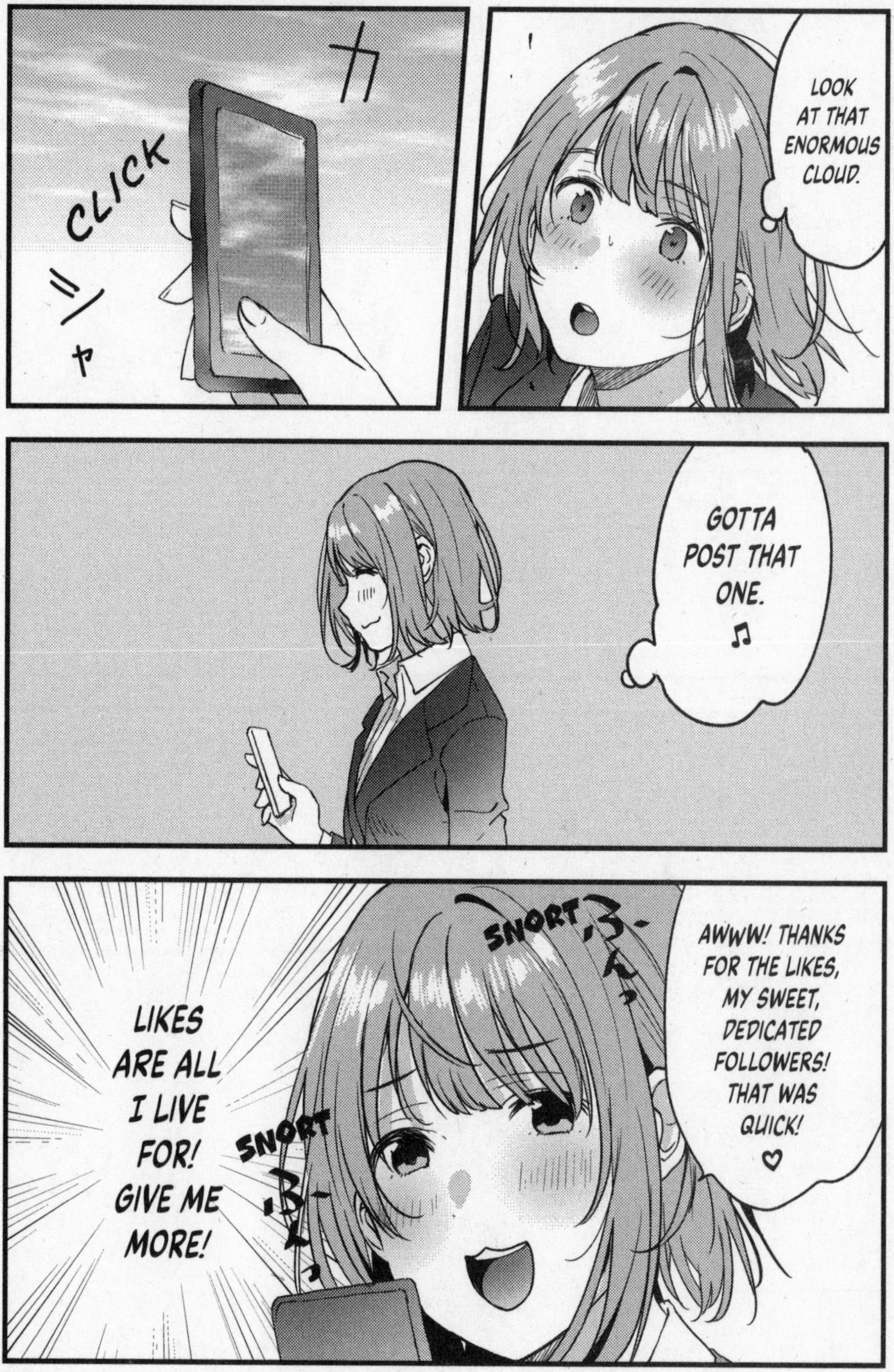
LOOK AT THAT ENORMOUS CLOUD.
CLICK
GOTTA POST THAT ONE. ♫
AWWW! THANKS FOR THE LIKES, MY SWEET, DEDICATED FOLLOWERS! THAT WAS QUICK! ♡
SNORT
LIKES ARE ALL I LIVE FOR! GIVE ME MORE!
SNORT

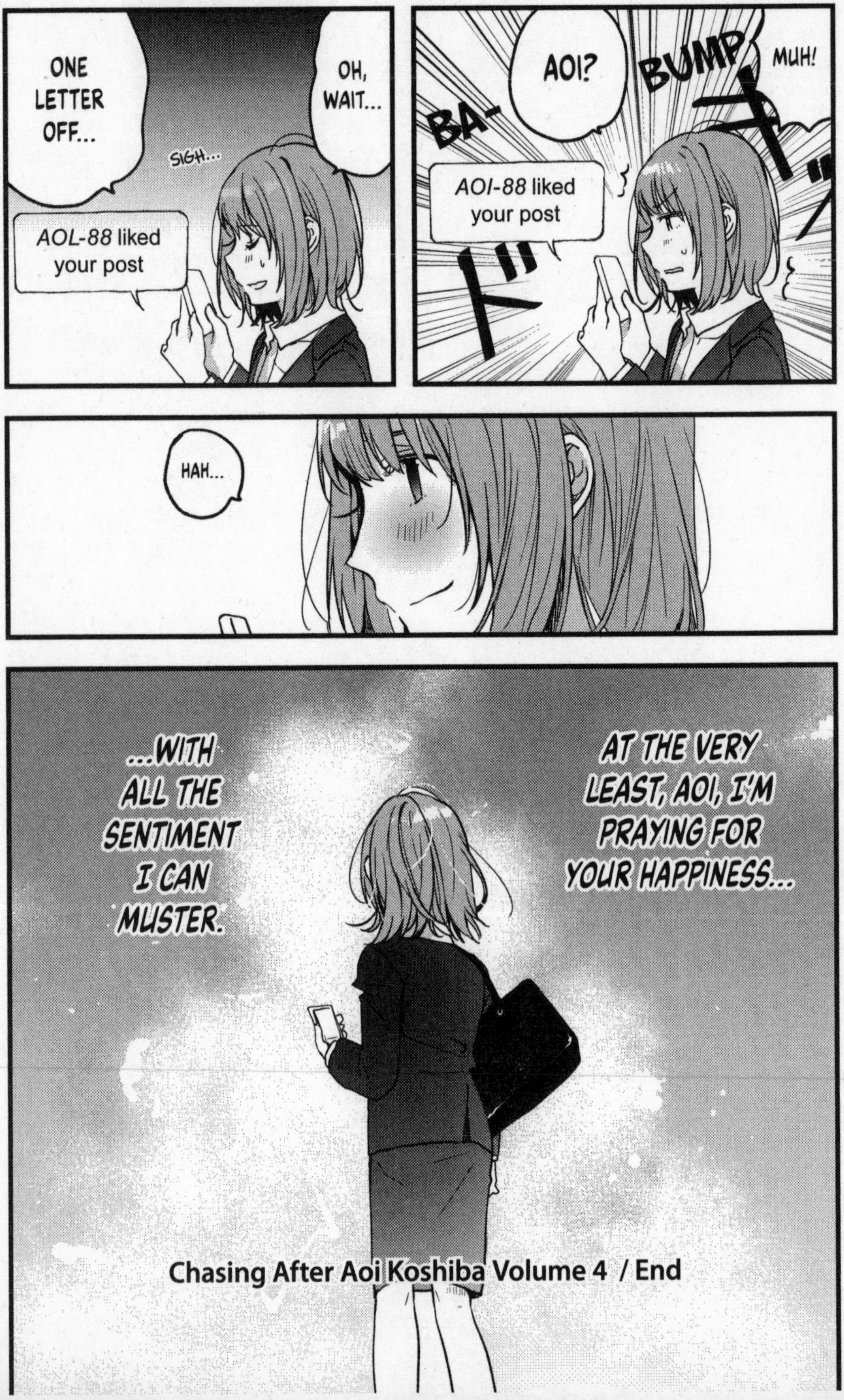
MUH!
BA- BUMP
AOI?
AOI-88 liked your post
OH, WAIT...
ONE LETTER OFF...
SIGH...
AOL-88 liked your post
HAH...
AT THE VERY LEAST, AOI, I'M PRAYING FOR YOUR HAPPINESS...
...WITH ALL THE SENTIMENT I CAN MUSTER.
Chasing After Aoi Koshiba Volume 4 / End

CHASING AFTER *Aoi Koshiba*

Summer, Fourth Year of University

The pieces of the past are fit into place, and now they'll be walking forward in the present. Thank you for sticking with us all the way!
Hazuki Takeoka

This is the final volume. Thanks to all the readers who followed us to this point. Imagine where Aoi and Sahoko might ultimately wind up!
Fly

Translation Notes

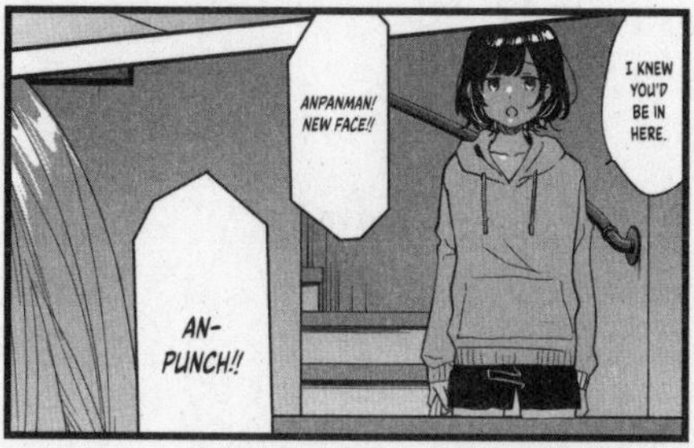
I KNEW YOU'D BE IN HERE.
ANPANMAN! NEW FACE!!
AN-PUNCH!!

Anpanman, page 65
A classic hero of Japanese children's TV. Anpanman is a long-running animated hero, based on anpan, a kind of pastry with sweet red bean paste inside. Anpanman fights a variety of germ villains in the series, and helps the wounded by giving them pieces of his own head to eat.

Oden, page 68
A traditional wintry hot pot dish, consisting of a variety of ingredients (meat, fish cakes, vegetables, tofu, mushrooms, and so on) simmered in a mild broth and served piping hot.

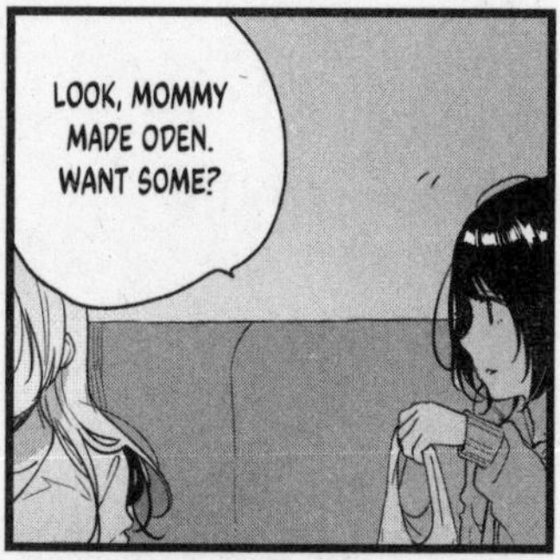
LOOK, MOMMY MADE ODEN. WANT SOME?

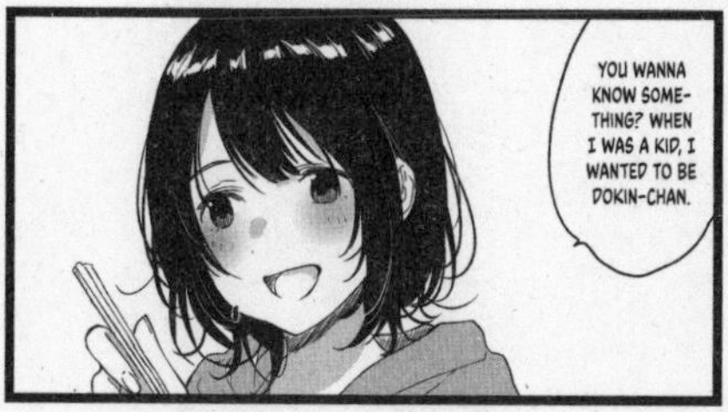
YOU WANNA KNOW SOME-THING? WHEN I WAS A KID, I WANTED TO BE DOKIN-CHAN.

Dokin-chan, page 69
An antagonist of Anpanman, usually partnered with Anpanman's primary nemesis, Baikinman (germ man). Dokin-chan is greedy and self-centered.

Izakaya, page 156
A type of Japanese pub that serves finger foods and other lighter fare in addition to drinks. A popular place for after-work gatherings and events of that nature.

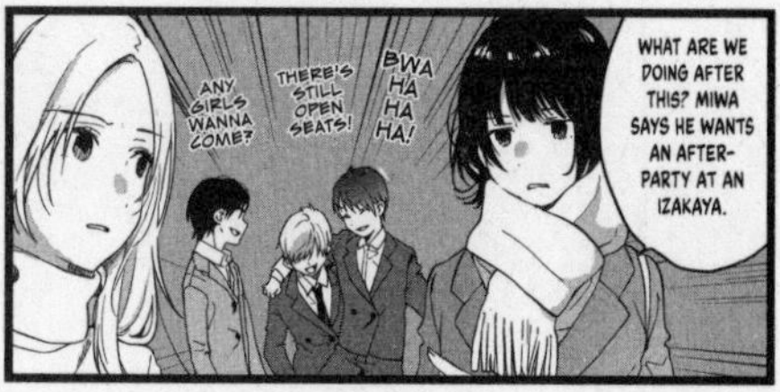
WHAT ARE WE DOING AFTER THIS? MIWA SAYS HE WANTS AN AFTER-PARTY AT AN IZAKAYA.
BWA HA HA HA!
THERE'S STILL OPEN SEATS!
ANY GIRLS WANNA COME?

THE SWEET SCENT OF LOVE IS IN THE AIR! FOR FANS OF OFFBEAT ROMANCES LIKE *WOTAKOI*

Sweat and Soap © Kintetsu Yamada / Kodansha Ltd.

In an office romance, there's a fine line between sexy and awkward... and that line is where Asako — a woman who sweats copiously — meets Koutarou — a perfume developer who can't get enough of Asako's, er, scent. Don't miss a romcom manga like no other!